In Praise of *Beyond Politics*

"*Beyond Politics* is a superb, thought-provoking and penetrating book, analyzing the real, as opposed to the presumed, effects of government regulation. It effectively turns the orthodox view that government regulation 'corrects' private 'market failures' on its head. The book deserves to be read by all serious students of public policy."
—**Sam Peltzman**, Ralph and Dorothy Keller Distinguished Service Professor of Economics Emeritus, University of Chicago

"*Beyond Politics* is a lively book that very effectively analyzes the very real phenomena of government failure. . . . The author makes a significant contribution by dealing informatively with the side of the matter that welfare economics tends to neglect and makes a vigorous case for the view that government intervention in the workings of the market should never be taken lightly."
—**William J. Baumol**, Director, C. V. Starr Center for Applied Economics, New York University

"*Beyond Politics* is a major contribution to informed comment. The book is so well written and the subject is so important and exciting that a great many people will find it very entertaining even if they do learn while reading it. We can welcome the book as a major step forward in understanding the dynamics of government and markets, and how both affect us all."
—**Gordon Tullock**, University Professor Emeritus of Law and Economics and Distinguished Research Fellow, George Mason University

"Public dissatisfaction with government by now seems a nearly inescapable part of our age of instant communications and an integrated world economy. Throughout the world, publics are looking for a new conception of government and its role. Happily, there is a whole new theory that fills the bill, which economists call 'public choice,' and which is clearly and persuasively presented in the excellent book, *Beyond Politics*."
—**Robert L. Bartley**, Pulitzer Prize-winner and late Editor, *The Wall Street Journal*

"*Beyond Politics* is so well written and interesting that it appeals even to those, like me, who may disagree with several of its arguments."
>   —**Mancur Olson, Jr.**, late Distinguished Professor of Economics, University of Maryland

"There is a need for a public philosophy that would provide a framework for discussion of appropriate spheres for markets and government. One such philosophy might begin with recognition of the desirable features of markets and also of the possibilities of market failure. But it would build on material such as is in this book to identify the risks of government failure, that is, the possibility that government intervention may well make things worse. Such a philosophy could provide a basis for communication and discourse and a framework for reasoned disagreement between people with diverse points of view about the goals of public life. The seeds of such a public philosophy are to be found in this book."
>   —*American Political Science Review*

"The book is well written. . . . That is why this book should be highly recommended for a course in economics at the junior or senior level. In fact, a curriculum in economics that does not include the subject matter covered by Simmons will be, at least, questionable in its quality. Those who do read the book will come out with what may be considered the most important lesson of *Beyond Politics*: Governments rely on force, and when force is wielded for political purposes the government becomes the worst violator of individual rights. Such lessons in liberty and freedom are badly needed in contemporary American economic education. This book fills this void more than satisfactorily."
>   —*Public Choice*

"*Beyond Politics* is a valuable analysis, making a cogent case for thoroughly rethinking what government should do. The book deserves wide reading."
>   —**John Engler**, former Governor of Michigan; President, Business Roundtable

"*Beyond Politics: The Roots of Government Failure* is the best non-Ph.D.-level summary of the basic insights of public-choice scholarship."
>   —**Donald J. Boudreaux**, former President, Foundation for Economic Education; Professor of Economics, George Mason University

BEYOND POLITICS

THE INDEPENDENT INSTITUTE is a non-profit, non-partisan, scholarly research and educational organization that sponsors comprehensive studies in political economy. Our mission is to boldly advance peaceful, prosperous, and free societies, grounded in a commitment to human worth and dignity.

Politicized decision-making in society has confined public debate to a narrow reconsideration of existing policies. Given the prevailing influence of partisan interests, little social innovation has occurred. In order to understand both the nature of and possible solutions to major public issues, the Independent Institute adheres to the highest standards of independent inquiry, regardless of political or social biases and conventions. The resulting studies are widely distributed as books and other publications, and are debated in numerous conference and media programs. Through this uncommon depth and clarity, the Independent Institute is redefining public debate and fostering new and effective directions for government reform.

100 Swan Way, Oakland, California 94621-1428, U.S.A.
Telephone: 510-632-1366 • Facsimile: 510-568-6040 • Email: info@independent.org • www.independent.org

BEYOND POLITICS

THE ROOTS OF GOVERNMENT FAILURE

RANDY T. SIMMONS

FOREWORD BY GORDON TULLOCK

REVISED AND UPDATED

The INDEPENDENT INSTITUTE

Oakland, California

The Independent Institute
100 Swan Way, Oakland, CA 94621-1428
Telephone: 510-632-1366 • Fax: 510-568-6040
Email: info@independent.org
Website: www.independent.org

Cover Design: Tony Wan
Interior design and composition by Leigh McLellan Design

Library of Congress Cataloging-in-Publication Data

Simmons, Randy T.
  Beyond politics : the roots of government failure / Randy T. Simmons. -- Rev. and
updated ed.
      p. cm.
  Rev. and updated ed. of: Beyond politics : markets, welfare, and the failure of bureaucracy / William C. Mitchell and Randy T. Simmons. 1994.
  ISBN 978-1-59813-050-8 (hardcover) -- ISBN 978-1-59813-042-3 (pbk.)
  1. Social choice. 2. Bureaucracy. I. Mitchell, William C. Beyond politics. II. Title.
HB846.8.M57 2011
351--dc23
                                    2011024633
15   14   13   5   4   3   2

Contents

Illustrations and Tables

Acknowledgments

THE EARLIER VERSION of *Beyond Politics* was produced by the Independent Institute with help from the Political Economy Research Center (now the Property and Environment Research Center— PERC), Utah State University's Institute of Political Economy, and the Earhart Foundation. This version benefitted greatly from my continuing conversations with people affiliated with PERC and my colleagues in the departments of Political Science and Economics and Finance at Utah State University—particularly Roberta Herzberg, Ryan M. Yonk, Christopher Fawson, and Diana and Michael Thomas were generous with their time and comments. Our Thursday political economy lunches generated ideas as well as important criticisms.

One person whose assistance and constant prodding were especially useful in getting the first and now this version finished is David Theroux, President of the Independent Institute. Thank you, David, for the telephone calls and emails that continued to remind that this was an important project. Alex Tabarrok, Research Director for the Independent Institute, provided invaluable criticisms and suggestions.

An ongoing procession of students in my classes and as research assistants generated ideas, research findings, and commentary as the draft was developed and sharpened. Bob Fawson, Chris Martin, and Kayla Harris, in particular, had significant effects on the quality of the final product.

As always, my wife Janet is my anchor and my sail. She supports while reminding about what is really important.

Preface

IN 1994 WILLIAM C. MITCHELL (Bill) and I coauthored
Beyond Politics: Markets, Welfare, and the Failure of Bureaucracy. We intended
to write a revision together and we talked about potential changes, additions,
and deletions but sadly my friend died in 2006. The book you are reading owes
a great deal to *Beyond Politics* and thus to Bill. I have written and revised as if
I were sending chapters to him for his additions and corrections. I think Bill
would have liked this book but I know that it would have been a different and
no doubt even better book had Bill been able to co-author. Listing myself as
sole author was a difficult choice because Bill was more than a collaborator—
he was mentor, friend, and valued critic; but the deletions, changes, revisions
and new material are substantial enough that I think this is what Bill would
have wanted. The usual disclaimer, "any errors are the sole responsibility of the
author," applies with more than the usual force in this case.

After Bill died I wrote a short piece in memoriam for the journal *Public
Choice* (April 2006, pp. 1–3). The following is part of what I wrote. I saved
the last part of it, a long quotation from Bill about his work, to end the final
chapter of this book.

> William C. Mitchell died January 2, 2006, at his home in Eugene, Ore-
> gon at the age of 80. Bill was one of a small number of economists, so-
> ciologists, and political scientists who participated in the first (1963) and
> subsequent meetings in Virginia of the group originally called the Com-
> mittee on Non-Market Decision-Making. After several meetings Bill
> suggested the shorter, less awkward name "Public Choice" for the new
> society and its journal. In 1988 he was selected as the first Distinguished
> Fellow of the Public Choice Society.

Bill often appeared distant and impersonal to many students and even colleagues and was a difficult person to know. He admitted he had what he called a "forbidding Nordic countenance," but claimed to have the "passionate heart of an Italian—Vince Lombardi . . . and Pareto, Puviani, and Mosca." When I heard his health was failing I immediately flew to Eugene where he met me literally, with open arms. The students who considered him austere would have been shocked at the ferocity of his bear hug. He insisted I stay at his home where he proudly showed me his stock certificate for his share of the Green Bay Packers. We talked of life, loves, art, friends, and dreams. He went into the hospital the day after I left, had a stroke, and died a few weeks later. The following is an incomplete portrait of this man who so strongly influenced my academic life, but I believe it captures the essence of his intellect and something about his soul.

One of Bill's core interests was to compare the efficiency and equity of political processes with market economy processes. His work in policy analysis and evaluation led him to conclude that political processes are perverse, not just in practice but in essence, and seldom improve on market processes. This theme influenced his work so much that the working title of our book that was eventually named *Beyond Politics* (Westview Press, 1994) was "On Making Things Worse: Government Responses to Market Failure."

A source of deep pride that he only wrote about late in his career was his service in the U.S. Airborne in World War II. Few of his students or colleagues knew that he made several combat jumps with the 513th Parachute Infantry Regiment of the 17th Airborne Division. Bill edited and completed (with an introduction and concluding chapter) a memoir of World War II experiences written by Kurt Gabel who served in Bill's own battalion and regiment, but who died before publication: *The Making of a Paratrooper: Airborne Training and Combat in World War II* (Lawrence, Kansas: University Press of Kansas, 1990). Bill framed and hung in his home the letter he received from historian Stephen Ambrose praising the book and Bill's contribution to it. Ambrose wrote of the book, "I laughed, I cried." Bill wrote his own analysis of the group solidarity in airborne units in his 1992 article, "Airborne We Fly the Sky—Paratroopers Do or Die" (*Crossroads: A Socio-Political Journal*).

In his academic paper, "Shape of Things to Come," Bill complained about economists and political scientists not developing a "body of systematic, explicit normative propositions." This concern stuck with him, which may be why he was much more attracted to Virginia Public Choice than to the Rochester or Chicago varieties. It led him to write in ways that some described as polemical and his response was, "What is wrong with that? Political Science needs some passion."

Our purpose in *Beyond Politics* was to provide students of economics, politics, and policy with a way to think in positive and normative terms about government. Identifying actions that are *beyond* politics—beyond the abilities of government to perform—is the positive part of this purpose. The normative part is to think seriously about what kinds of policies and rules *ought to be beyond politics*. Bill believed, as do I, that by identifying problems and suggesting solutions we will improve the lot of those who should be the ultimate sovereigns in a democracy—the citizens.

Foreword to the First Edition

THE STUDY OF POLITICS has initiated a revolution in recent years. That this revolution has hardly begun is attributable not to any caution or incompleteness but to the fact that most people are ignorant of it.

The new approach begins by assuming that voters are much like customers and that politicians are much like businesspeople. Bureaucrats in the federal government are much like bureaucrats in many large corporations. These statements seem simple and straightforward. One would think few would disagree.

Nevertheless, this approach is, rather mysteriously, very controversial. I have been denounced with great vigor for saying simply that the customer in the supermarket and the voter in the voting booth are the same person.

On the basis of these assumptions, it is possible to develop a new theory. Although the theory, called public choice, is based on economics and uses many of its tools, it is a genuinely original creation of political science rather than simply a transfer. (It should be noted that awareness of the new theory is fairly common in economics departments, though the subject is regarded as a little odd because economists are, after all, not students of politics.) The economic conceptions and tools, although helpful, were inexact for use in political theory, and hence it was necessary to develop new ones.

For this approach, the government is not a romanticized generator of public goods or a protector of virtue but simply a rather prosaic set of instruments for providing certain types of goods and services that may be hard to provide. Instead of thinking of the government as something that stands above the market, public choice theorists regard the government and the market as parallel organizations sharing a basic objective: filling the demands of the citizens.

Some of these demands, that for food for example, are no doubt best served by the market. Nonetheless, governments around the world are involved in the food production business. They make bread more expensive and transfer funds from the rather poor consumer of bread to the much-better-off farmer in Western countries. Interestingly, in Africa, where the farmers are poorer than the consumers, the system is used to transfer money from the farmers to the consumers.

In contrast, such problems as air pollution are widely viewed as properly handled by government even though they are resistant to both market and government solutions. People do not hold this view because air pollution is a more important matter than bread—on the contrary, food is fundamentally more vital to our lives than cleaner air—but because they see government rightly or wrongly as a better instrument for coping with it. Once again, society maintains two parallel organizational structures in the hope that they will provide for citizens' wants better than either one could by itself.

Most public choice theorists do not think the government provides very high-quality service. Nor do they think that the market is perfect. In economics, the theory of perfect competition is considered by many to be a mathematical convenience that permits analysis of some economic problems with greater speed than is permitted by the classical economics of Smith and Ricardo; the theory does not fit the world perfectly.

Similarly, the new theory of how politics works does not yet fit the world perfectly. We hope for its improvement. One of the advantages of being in a new field is that we can legitimately blame gaps and holes on the newness of the work. Economics has been around for a long time, and expectations of further revolutionary change are not so easy to come by.

There is a subdivision of public choice with a good deal of elaborate mathematical work. It is normally called "social choice." The bulk of the authors in public choice are not particularly mathematical and resemble Ricardo more than they do Hurwiez. Whether the mathematical complications in either public choice or economics are pioneering in important new areas or practicing mere escapism is an open question.

However, this book is about a new approach, one just making its imprint. There are now public choice societies in the United States—where the field has reached its highest development—as well as in Europe and Japan.

The originator of the subject was an Englishman, Duncan Black, but its first major development occurred in the United States. The American journal *Public Choice* is now twenty-five years old and the American Public Choice Society has almost 1,000 members. The European Public Choice Society is smaller, but nevertheless flourishing, and has its own journal, *Scelte Pubbliche.* The Japanese have also vigorously entered into this field, although they have not yet established structures as formal as those provided by either the American or the European societies. The Japanese journal is *Public Choice Studies.* In January 1994, public choice scholars from Japan, Taiwan, and Korea met in Hong Kong, where they were attending the Pacific Rim Conference of the Western Economic Association. They decided to establish an Asian Public Choice meeting and were hopeful that it would draw participation from more than just those three countries.

The flourishing state of the field in the past few years as been evident especially in the United States, where four additional journals have been started: *The Journal of Constitutional Political Economics, Rationality and Society, Journal of Theoretical Politics,* and *Economics and Politics.* Thus, the academic side of public choice is now well established at the higher levels. There are many scholars actively writing, publishing, and doing research in the field.

Some gaps exist, however. It is possible to teach excellent graduate courses in political science using a number of specialized books. However, we badly need more college courses in public choice at both the graduate and the undergraduate levels. It is therefore fitting that the authors of *Beyond Politics* are both political scientists. This book will go a long way toward improving on the thinly scattered material found in political science courses.

If the new approach is to have impact on our political system—it does, after all, give a more accurate and useful picture of government than the old approaches did—then people without graduate degrees need access to it. We need a book for the general reader, the kind one might find in the popular bookstore chains.

Mitchell and Simmons again come to our rescue. This book clearly is excellent for the ordinary informed citizen. I cannot truthfully say that it is an easy book, because the ideas included will be new to a great many of its readers. It is, however, not written as a book to be studied instead of read. Ordinary readers who are willing to temporarily leave aside the conventional wisdom about our politics will find that they can go through this book quickly and productively.

The book is a major contribution to informed public comment. There are many very difficult problems in connection with government, and we should try to solve them on the basis of the best learning available. This book will make that learning available to almost anyone who has a normal education and who is willing to devote a little effort to the task.

In fact, the book is so well written and the subject so important and exciting that a great may people will find it very entertaining even if they do learn while reading it. We can welcome this work as a major step forward in understanding the dynamic of government and markets and how both affect us all.

Gordon Tullock
George Mason University

Introduction

POLITICAL ECONOMY IS a term that covers many analytical approaches to the study of human behavior. Some political economists are Marxists, others are market socialists, others are political conservatives, and still others are libertarians. During the 1930s and 1940s, economists with a more positive view of markets than Marx, but who believed that socialism had great possibilities, developed theories of "market socialism." These, mostly European, economists argued that markets were wonderful public devices for directing private actions but needed to be directed centrally so they would produce desired public outcomes. They were countered by other, usually Austrian, economists who argued that the information problems inherent in attempting to manage markets were simply too great to be overcome, even if computing powers were expanding greatly. Other, usually American, economists countered the market socialist argument with normative arguments about the loss of individual freedom inherent in central design and control.

A new set of arguments and concerns about markets emerged alongside the market socialism debate. Welfare economics, a branch of economics that studies imperfections in markets, or "market failures," developed theories and principles about how markets ought to function and then compared those theoretical markets with actual ones. When welfare economists found markets failing to meet their expectations they identified causes of market failures and called for political intervention to make corrections. By identifying the causes of failure they thought they could identify ways to fix the causes.

While market socialists were attempting to control and direct markets and welfare economists were identifying market failures and their causes, political scientists were busy doing "thick description." They organized mountains of information about the workings of government but had few theories to use to unify or interpret the information. At mid-century, for example, a typical political scientist might describe in great detail the powers of the Speaker of the U.S. House of Representatives and assert that the Speaker was "too powerful." Few asked, however, why the speaker was so powerful. Why was power centered on the Speaker and committee chairmen? What would happen if power were decentralized? Political scientists had no analytical tools for answering those questions, but they had strong opinions.

Theories of government that did exist or were developing were based on the assumption that any problems with government could be fixed with more government. Some saw government as a forum for competing interests. If the government was not meeting the values of a particular interest, the reason was usually that the interests were underrepresented in the polity. Solution? Expand the number of competing interests. Others saw government as a system of elite rule in which the elite's excesses could be controlled by strict political rules. The prevailing view among political scientists was that government is generally benevolent, often benign, and seldom dangerous. To them, politics is where conflicts of values are resolved, inequalities narrowed, inequities solved. According to some, participating in politics is noble. The state builds character and creates civic and personal virtues. Most political scientists' faith in government is matched with skepticism of markets, skepticism fueled by the market failure literature and, for some, even rooted in a longing for market socialism.

Countering these visions of the economy and the polity is a relatively new political economy known as "public choice." Public choice applies the assumptions and methods that economists use to study private choices to the study of public choices. It questions the purported causes of market failures and the competence of governments to cope with alleged difficulties. Public choice analysts have identified perversities of majority rule and have shown that the polity has a powerful propensity to adopt inefficient policies and to restrict personal liberty—all in the interest of special interest groups or equalization of wealth and income. Perhaps the most important public choice development is a theory of government failure that raises questions about the ability of governments to respond to market failures. The conclusion is that government responses to market imperfections may, in fact, make things worse.

In addition to public choice, economists developed other arguments that cause us to question the ability of governments to accomplish all that people expect of them. These arguments center on property rights and the economic value of different institutions. Property rights are civil and even natural rights, something that was acknowledged for centuries, although many social scientists now dispute that argument. What is new about the study of property rights is that they are understood as an evolved and natural way to provide social stability and to include the future in current decisions.

Economic history was redefined by Nobel-prize winning economist Douglass North's studies of the economic performance of political institutions. What became the New Institutional Economics emphasizes how and why property rights and the institutions that support them succeed and fail. That understanding provides important insights into and contradictions of the welfare economists' assumptions and conclusions.

Another innovation in economics, although many would argue it is a rediscovery of the core of economics, is Austrian economics. The Austrians adhere to Ludwig von Mises's rule: the first job of an economist is to tell governments what they cannot do. They emphasize that knowledge is generated, spread, and used within the economy through ongoing processes. Like the New Institutional Economists, the Austrians focus on institutions, especially how institutions emerge in a world where people lack perfect knowledge. Although I do not consider myself to be an Austrian economist, I have learned a great deal from them and often, even unwittingly, use Austrian arguments in my own analyses.

My purpose in this book is to provide students of economics, politics, and policy with a concise explanation of public choice, markets, property, and political and economic processes and, from that explanation, identify what kinds of actions are *beyond politics*—beyond the ability of government. Combining public choice with studies of the value of property rights, markets, and institutions produces a much different picture of modern political economy than that accepted by mainstream political scientists and welfare economists. Citizens ask their governments to do more than is possible, to interrupt markets in ways that reduce net benefits while increasing costs, and to redistribute wealth and income even when redistribution decreases wealth and freedom. This book explains why such perverse policies are sought and enacted.

Identifying actions that are beyond the abilities of government to perform is my positive purpose. The normative purpose is to think seriously about what kinds of policies and rules *ought to be beyond politics.* Thus, besides identifying problems I suggest solutions to improve the lot of those who should be the ultimate sovereigns in a democracy—the citizens.

Students of economics and politics who read this analysis will find that it challenges cherished assumptions and conclusions about market failures and government successes. They will acquire positive and normative measures for evaluating claims about government and markets and, regardless of their ideological leanings, gain a foundation upon which rational policy may be built.

PART I

Market Failures and Political Solutions
Orthodoxy

"MARKET FAILURE" is the modern justification for government action. And that justification has been used by consumers, activists, politicians, special interests, and bureaucrats to produce broad-ranging programs, rules, and agencies to control and influence economic choices. Political control over private economic action became a fact of life during the last century. Rent control, pollution regulation, safety rules, import restrictions, fuel economy standards, and thousands of other controls have been enacted to overcome perceived imperfections in markets.

The vision underlying this expansion is that government succeeds where markets fail. It is a vision I do not share. I believe that economic reality is incredibly complex and that any attempts to explain how economies work are doomed to failure. I also take a sober, non-romantic view of government, and since I believe that economic reality is scarcely knowable, I am wary of those who pretend to know how to manipulate it for social benefit. To understand why I hold these views of markets and politics, it is necessary to understand the justifications and assumptions of the pro-government position. Let's begin.

1

Market Failure and
Government Intervention
The View from Welfare Economics

EVEN THE MOST elementary of modern economics texts routinely inform the reader that markets suffer from serious and inherent imperfections. We are told of undersupplied public goods, exorbitant and ubiquitous social costs of private actions, inevitable business cycles, unprotected consumers, and unfairly distributed wealth and income.

Concerns about markets are widespread among economists. The *Wall Street Journal* (Sept 3, 2004) asked several Nobel economists, "In what sphere of life, if any, do you think it most important to limit the influence of market forces?" Most replied with the standard arguments of welfare economists about supposed market failures. One did not, however. Vernon Smith, who shared the Nobel Prize in 2002, answered:

> None, because "markets" are about recognizing that information is dispersed in all social systems, and that the problem of society is to find, devise and discover institutions that incentivize and enable people to make the right decisions without anyone having to tell them what to do. The idea that market forces should be limited stems from a fundamental error in beliefs about markets. This is the wrong question.

The other Nobel economists' worries about market failure have a powerful impact because such worries are intuitively appealing and understandable to the general public and especially to idealistic students. And when these worries about markets lead to proposed solutions, most people ignore Professor Vernon Smith's concerns about wrong questions because the causes of failure are seemingly clear and the solution readily at hand. When markets fail, this argument goes, we must resort to and can rely on politics and governmental administration. Resources will be allocated efficiently and wealth and income will be fairly distributed, that is, more equally divided. Furthermore, political activity ennobles individual citizens while the unseemly, raucous, and self-interested competition in the market debases them.

Many economists now agree that models of market failure need to be coupled with models of government failure. Yet, even the Nobel economists interviewed by the *Wall Street Journal* quickly slip into worries about market failures. Moreover, non-economist social scientists and the general public are even more inclined to take a jaundiced view of the workings of a market economy. For them any activity motivated by self-interest is at best suspect and at worst contaminated. Adam Smith's unseen hand is widely regarded as a contradiction in terms; public benefits cannot emerge from competition and self-interest. In contrast, since political man is considered selfless and well informed, the public interest can be readily and accurately divined; since the political process is considered costless, the public interest is easily achieved. And political conflict debases no one.

I reject this simplistic political view and contend that market failure is seriously misunderstood. Further, I maintain that normal political responses to alleged market failures usually make things worse and that our chief problems stem not from market difficulties but from political intervention in otherwise robust markets. To set the stage for my arguments, I begin by exploring how markets work and discuss how mid-20th century critics—led by welfare economists—criticized them and justified the government intervention so prominent today.

The Market Process

"The market" is an abstract concept referring to the arrangements people have for exchanging with one another in all aspects of economic life. Thus, it is a process rather than a clearly defined place or a thing that we can observe easily, although some markets are in particular places. Markets can be as formal and well organized as the stock market and as informal and unorganized as Saturday garage sales or even singles bars.

Markets coordinate human activity by taking advantage of self-interest, as Adam Smith ([1776] 1981) famously pointed out. In the "bartering and trucking" of the market, a person is "led by an invisible hand to promote an end which has no part of his intention" (IV.ii.9). In one of Smith's most famous passages, he asserted:

> It is not from the benevolence of the butcher, the brewer, or the baker that we expect our dinner, but from their regard to their own interest. We address ourselves not to their humanity, but to their self-love, and never talk to them of our own necessities but of their advantages (I.ii.2).

Notice that Adam Smith's example shows how markets use self-interest to cause people to act as if they care about others. We get what we want from the butcher, brewer, and baker by making them better off. Conversely, they improve their own wealth by making us better off and they seek to do so, not because we necessarily like each other (although brotherly love is not precluded) but because they do "well" in markets by doing "good" for others. The chief characteristic of markets, then, is cooperation with others.

All of the cooperation between buyers and sellers and competition for products and for buyers means that no one is in direct charge of markets—no one declares how much of a product will be produced, by whom, in what quantities, and what will be the price. There is no one in charge of the market for shirts or coffee or pens or shoes, or bread or the myriads of other products we buy and sell every day. They are all produced and their prices are set spontaneously, without central direction and central planning. Individual companies and entrepreneurs, however, do a great deal of planning while coordinating their activities across time and space with little or no knowledge of each other.

Not only is no one in charge of markets, no one knows how to produce the vast majority of products sold in markets. The classic essay explaining how decentralized knowledge is coordinated spontaneously is "I Pencil: My Family Tree as told to Leonard R. Reed (1958)." In the essay the pencil makes a startling statement: ". . . not a single person on the face of this earth knows how to make me." He means that although billions of pencils are made each year no single person knows how to do all the steps in the process—creating saws, cutting trees, building trucks to haul logs, mine and smelt ore, and on and on. "I Pencil" has been updated by Matt Ridley in his book *The Rational Optimist: How Prosperity Evolves* (2010). "No single person," Ridley writes, "knows how to make a computer mouse." Many people know how to *assemble* a computer mouse, yet they know nothing of the processes of producing plastic from oil, drilling for the oil, or creating the materials needed for circuit boards. Ridley describes the computer mouse as "a complex confection of many substances with intricate internal design reflecting multiple strands of knowledge."

Markets develop and expand by relying on voluntary exchange as a way for people to obtain what they want. Markets promote exchange by providing information about the qualities of a particular product, especially compared with the qualities and costs of competing products, and the cost of agreeing on a price. When the costs of making decisions and trades are reduced, new opportunities can be exploited, and as the new opportunities are exploited wealth increases and economic growth occurs. More opportunities mean more wealth.

A simple classroom experiment illustrates the power of exchange in making people better off. As students enter the room they receive a plastic sandwich bag containing different combinations of candy. Each student identifies the value of his or her bag and the individual values are totaled. Then, students are allowed to exchange any of their candy with other students. After exchanges are made the students place a monetary value on their bags and those values are totaled. The bags are now worth more to them than they were before trading. That is, the trades produced more wealth even though the total amount of candy did not change.

Markets provide information, in part, by generating prices. Each price is a piece of potentially valuable information about available opportunities. The more prices there are and the more widely they are known, the wider the range of opportunities available and the more wealth that is generated. The prices consumers are willing to pay at a particular time and place indicate the relative value the consumers place on goods and services. As prices become known, individual suppliers send goods and furnish services where they are wanted most; that is, where they bring the highest price.

Because prices indicate the relative values other people place on goods, prices discourage wasteful use of scarce resources. The fact that something is expensive is an indication that others value it highly and that it is costly to replace. The fact that something is inexpensive or even free for the taking—if it has a zero price—indicates that it has little value to others and can be replaced easily. Low prices encourage consumption. High prices discourage it.

Markets, then, are decentralized processes for directing human activity. No central committee or decision-maker determines how or when resources will be used. Instead, values are expressed by monetary bids, and self-interest is usually the dominant motive for participation. When such a process produces outcomes that seem unacceptable or less than what is believed possible, many people—economists and non-economists—tend to support attempts to impose the visible hand of government on the invisible hand of the market.

Markets function best within a stable legal structure containing a set of well-defined rights. These rights include the freedom to contract with one another, the right to property, and the right to have contracts enforced. Protecting rights and contracts against fraud, deceit, destruction and theft is a necessary part of such a legal structure. Without these minimal activities by government, markets could exist only with great difficulty.

Legal systems establish frameworks for exchange—they set the rules of the game. Establishing this framework does not require that government officials or agencies intervene into the people's voluntary exchanges. It means there is a power to which people may appeal if contracts are breached, if fraud occurs, or private property is taken.

Establishing a stable legal structure while protecting rights and enforcing contracts is a widely recognized and accepted role for government. Some forms of government are, obviously, better at fulfilling those functions than others. Justifications for other appropriate functions for government are based on claims that markets, although useful for directing some human choices and behavior, are ill suited for directing others. Put bluntly, the claim is that markets fail and that failure justifies government action.

Market Failure as Justification for Restraining the Invisible Hand

Students of market failure begin their investigations of markets and market activity by postulating a perfect market; that is, one in which all opportunities for mutually advantageous exchange are being exploited. Under a set of rigorous assumptions about preferences, motivations, and technology, they show that markets will reach a point at which no one can be made better off without making anyone else worse off. Market failure simply means real-world markets failing to achieve the standards of the imaginary, perfect market.

Those economists most active in developing theories of market failure are welfare economists, one of whom was A.C. Pigou. In *The Economics of Welfare* (1932), which built on earlier work by Sidgwick (1883) and Marshall (1920), Pigou showed that the performance of markets in supplying social amenities is likely to be unsatisfactory. By 1952, the arguments were well enough developed for William Baumol to bring them together in his book, *Welfare Economics and the Theory of the State*. Baumol's work became the economic profession's standard for the study of market failures and provided an intellectual foundation on which to base proposals for government programs designed to improve on markets.

Baumol's work on the theory of market failures was followed by many of the other leading economists of his time. One notable contribution was made by Francis Bator (1958) whose essay, "The Anatomy of Market Failure," summarized what was developing into a large body of literature as well as analytical consensus.

Bator and others identified a set of market failures that eventually became central to modern economic analysis. Specifically, they clarified the characteristics of "public goods" and the reasons why markets are expected to underproduce them. They explained the nature and reasons for overproduction of negative externalities. They identified market power, lack of information, and market instabilities as having ruinous effects on the efficient operation of the private economy.

In the following pages, I briefly discuss the most commonly accepted forms of market failure developed in the welfare economics literature. I also identify the orthodox policy solutions. As later chapters make clear, I seldom agree with the diagnoses of market failure or with prescriptions for cure.

Ubiquitous Externalities

One seemingly pervasive market failure results from "spillover" or "external" costs of a private action. That is, one or more person's activities may create costs for a second person without the second person's permission or, sometimes, knowledge.

Private costs are the portion of the costs paid by the individual taking action. The spillover costs of an action are that portion of the total costs passed on to others. For example, if you neglect to change the oil in your automobile and the engine is damaged, you must have it repaired. Your negligence has produced private costs. If, however, your negligence causes the engine to emit noxious fumes, some of the costs of your failure to keep your car in good repair will spill over to all those who breathe the air contaminated by the fumes.

People generally undertake only those activities for which they expect the additional personal costs will be less than the additional personal benefits. When there are no costs created for others, an individual comparing costs and benefits avoids waste and searches for efficiency. But if some of the costs of your action spill over to others while you capture the benefits, then comparing private costs and benefits will lead to actions that are costly to society.

Let's return to the example of your automobile. If all of your auto's exhaust fumes were pumped into the interior of your car so that you were the only one to breathe them, you would drive very little if at all or you would find a means of making the emissions breathable. But if you are able to vent your exhaust fumes into the atmosphere, where others will breathe them, you are not likely to reduce your emissions voluntarily because your cost of reducing emissions outweighs your benefits. That is, since other people, plants, and animals who use the air share the cost of your pollution, you get a net benefit from polluting. Furthermore, your emissions by themselves will have a negligible effect on air quality regardless of whether others use the air as a waste repository or not.

Spillover costs are also known as negative externalities. When costs can be socialized—externalized, as in the automobile example—the individual weighs the total benefits against only a portion of the costs (the ones he or she bears) and improves his or her own position at the expense of others. Socialized costs and privatized benefits mean that people get a "free ride" at others' expense.

Where such spillovers do occur, most economists assume the market will respond imperfectly, *if at all,* to the desires of the public. The belief in the pervasiveness of negative externalities and the dangers they pose, as well as the implied need for government action, is demonstrated by a June 2010 Google search of the Internet for "ubiquitous externalities." The search yielded scholarly articles on electrical transmission, urbanization, water quality and quantity, political and economic interdependence, arms control, biodiversity, ecosystem management, waste disposal, and on and on. Apparently, those who seek for externalities find them everywhere.

Proponents of governments acting to control externalities commonly advocate four broad categories of policy instruments. The first three aim at influencing the behavior of the externality producer: regulation through direct controls, regulation that relies on market incentives, and persuasion. The fourth is direct government expenditures, generally for large construction projects such as sewage treatment plants to correct the externality at taxpayer expense.

Regulating externality production through direct controls—commonly known as "command and control"—is central to public policy in most countries. A government agency prescribes certain procedures and places limitations on the kinds of activities that may be undertaken. The thousands of valves and flanges, the hundreds of pumps, the drains, and flares of a petroleum refinery, for example, are subject to individual rules established by the government. In addition, the command and control approach often requires a specific technology or a specific treatment procedure. Thus, government decides on the kind of control, the appropriate standard of measurement, and the level of control.

A central argument against command and control regulation is that it takes little advantage of the skill and enterprise of company managers. Once a specific technology is mandated, little incentive exists to search for more effective or less costly technological improvement. There is also the often-overwhelming administrative problem of prescribing procedures and issuing permits individually tailored to thousands of different companies or individuals. (The administrative problem may be overwhelming but it does not stop bureaucrats from trying. In the G.W. Bush administration, for example, 250,000 bureaucrats were busily devising and implementing regulations and total U.S. government regulation increased by 7,000 pages.)

Instead of direct regulation, some economists have proposed that externalities can best be corrected by having government mimic the market through a system of pricing measures—user fees, taxes, and penalties or by creating new environmental rights. The government should place a charge (price) on pollution equaling the value people give to environmental quality or allow the creation of tradable pollution rights, for example. Firms can then respond to prices and achieve levels of environmental quality selected by market-like force rather than by political fiat. These policies, according to proponents, create incentives for firms to seek more efficient ways of reducing pollution, encourage innovation, and cause the people creating the spillover costs to recognize those costs. Polluters are then less likely to produce beyond the point where the costs of more production exceed the benefits. Some examples of environmental policies proposed and enacted rather widely during the last several decades include emissions trading; "bubble" and "offset" policies, which allow firms to build new pollution creating facilities in exchange for similar reductions at other sources; and "banking," which allows discharge reductions to be stored for future use (see Chapter 13 for an extended discussion of these ideas as well as something far more radical—"free market environmentalism").

Direct regulation and market or market-like incentives are attempts to change behavior. For many, simply changing behavior is not enough; they want to change people's hearts. In terms an economist might understand, they want to change internal incentives, not just external ones. Campaigns to encourage individuals to voluntarily stop littering, recycle trash, and join carpools; or calls to industry to recognize its social responsibility are crusades to persuade people to internalize the costs of their actions, to develop an environmental conscience. The hope is that people who produce externalities will subject their immediate self-interest to a general group interest. Such appeals rely on a moral resurgence and usually fail in the long run although there are occasional short-term successes.

Most economists are highly skeptical of appeals to conscience because economic analysis emphasizes the importance of making individual self-interest coincide with the group interest, rather than remaking human nature. In his classic book, *The Public Use of Private Interest,* Charles L. Schultze (1977) reflected this view nicely:

> If I want industry to cut down on pollution, indignant tirades about social responsibility cannot hold a candle to schemes which reduce the profits of firms who pollute. . . . In most cases the prerequisite for social gains is the identification, not of villains and heroes but of the defects in the incentive system that drive ordinary decent citizens into doing things contrary to the common good (p. 18).

Governments also attempt to control externalities through direct expenditures. Two clearly visible examples are sewer treatment facilities and waste disposal sites. Sometimes government policies create externalities that, in turn, generate programs and expenditures to control the externalities. Some U.S. federal water projects, for example, increase salinity for downstream water users. In one case salinity levels were so high that the U.S. government built a desalinization plant near the border with Mexico so that water flowing from the U.S. to Mexico is usable.

Public Goods

Welfare economists argue that private goods (consumer products such as pencils and automobiles are examples) are efficiently produced and allocated by markets—as long as externalities are controlled. Because a private good is exclusive—that is, non-owners can be kept from using it unless they pay for it, and suppliers can obtain the full value of the good from those who want it—it is distributed to the people who want it the most. Another characteristic of a private good is that one person's consumption prevents or reduces another's consumption of that good. If a person wants to consume a private good, he or she usually has to pay for it. (Note that many government-supplied goods such as food stamps and saw timber from the national forests are also private goods.)

But public goods differ greatly from private goods in ways that make their provision through markets problematic. In Paul Samuelson's (1954) original formulation, public goods have two distinctive characteristics. First, a public good is non-exclusive; it cannot be withheld from any member of a group once it is supplied to the group. One commonly used example of a public good is national defense—once a protective missile is supplied, all the people in the nation benefit, whether they pay for it or not. If it is available to one, it is available to all. Second, one person's consumption of a public good does not affect another's consumption. That is, the enjoyment or benefit of a public good is shared by all members of the group receiving the good whether the individual members choose to make a payment for it or not. Because one person's consumption of a public good does not preclude anyone else's consumption, the cost of providing the public good to an additional consumer is zero. If it is provided for one it is provided for all, and all can benefit without reducing its value to others. Police protection, parks, roads, and aids to navigation are commonly cited examples, as are flood control and sanitation.

Since people obtain the benefits of a public good regardless of whether or not they pay for it, there is a powerful incentive to offer nothing or little in exchange for the good. Consider the problem facing a potential mosquito control entrepreneur in an area like the Cache Valley in northern Utah. Several rivers and streams converge in the valley to form extensive wetlands that are home for all kinds of wildlife and insects, including mosquitoes—lots and lots of mosquitoes. Our hopeful mosquito controller believes people will pay for him to spray and kill the adult and larval mosquitoes. But if he sprays and then seeks payment from his potential customers—the people in the Cache Valley who prefer to have fewer mosquitoes—he will face the free-rider problem.

It is in the interest of each person from whom payment is requested to understate the amount of benefit he or she received or is willing to pay. Once the number of mosquitoes is reduced everyone benefits, whether they pay or not. Also, one person's payment is a relatively unimportant part of the total bill and whether he or she pays will not determine how many mosquitoes and their larvae are killed. So, each customer reasons, "Why pay?" Few or none pay and Cache Valley Mosquito Control, Inc. fails for lack of funds. A relatively inexpensive service that most people want is not provided because it cannot be produced profitably if the provider relies on voluntary payments.

Mosquito abatement illustrates a central problem with public goods. Because the benefits of a public good are received upon production, not upon payment, people can benefit without paying. They get a free ride because benefits are socialized while costs are privatized.

Public goods pose several serious problems for markets. First, how can one charge for a product when many "free riders" can refuse to pay? And even if it is possible to charge for the good, how can the appropriate price be established? Finally, without the guidance of prices, how much of the good should be produced? Although a bridge is an imperfect example of a public good because of crowding and because it is possible to exclude users, bridges do illustrate the pricing problem. If a bridge has excess capacity, the cost to other users of allowing an additional person to cross the bridge is zero. Charging a toll in this situation would discourage some people from using the bridge who would otherwise use it—even though their use would not decrease other people's use. The result is that total social welfare is less than what it could be.

Increasing total social welfare is a justification many welfare economists use for government providing goods that have a public nature. Francis Bator (1958), the originator of the bridge example, claims the pricing problem is so difficult to make that "[a]s long as activities have even a trace of publicness, price calculations are inefficient." In a footnote to this conclusion, Bator noted, however: "This is not to say that there exist other feasible modes of social calculation and organization which are more efficient" (p. 64). Regardless of such caveats, many presume that government intervention is necessary to provide public goods and to price them appropriately.

The argument that government should produce public goods did not originate with welfare economists. David Hume ((1739–40) 1898), for example, provided part of the foundation upon which modern scholars justify government activities. Hume maintained that individuals left to themselves, "would lay the whole burden on others." The solution was obvious to Hume because:

> Political society easily remedies . . . these inconveniences . . . thus the bridges are built; harbors open'd; ramparts rais'd; canals form'd; fleets equip'd; and armies disciplin'd; everywhere by the care of government (538–39).

In order for "political society" to remedy the inconvenience of free riding, it must find a means of paying for the public goods. Government's answer is to turn free riders into forced payers through taxation. The presumption is that forced taxation is often the only way for individuals to receive the benefits of the public goods they desire. And, in fact, Cache Valley, Utah has a government imposed mosquito abatement district funded through forced taxation.

No one claims there are many pure public goods. National defense is one of the few possible ones. However, less rigorous or partial definitions are frequently used to justify government supplying goods and services. Paul Samuelson argues, for example, that the public should finance any good whose (marginal) cost of supply is zero. The idea of marginal cost is easily understood by referring back to Bator's bridge example; once the bridge is constructed and until capacity is reached, there is no cost created by another person using the bridge. The cost at the margin is zero. This approach suggests bridges, roads, harbors and a host of other similar goods should be sufficiently "public" to require provision through taxation.

Another potential market failure is option demand—demand for the option to consume a good or service in the future. I frequently hear colleagues complain that the small university towns they live in do not provide them with all the amenities of civilized life they may once have experienced while graduate students in Cambridge or Berkeley. One such complaint is that cultural facilities and events are lacking; another is that there is little or no public transportation.

Smaller cities lack such facilities and services because no entrepreneur can make a profit from the limited demand for the services. My colleagues, however, want the facilities even though they do not make extensive use of them. The option for which there is a demand is valuable, but there is no way to collect sufficient fees to pay for it. Suppose that my colleagues live several miles from campus and own private cars, but that the cars now and then fail to function. If a bus costs 50 cents one way and the only alternative is a cab at ten dollars, a professor with a car that malfunctions say five times a year would pay $100 for five round-trips by cab. But if a bus were available, the annual cost would be just five dollars for the five emergency trips. The annual savings would amount to $95. A professor should then be willing to pay up to $95 annually to ride the bus. But how is the public bus company going to collect that $95? The value of the option is not the $5 for five fares, but $95.

Option demands present similar problems to those created by public goods. If they are to be provided, some way must be found to collect the fees so that the service can be offered. One obvious way is to tax the public to subsidize those who want the service. The result is half-full municipal buses and seldom-used city-owned concert halls.

The bus and concert hall examples preview our arguments in Chapter 5 about the difficulties governments face in providing public goods. If non-excludability means free riders exist when markets supply a public good, it also means free riders will persist if government supplies the good. Government can coerce payment from taxpayers, whether they consume the good or not, even if they simply want to, but there is still no guidance as to the optimal amount to produce or the appropriate price to charge. Given the other limitations faced by government, the arguments for publicly providing public goods are not as compelling as their face value might indicate.

Imperfect Competition

One of the most widely accepted and especially feared forms of market failure is imperfect competition, especially given fears it leads to monopoly power. Economists' concerns differ somewhat from those of the general public; economists recognize that monopoly power can lead to prices higher than they would be under perfect competition, while the voters and politicians worry about the effects of concentrated market power on the "little guy"—small businesses and working people. The U.S. Supreme Court reflected this general sentiment in the following famous passage from an 1897 decision:

> [Large business combinations] may even temporarily or perhaps permanently, reduce the price of the article traded in or manufactured, by reducing the expense inseparable from the running of many different companies for the same purpose. Trade or commerce under these circumstances may nevertheless be badly and unfortunately restrained by driving out of business the small dealers and worthy men whose lives have been spent therein and who might be unable to readjust themselves to their altered surroundings. Mere reduction in the price of the commodity dealt in might be dearly paid for by the ruin of such a class. (*United States v. Trans-Missouri Freight Ass'n,* 166 U.S. 323 [1897])

Economists, as opposed to judges, are concerned that monopolists make consumers worse off. If a competitive industry is monopolized, prices increase, quantity produced goes down, or both. These losses in consumer welfare can be avoided, at least in theory, if regulatory agencies prevent monopolies from forming in the first place.

There is another and possibly more compelling argument against monopoly than the misallocation of resources. Competition is the force compelling people in business to seek new and more efficient production techniques, to produce new products, and to take risks. Given the relative security of monopoly power, these incentives are reduced and the monopolist drifts into managerial and technical stagnation and the creativity that would produce new goods and services in the presence of competition does not exist. Thus, according to this argument, the major cost of monopoly is not necessarily reduced output and higher prices than would be obtained under competitive conditions; rather, it is the lost wealth that would otherwise occur because of competition spurring the creation of new ideas.

The traditional political response to monopoly power has been antitrust laws. There is, however, not a close connection between the economists' concerns and the antitrust laws, because the laws were established during the nineteenth century before the economic theories of imperfect markets were developed. Besides, the size of corporations has been unaffected by the existence of antitrust laws. Perhaps antitrust laws are used as a policy tool because they achieve political ends, not economic ones. As we will learn in Chapters 9 and 10, antitrust may be redundant since the economy is far more competitive than the supporters of antitrust recognize and consumers benefit far more from these contestable markets than many welfare economists and consumers, themselves, recognize.

Inadequate Information

Models of market competition typically rest upon the assumption of perfect information. They assume the consumer knows everything needed about the product's quality and the quality and price of competing products, etc. Such an assumption is unrealistic partly because the costs of obtaining such information outweigh the expected benefits. Consumers prefer to make purchases with imperfect information because the cost of obtaining full information would be too great.

One consequence of this choice on the part of consumers is that prices of certain commodities are not uniform across the market. Some sellers will be able to charge higher prices than others. But as long as prices are not outrageously out of line, consumers will pay them rather than pay the price of reducing their ignorance.

Why does inadequate information or uncertainty exist in the first place? There are many reasons. Products may be too complex to understand or their effects may be felt only in the longer run when it is too late to change one's decisions. Products may also have serious unknown side effects (as in the case of some prescription drugs). Of course, it is not unknown for sellers to exaggerate claims for their products and services. Buyers who do not make repeat purchases from the same seller may be at the mercy of unscrupulous persons.

For such reasons, information problems do arise. And while consumers devise handy rules of thumb and other protections to prevent fraud or reduce the costs of information, welfare economists and politicians have been all too willing to offer consumers the services of government. The question remains: are consumers better protected by reducing their information costs or by prohibiting producers and sellers from marketing inferior goods? I attempt an answer in Chapter 10.

Ensuring Economy-Wide Stability

The overall business climate experiences fluctuations known as business cycles, which are recurrent (but not periodic) fluctuations in general business activity over a period of years, usually measured in terms of unemployment levels, inflation, and income. Business cycles are often taken as evidence of market failures requiring government attention.

Governments claimed no particular advantage at combating business cycles until John Maynard Keynes published his *General Theory of Employment, Interest and Money* in 1936. He argued that markets are not self correcting—that some swings in the business cycle will not be corrected unless governments take action. To bring the economy out of depression, the government must find some way to stimulate consumption, investment, and capital expansion. He proposed that a combination of fiscal policies—deficit spending and manipulating tax rates and the money supply—would allow governments to fine tune economies so that full employment and stable prices could be achieved. Keynesian policies have been adopted widely since the *General Theory* was published and were the economic arguments behind the U.S. government's 2009 economic stimulus package titled the American Recovery and Reinvestment Act.

Keynes attributed unemployment to inadequate demand for labor. This view reflected his interpretation of the cause of the economic Depression of the 1930s during which the unemployment rate in Britain rose to more than 30 percent and many remained unemployed for more than a year. He claimed the unemployment of the Depression was caused by a lack of spending—too much saving. Keynes's reputation and the power of his theory combined to convert a new generation of economists to the view that markets could fail to correct economic fluctuations. The prolonged depression provided evidence for this view, and traditional theories were insufficient to explain economic fluctuations or to provide sufficient guidance for designing political responses.

The prevailing view of how the government should respond to business cycles is based on Keynesian economics. A simple explanation of the Keynesian view of the business cycle is that both economic expansion and contraction will be magnified if a market economy is left to its own direction. Erratic fluctuations in aggregate demand will lead the economy to waver between inflationary overexpansion and recessionary unemployment. A deficient level of demand results in abnormally high unemployment; excess demand produces inflation.

The simple Keynesian formula for aggregate demand can help make clear the potentially non-intuitive policy proposals. Aggregate demand is gross domestic product (GDP) and is referred to in the standard GDP formula as Y. Y is made up of the sum of consumer's expenditures on goods and services (C), government expenditures (G), investment (I), and net exports (NX). Thus, GDP or Y=C+G+I+NX. To keep aggregate demand from erratic fluctuations Keynesians claim that government can and ought to manipulate the variables on the right side of the formula by adopting flexible fiscal and monetary policies. That is, when C, I, and/or NX decline, government can increase demand by increasing G. Government can also encourage an increase in C by reducing the taxes so that consumers have more disposable income. Decreasing taxes and/or increasing spending results in deficit spending but during a downturn the government should not run balanced budgets, but should run a deficit to stimulate the economy and move it toward full employment. Government can also stimulate demand by expanding the money supply, which increases C, I, and NX.

To deal with inflation, government must do the exact opposite of what is required to increase employment. Once full employment is reached, taxes should be increased, the money supply tightened, and the government should run a budget surplus, not deficit. Such policies will counteract the wave of business optimism and consumer spending that is pushing aggregate demand beyond a level consistent with stable prices. Restrictive fiscal policies will restrict C, I, and NX by reducing disposable income, which will cause consumption to decline and will dampen investment. In addition, reduced government spending (G) will diminish aggregate demand (Y) directly. The combined result should maintain both full employment and price stability.

Attempts to manipulate the economy in this manner are relatively recent phenomena that required a revolution in thinking about government budgets. Widespread popular and political support for the view that the budget could be used to dampen fluctuations in the economy occurred only after the balanced-budget norm was destroyed or at least undermined. The extent to which Keynesian manipulations replaced other views about government's proper role is suggested by President George W. Bush's request to the nation to visit Disney World as a response to the economic downturn immediately after the terrorist attacks on 9/11/2001. President Bush also requested and Congress passed a 2008 stimulus package of tax rebates and encouraged Americans to spend them to help the economy. The $787 billion American Recovery and Reinvestment Act of 2009, passed under President Obama, is rather massive evidence of the depth of political acceptance of the Keynesian solution to fluctuations in the business cycle. In terms of the aggregate demand formula, Bush was trying to increase C while Obama increased G.

Critics of the Keynesian approach doubt the practicability of Keynesian policies, in part because workers and entrepreneurs use available information, including their expectations about government policy, and make decisions based on those "rational expectations." Thus, a counter-cyclical policy will have been anticipated by those in the market and the policy will not have its intended effect. Although many economists reject Keynesian policies based on a rational expectations analysis, politicians and the press seem to still be Keynesians. Our response to Keynesian arguments in later chapters (especially Chapter 15) is that even if the Keynesian analysis of the causes of inflation and recession is correct, governments will be unable to implement the policies necessary for Keynesian economics to work. I also conclude that Keynesian policies exacerbate some of the problems they are intended to cure.

Distributive Inequities

The distribution of income in the United States depends largely on the operation of market forces. Markets reward people in accordance with their contribution to the production of goods and services that consumers wish to purchase. Thus, a person whose productivity is low will earn little, regardless of whether the low productivity is attributable to lack of effort, lack of skill, or low demand for the skill.

Just as a university professor grades an exam according to the quality of the answers, not according to the effort that went into studying for the exam, markets reward output, not effort. People who lack skills, people with poor intellectual ability or poor health, and those who produce goods and services for which there is little demand or for which there is a large supply and low prices are likely to earn less than the more fortunate and the better educated.

There are two main arguments against relying solely on markets to allocate wealth and income: market failures and injustice. These two arguments are summarized in Arthur Okun's (1975) book, *Equality and Efficiency: The Big Tradeoff* (no one has really improved on his argument either in terms of logic or writing quality). He began by describing the outcomes of a perfectly competitive market that pays "workers and investors the value of their contributions to output." But, he argued, real markets are not perfectly competitive. Imperfections such as inadequate information, discrimination, inequality of opportunity, and monopoly power prevent the distribution that would be reached in the perfect market. A conclusion drawn from this argument is that rewards based on productivity are just, but that markets are imperfect. Therefore, ways must be found to make markets more competitive, to provide adequate information, and to prohibit discrimination.

Okun's second argument addresses the notion that rewards based on productivity are unfair. Since people's natural abilities are genetically based, they have in no sense "earned" them and those with a superior genetic heritage enjoy an undeserved and unfair advantage over their less fortunate fellows. Thus, Okun claims "society should aim to ameliorate and certainly not to compound, the flaws of the universe. It cannot stop rain, but it does manufacture umbrellas. Similarly, it can decide to restrict prizes that bestow vastly higher standards of living on people with greater innate abilities." Thus, the arbitrary distribution of natural abilities calls not for rewarding those endowed with superior ability, but for rewarding those endowed with lesser ability.

To summarize this redistributionist view: markets do not distribute income and wealth—as they ought to—even if we accept the premise that the allocations by a perfect market are justified. What is more, even perfect markets will fail to "justly" allocate the rewards of labor.

By the mid 1970s, one of the single greatest forces changing and expanding the role of the federal government in the United States was the push for equality. The federal government expanded its role through a series of income redistribution programs that had the explicit goal of reducing inequality by aiding the poor.

Retired and unemployed persons benefit from social insurance programs providing income payments in prescribed situations. The best known of these is Social Security, which is essentially a program of forced saving financed by compulsory payroll taxes levied on employees and employers. Although Social Security was originally envisioned as a social insurance that workers paid for themselves and received benefits that varied according to the level of contributions, it evolved into a system for transferring wealth from those who work to older retired persons regardless of the personal wealth or income of the retired person, or of the personal wealth or income of the younger, working person.

Poor people who do not qualify for Social Security benefits are provided for through other programs. These include the federally financed and administered Supplemental Security Income program, and the state administered but partially federally funded Temporary Assistance to Needy Families (formerly Aid to Families with Dependent Children) program. These programs attempt to provide a minimum income for the aged, the blind, the disabled, and to dependent children who do not have the financial support of a father because of desertion, disability, or death.

In 1964, just after the Johnson administration's "War on Poverty" got under way, there were 367,000 Americans receiving food stamps. This program expanded to the point that by February 2010 there were 39.7 million recipients, and the annual cost had increased from its original $860,000 ($5.9 million in 2009 dollars) to more than $53.7 billion (2009 dollars). Along the way, more than one in every seven persons has become a regular user of food stamps, or since stamps are no longer issued, electronic benefit cards. Eligible recipients now include striking workers and college students as well as those normally considered poor.

In order for government to redistribute incomes, it must tax from some and give to others. A variety of tax tools is available, including taxes on income, sales, property, and corporations as well as Social Security taxes. The favorite of these taxes for redistribution purposes is the income tax because it can be used to take more from those who have a greater ability to pay. The principle of ability to pay has been used to justify progressive tax rates, that is, rates that require those with high-incomes to pay proportionately more than those with lower incomes.

Redistributing wealth and income has become the major activity of government, supplanting the traditional functions of supplying public goods and controlling externalities. It is my view that this development has been spurred by the reasoning of welfare economists. It is too presumptuous to assume that policy makers pay enough attention to economists for us to claim that economists caused many, if any, policies. But we can safely say that the intellectual justification for redistribution comes directly from welfare economics and, therefore, that welfare economics is a spur to the development of the redistributionist state. For many, the chief failure of the market economy is its maldistribution of income and the most effective instrument for correcting this lamentable situation is to use the political process. Those who do not do well in the economy can exert influence through sympathetic political representatives in the political process and thereby increase their share. Unfortunately, experience shows that the political process rarely works this way; politicizing redistribution does not prevent those who do well in the economy from doing even better through the political process. Chapter 3 documents this conclusion.

Transaction Costs

Some potentially formidable barriers to well-functioning markets are transaction costs—the costs of negotiating and monitoring agreements to exchange. Transaction costs are part of every sale or contract: buyers and sellers must search out each other, agree on what it is they are exchanging, and gain some assurance they are getting what they bargain for. If sellers are to get the whole value of their product, they must incur the transaction costs of excluding nonpayers. Buyers must have a way of measuring or evaluating the product so they know they got full value for their money.

Transaction costs are used to justify a substantial amount of government regulation. If for every purchase of gasoline you had to bring a set of containers and a measuring device to measure gallons and determine octane ratings, for instance, you would waste time and money and face additional dangers from exposure to gasoline and its fumes. You can take your tape measure to the lumberyard to measure the length of a 2×4, but you are less able to measure the load that can be supported by a pre-built truss or glue-laminated floor joist. But with government regulation of weights and measures you buy gasoline without worrying about whether the amount on the pump is what really goes into the gasoline tank and whether the posted octane rating is accurate. Government inspections allow you to purchase pressure-treated or kiln dried lumber without having to certify for yourself that the advertised treatment processes actually happened. Building regulations allow you to build your roof with the pre-built trusses without having to hire an engineer to check the structural capacities of the trusses or joists. In short, government regulation facilitates trust. This justification for using government coercion is that the costs to you of acquiring information are reduced dramatically. It also assumes that markets will fail to provide information of similar quality.

The transaction cost defense of regulation must be modified, however. If sellers are intent on taking advantage of buyers because of the sellers' superior information, we must account for the enthusiasm with which sellers seek to be regulated. The demand for government regulation most often arises from sellers. As we learn in upcoming chapters, regulation is a way for sellers already in the market to use government coercion to restrict competition, choice, and opportunities. In addition, private entrepreneurs have become quite inventive at devising new ways to provide information and reduce transaction costs. There are superior alternatives to government regulation and I provide several examples in Part IV.

Conclusions

When most economists consider the market economy they usually do so by examining the market environment within which economic agents—consumers and producers—make decisions. They ask whether any improvements can be made. Are there artificial barriers to entry that reduce competition? What are the relevant externalities? Are there inequities? Is the market responding to demand? These are legitimate questions.

The analysis of markets usually encourages the welfare economist to recommend government policies to change the offensive or inefficient situation. As they dethrone markets they crown government by finding "solutions" that require government intervention: more and/or different taxes; price controls; subsidies and tariffs; penalizing collusion through antitrust laws; more controls over private property; and, of course, more government-directed planning.

Government responses to perceived market failures produce a steady increase in the size of government budgets, regulatory agencies, and legislative staffs. Government growth results from faith in government activism: the belief that the government can correct market failures by appropriate regulations, discretionary fiscal policies, and redistribution. The role of government is no longer limited to providing necessary public services like a legal system and national defense. Instead, government is expected to use its power to cure social ills that are not adequately addressed by private markets.

This view of government contains implicit assumptions about the motives and abilities of people who hold positions of power in government and who carry out government policies. It is based on faith that government can and will carry out the strategies necessary to correct market failures. Chapter 2 describes and analyzes these assumptions as a prelude to discussing, in subsequent chapters, the actual effects of political responses to market imperfections.

Bibliographical Notes

Despite the joke that if we laid all the economists in the world end-to-end we would not reach a conclusion, economists are remarkably consistent when it comes to the basics of their paradigm. They make the same general assumptions about human nature, how markets function, the role of prices, and the effects of changes in supply and demand. In fact, it has been said that a demand curve is the closest the social sciences come to an analog to the law of gravity. Except in extremely rare circumstances, demand curves are downward sloping to the right, meaning that quantity demanded increases as price falls.

I suggest one classic article and two introductory texts for those wishing to better understand the basics of economic analysis. The article is F.A. Hayek's definitive, "The Use of Knowledge in Society" (*American Economic Review*, 35,

September 1945, 519–30). It is the best description I know about how prices co-ordinate human activity and, incidentally, why markets coordinate better than politics. *Common Sense Economics: What Everyone Should Know about Wealth and Prosperity* (St. Martin's Press, 2010) by James Gwartney, Richard Stroup, Dwight Lee, and Tawni Ferrarini is an introduction to economic thinking that you can give as a present to friends and family. Its purpose is to reduce economic illiteracy and it succeeds. The authors identify twelve "key elements of economics that are easily understood while being powerful descriptors of how economies work and how wealth is generated. There is even a section of twelve key elements of practical personal finance. Although there are now several good introductory textbooks I recommend, the one I find most pleasurable: *The Economic Way of Thinking* (Prentice Hall, 2009) now in its 12th edition. Paul Heyne wrote the first several editions of the text and after his death Peter Boettke and David Prychitko have continued to update it. The writing style is conversational and the examples are easily understood and compelling.

Anyone beginning to read about free riders and collective action should begin with the book by economist Mancur Olson, *The Logic of Collective Action* (Cambridge: Harvard University Press, 1965). Olson describes the incentives to free ride and how successful groups provide "selective incentives" to overcome free riding.

The classic work on externalities and the environment is Garrett Hardin's "The Tragedy of the Commons," first published in 1968 by *Science* 162 (December, 1968), 1243–48. Hardin's article, one of the most reprinted articles on the environment, describes how rational, individual action can destroy commonly owned property. H. Scott Gordon's earlier article, "The Economic Theory of a Common Property Resource: The Fishery," in *Journal of Political Economy* 62 (April 1954), 124–42 provides a more mathematical and scholarly treatment of the same subject. Of course, instituting defined, enforceable property and use rights solves the problem of the commons. I suggest a collection edited by Nives Dolsak and Elinor Ostrom for examples from several different cultures. The book, *The Commons in the New Millennium: Challenges and Adaptation* (Politics, Science, and Environment: Cambridge, MA: MIT Press, 2003), contains eleven chapters describing management of common property resources.

For a thought-provoking treatise on distributional questions I refer readers to Charles Murray's *In Our Hands: A Plan to Replace the Welfare State* (Washington DC: AEI Press, 2006). Murray suggests replacing all welfare transfer programs with an annual $10,000 cash grant to everyone age twenty-one or older. Part would have to be spent on health insurance and saving a portion would be strongly encouraged. Low-income people would be able to change jobs more easily under Murray's proposal than under current welfare programs.

An extensive discussion of market failure can be found in Tyler Cowen's and Eric Crampton's edited volume, *Market Failure or Success: The New Debate* (Cheltenham, UK and Northampton, MA: Edward Elgar for the Independent Institute, 2002). They include classic articles showing market failures and use newer articles raising questions about the extent of market failure. The article on the QWERTY keyboard, for example, shows the supposed market failure story to be false. The book led Nobel Laureate in Economic Science Vernon Smith to suggest that the theory of market failure is just an empty box.

I suggest a book that captures the conventional wisdom about politics and markets as well as any I know. The title is, appropriately enough, *Politics and Markets* (New York: Basic Books, 1977) by Charles E. Lindblom. He writes of the limited competence of governments, but especially of markets, and the virtues of policy making and planning. I believe the book to be badly flawed and refer the reader to James M. Buchanan's critical review in *Journal of Economic Issues* 13 (March, 1979), 215–17, but recommend the book for readers wanting to understand the vision of politics and markets that continues to be popular among many academics, especially political scientists.

Reading Keynes is the best way to learn what he has to say. But I have a shortcut to suggest for the faint-of-heart. Purchase the Palgrave Macmillan 2007 reprint of Keynes's *The General Theory of Employment Interest and Money,* if for no other reason than to have it on your shelf. Before putting it on your shelf, read Nobel laureate Paul Krugman's introduction. It is an excellent summary and is eloquently written. It is also a roadmap to reading the text. Krugman says, "In telling people how to read *The General Theory,* I find it helpful to describe it as a meal that begins with a delectable appetizer and ends with a delightful dessert, but whose main course consists of rather tough meat. It's tempting for readers to dine only on the easily digestible parts of the book, and skip the argument that lies between. But the main course is where the true value of the book lies."

References

Bator, Francis. "The Anatomy of Market Failure," *Quarterly Journal of Economics, 72* (August 1958) pp. 351–79.

Baumol, William J. *Welfare Economics and the Theory of the State,* rev. 2nd ed. (Cambridge: Harvard University Press, 1952; 1965).

Baumol, William J. and Wallace E. Oates. *Economics, Environmental Policy, and the Quality of Life.* Englewood Cliffs: Prentice-Hall, Inc., 1979, 77 and 79.

Boettke, Peter J., Paul Heyne, and David L. Prychitko. *The Economic Way of Thinking.* 12th ed. Alexandria, VA: Prentice Hall, 2009.

Cowen, Tyler and Eric Crampton. *Market Failure Or Success: the New Debate.* Northampton, UK: Edward Elgar, 1980.

Dolsak, Nives and Elinor Ostrom. *The Commons in the New Millennium: Challenges and Adaptation* (Politics, Science, and the Environment). London: The MIT Press, 2003.

Gordon, Scott H. "The Economic Theory of Common Property Resources." *Bulletin of Mathematical Biography* 62 (1954): 124–42.

Gwartney, James D., Richard L. Stroup, Dwight R. Lee and Tawni H. Ferrarini. *Common Sense Economics: What Everyone Should Know about Wealth and Prosperity.* New York: St. Martin's Press, 2010.

Hardin, Garrett. "The Tragedy of the Commons." *Science* 162, no. 3859 (1968): 1243–248.

Hayek, Friedrich A. von. "The Use of Knowledge in Society." *American Economic Review,* 35, No. 4, pp. 519–30.

Heyne, Paul. *The Economic Way of Thinking.* Chicago: Science Research Associates, Inc., 4th ed., 1983, 125.

Hume, David. *A Treatise on Human Nature.* Oxford: The Clarendon Press, 1898, 300–04.

Keynes, John Maynard. *The General Theory of Employment, Interest, and Money.* New York: Harcourt, Brace, & World, 1936.

Keynes, John Maynard. *The General Theory of Employment, Interest and Money.* New ed. New York: Palgrave Macmillan, 2007.

Lindblom, Charles Edward. *Politics and Market: The World's Political Economic Systems.* New ed. Boulder: Basic Books, 1980.

Marshall, Alfred. *Principles of Economics.* Library of Economics and Liberty, 1920. http://www.econlib.org/library/Marshall/marP.html.

Murray, Charles. *In Our Hands: A Plan To Replace The Welfare State.* Washington: AEI Press, 2006.

"Nobel Laureates Offer Views on the Economy." Business News and Financial News, the *Wall Street Journal,* 3 (Sept. 2004). http://online.wsj.com/article/SB10941568639 808339-email.html#articleTabs%.

Okun, Arthur. *Equality and Efficiency: The Big Tradeoff.* Washington, DC: The Brookings Institution, 1975.

Olson, Mancur. *The Logic of Collective Action: Public Goods and the Theory of Groups.* Revised ed. Cambridge: Harvard University Press, 1971.

Pigou, Arthur C. *The Economics of Welfare.* Library of Economics and Liberty, 1932. http://www.econlib.org/library/NPDBooks/Pigou/pgEW.html.

Read, Leonard E. "I, Pencil: My Family Tree as told to Leonard Read." Irvington-on-Hudson, New York: The Foundation for Economic Education, Inc. 1958. http://www.econlib.org/library/Essays/rdPncI1.html.

Ridley, Matt. *The Rational Optimist: How Prosperity Evolves.* New York: HarperCollins Publishers, 2010.

Samuelson, Paul A. *Economics.* 7th ed. New York: McGraw-Hill, 1967, p. 47.

Samuelson, Paul A. "The Pure Theory of Public Expenditure," *Review of Economics and Statistics,* 36 (November, 1954), 387–89.

Schultze, Charles. *The Public Use of Private Interest.* Washington, DC: The Brookings Institution, 1977), p. 18.

Sidgwick, Henry. *The Principles of Political Economy—1883.* Cornell: Cornell University Press, 2009.

Smith, Adam. *An Inquiry into the Nature and Causes of the Wealth of Nations.* Indianapolis: Liberty Fund, Inc., 1981. Reprint. Originally published: Oxford: Clarendon Press, 1979. (Glasgow edition of the works and correspondence of Adam Smith, vol. 1).

"SNAP Annual Summary." Home Page. United States Department of Agriculture, 30 June 2010. http://www.fns.usda.gov/pd/SN.

"Stop!" *The Economist.* 23 Jan 2010: 11–12. Print.

U.S. v. Trans-Missouri Freight Ass'n., 166 U.S. 290 (1897).

2

Political Presuppositions
of the Idealized State

POLITICAL SCIENCE IS an odd discipline in that arguments are ongoing and often expanding, rather than leading to consensus. Charles Lindblom, former president of the American Political Science Association, noted that political science "is a name given not to a field of conventional scientific inquiry but to a continuing debate." The claims by various sides in the debate do not get resolved: "On any given issue of fact or value, debate in political science tends to be endless rather than declining (or terminating in a finding)" (Lindblom, 1997, 260–61). What this means for this book, is that, unlike for economics, it is difficult to identify *specific* claims about the state and the economy that are agreed on by political scientists.

Some broad assertions hold, however. The normative basis of political science, at least on both sides of the Atlantic, has been political liberalism—a vision of the state based on civic and political rights that should not be restricted by others. Included in these rights are the familiar ones delineated in the U.S. Bill of Rights including defense against arbitrary government; freedom of speech, press, assembly; property rights; and protection of minorities from majorities.

Political scientists value democracy over other forms of government while recognizing inherent tensions between liberalism's rights and the powers of democracy. Thus, political scientists are concerned about who participates in democracy and who does not. How are power and resources allocated? Which institutions best protect individual rights? Which rights ought to be protected? What about communal rights? Although members of the discipline were once concerned with constraining government, most are currently interested in expanding it. Where once there were many voices warning about the power of the state and claiming that many things were "beyond politics," most voices today believe that democracy ought to be expanded and the state along with it. In essence, there is little that is beyond the power of democratic politics.

Political scientists readily admit that self-interest drives market choices but they appear to assume that people shift mental and moral gears (or at least they should shift gears) when moving from the economic to the political aspects of life. Some argue that while market choices are based on simple preferences, political choices require complex judgments, sometimes based on moral or ethical rules. Thus, to many political scientists, bureaucrats are well meaning, dedicated civil servants who apply their professional training and expertise in the public interest. Politicians balance the claims of competing interests and trade votes to produce socially beneficial outcomes. Interest group competition resembles market competition in that it appears an invisible hand guides results. Voters seek to enhance the general welfare by choosing carefully among competing politicians and ballot proposals. One product of all this is a process that enables the participants to become part of a cause greater than themselves.

Government, therefore, is basically passive, waiting to be acted upon by voters and interest groups, while politicians and bureaucrats are middlemen who arrange exchanges and deals for others and protect the public interest. In this view, politics is a benign, competitive process having close parallels with competitive markets, with people participating primarily to serve interests other than their own, although serving their own interests is not precluded from the analysis.

Political scientists prefer politics to markets because they tend to think that politics, at least in a representative democracy, is more just and equitable than are markets. The political science preference for politics over markets is intellectual support for the economists' often implicit although sometimes explicit claim that government can remedy market failures and imperfections. And the economists need that support for, as George Stigler (1975, 103) put it:

> Economists have long had a deeply schizophrenic view of the state. They study an elaborate and remarkably complex private economy, and find that by precise and elegant criteria of optimal behavior a private enterprise system has certain classes of failures. These failures, of which some are highly complex in nature and all are uncertain in magnitude, are proposed for remedial or surrogate performance by the state.

Simultaneously, the economists—along with the rest of the population—view the democratic state as a well-meaning, clumsy institution all too frequently diverted by emotion and administered by venality. The state is often viewed as the bulwark of "vested interests"—and in fact where else can an interest vest? The state is thus at one and the same time the corrector of subtle disharmonies between the marginal social and the marginal private products of resources, and the obstinately unlearning patron of indefensible protective import quotas and usury laws.

Economists who take such a schizophrenic view have not applied their own, powerful tools of analysis to the state. When they do, they are less likely to assume the state can easily improve on markets. Part II presents such an analysis. But before undertaking that analysis, I provide an overview and discussion of the presuppositions that underlie economists' and political scientists' faith in political processes.

Politics as Market

The most widely accepted model of the governmental process comes from the pluralist tradition begun by David Truman (1951), Robert Dahl (1956) and Charles E. Lindblom (1977). Although Truman's pluralist democracy differed from Dahl and Lindblom's polyarchy, each built on the view of government developed by James Madison in *Federalist 10* in which Madison argued that it is impossible to stop factions, or—in today's terminology, "interest groups"—from organizing and attempting to use the political system to their own ends. The effects of one faction are controlled by vigorous competition from other factions. An existing multiplicity of interests competing with one another in the political arena produces a market-type competition, which becomes the collective choice version of Adam Smith's "invisible hand." It produces socially beneficial policies—policies that no one necessarily intended but which are in the public interest. Although this political market is seen as suffering from some inherent limitations, the process is judged to be essentially healthy. Consider Robert Dahl's (1967) arguments:

> Because one center of power is set against another, power itself will be tamed, civilized, controlled and limited to decent human purposes,

while coercion, the most evil form of power, will be reduced to a minimum. Societies are collections of competing, organized factions, each headed by an elite. These "plural elites" interact, compete, strike bargains and manage conflict within their own units.

According to Charles Lindblom (1977, 137), "constant and varied interaction between leadership and citizenry . . . enables citizens to form coalitions and guides leadership's response to them." He further claims the key process is leaders persuading masses of voters. The process of persuasion is not simply the leader communicating to a homogeneous citizenry. Instead, leaders communicate with intermediate leaders, who, in turn, attempt to persuade lesser leaders. These leaders include other local politicians, writers and broadcasters, religious leaders, union officials, and finally active, informed citizens who are opinion leaders in their neighborhoods.

This form of democracy, labeled pluralism, is clearly not a system of majority rule, nor is it a system of elite rule. A political party is a coalition of political leaders who cooperate to win elections. The parties agree on those issues for which there is massive, clear support. They divide on issues over which there is not a clearly perceived majority. The outcome is that majority positions prevail when they are clear and unmistakable. Where they are not clear, elected and appointed officials are able to pursue their own agendas which may or may not be in the public interest.

Some criticize polyarchy because they claim the organized can benefit at the expense of the unorganized. Furthermore, leaders are able to use rather than serve the membership of their groups and majority rule is not always followed. Even so, political competition is generally seen as an effective form of political organization. Competition among leaders and groups causes pertinent information to reach decision makers. The abuse of power is controlled by ordinary citizens' choosing and removing officials; elected officials sharing authority with bureaucrats; and alliances forming between interest groups, legislative, bureaucratic, and executive leaders. Lindblom (1977, 140) described it as "a vast process of mutual accommodation to win votes, to assemble the votes of smaller groups in ever larger blocs and, for some leaders, to achieve influence by delivering votes to others."

The pluralist position is supported, surprisingly enough, by two prominent members of the Chicago School of Political Economy. Gary Becker and George Stigler each argued at length and in detail that present policies are politically efficient, that is, nothing better can be done under existing rules. Protectionist policies are the rational outcomes of the current political process. Politicians and voters adopt the more efficient or less inefficient policies (a rather startling claim in view of all the rent-seeking evidence I summarize in later chapters, starting in Part II). In any event, while the pluralists surely would not employ the same reasoning process as Chicago analysts it is clear that both share an essentially benign view of politics.

Anyone can see that these assumptions, like those of the perfect market, are unrealistic. Balancing all these interests is cumbersome, tedious and costly, especially since the medium of exchange is comprised of votes, support, status, and time rather than something as simple as money. Another complication is the sheer number of participants in the process. As interest group numbers increase, the costs to achieve agreement also increase and the ability to make efficient decisions declines. Besides, no one is currently willing to argue that today's interest groups generate anything approximating the public interest or that they successfully moderate each other's actions or influence.

Such considerations are irrelevant in the pluralist tradition. Truman argued, for example, that efficiency is not an appropriate tool of analysis or an appropriate criterion for evaluating the governmental process. Instead, stability of the political system, equality, and control by "the people" are the valued criteria. These concepts become both positive statements describing the governmental process and normative statements describing how it ought to function.

Pluralism is challenged by some political scientists not because they disagree with how it works, but because they want to replace it with something superior. That something is deliberative democracy. Unlike *Federalist 10*'s suggestion that the competition of ideas would preserve liberty and promote the public good, proponents of deliberation believe that informed, educated deliberation will transform preferences. Then the polity will not need to add-up votes to decide the common good because of general agreement on the issues. This idea echoes Rousseau's "general will" and is an attempt to move beyond "adversary democracy" (Mansbridge, 1980).

Shapiro (2002) explains:

Deliberative remedies are put forward in response to various maladies that are perceived as pervading contemporary democracy. Poor quality of decision-making, sound-bite politics, low levels of participation, legitimacy of government, and ignorant citizens are among the more frequently mentioned. The assumption is that if people talk for long enough in the right circumstances, they will agree more often and this is a good thing (Shapiro, 2002, 238; For sources on deliberative democracy see Gutmann and Thompson (1966) and Ackerman and Fishkin (2000)).

Proponents of deliberative democracy believe that politics improves the capacity for individual fulfillment and improvement. This Aristotelian and Tocquevillian theme is at the core of modern discussions about civic engagement. According to this view, participating in the political process is a way to lift oneself above the crass self-interest many believe characterize market transactions. People are not able to reach their highest potential *unless* they participate in political and civic processes. In fact, such participation is necessary for human moral development. Only by connecting oneself with others through participation in political processes does one become whole. A central purpose of political participation is, therefore, to cause people to change:

. . . from seeing themselves and acting as essentially consumers to seeing themselves and acting as exerters and enjoyers of the exertion and development of their own capacities. . . . For the latter self image brings with it a sense of community which the former does not. One can acquire and consume by oneself, for one's own satisfaction or to show one's superiority to others; this does not require or foster a sense of community; whereas the enjoyment and development of one's capacities is to be done for the most part in conjunction with others, in some relation of community (C.B. Macpherson, 1977, 99).

Tocqueville emphasized associational life as being necessary for democratic life. One restatement of this position is Robert Putnam's historical study of Italy, *Making Democracy Work* (1993) in which he emphasized the importance of civic community in developing civic institutions. In more recent work, Putnam emphasizes how participating in the political system, even if it is simply to vote in recurring elections, builds "social capital."

> Whereas physical capital refers to physical objects and human capital refers to the properties of individuals, social capital refers to connections among individuals—social networks and the norms of reciprocity and trustworthiness that arise from them. In that sense social capital is closely related to what some have called "civic virtue." The difference is that "social capital" calls attention to the fact that civic virtue is most powerful when embedded in a network of reciprocal social relations. A society of many virtuous but isolated individuals is not necessarily rich in social capital (Putnam, 2000, 19).

Social capital, civic participation, a sense of community, and interconnectedness are all terms used to validate the transforming power of being part of a political community. The underlying assumption is that, "Civic engagement brings people together; interacting enables them to communicate their preferences and expectations, and working together builds bonds of trust and mutual obligation" (Fiorina, 2002, 515). Bonds of trust and mutual obligation lead to political participation that transcends self-interest.

Many of the political reforms instituted during the last century in the United States and elsewhere were intended to increase civic engagement. The argument was that government by the people required empowering citizens and opening political and civic procedures and processes. Reforms to accomplish these ends included opening up presidential nominating processes, centering politics on candidates rather than parties, requiring open meetings and recorded votes, creating more interest groups, reducing institutional impediments to initiative and referendum processes, relying on public opinion polls, increasing the number of local political bodies, opening bureaucracies, requiring public hearings and comment, and registering more voters.

Omnicompetent Scientific Managers

In order for a democratic government, whether it be polyarchal or deliberative, to carry out its ends, it must rely on managers. Information must be gathered, policies reviewed, and programs implemented and administered. The managers who undertake these tasks are known as civil servants, public administrators, or bureaucrats. They are an essential part of any attempt to manipulate markets, and an understanding of the conventional understanding of their capabilities and expected tasks is important to analyzing their ability to correct market failure.

For more than one hundred years the basic vision of bureaucracy has been that efficiency is promoted by professional, nonpartisan administration directed and coordinated by a strong executive. Although no one cited his article until after its republication in *Political Science Quarterly* in 1941, an 1887 article published by a young political scientist who later became President of the United States—Woodrow Wilson—summarized the basic vision. To Wilson:

> The field of administration is a field of business. It is removed from the hurry and strife of politics; it at most points stands apart even from the debatable ground of constitutional study. It is a part of political life only as the methods of the counting-house are a part of the society; only as machinery is part of the manufacturing product (p. 18).

Wilson's essay reflected what became known as the politics-administration dichotomy, the distinction between the proper sphere for partisan politics and the proper sphere for non-partisan administration. He asserted, "More important to be observed is the truth already so much and so fortunately insisted upon by our civil service reformers; namely that administration lies outside the proper sphere of politics." And he believed "this discrimination between administration and politics is now, happily, too obvious to need further discussion" (p. 13).

The politics-administration dichotomy was part of the civil service reform movement and fit well with the arguments of muckrakers like Lincoln Steffens, Ida Tarbell, and Upton Sinclair. In addition, Frederick Taylor and other advocates of scientific management were, at the time, developing techniques of factory management and these ideas of "scientific management" were adopted by promoters of a scientific, non-partisan, public administration.

Scientific management of public agencies became an ideal of both the left and the right. It is based on the belief that "right-minded" managers, who are not motivated by profit or other selfish goals, will protect the public interest while managing government agencies, programs and properties. In order to accomplish this purpose, however, managers need to be insulated from politics. Once the political system has produced policy direction, scientific managers need to be left alone to manage according to their professional training.

Public administration, as viewed by its proponents, allows a well-trained, competent bureaucracy to apply technology and expertise to eliminate the waste commonly found in market transactions, to protect the people from the excesses of business, and to distribute society's wealth fairly. One of the purported virtues of public administration is its ability to divine not only what people want, but what is good for them. Consumer sovereignty, or the preference of citizens, is not valued as highly as the truths of science wielded by powerful, non-partisan administrators. Examples include regulation of individuals and business by government agencies. Ordinary citizens must be protected from themselves in a host of activities: motorists must purchase automobiles with bumpers that pass government-imposed crash tests, seat belts that activate a buzzer when not hooked up, and set rates of fuel efficiency; new homes and additions to existing homes must be built according to standard building codes; lawnmowers must have devices to automatically stop the blade when the operator lets go of the handle.

Citizens must be protected from business as well: meat cannot be purchased without a government inspection, medical services cannot be bought from someone who has not graduated from an accredited medical school, businesses must pay their employees a wage at least equal to the minimum set by the government; advertising messages must conform to the guidelines established by the Federal Communications Commission, new drugs must meet tough standards and testing and undergo extensive reviews by the Food and Drug Administration. Science establishes the standards for protecting individuals from themselves and from others and the standards are then enforced by the government.

Today's students of public administration recognize that Wilson's scheme for separating politics from administration was impossible. In fact, introductory textbooks now emphasize the political dynamics of public administration. One text argues for facing the political nature of public administration "maturely." The authors go on to say,

> Just as the first stop in arresting alcoholism is to have the alcoholic admit
> that he or she is an alcoholic and will always be an alcoholic even after he

or she stops drinking, the first step toward putting public administration operations on a more realistic footing is for public managers to admit public sector administration is an inherently political process (Shafritz and Russell, 2010, 26).

Modern analysts emphasize that bureaucracy has to be much more politicized than proponents of scientific management had thought. Agencies, for example, have to build and curry the favor of a clientele in order to survive. They must mollify chairs of appropriations committees while carrying out unclear and often underfunded legislative requirements.

In addition, administrators do not have perfect information or certainty. Rather than choosing the best course of action from among a complete and certain list of alternatives, administrators must seek improvement by making what Herbert Simon (1976) called "satisficing" choices among a limited number of alternatives.

Whether the description of bureaucracy is made by an old scientific manager or a new systems theorist, the same model of political behavior underlies the argument. Managers may maximize or suffice with perfect or imperfect information, they may be caught in difficult political pressures, politics internal to their agency may reduce their options, but they try to act in the public interest. The following paragraph from the authors of the introductory text cited above summarizes:

> The U.S. Navy once used this recruiting slogan: "It's not just a job, it's an adventure." So it is with public administration. A public service career is often the most exciting thing individuals can do with their lives. Walter Lippmann often observed that "the joys of private life" are much overrated. "For the truth is that public life, once a man [or woman] has been infected with its excitement and importance, is something that few ever get over." Whether one comes to a capital to expand government or to contract it, it is a worthy personal quest, a great personal adventure—and equally worthy and adventurous if you serve in a national capital, a state capital, a city hall, or a neighborhood association (Shafritz and Russell, 2010, 27).

The Planning Ideal

Using the state to remedy market failures requires planning, not necessarily the central planning of production that was attempted in Communist countries, but planning that is supposedly less political, more scientific, and more targeted to specific problems. Examples abound: fiscal policies, plant closings, accident prevention, income security, pollution, endangered species, investment, development, transportation, housing, employment, smart-growth and on and on. Notice that these types of planning are far more extensive than the "good government" planning advocated by the Progressives who were primarily concerned about political corruption and their fears of concentrated economic power.

Although welfare economists are generally reticent about expanding government planning to include planning and coordination of economic activities beyond the control of externalities, this expansion has broad support across the political spectrum. The most visible arena for planning is land use. Almost every city and county in the United State has a planning department and a planning commission to direct land use in their jurisdictions. State and federal agencies produce elaborate plans affecting many private actions that might affect the physical environment. Historic preservation commissions make plans that affect actions that might affect the aesthetic environment. Two-thirds of the 30,000 members of the American Planning Association work for government agencies. Democrats and Republicans agree that "smart growth" must replace market directed growth. Instead of markets directing, governments must plan and direct housing types, mass transit, and walk-able communities. Government-directed smart-growth is advanced as a means of replacing "mindless growth" and "excessive development" arising from uncontrolled market activity. Government is the appropriate tool to control everything from aesthetics of house design to the location and timing of economic development.

Conclusions

Many advocates of greater government planning and direction see exchange as a competitive activity producing winners and losers. The "little guy" is at the mercy of the "big guys"; consumers are manipulated by advertisers into buying products they don't need or even really want; buyers are at the mercy of sellers; and labor loses to management. Although mutually advantageous gain is considered a possibility, the usual expectation is that someone's gain is often someone else's loss.

Politics presumably makes things better. Political processes distribute wealth more equally with the result that the political and economic power of those who operate the economy is reduced. Political interference in the workplace protects labor from being victimized by management, and political actions afford consumers greater protection. This idealized democratic state is guided by the visible hand of government that improves on the chaos of the market. It lifts people from the morally degenerating or, at best, amoral self-interest of the market into more responsible and more socially beneficial activities. Government becomes the tool allowing for the expression of competing values and for resolving conflicts between them. Competent, scientific managers protect citizens from themselves, from organized interests, and from big business.

Economists who advocate government intervention to reverse a market failure are not as optimistic or as naive as the preceding summary suggests. The summary does reflect the view animating discussions promoting government to resolve market failures. The problem is that few economists have applied their powerful tools for analyzing market processes to an analysis of government processes. Those who argue that market failure justifies government action don't stop to ask: What incentives exist in government? Who wins and who loses? Are the actual outcomes different from those we hope for? Do good intentions in government produce good results?

The following chapters provide such an analysis. They show the idealized democratic state to be just that—idealized but not realized and with no potential for realization. They also show the earlier claims of market failure to be far weaker than supposed even just a few years ago, so that the initial justifications for relying on the state, ideal or not, are seldom justifications at all.

Bibliographical Notes

This chapter identifies some of the most important and classical works for understanding the pluralist vision of the state. They are: Robert Dahl's *A Pref-*

ace to Democratic Theory (Chicago: University of Chicago Press, 1956), David Truman's *The Governmental Process* (New York: Alfred A. Knopf, 1951), and Charles E. Lindblom's *Politics and Markets* (New York: Basic Books, 1977). An excellent slim volume on interest groups is Alfred O. Hirschman's book *The Passions and the Interests* (Princeton: Princeton University Press, 1977).

Anyone wishing to be at least conversant with discussions about social capital and civic engagement must read Robert Putnam's *Bowling Alone: The Collapse and Revival of American Community* (New York: Simon & Schuster, 2000). Putnam's thesis is that thousands of Americans once bowled in leagues but now are more likely to bowl alone. Bowling alone is his metaphor for his claim that Americans are becoming less connected with their families, neighbors, communities, and nation. They are less likely to take Sunday picnics and more likely to give "the finger" to other drivers. All this is evidence, he claims, that "the bonds of our communities have withered."

Public administration is its own academic field complete with academic journals and professional conferences. Thus, the literature on the subject is voluminous. I suggest a few I find interesting and useful. First, I suggest Herbert Simon's *Administrative Behavior: A Study of Decision-Making Process in Administrative Organization* (New York: The Free Press, 1976) first published in 1947. Simon, who later won the Nobel Prize in economics for his work on decision-making theory, provides the basis for much of the modern study of bureaucracy. Second, I recommend James Q. Wilson's *Bureaucracy: What Government Agencies Do and Why They Do It* (New York: Basic Books) as a "must read" about how bureaucracy functions. First published in 1989, a new edition was released in 2000. His strongest contribution is identifying four political environments that determine how outside interests influence bureaucracy—client politics produces a client agency, grass roots social movements produce entrepreneurial agencies to "solve" problems, rival interest groups result in interest group agencies who must pick the right interest group at the right time, and majoritarian politics produce majoritarian agencies whose major concern is to not create enemies. Finally, *The Encyclopedia of Public Administration and Public Policy* (Rabin, Dekker Encyclopedias, Supplement Edition 2002) is far too expensive for most personal libraries, but it is available online and should be in most university libraries. If you want to understand the field of public administration, this is the place to start.

References

Dahl, Robert. *A Preface to Democratic Theory*. Chicago: University of Chicago Press, 1956.

Dahl, Robert. *Pluralist Democracy in the United States: Conflict and Consent*. Chicago: Rand McNally, 1967, p. 24.

Fiorina, Morris P. "Extreme Voices: A Dark Side of Civic Engagement." *Civic Engagement in American Democracy*, ed. Theda Skocpol and Morris Fiorina. Washington, DC: Brookings, 1999.

Fiorina, Morris P. "Parties, Participation, and Representation in America: Old Theories Face New Realities." *Political Science: State of the Discipline*. New York: W.W. Norton & Company, 2002.

Fishkin, James S. et al., *Does Deliberation Induce Preference Structuration? Evidence From Deliberate Opinion Polls*. Presented at American Political Science Association. Oct. 30, 2000: 1–22.

Gutmann, Amy, and Dennis Thompson. *Why Deliberative Democracy?* Princeton: Princeton University Press, 2004.

Hirschman, Albert O. *The Passions and the Interests*. 20 ed. Princeton: Princeton University Press, 1997.

Lindblom, Charles, E. *Politics and Markets*. New York: Basic Books, 1977.

Macpherson, C.B. *The Life and Times of Liberal Democracy*. Oxford: Oxford University Press, 1977, p. 99.

Mansbridge, Jane. *Beyond Adversary Democracy*. New York: Basic Books, 1980.

Putnam, Robert D. *Bowling Alone: The Collapse and Revival of American Community*. New York: Simon & Schuster, 2000, p. 19.

Putnam, Robert D. *Making Democracy Work*. 2 ed. Princeton: Princeton University Press, 1994.

Rabin, Jack. *Encyclopedia of Public Administration and Public Policy*, First Update Supplement (Public Administration and Public Policy). Supplement ed. Boca Raton: CRC, 2005.

Shafritz, Jay M. and E.W. Russell. *Introducing Public Administration*. New York: Pearson Education, 2010.

Shapiro, Ian. "Problems, Methods, and Theories in the Study of Political Science or What Is Wrong With Political Science and What To Do about It." *Political Theory* (2002), p. 238.

Simon, Herbert. *Administrative Behavior: A Study of Decision Making Process in Administrative Organization*. New York: The Free Press, 1976.

Stigler, George. *The Citizen and the State: Essays on Regulation*. Chicago: University of Chicago Press, 1975, p. 103.

Truman, David B. *The Governmental Process: Political Interests and Public Opinion*. New York: Alfred A. Knopf, 1951.

Wilson, Woodrow. "The Study of Administration," *Political Science Quarterly*, 2 (June, 1887), pp. 197–222.

In Dispraise of Politics
Some Public Choice

GOVERNMENT FAILURE IS the topic of Part II and is a central research topic of the academic discipline known as public choice. Public choice scholars apply economic reasoning and analysis to the study of collective or public choices. Their conclusions quickly disabuse one of the notions of the idealized state explained in Part I.

Public choice scholars have shown that governments do not easily fix market failures; they usually make things worse. The fundamental reason is that the information and incentives that allow markets to coordinate human activities and wants are not available to government. Thus, voters, politicians, bureaucrats, and activists who believe themselves to be promoting the public interest are led by an invisible hand to promote interests other than the public interest.

This analysis is confined to democracies, not authoritarian regimes and the criticisms of democracy should not be taken as support for those regimes. I believe strongly in self-government. Democracy can be structured to provide appropriate protections for individual rights and opportunities for voluntary, collective action. But, modern democratic politics is often exploitative, wasteful, and destructive of individual rights. The analysis presented here prepares the reader to understand the case studies of Part IV and anticipates the reforms I propose in the final chapter.

3 | Undemocratic Side of Democracy

IN THE DECADES following Pigou's *The Economics of Welfare* economists viewed government as a disinterested agency for correcting market failure while political scientists generally viewed government (at least *democratic* government) as a means of reflecting the general will. This chapter introduces a less romantic theory of government known, somewhat inelegantly, as "public choice." The name "public choice" emerged from a 1967 meeting of the Committee for the Study of Non-Market Decision Making, which renamed itself the Public Choice Society.

Public choice is the study of political or public choices using the tools and assumptions of economics. The unit of analysis is not the state, legislature, committee, or bureaucracy—it is the individual citizen, legislator, committee member, or bureaucrat. And those individuals are not passive, other-regarding political eunuchs. They have passions, interests, and values that they pursue through the political process. Governments, in public choice theory, are collections of individuals interacting to achieve outcomes consistent with their self-interest.

In its assumptions public choice is just common sense. As the old joke about politics in a state known for political corruption goes, "We don't expect our politicians to be corrupt, we demand it." Common sense suggests we should not expect people to defy human nature when they move from the grocery store to the voting booth or mayoral seat. Oddly enough, that is exactly what many economists, political scientists, and citizens expect. Public choice moves us out of that romantic, "mythful" thinking into a more realistic and insightful view of the political world. It does not deny that acts of political courage and altruism occur; it does suggest we ought not to expect or rely on them. Perhaps the major discovery of public choice is the welfare diminishing propensities of real-world politics. These propensities, known as government failures, are as ubiquitous, as market failures and may be more difficult to cure. Because government fails, government attempts to fix market failures may make things worse.

The Polity as an Economy (of Sorts), or, Applying Economic Concepts to Politics

The Simple Model

The public choice model of politics and democracy is actually quite simple. Politics is a system consisting of four groups of decision makers—voters, elected officials or politicians, bureaucrats, and interest groups. The individuals making up those groups seek benefits from the political system. Politicians seek votes while bureaucrats seek job security and budgets. Interest groups and voters seek more wealth and income. Although there are serious limitations in the political institutions of exchange, each actor wants something possessed and/or controlled by others. Voters and interest groups want services from politicians and bureaucrats while bureaucrats want greater revenues or budgets from politicians and taxpayers. And, of course, politicians want votes and other forms of support from citizens and interest group members. For convenience the system is depicted in Figure 3.1.

Like markets, politics operates in an environment of scarce resources and uncertainty. And, like the market, the polity offers a means for allocating these

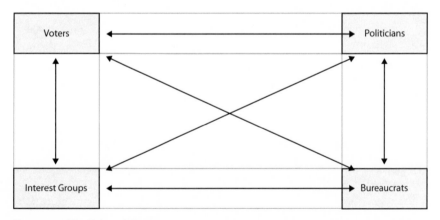

Figure 3.1 The Political System

scarcities, distributing income and wealth, and providing for the common welfare. In one sense the polity is a substitute for the market; in another sense it is a complement designed to fulfill certain tasks markets find difficult to perform.

In our model, each individual controls certain assets, is self-interested and purposively oriented, and is a rational decision maker. Unfortunately, and precisely contrary to markets with well defined and defendable property rights, political processes have certain properties that lessen the achievement of efficiency and discourage harmony among the self-interested.

Self Interest

In assuming self-interested political agents, I am simply asserting that most people identify more easily with their own concerns than those of other people; I am not saying individuals are without interests in others (e.g., their family) and their welfare. Still, most of us get up in the morning asking what we must do for ourselves, not what we can do in the public interest, or for the GDP. So long as we operate within well-designed economic and political institutions such self-interest is not bad; in fact, such institutions will, like Smith's "unseen hand," serve to convert self-interest into general good. Most people, most of the time, find it impossible to argue for any sustained period against their manifest best interests. Few people possess the wisdom and information to divine the best interests of others, and still fewer offer to continuously sacrifice themselves so the well being of others may be improved. People find the most time to do the things they value most and find the least time for the onerous, or those that show little promise of significant payoff for themselves. I do not claim every normal individual always knows his or her own best interests, but that no one else is likely to know them better. As Aristotle put it, the wearer of shoes knows better than the cobbler whether a shoe pinches.

As citizens follow their own strongest (but not necessarily most noble) ends, they act much like economic agents in the economy. Whether consumers or citizens, they seem capable of organizing their objectives in some order of relative importance. Like consumers, citizens prefer more to less, other things remaining constant or equal.

Analyses of markets focus on supply of and demand for products, labor, expertise, etc. The same dual focus is useful in analyzing politics as well. The conventional wisdom about markets is that, controlling for market failures, the demand and supply sides will equilibrate and the optimal amount of a product or service will be produced and consumed. The conclusions from public choice are that neither the demand or supply sides of politics are likely to reflect the public interest.

Focusing on the decision-makers leads inevitably into considering the environment of choice and how that environment affects both individual and collective choices. In politics and markets resources are, at any given time, scarce relative to demands for their use. Because our time, money, energy, and other resources are limited or scarce, we limit our potential returns if we do not use them efficiently. We accomplish less or have less discretionary time or money, for example. In short, scarcity poses opportunity costs and unlike benefits, such costs increase and usually at an increasing rate. That is, because of the law of diminishing marginal returns, getting the same amount of benefits a second time costs more than it did the first time. If the law of diminishing marginal productivity did not operate, the world could be fed from someone's backyard garden since adding labor, water, and fertilizer without limit would cause unlimited production. In reality, production (benefits) increases but at a decreasing rate while costs increase at an increasing rate! That is, it takes more and more fertilizer, water, weeding, and care to get the next little bit of production.

Additionally, the decision environment is best characterized by varying degrees of uncertainty; that is, we only rarely know with confidence what will happen. We always choose in varying states of ignorance with respect to what nature and other rational, self-interested people are contemplating. Thus we cannot accurately predict and control the future, nor undo the past. Try as we might through science and hedging our bets (insurance), we cannot know all there is to know. Fortunately, we need not be omniscient or omnicompetent.

Imposing various forms of order through political rules is one way people seek to reduce uncertainty and advance their self-interests. Such rules structure the behavior in the political game. Among those rules are constitutions that prescribe how subsequent policy choices and decision changes are to be made. Civil rights, property rights, contracts, etc., serve to better define who commands which resources and how they may be employed and transferred. The important point is that collective institutions are highly important matters with good and bad consequences for individual and joint welfare.

The Fundamental Nature of Collective Choice

On the basis of these elementary but fundamental considerations about decision makers we are ready to explore the nature of politics itself. In the first place, to have a government and a system of democratic processes is to decide that henceforth certain choices will be made not by individuals in the isolation of markets but *jointly with others.* In order to decide with others, rules must be adopted enabling authoritative, joint choices to be made in spite of differences among those choosing. Plurality is one such rule; simple majority and supra-majorities are others. Such rules necessarily imply that when choices are made there will be relative losers and winners. To put it another way, a voter on the losing side is required to comply with the winning decision because government has coercive power to impose its will on the dissidents and majorities may use the power of government to exploit minorities. Noting the coercive power of political systems suggests that government is a monopoly—control over which is desired by many and protected by those in control. Social scientists have long noted the jealousy of rulers in harboring their authority. Even elected rulers do not cheerfully tolerate competitors, and reward friends and punish enemies.

Although governments are best thought of as monopolies, it is important to remember they are rather peculiar monopolies. They are *not* profit-oriented in the same sense as the market monopolist. They conduct their fiscal operations in ways radically different from the private firm and even the private monopolist. Governments rarely seek profits for their "owners" by selling goods and services at prices that enable costs to be met and profits earned. As we discuss later, these differences make governments act much differently than private monopolies.

Chapter 2 identified the production of public goods as a justification for governmental action. Since public goods are really gratuitous or indiscriminate goods once they are produced, non-paying citizen-consumers cannot be easily prevented from making use of or enjoying the benefits. Thus, special problems of pricing and supply are created, which are not easily resolved by government. How much is enough? Who shall pay how much? How should payments be made? Since price tags are not found on individual units of public goods, tax systems are devised to meet the costs of offering these public goods. But, again, when everyone has equal access to the same quantities of the same good how are we to tax in order to provide them? In the market, consumers or buyers confront price tags to which they can relate their own estimates of the value of the good. Not so in the polity where there is no direct connection between the costs and benefits of a good or service. As a consequence those who benefit most may not be taxed while those who are taxed most may not place high values on or use the service.

These several attributes of collective choice at once distinguish the political process from the market where free, independent, individual choice is the norm. Politics inevitably involves conflicting preferences, majorities versus minorities, coerced participation, enforced sharing, and as we shall see, extraordinary inefficiencies and inequities. That so many citizens wish to extend these attendant controls over their personal lives appears paradoxical, but we will resolve that dilemma shortly. How monopolistic governments can be restrained also becomes an important issue, one reserved for the last chapter.

Voters and Ballot Box Logic

In Latin "votum" or vote means "ardent wish." But obviously many American voters are not terribly ardent and are, in fact, highly frustrated, which explains why the right to vote is not regularly exploited by many citizens. Apparently, voting is viewed as neither a highly rewarding nor efficacious activity. Without substantial reforms electoral participation will remain low, and even with reforms voting can never provide a truly effective means of representing citizen preferences. In brief, electoral choices are made but without much individual influence over policies.

The voter is a citizen who commands a number of civic assets or rights enabling participation in civic endeavors. Like all assets, these assets vary in value even though we often speak of the vote as free, implying, therefore, that it is value-less. But, the expenditure of time, effort, and money by both voter and contending politicians suggests a vote is worth a good deal to those involved. Although most citizens acquire the right to vote as a matter of birthright, their votes (rights) are distributed universally, equally, and (unlike most market assets) are non-transferable. This precious right to vote provides the legal basis on which each citizen may express, however inadequately, civic preferences. Undergirding the vote is an entire set of constitutional freedoms including speech, print, religion, and organization that enable the individual to function as a sovereign member of the polity. Without these freedoms democracy could not exist. Even so, these valued assets do not necessarily promote effective and efficient choices. The high cost of information combined with the low pay-off for casting an informed vote, for example, encourages people to remain uninformed. The fact that we cannot sell votes prevents resources from being transferred to their highest-valued uses. Furthermore, voters cannot choose among specific policy results, but must rely upon political promises—promises that cannot be legally enforced. If politicians could be sued or otherwise penalized for failure to honor commitments, politics would be a great deal different.

We must recognize the dual roles played by the voter—beneficiary and taxpayer. While these roles or positions are mutually contradictory in the abstract, no contradiction exists in the concrete world of politics; one role does not discipline the other as in the market. In the market, prudent consumers must consider income and prices before deciding to buy, which must be done at the margin with an eye to one's future prospects and obligations. In the polity, on the other hand, citizens are not constrained by income or prices. The goods and services of government are provided whether one wants them or not. And frequently we vote for goods to be consumed by others and paid for by still others. Voting for more spending may be appealing because of the intended beneficiaries, but such good intentions are not immediately disciplined by the knowledge that someone must pay for the additional spending; and if taxation is recognized, some other taxpayer (preferably a wealthy one) can be forced to finance one's private desires and altruistic impulses. The voter should not be indicted for extravagance when nothing in the voting decision requires considering income and prices.

The situation is even worse: in playing out the taxpayer role, well-meaning, public spirited voters have every incentive to opt for reductions in their own tax payments and every incentive to pursue private gains at public expense. Ignoring the public cost of one's own demands is highly rational; then too, a prudent citizen must pay a steep price to even be informed about the costs and benefits of policy options. That most voters choose to remain ignorant is hardly surprising. Only in politics can a person make ethical imperatives of logical contradictions such as a citizen advocating more defense, increased spending on social programs, and consumer protection while also promoting lower taxes, balanced budgets, and reduced government controls. When the price of something in the private market changes, consumers can alter their consumption, that is, buy less when the price increases and purchase more when the price decreases. Given fixed quantities of publicly supplied goods and public sharing of the costs, individual citizens cannot follow this sensible course of action. Coerced collective consumption does not permit, let alone encourage, responsible marginal adjustments by the citizen-consumer.

Certain consequences of irresponsibility for the citizen and polity are fairly clear. As a taxpayer, the citizen is interested in the aggregate size of the budget and supports reduced spending, reduced inflation, and increased economic growth. As a beneficiary of governmental spending, the same citizen supports an increase in subsidies or favors for his occupation, governmental regulation of his profession that creates barriers to entry, and has little interest in the total size of the budget. Predictably, these latter interests are generally apt to be more intensely felt than taxpayer commitments.

By this analysis, we should expect the spending incentives to outweigh the revenue considerations not only for the individual but for society as well. Still, there is more to be said; the situation is complex. The citizen/beneficiary must appeal primarily to legislative bodies to obtain government services. Legislators usually represent localized interests and have a constitutional mandate to enact appropriations. Thus, citizens and interest groups appeal, first, to Congress, their state legislatures, and city councils to voice demands for funds, programs, and other privileges. They also appeal to the President, governors, mayors, and the bureaucracy. Although the President, governors and mayors are subject to spending forces and incentives, they are more sensitive than legislators to taxpayer complaints—taxpayers are strongly more inclined to blame chief executives than legislators for tax increases. In addition, almost all chief executives are elected every four years so they are apt to respond to a longer time horizon than do those legislators who are elected every two years.

Concentrating on the fiscal aspects of voting and elections should not, however, overshadow other considerations having important consequences for public life. Although the vote is a visible, central feature of democracy, we should recognize how really insignificant it is in the entire process of collective choice; we sometimes overestimate what can be accomplished by spasmodic attendance at the polls. The limitations are as dismaying as they are pronounced. As voters we are normally confronted not with marginal choices—a little more or a little less—but with either/or decisions, which usually consist of "tie-in purchases": in order to obtain one good, we must also accept a variety of other commitments we view as less desirable or even bad. To get a labor policy I like, I may also have to accept a foreign policy I abominate. To have a President of my choice, I must accept his selection of a Vice President. Of course, markets create similar situations for consumers. Complex products and services do pose such dilemmas, and we should not minimize them. But these dilemmas are more easily resolved than their electoral counterparts.

Voting is a painfully limited way to express one's values and preferences. It accomplishes its results only indirectly; the vote does not immediately call forth that which is voted for. In fact, if we vote for something but are in the minority we do not get it at all, while if we vote against something and are in the minority, we get it and are compelled to pay for the unwanted candidate or services. Furthermore, because of secrecy in casting a vote, a voter cannot collect on her vote, and even if she could collect, her vote is practically worthless in the sense that one vote among thousands and millions of other votes ensures worthlessness. Rarely can one vote swing an election. Such is the paradox of participation: the more voters participate, the lower the power/value of the individual vote. This dismal prospect is made even more discouraging by voter free riding. If everyone believes his candidate will win, few will go to the polls thereby encouraging the candidate's defeat. Likewise, if everyone thinks her candidate is without a chance of winning most will fail to vote and thus produce the same result.

If information is expensive and even if a voter has sufficient information to cast an informed vote, she still faces the fact that her vote is practically worthless. But many still vote. Why? One possibility is that voters are motivated by something other than the chances of getting their preferred policies. It may be that voting is like cheering and jeering at a sports event. Fans at a baseball game stand and cheer even though their individual voices have no effect on the total amount of noise generated by the crowd or on the outcome of the game. They cheer to express their loyalty or enthusiasm for their team. Other fans come to games to express their dissatisfaction with their team or especially the team's management. The paper bag-wearing New Orleans "Aints" fans are a prime example. Those fans came to games wearing paper bags to express their frustration with season after season of losing. Despite the fact their team did not win, they kept coming. Voters may be the same way, they know their vote will not count but they vote anyway in order to express their enthusiasm or distaste for their political system and its outputs (Brennan and Lomasky, 1993). The fact that there is more to cheer for or against in national elections might explain why national elections in the United States turn out about half of the eligible voters while municipal elections turn out about 20 percent, despite a local vote being more likely to actually affect the outcome.

Expressive voting sheds new light on the effects of voter irresponsibility in two ways. First, if an individual's vote does not determine the outcome, yet he still chooses to vote, he is freed from having to gain expensive information about a policy or candidate. The least expensive information is found in candidate characteristics, such as gender, height, hairstyle, race, and religion. Only slightly more expensive is information gained from sound bites and campaign slogans. Ambiguous but ringing slogans like "Change" tell the voter nothing about what a candidate will actually do but allow voters to project their own meaning into the slogan. Adlai Stevenson, the Democratic candidate who ran against and lost to Dwight Eisenhower in 1952 and 1956, was talking about the difficulty of campaigning about issues rather than slogans when he said, "I have tried to talk about the issues in this campaign . . . and this has sometimes been a lonely road because I never met anybody coming the other way." Actually discussing issues does not generate votes as few voters pay attention.

Second, expressive voting frees voters to choose irrational policies. If their votes really mattered, there would be an incentive to understand the effects of the policies they prefer. But their votes do not matter and such information is expensive. Instead of voting their private interests they vote their emotional and symbolic interests, even if they know those interests are inherently contrary to their private interests or to the public interest. A voter may know, for example, that tariffs make consumers worse off yet vote for protectionist politicians out of a sense of national pride.

Things may be even worse than suggested by the expressive voting model as that model inherently assumes that the voters know when their emotional interests are contrary to good policy and would change their vote if they were properly educated. But because one vote has so little value, even informed voters can vote against their best interests. That is, they can be rationally irrational (Caplan, 2007).

Basic economics tells us that people will purchase more of a valued good as its price drops. In private and public life we should, for example, see more altruism when the "price" or cost of "doing good" is low. In private life, people must pay the costs of their altruism by writing checks or donating time. In public life, however, voters can cast a nearly worthless vote for a lot of altruism such as minimum wage laws, job-protection bills, old-age security, and environmental restrictions, with the knowledge that their choice will cost them nothing. As Brian Caplan (2007, 151) puts it,

> Correctly interpreted, the simple economic model *specifically predicts* that people will be less selfish as voters than as consumers. Indeed like diners at an all-you-can-eat buffet, we should expect voters to "stuff themselves" with moral rectitude.

Even a voter fully informed about undesirable effects of policies can and will vote in favor of those policies. And many vote for them knowing that their choices as consumers will be limited or their tax bills will rise if the policies are implemented. They choose to vote for irrational policies because their nearly worthless vote will not affect the outcome. They can at least feel good about their vote by casting it for the more moral position. They choose to be rationally irrational.

Whether voters are sovereign or manipulated, restless or stable, apathetic or interested, ungrateful or appreciative, prospective or retrospective, maximizing or satisfying, expressive or calculating, rationally ignorant or rationally irrational, they are put into an unpromising choice situation. Without a convincing cost/benefit nexus to discipline choices, voters are led necessarily to practice that most ancient art—the art of having it both ways. The ambiguous status of the vote reminds us that Eugene Debs, the nineteenth-century labor organizer and socialist was, perhaps right: "It's better to vote for something you want and not get it than to vote for something you don't want and get it."

The Impassioned Organized Interests

Rational citizens in pursuit of private desires quickly learn the superiority of organized groups over individual pursuit of welfare through the ballot box.

By organizing into an interest group, voters can pursue their concerns with the greater efficiency that results from concentration on single goals, a division of labor, specialization, and the power of concentrated passion and incentives. Surely, by coordinated effort, two people can lift more than the sum of what each might lift independently.

With more than seventeen thousand interest groups now actively involved in our political process we can readily appreciate the power of the above arguments. Favor seeking, or as the economists call it "rent seeking" (trying to collect rents from capital not owned by the rent seeker; that is, obtaining more wealth and income through political action) is now a major activity of virtually all organizations. As more interest groups discovered that they could do better by working the halls of government than the shops of industry, government became more powerful in deciding questions of allocation and distribution; the more the government's power was enhanced, the more active interest groups became. Political competition supplants economic competition when incentives are altered, and they have been altered, probably permanently, in the direction of political entrepreneurship and political competition and conflict. The tragedy is that gigantic short-run gains by individual groups create mostly long-run dangers of economic paralysis and decline (see Olson, 1982).

Despite their rhetoric, interest groups are not organized for the intention of improving the working of the economic order; they form for the sole purpose of increasing their members' welfare and will do so knowing full well that it comes at a cost to others. Interest groups do not, then, seek public goods for the nation but to obtain more private goods that could not be gained in the private economy. Special interests and especially those representing producers seek to have income and wealth redistributed to themselves. And because hundreds of billions of dollars can be redistributed, interest groups are only too willing to make political investments of a substantial magnitude.

All of the better-known interests now have headquarters in Washington DC, and in our state capitals, and all make contributions to political candidates and play politics every day of the week, fifty-two weeks of the year. Such organizations have impressive bureaucracies and highly paid consultants to devise political strategies for the attainment of their objectives. While interest groups work on behalf of their members, their staffs have even greater interests to advance—their own.

I do not wish to exaggerate the influence of the interests because certain notable constraints operate to limit their power. In the first place, competition can serve to restrain their gains if not their demands. It is also true that organizing groups is not simple, cheap, or easy; interest groups are hardly immune to free riding. Because their claims impinge on others, smart politicians can mobilize the disaffected into winning electoral coalitions. Finally, the inevitable abuses and corruption that occur in such settings may arouse citizens who demand reform and additional constraints on group activities.

Politicians and the Universal Political Touch

Politicians are elected for set terms of office, provided a fixed salary, and expected to enact public laws and policies binding on all. Their formal roles are defined in constitutions and often surrounded by considerable pageantry, pomp, status, and titles. As long as they are in office, they are important and powerful people.

Fiscal Orientations of Public Office

Like all political agents, the politician spends other people's money and spends it on still others who may not have contributed to the common treasury. Officers of private corporations also spend the money of others (stockholders) but the constraints on their behavior are considerably more direct and powerful than those experienced by politicians. In brief, anyone who spends money that is not his own on others than himself will not have as powerful an incentive to get his money's worth as the person who spends his own money on himself.

A business owner attempts to obtain sales receipts that exceed payments to produce the goods; if successful, a profit is earned that can be retained and used as that businessman deems wise. The politician is under no similar constraint. The politician who invents a new way of doing something may be rewarded by the voters at the next election but is not allowed to recapture any profits his civic innovation may produce. In fact, saving money for the government and taxpayers may defeat the politician because those citizens who will receive fewer government resources will be more likely to coalesce and vote in opposition than are the many taxpayer-gainers—each of whom will realize but a small saving, one not worth the costs of organizing to reward the helpful politician.

The difficulties of supporting the general interest are compounded when concentrated interest groups are considered. A reason the politician faces more powerful incentives to spend than to economize is the one just given—small groups who benefit from government expenditures have more incentives and cheaper means of organizing than do the diffused taxpayers. If a politician has a choice of dividing a million dollars equally among a million citizens or equally among a thousand people she will rationally opt for the latter option because she is more likely to win the gratitude of those who gained $1,000 than of those getting but one dollar apiece. Conversely, if the same politician has to choose between taxing a million taxpayers a dollar apiece and taxing a thousand taxpayers a thousand dollars each she will under most circumstances choose the former option. The logic is similarly clear; the electoral implications of concentrated gains and dispersed losses prevail.

In discussing the citizen-voter, I emphasized the absence of a constraint to inform and discipline fiscal choices. The same is true for the politician. Spending the public's money to buy votes is considered unethical. But in administering the public's money, spending and revenue decisions are not treated together in one and the same process as in the market; instead, these crucial decisions are divided into two distinct choices, often made at different times, by different people serving on different committees in separate offices. Wouldn't we all spend more in our private lives if we were not faced with price tags and monthly bills? In some families that is how fiscal matters are handled: one spouse worries about the income while the other spouse deals with expenditures and neither talks to the other. Inevitably, and unhappily, such a family soon finds itself dealing with creditors, financial consultants, lawyers, and bankruptcy court. Governments, we must remind ourselves, rarely permit their creditors to sue them and seldom go bankrupt.

The foregoing describes in somewhat abstract terms the political setting within which politicians seek office, make policy choices, and how this setting contrasts with the marketplace. Next is an examination of the strategies, tactics, and other practices followed by the politician in everyday political life. These matters need attention if for no other reason than to sharpen our familiarity with real-life elected officials and policy-making. Then, too, the daily practices and rules of thumb followed by political entrepreneurs are their adaptations to political settings imposed upon them. These job adaptations are as rational as those of the consumer, producer, and middleman.

Competition, Compromise, and Bargaining

Because votes are so crucial to political success, politicians are required to be competitive, to bargain, and to compromise. Rarely can the individual politician achieve his and/or his constituents' goals without allies. Workable public policies for divided constituents and live-and-let-live arrangements with colleagues become all-important goals. Accordingly, politicians are fond of such expressions as "I can buy that," "I can live with that," or "Let's run it up the flagpole and see if anyone salutes." Seeking allies and compromises are important activities for most politicians and necessarily so, because power is divided and decision-rules require some minimal agreement. In fact, one of the textbook definitions of politics is "the art of compromise."

At the same time, politicians are competitors for office. They compete over final terms of agreements and have diverse interests to protect and advance, not only including their own, but also their constituents,' party followers,' and financial contributors' interests. Like all bargainers, the individual politicians are enmeshed within a game of mixed motives, that is, a game characterized by both shared and competing interests. The task then is to advance one's own interests without driving other politicians from the bargaining table. Everyone can be made better off by some agreement but not all agreements are equally valued. The situation is roughly analogous to that of buyers and sellers haggling over a selling price and other considerations in a market exchange. Unfortunately, the political market does not provide as facilitative and efficient a mechanism as market prices for resolving disagreements. Legislating tax policy is a process of give and take, but those being taken from are seldom part of the conversation. The process also seems to generate some less admirable personal behavior. Successful politicians become the mirror image of what they do; shifting, smoothing, evading, concealing, lying, and diffusing hostility. Insincerity and flattery are common forms of political behavior; so, too, are paranoia, hatred, envy, and cynicism. Examples abound. President Nixon promised the nation "I will not take this nation down the road of wage and price controls, however politically expedient they may seem . . ." Two months later he enacted the very controls he said he would not enact. Admittedly, the popular wage and price controls played just a small part in the election, but Nixon was reelected two years later by the largest margin in history! In the campaign of 1988, Vice President George H.W. Bush promised not to raise taxes; in 1990, he agreed with Congress to do so. During the 2000 presidential campaign George W. Bush was a champion of free trade. In March 2002 he instituted 30 percent tariffs on foreign steel. President Obama pledged to take sweetheart deals out of his health care bill, yet he ended up supporting $300 million in extra Medicaid funds for Louisiana (the Louisiana Purchase), the permanent exemption for Nebraska's share of Medicaid expansion (the $100 million Cornhusker kickback), and an exception that allows Florida Medicare recipients to stay in Medicare Advantage although retirees in every other state will lose that option (Gator Aid).

Courting voters forces practitioners to adopt tactics rivaling those of Machiavelli's Prince. Successful politicians garner credit for popular programs and policies while simultaneously diffusing their responsibility among underlings and opponents for whatever goes bad and concealing mistakes and embarrassments. They deploy "trial balloons" to reduce the risk of innovation and they never knowingly allow opponents to define themselves, the issues or monopolize attention. They usually avoid flat, forthright statements and commitments about uncertain futures and unabashedly steal popular issues and proposals whenever possible. They trust few and pick their enemies with care, for competing politicians are highly valuable targets. And they always honor the self-interests of those to whom they appeal but cloak those same interests in the language of the national interest, social needs, and entitlements.

Successful politicians must be good tacticians. When seeking allies they usually seek only as many as are necessary to win and prefer those who can be dominated. They treat coalitions as temporary, unstable groupings and today's opponent as tomorrow's ally. If losing, they broaden the scope of the conflict in order to enlist supporters. When ahead in a race, they ignore their opponents.

Politicians are never all-powerful; they must contend with demanding and conflicting voters and competitors, real and potential. To some extent they must become responsive to the wishes of the voter at the center of the political spectrum. Still, political institutions are imperfect devices for registering the popular will, and politicians do have distinct advantages in their relationships with voters. If the politician is engaged on a full-time basis while the citizen is a part-time, inattentive bystander, how could it be otherwise?

Buying Votes with Public Money

Spending money on voters has obvious appeal, but politicians quickly learn that maximizing votes does not result from simply throwing words and funds at citizen demands; something more sophisticated is required. There is a basic calculus enabling the politician to minimize vote losses for enacting or supporting tax legislation while at the same time maximizing favorable votes for money spent. In short, the politician asks two questions: (1) How many additional votes will I receive for each additional dollar spent? (2) How many additional votes will I lose for advancing the welfare of some groups at the expense of others? If politicians must choose among alternative spending projects, they attempt to equalize the added votes from each added dollar of spending per project and that guarantees the maximization of votes. Minimizing votes lost from increasing taxes is assured by the same logic, that is, when choosing among alternative taxes, the best thing to do is match the marginal votes lost from each tax. Chapter 4 shows how this impeccable logic for promoting the self-interests of the politician leads to logrolling and a diminishment of the public welfare.

The general rule of marginal calculation must, however, be extended to particular programs of spending as well as taxation. The politician deals not in the vast and mystifying aggregates of national income but with particular spending and taxing proposals. Some spending is politically more profitable than others. Perhaps, the basic consideration is this: spend money on private benefits that are not only highly visible but sufficiently large to make a difference to recipients. Likewise a payment received now or in the near future is better appreciated than a larger, but uncertain future installment. Furthermore, to ensure lasting gratitude, the flow of income or other benefits ought to be more or less continuous. Spending on public goods may be highly useful in the long run, but individual gains are not easily nor readily appreciated by most citizens. Our supply of public goods is assured, however, by the fact that their production confers considerable benefits on the holders of contracts for their provision (for example: highway construction and defense expenditures). It should also be observed that most people receiving monies from the public treasury rarely appreciate having them described as outright pork barrel or subsidies; better that they be considered entitlements or needed investments in the public interest. In recent years these "investments" have included such pet projects as $25,000 for mariachi lessons in Las Vegas schools, $100,000 to fund a Groundhog Day "weather museum" in Punxsutawny, PA, and $2 million to buy back an old presidential yacht which was sold 27 years prior to cut costs in the first place (*USA Today*, 11/22/04). Earmarks in the 2009 U.S. federal budget included 11,914 earmarks at a cost of $28.9 billion, the second most earmarks and the second highest cost in American history (Heritage Foundation, 2009).

Politicians recognize that spending must also take into account the status positions of recipients. Nothing irritates people more than a belief that the undeserving—poor or wealthy—are being made better-off. Advantages must not only be cloaked in the public interest but also conveyed in less visible but legitimate ways. Rarely are the rich given outright grants; instead their gains are provided indirectly through the tax code and market advantages. Whether beneficiaries get their government income in the form of a check through the mail or through a reduction in their income tax, the same result in net income and wealth is produced. But, if the less well off do not know that is happening, the beneficiary and politician are both better off.

Spending on the less well off cannot be hidden through tax privileges since they pay little or no taxes. Thus, spending on the poor is more visible, making the task of the politician more difficult and the status of the poor more demeaning. One political way out for the politician has been to provide the poor with more direct aid-in-kind such as housing, clothing, food, medical services and education. With certain strings attached, these forms of aid satisfy the need of the politician to show middle class taxpayers they are getting their money's worth and that taxpayer support is not being used for immoral, frivolous, or unhealthy endeavors. To gain the support of private producers and government bureaucrats, programs are administered with innumerable controls, checks, and red tape.

Since depressions and recessions temporarily reduce the revenues of government, budgetary crises arise, challenging the ingenuity of our leaders. If budgets must be reduced, they will be lowered by the smallest amount politics will permit. The programs reduced least will be the big-ticket items that confer well-known, substantial benefits on many people. As reformers of the Social Security program have learned, flows of benefits, once begun, are virtually impossible to terminate or even be reduced. Once installed, they become habitual to both recipient and conveyor or bureaucrat. Threats to terminate programs are perceived as imposing greater losses than the long-term gains to the many more taxpayers. But the former's losses will inspire them to organize in defense faster and more effectively than will the greater but more amorphous gains for taxpayers. It is for this reason that old programs rarely die or fade away; the fact is they get bigger as officials devise attractive new programs to add to the old.

But suppose that sacrifices must be made. One strategy is to undertake "meat axe" or across-the-board reductions. This strategy rings the bell for equality or fairness. While it ignores the size of programs and their differential social value, this approach has undeniable political appeal. The politician will not appear to be picking on some while protecting others. Finally, if cuts must be made on some other basis, the best approach from the politician's perspective is to cut back on those beneficiaries offering the least resistance. For instance, in universities it is the maintenance department and the libraries and not the professors and chief administrators. Public investments, no matter how sound, are deferred. And, to create the impression of cutting back, the government may publicize how many employees are removed from the rolls. Of course, most will be retirees, transfers, resignations, and those who die but are not replaced. Salaries are not reduced, but increases are delayed. Some sacrifices are made, but mostly by the less powerful.

These propensities of government strongly suggest that the politician's compassion for meeting ever-increasing social wants is being translated into legislation with ever-increasing price tags. Unfortunately, but understandably, public opinion is less preoccupied with checking public expenditures than with redistributing the burden of taxation, perhaps because average people feel they have little influence over expenditures. Accordingly, most citizens voice far more concern over personal taxes than over increased expenditures, most of which go to other citizens. After all, taxes decrease someone's welfare and expenditures make someone better off. In addition, taxes are necessary evils, while something good can always be said about every spending proposal. The fact that expenditures lead to tax increases is usually lost in the discussion of the expenditure's benefits.

The Exchequer Against Taxpayers

Given the obvious fact that a conflict of interest exists between the government and the taxpayer, politicians have an incentive to devise tax stratagems that will lessen the apparent conflict of interest. Taxes are resented more than market prices because they are not directly related to one's benefits and, furthermore, are imposed. Understandably, taxpayers believe a good tax is a small tax and if taxes must be enacted, the best one is paid by someone else. Since the politician must take account of these sentiments, we should hardly be surprised to learn that politicians are even more Machiavellian about tax policies than about their spending habits. After all, politicians want people to know about the good they are doing while concealing the costs. Thus, a premium is placed on deception. Still, as George Harrison of the Beatles wrote:

If you drive a car I'll tax the street
If you try to sit I'll tax the seat
If you get too cold I'll tax the heat
If you take a walk I'll tax your feet.
   (from "Taxman")

As noted above, politicians follow a calculus of revenue gathering that in form is identical to the one observed in choosing spending activities. Again, the most powerful concern for the politician wishing to remain in his office is how many votes will be lost by the added dollar of taxation? When choices are made among revenue instruments the idea is to balance these vote losses among the different taxes so that the total vote loss is minimized. This is not as difficult as it may seem since economists and politicians have learned much about the real and perceived incidence of different taxes. And worse, government is in the unique position of being sufficiently powerful and informed to manipulate citizen perceptions. The fact that in all democracies tax loads have increased enormously over the past eighty years is powerful testimony to the abilities of politicians and the capacities of governments to extract revenues. How is it accomplished?

When legislators assemble to levy taxes the first thing they do is denounce taxation, huge budgets, and deficits. Once this charade is over, tax bills are designed in such a way as to distract attention from the proceedings. Since old taxes are usually considered more palatable than the new, the goal is to increase either the base and/or the rates of the familiar tax and to do so in minute ways that escape immediate attention. Still an annual increase of even 0.01 percent can add up to a hefty sum over the years. If taxes can be levied on unpopular activities and persons, so much the better because sin can ostensibly be discouraged while the coffers are expanded. And if tax increases must be enacted, it is best to do so during crises (particularly during popular wars) as happened with the enactment of the income tax during World War I and the withholding provision during World War II.

Equally popular from a political perspective are taxes levied on the rich and/or giant, impersonal corporations. Taxing corporations is especially valued because of the widespread misperception that companies rather than their customers pay taxes. Tax increases also seem more widely acceptable when they are accompanied by tax reforms allegedly designed to simplify and rectify past inequities or unfairness. Although genuine tax reform is rare, many important alterations are adopted. A "technical" change designed to conceal new privileges is the favorite strategy for "correcting errors" in tax codes. Local and state governments find it highly useful to earmark certain taxes for specific purposes thereby gaining the approval of those who make extensive use of the facilities and activities supported by the earmarked revenues. Gasoline and liquor taxes are prime examples. Since the income tax is a major source of federal revenues and income is taxed directly, taxpayers are quite sensitive to alterations and especially increases. In order to appease all concerned, including the tax collector, revenue-maximizing legislators will take special pains in revising the income tax. Although progressive rates are a political necessity, they are often illusory. The government has two rates, the legal or nominal and the real rate, with the nominal rate being much higher than the real rate which is much less known to the average taxpayer. Legislators prefer to enact progressive income tax rates but qualify them with numerous loopholes and exemptions. With the aid of an accountant, the taxpayer is then able to reduce his tax bill by substantial amounts. At the same time, the taxpayer has only the vaguest notion of how the loopholes affect others and appears at least partially satisfied that the rich are paying much more; how much more remains a mystery to all but the rich. Because they are hidden, these tax breaks are politically more acceptable than outright subsidies of the same amount.

Note too that the government forces the employer to collect the income tax and collect it not once a year but at every pay period thus assuring or stabilizing the continuous flow of revenues. By using automatic deductions, the sacrifice of payment and inconvenience seem somewhat less onerous than if paid in cash in person every week or every month. And, it is a cheaper and more reliable means of collection. Much the same logic of collection is incorporated in other payroll taxes, including the most important one—Social Security. Social Security brings to our attention still other political considerations including the very name of the tax itself. Unlike the income tax, which is so labeled on our salary stubs, the Social Security tax is identified by an acronym that baffles all—FICA (Federal Insurance Compensation Act). To this day, the founders of the program and its administrators have preferred to call the tax a "contribution" or "premium." It is neither and cannot be so; it is an involuntary payment or tax. Still the practice of finding euphemisms for taxes continues with such beauties as "revenue enhancement," "tax incentives," "tax expenditures," and "surcharge." Another patent tactic of the tax writers is to levy the tax on two different groups—the employer and employee—with the expectation that the employee will never realize he or she is the ultimate payer. The Social Security payroll tax that is presumably shared equally by worker and boss is, mostly in fact paid by the worker.

When seeking additional sources of revenue, politicians prefer those taxes that do not disrupt the continuous supply of revenue. In the language of the economist, the politician prefers to tax those goods and services the demand for which is inelastic, meaning that increases in their prices as a result of the tax have less than proportionate effects on sales and, therefore, tax revenues. Many so-called sin items fall in this category. The same might be said of taxes on such events as marriages, hunting and fishing, the occasion for which is a happy one and, therefore, not likely to be canceled or postponed by taxpayers having to pay some fee.

Since we live in a federal system, we should take note of effects generated by geographical dispersion of power, some of which are quite handy for the tax politician. A favorite practice among politicians is to mandate popular expenditures on the part of lower units but force the latter to find the tax revenues to pay for whatever good is to be accomplished. Local politicians, on the other hand, like to receive federal grants-in-aid with no strings attached and levy taxes that fall largely on non-resident taxpayers. Hotel and motel taxes are ubiquitous at the local level because the non-resident taxpayer is unable to vote in the tax-levying community. Of course, taxing non-residents creates incentives for the taxed to avoid visiting and doing business in the tax areas. Since convenience and necessity usually overrule the added cost of seeking pleasure or doing business, that seems a small deterrent to most tourists and business travelers.

Although important to locals, the above considerations pale in significance when compared with the two major means of financing government during times of inflation. We refer, of course, to borrowing and money creation. While there is no mechanical connection between these phenomena, it is quite clear that over the long run significant relationships hold. Because politicians prefer to tax by those means that lose the fewest votes, running deficits, borrowing, and making use of the progressive income tax provides a neat means of accomplishing that end. Richard E. Wagner and Robert D. Tollison (1982) explain it as follows:

> The political gains from deficit finance vary in direct proportion to the degree of diffusion of the costs of budget deficits among the population. A cost of $10 billion spread over one hundred million people will generally provoke less opposition than the same cost spread over only one million people. To the extent that budget deficits are financed by genuine government borrowing, the costs of deficit finance will be concentrated upon the investors who are crowded out. In contrast, money creation will diffuse the cost among the population. Therefore, since deficit finance accompanied by money creation will diffuse the cost more generally, it will evoke less opposition than deficit finance in the absence of money creation (p. 11).

Deficit financing and creating money can be complemented by using inflation as a tax on nominal income as it was during the 1970s. No formal increases in income taxes were enacted by Congress when the automatic progression of income tax rates enabled the government to obtain greater revenues as inflation sent more and more taxpayers into higher income brackets and, therefore, higher tax rates. Since most citizens are barely aware of the tax implications of democratic financing practices they can easily blame convenient scapegoats (Big Business, Unions, OPEC) for the inflation. That only government has the authority to print money and the political incentives to choose the politically optimal strategies of spending and taxing is a difficult lesson for most of us to master. The fact that government might abuse its sacred trust to establish and maintain a stable monetary system seems as obscene and unlikely to the ordinary citizen as to the Keynesian.

Implicit in much of our analysis of spending and taxing proclivities has been the recognition of two major sources of conflict in the polity: conflicting preferences among citizens for different expenditures and the allocation of tax burdens. Since expenditures on public goods generate spillover benefits for all or nearly all citizens, such spending is not apt to produce all-out conflicts among us. Not so with taxation. Taxation is something of a zero-sum game in that whatever reductions one taxpayer can obtain, another will have to pay. Taxpayers conflict to a far greater degree than beneficiaries. Should we be surprised that tax hikes are viewed by politicians as more costly in votes than expenditure reductions? Is it any wonder that tax rebellions occur? The wonder is that we have not had more, especially when governments engage in policies that can only exacerbate the situation. The case for constitutional fiscal constraint rests on just such considerations.

The historic tax reform of 1986 may seem to contradict much of what we have written but that would be a superficial judgment; the enactment of rate reductions, elimination of loopholes, and simplification of rate schedules, in fact, support our analysis. Congressional politicians, in effect, wiped the slate clean so that they could once more "auction" off tax exemptions and other privileges. The marginal value of the thousands of exemptions and loopholes had decreased enormously over the years; with fewer loopholes, their value increases sharply to the advantage of Congressmen and especially those on the tax committees. At the same time, the worth of tax lobbyists also increased since they are the experts in obtaining a renewal of old loopholes. What we have seen since those tax cuts is an annual reenactment of tax exemptions and political rewards in the form of increased campaign monies for compliant Congressmen. In fact, that began immediately after the passage of the Tax Equity and Fiscal Responsibility Act of 1986 with the addition of countless so-called "transition rules" to protect those interest groups essential to the reelection of important members of the Senate Finance and House Ways and Means Committees. By 2005, things had gotten so complicated again that the President's Advisory Panel on Federal Tax Reform reported,

For millions of Americans, the annual rite of filing taxes has become a headache of burdensome record keeping, lengthy instructions, and complicated schedules, worksheets, and forms—often requiring multiple computations that are neither logical nor intuitive.

The Advisory Panel recommended reenacting tax simplification. Rational politicians, especially in response to pressure from the 2010 Tea Party activists can look at the panel's report and see it as a justification for wiping the slate clean again so there are new tax benefits to "sell." Tax reform, after all, becomes a way for politicians to look for more donors.

Hard-Working Bureaucrats and Non-Working Bureaucracy

In political stereotyping the bureaucrat is usually portrayed as a faceless, lazy, and/or incompetent nitpicker. Although stereotypes are informed by elements of truth, this particular stereotype is misleading. The fact is, bureaucrats in general, particularly those holding higher ranks, are not only hard-working but dedicated servants and professionals. They are our permanent government. The paradox is that while bureaucrats are hard-working the bureaucracy is frequently believed to be non-working. The paradox is easily resolved when we distinguish at least two levels in the meaning of efficiency. Before getting into technical definitions, it is important to provide the institutional setting of a public bureaucracy, for without that knowledge we cannot understand bureaucratic behavior and outcomes.

As Max Weber said, a bureau is a formal, hierarchical organization staffed by persons, publicly paid, holding lifetime jobs won in open competition. The bureau's ostensible goal is providing civic services at zero prices—activities and services financed mostly by a lump-sum budget authorized by a legislative body. Historically, services provided the public consisted mostly of such public goods as domestic order and defense, but more recently, more private goods and income are offered through redistribution or transfer programs. This change in the mix of activities and services is fraught with significance for the bureau as well as the general public, not the least of which is increased favor-seeking by clients and bureaucrats alike.

Regardless of the particular services provided, bureaus are resolutely non-profit in their orientation. As a consequence, other—including political—criteria help to shape its major choices regarding allocations, internal operations, and responses to changing circumstances and innovation. Since the public agency is a creature of the polity, in general, and the politicians, in particular, its role and activities are suffused with politics, something civil service is supposed to reduce or eliminate but in practice leaves much to be accomplished. So, bureaus are major political actors.

Although most political scientists care little about the fiscal aspects of bureaucracy, public choice has made bureaucracy a focal point of their analyses. Unlike the business firm, a public agency gets its funds from elected representatives convened in legislatures, rather than contingent sales of its products or services. The critical question, then, is how the legislature decides how much money is to be allocated to each agency. Part of the answer can be briefly summarized without being superficial. Since we cannot ignore political institutions, politicians, voters, and interest groups, a theory of allocation among bureaucracies entails nothing less than a full-scale theory of public finance. All interact to make collective budgets and, incidentally, to ensure growth in governmental spending and taxation.

We must not be insensitive to the role bureaucrats play in shaping the demand for their own services nor in their power to influence the cost conditions under which they produce their services. Bureaucrats engage most directly and continuously with legislators serving on appropriations committees having authority to recommend budgets to the entire legislature. Such interaction and mutual dependence is certain to guarantee or reinforce powerful tendencies to spend more funds. These committees consist of largely self-selected politicians interested in winning the votes of grateful constituents. Since cooperating with the bureaucratic providers of services generates votes, we can hardly be surprised at joint efforts by politicians and bureaucrats to maintain the supply of services, expand offerings and, just generally, be helpful to voters. We have then a kind of benevolent conspiracy, or in the popular phrase, an "iron triangle."

The conspiracy may be benevolent but the outcomes are not. These fiscal outcomes, so insightfully analyzed by William A. Niskanen, Jr. (1971), are bureau budgets twice the size of an analogous private firm operating under competition and three times the size provided by a private monopoly. It isn't that public monopolies generate superfluous services although they frequently offer too much of a good thing, but that the outsized budgets finance padded costs. In short, the added funds go to over-staffed agencies employing costly procedures, providing higher incomes and unnecessary perks to employees, and underwriting a more pleasant life style. Still, we get too many services from too many bureaus—too many, given the opportunity costs. In a more perfect world, where we know the comparative values placed by citizens on government services, the funds could be spent by other agencies providing other, more valued services or, heaven forbid, taxes might even be reduced.

Citizens confront a bilateral monopoly operated by appropriations committees and bureaus whose only constraints are other bi-lateral monopolies competing, indirectly, to be sure, for a vaguely limited budget that is in turn conditioned by past budgetary allocations and the generalized constraint that taxation may have some limits in democracies. This somewhat pessimistic account must be softened by the recognition that few bureaucrats are outright thieves stealing public funds; most are dedicated servants disciplined by their professional training, civic duties, legal constraints that are not to be underestimated, and, of course, by a critical public. Nevertheless, the dedicated public servant wants to do good and that is best accomplished by ever larger not tighter budgets. Doing more good requires more money.

Since bureaus do not function within the demanding constraints of market competition, responsiveness and responsibility are most likely to be achieved through detailed oversight by other branches of government and whistle-blowers from within and without government. Such oversight is a two-edged sword for it also entails red tape, public hearings, appeal procedures, and tedious legalities. By contrast, the market registers complaints and dissatisfactions by reduced sales and direct action by irate consumers who confront store owners, car dealers, waiters, clerks, and the like. Such action normally brings forth a quick response, unless, of course, the firm is obligated to operate within a vast and costly consumer protection law or maze of regulations (see Chapter 9).

Given a politically determined budget, the bureau chooses its fiscal strategies of survival and growth. Without the yardstick of profit and information provided by the price mechanism, the bureaucrat acts so as to improve the agency's position vis-à-vis the legislative committee and the citizen clients of the agency. The preferred strategy is to insulate the agency from annual legislative scrutiny and control by obtaining earmarked funds, establishing uncontrollable benefit formulas for the clients, adding new supportive activities and services, and, as nearly everyone knows, spending all of the annual appropriations. These same bureaucrats will endeavor to convince the public and legislative committees that the demand for their services is greater than anticipated and costs higher than predicted. Supplemental funds are absolutely essential. While fortifying their budget, bureaucrats do everything within their power to avoid embarrassing errors that might reflect adversely on agency heads and their own mission. Caution is the key word.

Problems of internal administration and individual success within the bureau are strikingly similar to those found in large private firms or corporations since neither employs the price system within the organization and all members have their own ambitions and agendas. Without the discipline of prices, bureaus (whether managed by liberals or conservatives) substitute routine for rational economic calculation, which frequently contributes to still further allocative inefficiencies. The need to implement plans and programs, as well as to secure protection from angry clients, leads to an elaboration of procedure, rigidity, and inertia. Instead of removing the bad or at least inquiring whether it would be better to remove it (see Part IV for examples) they adopt additional controls. They assume, quite rightly, that where there is a plan, there are loopholes and that they will not go unused. And, unlike the private firm, program failure means the bureau can appeal to unmet needs as a reason for a larger appropriation. Discovering a critical, unmet need increases the motivation of the dedicated bureaucrat and provides something for that bureaucrat to do.

Another distinct difference between the public bureaucracy and private firms is that competitive firms protect their market share by improving consumer satisfaction while bureaus, at least in the short run, protect their budgets by *decreasing* consumer satisfaction. Since bureaus obtain their budgets from legislators, they must find ways to convince them that their budgets will be protected during times of economic downturn and increased in prosperous times. Thus, bureaus threaten to reduce the most essential of their popular services. Known as "the Washington Monument strategy," it was so named after the National Park Service, facing budget cuts in 1968, closed the elevator to the Washington Monument and told tourists they had to take the stairs because the Park Service could not afford to operate the elevator. The tourists were directed to take their complaints to their members of Congress. Agencies in cities and towns, for example, periodically claim they will need to reduce garbage collection and police protection if taxes are not increased. In 1996, Yellowstone National Park closed Norris Campground, one of the park's most heavily used campgrounds. The irony is that although campers paid fees that exceeded the cost of keeping the campground open, most of the money from the fees went to the U.S. Treasury, not the park. Thus, the park closed a moneymaking campground to save money. The Washington DC Metro proposed to cover a 2009 budget deficit by shutting down the subways at 10:00 p.m., a proposal designed to generate outrage given that the Metro is open until midnight weekdays and until 3:00 a.m. on weekends.

Our well-meaning public servants live outside the world of supply and demand in a culture where there almost never is an objective measure of the value of their work. The public firm has the additional advantage of not having to pay taxes, purchase licenses, or post bonds. They can be unfair competitors. Not unexpectedly, they remain inefficient. Without the goad of profit and bankruptcy they cannot be otherwise. Sadly, and all too often, they spend their time not in reducing costs but rationalizing higher ones.

The Argument Summarized

The political processes described here are seen in terms of the rational pursuit of individual ends but within an institutional setting replete with perverse incentives and costly, biased information. Collective choice is, accordingly, inherently coercive and irrational in the economic meaning of the term, that is inefficient, a notion to be developed at length in the next chapter. In the promotion of inefficiency, the influence of logrolling and compromise cannot be exaggerated.

Democratic politics are not really government by the people but rather an intense competition for power among voters, interest groups, politicians and bureaucrats. If voters are just rationally ignorant, then voter information campaigns might improve electoral outcomes. But if voters are voting to cheer on a candidate or cause or expressing inexpensive altruism there is little that more information can accomplish. Thus, voters make the rational choice to be ignorant, governed by ideologies, and to abstain from individual political participation. By joining interest groups voters can have a stronger voice in government, but private or public interest groups are likely to pursue inefficient policies. Bureaucrats protect their budgets and job security and seek political autonomy and prestige through their exchanges with the other players in the political game. Politicians find it highly rational to engage in obfuscation, play-acting, myth-making, ritual, the suppression and distortion of information, stimulation of hatred and envy, and the promotion of excessive hopes. Thus, in collective choice, everyone is exonerated from responsibility.

Bibliographical Notes

A number of scholars writing in public choice have made significant contributions to de-romanticizing government and the politics of democracy. The two best known and most prolific are James Buchanan and Gordon Tullock, whose work as co-authors and separately have defined the field. Liberty Fund Press has published *The Collected Works of James Buchanan* in twenty volumes and *The Selected Works of Gordon Tullock* in ten volumes. Buchanan won the Nobel Prize in 1984 and his work concentrated on understanding the institutional structures of society. Tullock's work is more eclectic, covering economics, political science, public choice, sociology, law and economics, and bioeconomics.

Their co-authored *Calculus of Consent* and *The Limits of Liberty* are the place to start. Among their single-authored works I highly recommend Tullock's *The Social Dilemma: Of Autocracy, Revolution, Coup d'Etat, and War.* The book demonstrates Tullock's inventive mind at work on the workings of the dictatorial state and the economics of war between nations. Also do not miss Volume 9, *Law and Economics.* It includes his book *The Logic of Law,* which was the first book to analyze the law from the perspective of economics and his controversial essay, "The Case against the Common Law." The first volume in the Buchanan series contains his essay, "What Should Economists Do?" and a section titled "Politics Without Romance" that I believe are must-reads. "Politics Without Romance" contains many of the arguments we made in this chapter. Here is how Professor Robert Higgs (1993) describes what Buchanan says about economics and economists:

> Mainstream economists cannot move the earth with a mathematical lever, because they have no place to stand—no "given" information about property rights, consumer preferences, resource availabilities, and technical possibilities. What neoclassical economics takes as given is, in real-

ity, revealed only by competitive processes. "Most modern economists," Buchanan aptly concludes, "are simply doing what other economists are doing while living off a form of dole that will simply not stand critical scrutiny."

The proper role of markets and politics was best delineated by Milton Friedman in his superb *Capitalism and Freedom* (Chicago: University of Chicago Press, 1962). Friedman was and always remained ahead of his time. His book should be awarded a prize for first-rate writing on critical matters of political economy. The ideas were controversial in 1962. Today, many are mainstream.

The most fun read I know about de-romanticized government is P. J. O'Rourke's *Parliament of Whores*. It was originally written at the end of the Reagan administration and has been re-released with an extensive forward by Andrew Ferguson (New York: Grove Press, 2003). As the jacket blurb says, "Although the players have changed, the game is still the same." I must warn that between the laughs, O'Rourke has a hard edge that can offend as he takes on all sacred cows and politically correct sensitivities. Perhaps his best line, among the thousands of great ones is "Giving money and power to government is like giving whiskey and car keys to teenage boys."

The view of self-interested voters was first explicitly laid out by Anthony Downs in his path-breaking *An Economic Theory of Democracy* (1957). Downs identified conditions for applying economic theory to political decision making. As such, he was one of the first modern public choice theorists. Downs thought voters vote according to their ideology and concluded that a two-party democracy is only stable if there is wide ideological consensus among the voters. To understand the rational voter and the ensuing rational ignorance theses, start with Downs.

Two of the books mentioned in the chapter deserve especially to be highlighted. This first is Geoffrey Brennan and Loren Lomasky's *Democracy and Decision: The Pure Theory of Electoral Preference* (1993). They discarded the idea inherited from Downs that voters vote to get a particular result and coined the phrase "expressive voting." Since one vote is practically worthless as a means of affecting the outcome of an election, they wondered why voters even bother to vote and concluded the reason is expressive or symbolic voting. That is, there are psychological benefits from voting that overwhelm self interest. They claim, in fact, that "Considerations dormant in market behavior become significant in the polling booth" (p. 16).

The second book is a highly readable frontal attack on the rational voter hypothesis. It is Brian Caplan's (2007) *The Myth of the Rational Voter*. Caplan goes one step beyond Brennan and Lomasky and claims that voters vote *irrationally*. That is, they choose ineffective and otherwise bad policies because voting is cheap altruism. Since their vote nearly does not matter to the outcome, they can vote their prejudices or misperceptions without fear that they are creating costs for themselves. Caplan develops the implications of rational irrationality for supply-side politics when he discusses how politicians exploit that irrationality, a topic taken up in the next chapter.

An obviously seminal work on interest group politics is *Federalist 10* by James Madison in which he famously argued that interest groups (he called them factions) cannot be controlled but it is possible to control their effects. He viewed politics as if it were a market in which competing interests would insure that policies in the public interest would be allowed while private interests would not. Of course he did not anticipate the rise of party politics nor logrolling, but his interest group competition argument continues to resonate.

Mancur Olson (1965) was the first modern to explain that interest groups do not form spontaneously; they are the product of political entrepreneurship that finds ways of reducing free riding on the group's collective product. Thus, he argues that groups concentrated interests would be more easily organized than groups with diffused interests. Olson was followed by two classic articles, one by George Stigler (1971) and the other by Samuel Peltzman (1976). Stigler showed how groups with concentrated interests could more efficiently influence government than groups whose interests were diffuse. He showed that organized groups would cloak their private interests in claims of public interest so that so-called public interest regulation was actually in their interests and that the main beneficiaries of regulation in the consumer interest were not consumers but the regulated groups themselves. Peltzman (1976) showed how politicians and bureaucrats would maximize their own interests along with those of the regulated, organized groups to take advantage of consumers. Among political scientists this three-way relationship between politicians, bureaucrats, and interest groups became known as the iron triangle. Notice that consumers and voters are outside the triangle.

The public administration view of bureaucrats as public servants was exploded by William Niskanen (1971). He assumed that bureaucrats were budget maximizers and built a theory of bureaucracy and representative government around those assumptions. He began by asking what it is that bureaucrats maximize since they are part of non-profit organizations. After considering several possibilities such as salary, prerequisites of the office, reputation, and power, he concluded that each of these is positively correlated with increases in the agency's total budget. Thus, bureaucrats are budget maximizers. Although there have been many additions and variations on Niskanen's model, it remains the core of studies of bureaucracy in public choice.

References

Acevedo, M. and J. I. Krueger. "Two Egocentric Sources of the Decision To Vote: The Voter's Illusion and the Belief in Personal Relevance." *Political Psychology,* 25 (2004).

Brennan, Geoffrey and Loren Lomasky. *Democracy and Decision: The Pure Theory of Electoral Preferences.* Cambridge: Cambridge University Press, 1993.

Buchanan, James M. *Cost and Choice* (Collected Works of James M. Buchanan). Indianapolis: Liberty Fund Inc., 1999.

Buchanan, James M., and Gordon Tullock. *The Limits of Liberty* (Collected Works of James M. Buchanan). Indianapolis: Liberty Fund Inc., 2000.

Buchanan, James M., Charles Kershaw Rowley, and Gordon Tullock. *The Calculus of Consent: Logical Foundations of Constitutional Democracy* (Tullock, Gordon. Selections. V. 2.). Indianapolis: Liberty Fund, 2004.

Caplan, Bryan. *The Myth of the Rational Voter: Why Democracies Choose Bad Policies.* Princeton: Princeton University Press, 2007.

Despeignes, Peronet. "Budget Bill Has $15.8b in Extras; Passages Delayed over Tax Privacy, Abortion." (2004, November 22) *USA Today,* p. A12.

Downs, Anthony. *An Economic Theory of Democracy.* New York: Harper, 1957.

Friedman, Milton. *Capitalism and Freedom.* Chicago: University of Chicago Press, 1962.

Heritage Foundation. http://www.heritage.org/Research/Reports/2009/03/Omnibus -Spending-Bill-Huge-Spending-and-9000-Earmarks-Represent-Business-as-Usual.

Higgs, Robert. "What Should Economists Do?" *Reason (*December, 1993).

Ingram, Helen, David Colnick and Dean E. Mann, "Interest Groups and Environmental Policy," in *Environmental Politics and Policy: Theories and Evidence,* 2nd ed., James P. Lester, W. Douglas Costain, Riley E. Dunlap and Helen M. Ingram, (Eds.) Durham: Duke University Press, 1995.

Moe, Terry. *The Organization of Interests: Incentives and the Internal Dynamics of Political Interest Groups.* Chicago: University of Chicago Press, 1988.

Niskanen, William A., Jr. *Bureaucracy and Representative Government.* Chicago: Aldine-Atherton, 1971.

Olson, Mancur. *The Rise and Decline of Nations.* New Haven: Yale University Press, 1982.

O'Rourke, P.J. *Parliament of Whores: A Lone Humorist Attempts to Explain the Entire U.S. Government.* New York: Grove Press, 2003.

Pigou, A. C. *The Economics of Welfare.* New York: General Books LLC, 2010.

President's Advisory Panel on Federal Tax Reform, *Final Report* (Washington: 2005) 1–272.

Rosenbaum, Walter A. *Environmental Politics and Policy,* 3rd ed. Washington: CQ Press, 1995.

Tullock, Gordon. *Law and Economics,* Volume 9. Indianapolis: Liberty Fund, 2005.

Tullock, Gordon. *The Selected Works of Gordon Tullock* (10-Volume Set) (v. 1–10). Indianapolis: Liberty Fund Inc., 2006.

Tullock, Gordon. *The Social Dilemma* (Selected Works of Gordon Tullock). Indianapolis: Liberty Fund Inc., 2005.

Wagner, Richard E. and Robert D. Tollison, "Balanced Budgets, Fiscal Responsibility and the Constitution," in Richard E. Wagner, Robert D. Tollison, Alvin Rabushka, and John T. Noonan, Jr., *Balanced Budgets, Fiscal Responsibility, and the Constitution.* Washington, DC: CATO Institute, 1982, p. 11.

Wilson, James Q. *Political Organizations.* Princeton: Princeton University Press, 1995.

4

Pathological Politics
The Anatomy of Government Failure

IDENTIFYING THE MAJOR actors, incentives, decision set-
tings, and basic interactions provides us with a foundation for the remaining
diagnostic analysis—the pathology of politics. Setting forth the failures of
markets as in Chapter 1 is a necessary but insufficient step; we must also identify
the failures of the polity and explain their occurrences. All this is preparatory
to showing why the polity chooses policies that fail to overcome alleged market
failures; most of these policies are highly inefficient and more often than not
patently inequitable. But that is getting ahead of the argument. This chapter
completes the analysis of government failure by showing how and why the political process is defective and examines further whether these defects are inherent in politics or in particular institutions that might be altered and improved.

Citizen Sovereignty and Efficiency

A pathology of politics is meaningless without a normative foundation—
in this case, efficiency, a much misunderstood and abused term among non-
economists. Here it refers to a measure of how well society provides for the
material wants of its members. This simple definition is in accord with the more
precise one of Pareto, namely, whether a given policy, action, or allocation is
able to improve the subjective well being of anyone without diminishing that
of others. Such a result is said to be a Pareto improvement. A polity or economy
producing huge quantities of *unwanted* goods and services even at the lowest
cost is not Pareto efficient since no one would be made better off. Indeed, many
would be worse off since the resources devoted to making unwanted goods
could be allocated for goods people actually want. So, the chief concern is with

allocative efficiency—improving people's subjective well being. I am second-arily concerned with technical efficiency, which is producing something at the lowest cost. Efficiency in politics, then, is concerned with meeting individual preferences, while employing resources in their most valued uses.

Despite the importance of individual preferences in democracies, a number of otherwise attractive political features have the unhappy facility of violating Paretian efficiency. The two most prominent involve redistribution of income. Redistributive gains dominate efficiency considerations in policy discussions, and democratic institutions encourage this redistributive propensity. In addi-tion, democracy has an unfortunate but a distinct penchant for enacting inef-ficient proposals—proposals that make some better off but at the expense of others or even worse, making everyone worse off in the long run. By choosing policies and rules that produce greater costs than benefits and failing to enact those having greater benefits than costs, citizens are made worse off, if not ab-solutely then worse off than they might be otherwise.

Sources of inefficiency in the political process may be usefully categorized in seven ways: (1) perverted incentives; (2) collective provision of private wants; (3) deficient signaling mechanisms; (4) electoral rules and the distortion of preferences; (5) institutional myopia; (6) dynamic difficulties; and (7) policy symbolism.

Perverted Incentives

Adam Smith's greatest accomplishment was demonstrating the beneficence of the hidden hand of the market in converting self-interests into collective good. Just how the invisible hand operates has preoccupied economists for more than 200 years. The great accomplishment of modern public choice has been to demonstrate the pernicious workings of the visible hand of politics. The same decision makers operating under market and political rules produce quite different results. One of the major reasons pertains to the incentives gov-erning choosers. Although both political and market participants are assumed to be self-interested, the incentives—objective rewards and penalties—differ profoundly. What the market and polity offer in the way of concrete awards, encouragements, discouragements, and costs contrast so much that people who have worked in both environments are puzzled at and sometimes exasperated by the variations. Businessmen in particular find working in the public sector frustrating.

In markets, the promise of profits fortified by the ever present risk of loss encourages entrepreneurs to improve their products and services, while lowering the cost of doing so. The wealth of customers and entrepreneurs is increased and innovative ideas are provided by other competitors. By serving himself, the producer serves others; by serving others, he profits. It is, in short, an exchange system enabling mutual gains.

Some students of politics, including well-known economists and political scientists, see parallels and argue that politics ought to also be viewed as a vast exchange system. One such economist, Donald Wittman (1995) referred to "an invisible-hand theory of efficient democratic markets." According to Wittman, "vote maximization leads to wealth maximization in democratic markets in the same way that profit maximization leads to wealth maximization in economic markets" (p. 160). One trouble with Wittman's analysis is that politics and government do not offer a full range of profit making activities to its participants. In fact, the abuse of authority is feared so much that profit making (as distinct from self-seeking) in politics is prohibited by extraordinary constitutional, statutory, and ethical limitations on public officials. These rules circumscribe discretion and even goals. In this respect, the American Constitution is (and was designed to be) a distinctly negative document.

Government officials are not permitted to sell their official services or goods. And since they must offer their goods and services to all at zero or less-than-cost prices, we can never learn the precise values citizens place on these activities and goods. Without a market, value becomes impossible to ascertain and implement. Since everything in the market acquires a price, comparative efficiency judgments can be made by buyers and sellers enabling each to make ready, fairly accurate calculations on the right thing to do. Political actors have no such guidance and without it efficient choices become, as Mises and Hayek argued, impossible. A mayor might know how much it costs to construct a neighborhood park requested by citizens in the neighborhood, but there is no way to know the efficient amount of park to supply or if one ought to be supplied at all. The mayor's measure of demand is the number of citizens who sign a petition or show up at a city council meeting and the citizens' measure of cost is the opportunity cost of their time spent lobbying. Without prices and market forces, at best, government officials and citizens know what it costs them to purchase resources and products; but they cannot determine the values consumers place on the government services produced. Thus, it is next to impossible for even the most skilled government economist to construct a valid demand curve for politically provided goods.

When choosing public policies, politicians—who wish to remain in office—must rank the vote impact higher than the efficiency impact of alternative courses of action. Their calculations are at odds with those of businessmen, their market counterparts. Whereas the latter asks *how much* people want something, the equivalent of asking what they are willing to pay, the politician asks *how many* people want something. Politicians count majorities first, and intensity of preferences and beliefs second, and indirectly. A firm does not have to win majorities in order to do business; the politician, interest group, and voter do. Since a vote is weighted the same as any other vote, they are all equal. But some buyers have more dollar-votes than others and their voices therefore, count for more. Since equal votes and unequal dollars are fundamental facts of the political economy they provide the crucial bases for debates and conflicts over the redistribution of income, wealth, status and power. Those who seek equality of outcomes wish to extend the realm of votes while those who prefer uncertain inequality tend to favor the market domain.

Separating Costs and Benefits

Perhaps *the* fundamental political fact—one characterized by inexpedient and untimely consequences—is the separation of cost and benefit considerations. The fact that few persons are forced to weigh them one against the other before making policy choices enables and encourages people to seek additional gains at collective expense.

As the number seeking favors from government increases, the government finds itself in the difficult position of having to cater to private desires rather than providing public goods, the goods governments are supposed to provide. The opportunity costs of devoting more time and resources to favor-seekers are that the provision of national defense, domestic law and order, and other genuine public goods is reduced. An analogy to government stretching to do more is the concept of "feature creep." As software programmers add more and more features to their products, the system becomes so overburdened that it cannot perform its basic and intended functions well. Recognition of feature creep has led several writers to worry about "governmental overload" and the consequent frustrations engendered by failure to provide basic services. Some writers claim that much of our alleged civic malaise and even cynicism results from governments attempting to do too many things and doing none well. The well-known conservative columnist George Will makes this a touchstone in his critiques of contemporary America. Although expressed in non-efficiency terms, his point is well taken.

More economically minded analysts would point out that citizens seeking collective provision of their private wants seek those goods for which they would not pay in the private market. So long as the goods come free, they demand more and, thereby, misallocate scarce resources from their higher valued uses. I spent six years as a city council member and four years as mayor of a small Utah city (yes, I understand the ironies) and saw such misallocations first hand. A nearby city of just 4,000 people, for example, received a road grant for $4 million. The money came because the city manager's daughter had served an internship in the U.S. House of Representatives and when spare, unexpected money showed up for road projects, the Congressional staff remembered her and called to see if her father's city could use the money. The city had planned and set aside money for a $1 million road but are quite happy to spend the $4 million instead to construct a four-lane road. The local officials most certainly would not have built four lanes if they had to spend their own restricted tax monies when other projects were more needed. And the local taxpayers would not have increased their taxes to build the road. But the four lanes were built not only because they did not burden local taxpayers but also because the expenditure of dollars from elsewhere provided a local contractor with additional work. They might as well have built pyramids or simply dug ditches and then filled them; the economic effects would have been the same. All the other mayors in the county were jealous of what they call the "lucky money" that came from the Congressional office and most are staying in close touch with Congressional offices in hopes of getting lucky money of their own.

The pervasiveness of this means of self-aggrandizement is saddening but understandable. How could it be otherwise when to sacrifice private goods in the public interest forces the sacrificer to pay all the costs while others enjoy the benefits? Divorcing costs from benefits induces not only a favor-seeking motive in each citizen but in the long run turns democracy into a constant search for a free lunch. But, as Milton Friedman (1962) reminded us TANSTAAFL!—"There ain't no such thing as a free lunch!" since someone always pays. Milton's son David Friedman (1989) describes the political free-lunch-seeking process in the following parable:

> Special interest politics is a simple game. A hundred people sit in a circle, each with his pocket full of pennies. A politician walks around the outside of the circle, taking a penny from each person. No one minds; who cares about a penny? When he has gotten all the way around the circle, the politician throws fifty cents down in front of one person, who is overjoyed at the unexpected windfall. The process is repeated, ending with a different person. After a hundred rounds, everyone is a hundred cents poorer, fifty cents richer, and happy (p. 107).

Divorcing costs from benefits is what happens in the familiar setting of a group dining together and agreeing to split the bill. The situation even has a name—*the unscrupulous diner's dilemma.* If the bill is being split evenly the self-ish diner will order an exceptional dinner in the belief that her fellows will order normally. But if everyone orders more in the expectation that others will help pay the cost they each end up with a far higher bill individually and severally than if they had agreed at the outset to each pay their own portion of the bill. If friends are willing to do this to each other in face-to-face sitting around a table, think how much more citizen-taxpayers are willing to do it to anonymous, other taxpayers. And in politics we cannot say as did Phoebe in Season Two, Episode five of the television series *Friends* when Ross tried to split the bill among them all, "No, uh uh, no way, I'm sorry, not gonna happen."

Political Signaling: Votes and Rhetoric

One of the greatest inventions is money, for it is a wonderfully convenient means of enabling persons with diverse interests to communicate in simple, precise, and rapid transactions. Without a monetary system, a modern society would soon dissolve into chaos. Without money we would not be able to avoid the double contingency problem of barter, that is, finding a trading partner who wants what you have and has what you want. Barter is extraordinarily cumbersome, imprecise, and inefficient. So are the substitutes for the pricing system that enable planners to play at market competition: price ceilings and floors, subsidies, tariffs, barriers to entry, quotas, make-work rules, rationing. Knowing these fundamental facts, however, has not dissuaded many political scientists from finding virtues in political systems that, in effect, employ barter and planning.

In democracies, the chief unit of account and medium of exchange is the vote. Now consider the vote itself as an analog to money. In the first place, everyone has but one vote and that vote is indivisible. Accordingly, the vote cannot express a voter's *intensity* of preferences. Without multiple votes or a weighted system of voting we cannot indicate to others just how much we prefer one candidate to another, or one policy over another. All we can say is that whomever or whatever we vote for is more preferred than the option not voted for. The vote, the mark, or "X" on the ballot can, therefore, convey little information and indeed when counted on Election Day, produces considerable ambiguity. What does the "X" mean? Both winners and losers can rationalize the outcomes. Is it a strong positive endorsement or merely a negative minimizing of a choice among bads? As guidance to policy-makers the "X's" are highly ambiguous. Reducing the mystery and improving elections has inspired many formal theorists of public choice and other reformers to devise intricate reforms of the ballot, electoral rules, etc. Few of their suggestions are ever adopted.

The above problems can be reduced somewhat through the use of vote trading, a form of barter better known as logrolling in legislatures. (Logrolling is a term from the American frontier for reciprocity in rolling heavy logs to build a cabin or to clear a field—"I'll help you roll your logs if you'll help me roll mine.") Although a good case can be made that vote trading offers an improvement over non-trading, the argument usually breaks down in practice because the skewed distribution of diffused costs and concentrated benefits dominates the aggregate size of those results. Vote trading will, therefore, favor projects in which total costs exceed total benefits. If everyone votes on each project separately, all will be defeated. Voting on them individually yet providing for vote trading will see them enacted into law and we will all be worse off.

An example will illustrate as well as demonstrate the logic of logrolling at its worst. Suppose three voters are confronted with two projects, a jail and a

Table 4.1 Inefficiency of Logrolling Voter's Net Benefit

Project	A	B	C
Jail	−$200	$300	−$200
School	−$200	−$200	$300
Net	−$400	$100	$100

school. Each project is to be voted on independently of one another, and the decision is to be made by majority rule. If the voters estimate their respective costs and benefits as shown in Table 4.1, we expect that both projects would be voted down: in the case of the jail by voters A and C while in the case of the school by voters A and B. Since both projects are inefficient, that is, costs exceed total benefits, it is clear that the election produced the correct result.

But consider what might occur if the voters discovered and practiced logrolling. In such an event, voter B would agree to support voter C's school, if C will support B's jail. The result is that the three-member polity has now adopted two inefficient projects with a total loss of $200. Although B and C must help pay for each other's project, they still come out as gainers, but, of course, this is accomplished at the expense of A who must bear $400 of the total cost of $800. We can just as easily construct further simple situations showing the opposite results, but I believe in the real world, logrolling is more likely to confirm the blackboard illustration. While vote trading among ordinary voters is effectively discouraged by prohibitive transaction and monitoring costs, the politicians have managed, quite rationally, to impose a form of implicit trading on voters through the use of issue packaging. The practice is simply one of combining individually popular proposals into a single package such as a party platform or, more commonly, through non-germane amendments to bills in legislature. The less popular proposals are attached as riders to popular ones; for a legislature and/or a President to reject the dubious rider entails rejecting all the good measures as well, and taxpayers are forced to suffer losses to support the gains of a few.

A variant on this form of vote trading is found in the strategy Anthony Downs (1957) termed a "coalition of minorities." Suppose that three issues are presented to voters with the division among them being 20 percent in favor of a particular subsidy and 80 percent opposed on each issue. One might superficially assume that political candidates would quickly announce their support of the overwhelming majorities on each issue and oppose all three subsidies. But they need not because supporting a combination of those 20 percent who favor each policy will garner a majority of sixty percent, a majority incidentally, that is much more likely to materialize and remain stable because the gains afforded individuals are apt to be greater than the individual losses suffered by those who oppose the subsidies. Realistically, we should also assume that some of the taxpayers/consumers who oppose subsidies other than their own will number among those who gain from one or more other subsidies. The Smoot-Hawley Tariff generally credited with deepening and extending the Great Depression, was produced through just such a process. Members of Congress joined the coalition supporting the tariff by gaining some concession, usually a tariff on something manufactured in his district. Eventually enough members joined the coalition to pass the bill and there were so many products protected that international trade was reduced to a fraction of what it was before Smoot-Hawley. Everyone was made worse off, although all members of Congress acted, they believed, in the interest of their constituents. Thus, we get the term "paradox of vote trading"—each voter in a coalition, like the diners splitting the check at a restaurant, makes others, and sometimes themselves worse off.

This problem does not arise in the private economy because coalitions and logrolling are irrelevant to making decisions. Each buyer and seller can and does act independently and normally without consideration of others; in fact, they compete not only across markets but on the same side of the market, consumer against consumer and seller against seller.

The signaling of intentions and communication more generally is conducted in polity and economy, alike, through the use of everyday language. The acquisition of a common language is a marvelous achievement especially appreciated when one visits a foreign country, or attempts to communicate with babies and domesticated animals. But language, as English teachers know only too well, can be used with varying degrees of skill. Some people communicate better than others. Scientists and technicians, for example, are able to employ the languages of mathematics and science with extraordinary precision and economy.

Because voters are rationally ignorant (the costs of gaining particular information are greater than the benefits since one vote is essentially meaningless) politicians must employ a language designed to evoke emotion, enough emotion to motivate the right people to turn out and vote. Thus, politicians rarely speak with precise meanings, marginal calculations, or logical reasoning; instead they manipulate affect, raw emotions, group identifications, and even hatred, envy, and threats. Because premature commitment to an issue can cause one to end up in a minority position, successful politicians equivocate, hint, exaggerate, procrastinate, "straddle fences," adopt code words, and voice *non sequiturs*. Understanding the politician is, therefore, extremely frustrating for those who value precise statements. Note that this is not the fault of the politician; it is rooted in the rational ignorance of voters, distribution of conflicting sentiments among voters, and the nature of collective endeavor.

What all this means is clear: political communication is rarely conducive to rational or efficient allocation of scarce resources. This does not mean that the individual politicians are irrational in their choice of language and symbolic activities. Waving the flag and kissing babies are practiced because of their tactical value in an activity that is at once a rational game and a morality play, which is the endless fascination and frustration of politics.

Institutional Myopia

A primary accusation by critics of markets is an alleged indifference of markets to the needs of future generations. This criticism never fails to be made because it has a profound appeal among those who really care about the future. Since market agents are selfish and short sighted how could they possibly pursue conservation goals? "Cut and run" is their guiding precept. It is assumed and claimed that only the political process and governments have the incentive and the ability to serve the future. Horror stories about the exploitation of our Eastern and Northern woods, wanton killing of bison, and callous over fishing of streams and the ocean, are cited as convincing examples and evidence of the failure.

The fact of the matter is that the historical examples are misunderstood, and the capacity of governments to enact protective laws is grossly overestimated. Markets are governed by persons, both buyers and sellers, constantly and necessarily engaged in comparing present and future values; if they did not make such comparisons we would have a difficult time explaining why many choose to make substantial investments during uncertain times. Profit maximizers serve themselves, but they do so by investing in uncertain future prospects. Thus, through their efforts to determine whether future generations of buyers will buy their wares, they may conserve now and/or invest in producing more resources for future use. In order to do this they must make estimates of future demands for present and possibly new demands. If private Louisiana logging firms believe future sales of lumber products will increase (for whatever reasons), they will choose to harvest fewer trees now and even plant more for future harvest. Private timber firms are even preserving wildlife habitat and scenic vistas because of their expected future value and, as many close students of the oil industry have pointed out, oil companies do not pump oil twenty-four hours a day; market signals dictate the holding of vast inventories of oil in the ground. All resource holders operating in a private property, free market context are *forced* to consider inventory policy and the future.

What of the political possibilities? The conventional wisdom is that informed voters and dispassionate but professional public officials will be more far-sighted. Deprived of making profits, officials are assumed to place higher values on the future than would entrepreneurs, but just why remains something of a mystery since future voters are either unborn or have yet to register their preferences at the polls. Common sense suggests that a citizen-voter deprives herself of a great deal in casting support for, say, conservation measures when all benefits are conferred on *unknown* future voters with *unknown* tastes. Politicians seem to understand this dilemma because historically they have not been in the forefront of the environmental movement. If government is so omniscient, why did it take so long to protect our environment? Socialist countries it seems are even more negligent. We must not forget that for the politician a week is an eternity, especially around elections. The reason for politicians' myopia is simple: voters are also myopic. Voters are shortsighted because most public policies confer either long-run benefits with immediate costs or immediate gains with delayed costs. In the first instance, political systems produce inaction, delay, and caution; while in the second situation speedy action is undertaken, but the action is usually ill considered, excessive and enacted under the strains of crisis (see Part IV for detailed examples). Legislation enacted during increasing unemployment may create the illusion of action and accomplishment but always at considerable, real, long-run cost in the operation of free markets. Price controls enacted during inflation are a singular example of such illusory gains and real costs.

There seems to be no compelling reasons why voters, politicians, and bureaucrats should be more future-oriented than selfish buyers and sellers. Removing property rights and the profit motive does not enhance the future's prospects; it actually diminishes the time horizons of political beings.

Dynamics: Uncertainty, Innovation, and Welfare

Facing uncertainty, governments understandably behave in highly uncertain ways, making prediction of their behavior problematic. On the one hand we observe that bureaucracies seem lethargic while legislatures and chief executives seem, all too often, to bounce from inaction to hyper-action and back again. Private firms appear to be somewhat more stable in their responses. Perhaps the reason for the variances between government and private firms has to do with the existence of profit and its connection with uncertainty in markets, and the absence of profit but the presence of uncertainty in politics.

Students of international politics and public planning have long observed that governments are woefully under equipped with vital information and theory having practical value. Unlike private firms, governments do not have a single purpose or goal such as profit maximization. Instead they pursue conflicting objectives and make trade-offs. Relating conflicting ends and highly uncertain means is inherently difficult. Economists might phrase it by saying society does not have a "social welfare function" or a single "public interest." Public planners facing this dilemma react with either excessive caution or haste. We see plentiful examples of both. Grandiose projects have been authorized overnight without much assurance of success, while promising programs are avoided and delayed. Few federal dam building programs, for instance, have positive cost-benefit ratios yet they were enacted with disconcerting consistency. And we should expect such misallocations as long as politicians continue to spend taxpayers' money, especially when interest groups can gain private benefits at public expense.

Elected officials respond to changing voter preferences in predictable ways, usually erratic over-responses while the bureaucrats held responsible for the implementation of hastily conceived plans behave in less dramatic (but equally inappropriate) ways of inaction and delay. Among bureaucrats the costs of errors are thought to exceed the gains from risky choices so excessive caution or prudence is the norm. Regulation provides good examples. Inadequate resources, due-process requirements, competing claims among clients, and fear of legislators all contribute to maximizing time wasted in performance of regulatory goals.

Policies, once adopted, come to have the status of sacred cows even when they are manifestly inefficient. This paradox, like many others encountered in public choice, can be easily unraveled once we understand that inefficient policies can be enacted if benefits are highly concentrated and costs widely distributed. Beneficiaries enjoying benefits have little difficulty keeping their gains because abolishing those gains would do great damage and confer but small gains on millions of taxpayers. So the latter do not act, while the former can be certain to mobilize enormous resources in defense of privilege. Apparently we will fight harder to keep a certain gain than fight for a greater, but uncertain gain.

Things may be even worse than the previous paragraph suggests. Bryan Caplan (2007) argues that concentrated benefits and dispersed costs may characterize most government programs, but the real reason those programs are adopted is that the voters want them. The average voter, according to Caplan, is motivated by biases against markets and in favor of government. Not only do voters have insufficient information about how markets and government work, they hold damaging and wrong-headed beliefs. No wonder the Social Security program remains with us. No wonder all the bankrupt farm programs are not only with us but grow. No wonder other subsidies hang on, and worse, multiply and increase.

Inefficient and even destructive policies continue to exist and grow because virtually every policy can be defended as having contributed some good to someone in need. Even those most disadvantaged by a certain institution or policy are often among those who defend practices such as minimum wages, equal opportunity laws, and rent control. Ironically, efficiency reforms have few constituents even during so-called conservative administrations. In fact, one might well contend that conservatives are particularly well suited to consolidate and legitimize past inefficiencies as well as serve the interests of the better off. None of the five Republican presidents since Lyndon Johnson's "Great Society" legislation started the escalation of the American welfare state have diminished its scope. Some wag has said "the Republican Party can only promise to do what the Democrats do, only do less of it." If so, innovation in the practical political sense is largely the prerogative of the political Left. Indeed, President Bill Clinton, a Democrat, proposed and got the Congress to enact welfare program reforms that are far more imaginative than any tried by Republicans since Richard Nixon proposed the Family Assistance plan, which would have been a negative income tax.

Once again Milton Friedman (1962) had some intriguing insights into the close connection between beliefs about the role of government, time perspective, and policy innovation.

> The liberal in the original sense—the person who gives primacy to freedom and believes in limited government—tends to take the long view, to put major emphasis on the ultimate and permanent consequences of policies rather than on the immediate and possible transitory consequences. The modern liberal—the person who gives primacy to welfare and believes in greater governmental control—tends to take the short view, to put primary emphasis on the immediate effects of policy measures. This connection is one of reciprocal cause and effect. The man who has a short time perspective will be impatient with the slow workings of voluntary arrangements in producing changes in institutions. He will want to achieve changes at once, which requires centralized authority that can override objections. Hence he will be disposed to favor a greater role for government. But conversely, the man who favors a greater role for government will thereby be disposed to have a shorter time perspective. Partly, he will be so disposed because centralized government can achieve changes of some kinds rapidly; hence he will feel that if the longer term consequences are adverse, he—through the government—can introduce new measures that will counter them, that he can have his cake and eat it. Partly, he will have a short time perspective because the political process demands it. In the market, an entrepreneur can experiment with a new innovation without first persuading the public. He need only have confidence that after he has made his innovation enough of the public will buy his product to make it pay. He can afford to wait until they do. Hence, he can have a long time perspective. In the political process, an entre-

preneur must first get elected in order to be in a position to innovate. To get elected, he must persuade the public in advance. Hence he must look at immediate results that he can offer the public. He may not be able to take a very long time perspective and still hope to be in power (pp. 16–17).

Electoral Rules: Paradoxes and Impossibilities

Among the numerous properties of democracy, one of the most important is the impact of formal rules on group decision making and especially rules pertaining to elections in which we choose candidates and policies. According to such famous theorists as Kenneth Arrow, Duncan Black, Charles Plott, William H. Riker, and a host of lesser-known formal analysts, rules matter. Because their work is highly technical, accessibility is achieved only by considerable translation and oversimplification.

Much (but hardly all) of the formal, technical mathematical analysis of politics is based on the path-breaking work of Kenneth Arrow (1951) and Duncan Black (1958), the former a Nobel Laureate in Economics. This discussion is based mostly on their efforts. For those who see little fault in democracy, Arrow's results are earthshaking because he proves that no democratic voting rule can satisfy five basic conditions—perfectly reasonable ones—simultaneously. One or more must be violated in the effort to arrive at collective results that are consistent with individual preferences. We learn that majority rule does not function well when voters have more than two options. If three options are offered and each voter is asked to rank the three, it is frequently the case that no one option will win a majority of first place rankings. And, if they were to consider their choices in pairs they would soon learn that voting cycles result in each option defeating all others and no one winning.

All this can be illustrated with the use of a simple table in which we suppose there are three voters and three options, which might be either policies or candidates. The voters rank their preferences as shown in Table 4.2.

If each option is paired or compared with each other, we clearly learn that a will beat b, and b will beat out c, but that c will in turn beat a. Thus, majority rule has some severe problems, for each option can beat every other option and no determinate winner emerges that can claim to be the majority preference. Cycling is the name of this phenomenon. Of course, there are ways out

Table 4.2 The Voting Paradox

| | Voters | | |
Ranking	A	B	C
1st	a	b	c
2nd	b	c	a
3rd	c	a	b

of the dilemma or ways of preventing it, and there is no necessity that cycling will occur. But it is true that as the number of options increases relative to the number of voters that the cycle will occur with increasing frequency. For our purposes it is sufficient to note that cycles are real and while they do not prevent us from employing majority rule, they do create difficulties that should not and cannot be ignored. Majority rule is no panacea.

An alternative to majority rule is the plurality rule—the candidate who garners the most votes among all those the voters consider is elected. Of course that can mean the winner receives less than a majority of all the votes while the losers represent a majority of all voters. Abraham Lincoln and Bill Clinton won office not with a majority but with a plurality—a majority of voters voted for other candidates. George W. Bush did not even gain a plurality in 2000 as Al Gore received more of the popular vote. Another problem with plurality rules is that the existence of a third option can change the relative ranking of the first two options. That is, one's choices can be influenced by whether or not there are more than two options.

An effect of having more than two options is shown by the 2002 French presidential election. Incumbent president Jacques Chirac was the highest vote getter in the three-person primary race between himself, Jean-Marie Le Pen, and Lionel Jospin. Le Pen was the next highest vote getter and Jospin was third. Chirac and Le Pen then ran against each other to select the president and Chirac won. Polling data indicated that in a two-person race, Jospin would have defeated Le Pen and could have also defeated Chirac. Thus, Le Pen's presence in the race changed relative rankings for Chirac and Jospin (Dasgupta and Maskin, 2008).

Another problem with voting is how to count the votes. No one who studies elections will forget Florida's "hanging," "dimpled," and "pregnant" chads in the

2000 U.S. presidential election. The state of Florida certified the vote and declared George W. Bush the winner after the U.S. Supreme Court stopped recounts ordered by the Florida Supreme Court. Independent recounts showed that Bush won in all legally requested scenarios but a statewide recount with different counting rules would have resulted in Al Gore defeating Bush. Additionally, the National Opinion Research Center examined nine recount scenarios based on different methods of interpreting ballots and concluded that Gore would have won under five of them and Bush would have won under four of them (Keating, 2002). How we count votes matters.

Some students of elections have advanced a variety of weighted voting schemes designed to overcome some of the difficulties of political choice, but they do not solve all. The big problem is how to weigh the votes, for that will affect the totaling of the various scores. So, technical ingenuity has yet to resolve all of Arrow's reservations. Then there is the agenda problem or the order in which options are voted upon, a problem that can be solved, but only through manipulation.

Of course, the American system does not operate by any such direct voting as suggested by Arrow's criteria; instead we vote directly on a few policy issues and mostly confine our voting to elections in which candidates for public office are selected. In these latter choices we encounter specific forms of electoral institutions peculiar to different democracies. For example, Americans select their presidential candidates through the use of party conventions and primary elections in which delegates to a national convention are chosen. The nominated candidates then compete in a national election. In forty-eight of the states the winning candidate receives the state's entire electoral vote whether won by a substantial majority or but one vote; it is a winner-take-all result. As political scientists know so well, the strongest candidate in the primaries need not be strongest in the general election; that is the case because the more committed voters who attend the party primaries select the more extreme competitors. An additional result of our system is that candidates for the U.S. Presidency tend to devote more of their attention to states with more Electoral College votes and ignore those with fewer votes.

Another consequence of the American electoral system is the frequent honoring of the so-called median voter, that is, politicians tend to adopt positions departing from those favored by more extreme voters and converge instead on

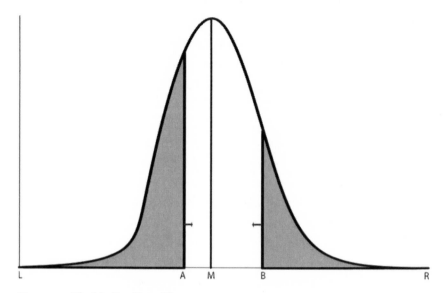

L   A   M   B   R

Figure 4.1 The Median Voter Theorem

the preferences of median voter(s). The logic of appealing to the median voter is seen in Figure 4.1. In this figure, voters are normally distributed across a standard left-right continuum. Since the mass of voters is located at the center of the distribution, vote-maximizing candidates will propose policies that appeal to those voters. In Figure 4.1, Candidate A will move right and Candidate B will move left, if they want to reach the median voter—if they want to win. Unless Candidate B moves, A will win easily. If A expects B to move, she will move to position M in order to beat B to the median voter. By appealing to the voters at the very center of the distribution, the candidates divide the vote equally. If either candidate moves away from the middle, the other candidate captures the votes in the middle and wins the election.

Seeking the vote of the median voter is said to drive candidates to a "tweedle-dee-tweedle-dum" strategy in which the median voter is indifferent between the candidates. Of course, minority voters out on the far-reaches of the normal unimodal preference distribution lose because they are minorities. At best they gain only vague rhetorical reassurances from the candidates. Since the median voter gets so much attention, it is to the advantage of concerned interest groups to shape voter preferences for one position or another. As Gordon Tullock (1967) argued, the name of the political game is shaping preferences and their distribution. That is why political advertising, even the uninformative, is such an important ingredient in the electoral process. At its worst, advertising tempts exaggeration, deception, and lies. Shaping the options and the agenda become additional subjects of intense scrutiny among activists—for on them depend the outcomes of the elections.

Earlier I alluded to the problem of the geographical distribution of voters suggesting that it might have something to do with final policy choices. Several studies have shown that majority voting does not necessarily reflect overall majority views if the voting is done in separate single member districts (a voting system in which only one person is elected from each electoral district). It is conceivable and quite likely under majority rule that the minority position will be underrepresented in a legislature or convention. For example, the overall minority position may win overwhelming majorities in a handful of districts, and lose by small margins in most other districts and end up placing few representatives in the legislature. Those who win bare majorities in the districts can, therefore, win a huge majority in the legislature. In California, for instance, after the 2000 Census Congressional district boundaries were changed to preserve party strongholds. The results of this were demonstrated in 2004, 2006, and 2008 when only one sitting Democrat and one Republican lost their seats to the candidate from the other party (those two candidates were undergoing corruption investigations). Almost all candidates won with more than 65 percent of the vote (*Harvard Law Review* Staff, 2009). All this is accomplished under majority rule! It becomes clear why politicians have such fierce fights over geographical boundaries for legislative districts; their own interests are at stake and so are those of voters.

Since most voting is for candidates rather than issues, and most of policymaking takes place between elections, there may not be much significance to the median voter beyond the symbolic and a few generalized constraints on government to elections. It is risky to argue that the policies of the center voters prevail. Instead, both theory and empirical outcomes strongly support the notion that most of the distributive policies enacted by government would not be favored by sovereign majorities if the voters were directly confronted in referenda with issues involving tariffs, quotas, make-work rules, barriers to entry, or government loans. The only way in which they might be adopted would be to allow logrolling among voters, and that would be prohibitively expensive. As Robert Dahl (1956) wrote more than fifty years ago, the democratic political process is not, "a majestic march of median-voter majorities but rather the steady appeasement of minorities" (p. 80). If this is true, surely we have a major failure of the polity.

Even a cursory review of a vast and highly intricate, technical body of theory and empirical studies illustrates the extensive perversity of electoral institutions, the cornerstone of democracy. Even if voters, politicians, bureaucrats, and interest groups are all altruistic and informed, their individual policy preferences will be distorted through the workings of the basic rules themselves. These rules create winners and losers and seemingly have no particularly rational or consistent basis. If we are concerned that pervasive market imperfections and failures be properly handled and improved, we are apt to be disappointed. No set of rules can guarantee the achievement of fair and efficient policies. Nor should we assume that politicians and others are indifferent to manipulating the rules themselves; they cannot afford disinterest. While generations of political theorists have often suspected these results, we could not place much confidence in their suspicions until formal public choice enabled us to better understand the actual mechanisms.

Justice and Redistribution

Continual reference has been made to the problem of equity or justice in the context of both markets and democracy, but without any sustained analysis. I have alluded to the fact that although government in liberal societies is often expected to rectify "unjust" market distributions of wealth and income, such governments more often than not exacerbate inequalities. Although this problem is addressed in detail in Chapter 10 some preliminary discussion is warranted.

An efficient distribution of income and/or wealth may or may not be considered just or equitable. If, for example, most wealth were in the hands of a single family and a government proposed to take some away and redistribute to the less well off, such a proposal would have to be termed inefficient since the wealthy family would object. Whether another distribution is equitable depends on the criteria we employ in making such judgments, and there is no widespread agreement on the appropriate criteria.

Regardless of our feelings about distributive outcomes, there remains the positive problem of determining how various political processes will, in fact, decide such issues. Many members of the Left are inclined to believe that not only should greater equality prevail, but also that under majority rule it *will* prevail. A good case cannot be made in defense of the prediction. The reasoning is as follows.

Suppose that a simple majority of voters is required to pass a redistribution bill and that 100 voters, each with a different income, participate in the decision. Under this arrangement the two median voters (income recipients) will decide. Those persons could support the wealthier 49 or the less well-off 49 voters. If they bargain, they may quickly surmise that they can command more of the redistribution by supporting the upper income group than by joining the poorer folk. On the other hand, they may reason that there is more to tax from the rich than from the poor so they will stand to gain more from that redistribution. In either case, the median voters will have the power to decide the outcome and in this case they could exact an outcome that would maximize their share. According to this theory, first advanced independently by Stigler (1970) and Tullock (1988), the middle class profits most from redistributive efforts of democratic governments. Whether or not the facts of empirical life support this theory is still in doubt because it is not easy to test; furthermore, it is complicated by the fact that much redistribution takes place within each income class. We do know that adopting welfare programs for the poor requires the support of the middle class, who provide their support in exchange for having welfare benefits extended to themselves. More than one study has demonstrated this to be so in such fields as housing, education, transportation, environmental improvements, and health services. And, of course, much tax policy is so designed as to confer tax benefits on the middle class.

The point is this: the political process not only promotes inefficiency but is skewed to advance the interests of those who are better off. Those who do well in the marketplace also do well in the polity.

Policy Symbolism

As explained earlier, voting sends mixed messages and political arrangements separate decisions about costs from those about benefits. One result of these conditions is that politicians can engage in "policy symbolism," making grand policy statements whose objectives will not be accomplished. There are at least two forms: (1) statements of sentiment, such as congressional resolutions, that have no legal policy effect, and (2) decisions that legally establish real policy objectives and potentially could have effects, but that have been designed *not* to achieve their objectives (Lyons, 1999: 286).

Regulatory law provides many opportunities for policy symbolism. A common tactic is to create grand-sounding legislation but not provide funds sufficient to accomplish its objectives. In addition, Congress often provides policy objectives that are completely unrealistic or gives agencies "lengthy lists of actions to take and deadlines to achieve that the agency cannot even begin to accomplish" (Bryner, 1987: 207). This approach gives little direction since "if everything is a priority then nothing is." Sometimes, politicians know their policies are so strict that they will be unenforced, especially by state and local officials who are fearful of driving out industry and employment. Thus, Congress passes laws and creates policies in anticipation that enforcement will be spotty and easily circumvented.

There are understandable political reasons for engaging in such symbolism. One is because "enthusiastic support is much more likely to be generated by dramatic promises than by modest, incremental proposals" (Bryner, 1987: 207). Another is to be able to place blame for failures on the bureaucracy (Fiorina, 1977: 72–79). Symbolism may also be designed to placate idealistic interest groups and rationally uninformed voters.

Agencies obviously find unrealistic and often unfunded promises impossible to achieve. Requirements for zero pollution discharges into navigable waters, non-impairment of worker health, and zero cancer risks make good political statements, for example, but cannot be achieved. These requirements provide no guidance about how inevitable tradeoffs are to be accomplished. Such rules deny that once policies have been implemented their marginal costs may outweigh their marginal benefits. Worse, they ignore the possibility that total costs may exceed total benefits. These policies are symbols meant to demonstrate to voters that their politicians are taking bold steps.

Some Conclusions

The unromantic and pathological properties of the democratic process have been explored in Chapters 3 and 4. The picture is not a pretty one, but readers should not draw easy and superficial conclusions from the examination and comparisons of real and idealistic worlds. While markets and polities are both imperfect, we do have some choices, and those choices are important for our individual and collective well being. The important caution is this: even imperfect democracies have far more to be said in their favor than do the non-democracies. Democracies honor individual sovereignty as a goal worth attaining. And whether we like a particular citizen's preferences in the market or polity makes no difference as compared to her opportunity to give voice to them. Even in this regard, obnoxious political preferences are more difficult to accept than are obnoxious market preferences. In short, the market has fewer externalities than does the polity. Nevertheless, I much prefer living in our flawed democracy to residing in any dictatorship. This must be thoroughly understood throughout my analysis of detailed policy imperfections in the following chapters.

Bibliographical Notes

In addition to the sources cited in the previous chapter, one really should consult the *Handbook of Social Choice and Welfare Volume 1*, edited by Kenneth Arrow, Amartya Sen and Kotaru Sazumura (North-Holland, 2002). The text summarizes the formal complexities of voting schemes and compares them with market processes. The book is hardly exciting, but it is a reliable source on these arcane and devilishly difficult matters.

Written with considerably more literary skill as well as attention to historical cases and data is a book by William H. Riker entitled *Liberalism Against Populism: a Confrontation Between the Theory of Democracy and the Theory of Social Choice* (San Francisco: W.H. Freeman and Co., 1982). Although the book was published more than twenty-five years ago, it is entirely applicable to today. Riker shows that voting is no simple mechanism that automatically registers both individual and social choices. No scheme of voting is immune to the pathologies of failure or, at the very least, imperfections. Elections are subject to manipulation, uncertainty, ambiguity, and outcomes that cannot be readily defended as just or efficient. This is not a defense of non-democracy; instead Riker advances a more sensible, reasonable set of democratic expectations by which to judge political institutions.

Still another dated but relevant volume is that of Hans van den Doel and Ben van den Velthoven, *Democracy and Welfare Economics* (Cambridge: Cambridge University Press, 1993). Although brief, this book is written more in the style of a text than an extended essay. Nevertheless, the authors advance sensible judgments on the nature of welfare, democracy, bureaucracy, representation, majority rule, and what they term "negotiation." The strengths and weaknesses of these alternative decision processes are set forth with brevity, but also insight and clarity.

Both students and professional analysts of public choice should remember that the field was not invented out of thin air. The way was scouted and hints offered by a number of precursors of whom the best known is surely Joseph Schumpeter. His book, *Capitalism, Socialism, and Democracy,* first published in 1942, contains four fascinating chapters on democracy, one of which advances a theory of democracy much in the vein of modern public choice. Its chief difference is that Schumpeter did not control his emotions as much as current analysts might, but he uses them to good effect. Still, his image of voters and possibly politicians is somewhat at odds with that of current thinking. On the other hand, the irrationality of voters is blamed on the rules of the game, an analysis very much in keeping with modern public choice.

Readers interested in obtaining a summary textbook statement of political failures can hardly do better than consult *Economics: Private and Public Choice* (New York: South-Western, Cengage Learning, 2010) by James D. Gwartney, Richard L. Stroup, David Macpherson, and Russell S. Sobel. The text is now in its 13th edition. Chapter 6, "The Economics of Collective Decision Making," lays forth the basic courses of political failures in an admirable fashion. The early editions of this textbook pioneered the way for a growing number of economics principles textbooks that fully appreciate the workings of a market economy and understand that perceived externalities are not an immediate justification for government action.

References

Arrow, Kenneth J. *Social Choice and Individual Values.* New York: John Wiley and Sons, 1951, rev. ed. 1963.

Arrow, Kenneth, Amartya Sen, and Kotaru Sazumra. *Handbook of Social Choice and Welfare Volume 1* (Handbooks in Economics). 1st ed. Paris: North Holland, 2002.

Black, Duncan. *The Theory of Committees and Elections.* Cambridge: Cambridge University Press, 1958.

Bryner, Gary C. *Bureaucratic Discretion: Law and Policy in Federal Regulatory Agencies.* New York: Pergamon Books, Inc., 1987.

Caplan, Bryan. *The Myth of the Rational Voter: Why Democracies Choose Bad Policies.* Princeton: Princeton University Press, 2007.

Dahl, Robert A. *A Preface to Democratic Theory.* Chicago: University of Chicago Press, 1956, p. 24.

Doel, Hans van den and Ben van den Velthoven. *Democracy and Welfare Economics.* 2nd ed. New York: Cambridge University Press, 1993.

Downs, Anthony. *An Economic Theory of Democracy* New York: Harper and Brothers, 1957, Chapters 4 and 9.

Fiorina, Morris P. *Congress: Keystone of the Washington Establishment.* New Haven, CT: Yale University Press, 1977.

Friedman, David. *The Machinery of Freedom.* La Salle, IL: Open Court, 1989.

Friedman, Milton. *Capitalism and Freedom.* Chicago: University of Chicago Press, 1962, pp. 16–17.

Friedman, Milton and Rose Friedman. *Free to Choose.* New York: Harcourt Brace Jovanovich, 1979, p. 19.

Gwartney, James D., David Macpherson, Russell S. Sobel, and Richard L. Stroup. *Economics: Private and Public Choice.* 13 ed. Mason, OH: South-Western, Cengage Learning, 2010.

Harvard Law Review Staff, "Political Gerrymandering 2000–2008: A Self-Limiting Enterprise?" 122 *Harvard Law Review* (2009), pp. 1468–488.

Keating, Dan. "Democracy Counts: the Media Consortium Florida Ballot Project." Paper presented at the 2002 American Political Science Association annual meeting. http://www.aei.org/docLib/20040526_KeatingPaper.pdf.

Lyons, Michael. "Political Self Interest and U.S. Environmental Policy." *Natural Resources Journal,* Vol. 39, No. 2, (Spring 1999), pp. 271–294.

Moe, Terry M. *The Organization of Interests: Incentives and the Internal Dynamics of Political Interest Groups.* Chicago: University of Chicago Press, 1988.

Olson, Mancur. *The Logic of Collective Action.* Cambridge, MA: Harvard University Press, 1965.

Riker, William H. *Liberalism Against Populism: A Confrontation Between the Theory of Democracy and the Theory of Social Choice.* Long Grove, Illinois: Waveland Press, 1988.

Schumpeter, Joseph. *Capitalism, Socialism, and Democracy. 1.* Reprint, New York: Harper Perennial Modern Classics, 2008.

Stigler, George. "Director's Law of Public Income Redistribution," *Journal of Law and Economics* (April, 1970).

Tullock, Gordon. *Toward a Mathematics of Politics.* Ann Arbor: University of Michigan Press, 1967, p. 2.

Tullock, Gordon. *Wealth, Poverty, and Politics.* New York: Basil Blackwell, 1988.

Wittman, Donald. *The Myth of Democratic Failure.* Chicago: University of Chicago Press, 1995.

5

Politics of Free and Forced Rides
Providing Public Goods

THE DIFFICULTY OF providing public goods through volun-
tary action has been long recognized. In 1740 David Hume stated the problem
and the conventional response quite clearly in *A Treatise of Human Nature:*

> Two neighbors may agree to drain a meadow, which they possess in
> common; because 'tis easy for them to know each other's mind; and each
> must perceive, that the immediate consequence of his failing in his part,
> is the abandoning the whole project. But 'tis very difficult, and indeed,
> impossible, that a thousand persons shou'd agree to any such action,
> it being difficult for them to concert so complicated a design, and still
> more difficult for them to execute it; while each seeks a pretext to free
> himself of the trouble and expense, and wou'd lay the whole burden on
> others. Political society easily remedies both these inconveniences . . .
> Thus, bridges are built; harbors open'd; ramparts rais'd; canals form'd;
> fleets equip'd; and armies disciplin'd; everywhere by the care of govern-
> ment (pp. 538–39).

The common assumption is that public goods will be undersupplied by
markets, better provided by government, and better financed by taxation. But
to turn to government to fund and supply public goods does not easily solve
the problem of free riding and, in fact, raises some unanswerable questions.
Governments cannot readily and accurately measure how much of a public
good is demanded, nor can they eliminate free riding.

Government funding and provision of public goods is subject to all the ills
described in Chapters 3 and 4. Prices do not direct actions; politics does. Thus,
some outcomes will be entirely arbitrary; others will reflect the desires of the best

organized and funded interest groups, efficient choices and means of provision will be rejected in favor of inefficient ones, demands will be exaggerated, citizen perceptions will be manipulated by the public servants whose responsibility is to reflect public wants, and deception will be prevalent. One result is that some publicly supplied goods will be oversupplied and others undersupplied. Few will be provided efficiently.

There are ways to reduce arbitrariness and even perversity in the provision of public goods. Recognizing that government provision is no more likely to produce optimal outcomes than leaving provision to markets provides some impetus to searching for and experimenting with those possibilities. Also, there are few true public goods. Hume's examples—bridges, harbors, ramparts, canals, fleets, and even armies—are not pure public goods since they allow for excludability, which means that they are amenable to market pricing. Technological advances, such as congestion pricing on toll roads, are also reducing the "publicness" of many publicly provided goods so that, just as the invention of barbed wire enabled free grasslands to become private property, many public goods can be transformed into quasi-private goods.

How Much to Supply

In markets, the interaction of supply and demand determines how much of a private good will be supplied. Prices coordinate the actions of individual suppliers and consumers and they, as well as society, achieve mutually beneficial outcomes. In politics, the interaction of legislators, voters, interest groups, and government officials determines how much of a public good will be supplied. And unlike private goods, which can be provided in varying amounts to individual consumers, the polity must decide upon a *single quantity* of the public good that will be *equally* available to all citizens regardless of individual preferences. Unlike private goods each citizen "receives" or "enjoys" the *entire* amount produced.

Agreeing on how much of a public good to produce when everyone wishes a different quantity is challenging for economists, legislators, and voters alike. Economists have determined that, given revealed demands, the optimal quantity is that amount at which total marginal benefits equal total marginal costs, while marginal benefits received by individual citizens are equaled by their respective marginal tax costs. Although the formal conditions of optimality can be identified precisely, they are practically impossible to implement because differential tax payments based on each taxpayer's valuation of the public good would then have to be enacted. And if taxpayers know they will be taxed on how much they claim to value the public good, they will have a powerful inducement to understate their valuations. But if taxpayers pay equal taxes, some will be upset because their own tax payment will exceed the benefits they receive. Clearly, institutions that enable or require people to be honest in their valuations would be valuable, but such institutions are difficult to implement and they would gain acceptance slowly and, perhaps, grudgingly.

Free Riders and Forced Riders

Because public goods are offered in single quantities and at fixed tax rates, some citizens receive more than they want; they are forced riders paying for quantities unwanted at the price they are forced to pay. Others receive less than they want and would be willing to pay more for the amount they receive; they free ride off the contributions of others. With private goods, each consumer adjusts quantities purchased, or when faced with a fixed quantity pays more or less depending on the quality. The polity offers neither of these adjustment possibilities to the citizen. Thus, the same citizen can and most likely will be undersupplied with some public goods and over-supplied with still others. Figures 5.1 and 5.2 illustrate this situation.

The situation of diverse preferences for both public and private goods is depicted in Figure 5.1 where Rush Limbaugh (rl) and Keith Olbermann (ko) are considered to have quite different preferences for government spending on welfare and defense. The indifference curves display these preferences by showing Limbaugh's and Olbermann's respective rates of substitution for these two goods. Given a fixed budget line, their preferences are irreconcilable. Irreconcilable differences do not prohibit a political decision from being made, however, and the outcome will depend on the voting rules. This becomes clearer by including more voters. With additional voters, a simple majority voting rule, and everyone voting, it is quite likely that the "median" voters—those with as many voters preferring positions above theirs as voters preferring positions below theirs in a preference distribution—will decide the respective quantities

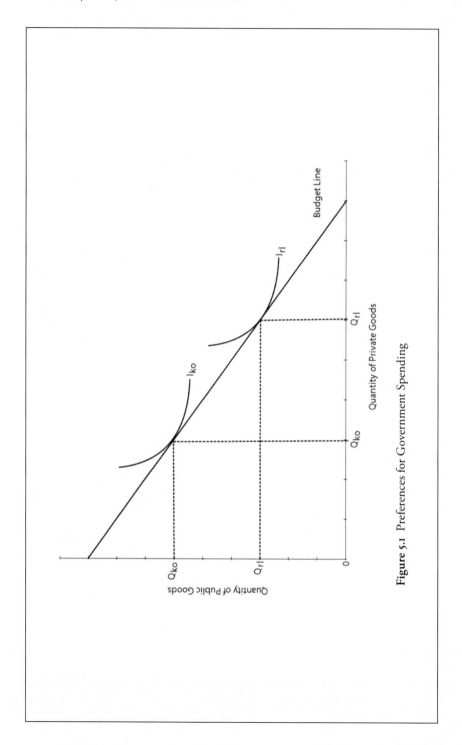

Figure 5.1 Preferences for Government Spending

of welfare and defense spending. Even though such a decision may be the best choice under the conditions, both Olbermann and Limbaugh will be unhappy with the outcomes.

Olbermann's most preferred combination of defense and welfare is shown at Q_{ko} on the vertical scale and Q_{ko} on the horizontal one indicating a distinct preference for approximately three times as much spending on welfare as defense. Limbaugh's preferences indicate a preferred ratio of twice as much spending on defense as welfare. Of course, each would prefer his positions be adopted and that even greater amounts of the more preferred good be chosen. The budget limitation of course makes that impossible. It is entirely possible and likely that while Olbermann would like to see the budget expanded (moved to the right), Limbaugh might well complain that it is too large and should be further reduced (moved inward to the left). In politics, the budget line is as subject to varying preferences as are individual indifference and demand curves.

With the use of another bit of elementary geometry, we can make the point still more vivid. In Figure 5.2 we extend our analysis by showing the preferred amounts of welfare spending among three voters—Olbermann, Limbaugh, and

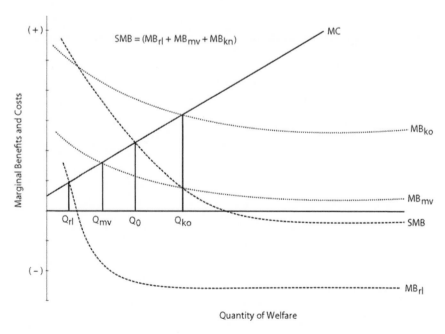

Figure 5.2 Preferred Amounts of Welfare

a median voter. The optimal quantities for each voter occur at those junctures where marginal costs (MC) equal marginal benefits (MB), just as is the case in markets offering private goods. Unfortunately, each voter is unable, as he or she would in markets, to simply purchase preferred amounts; only one quantity can be supplied by government and that prevents any easy and exact matching of individual MBs and MCs. For example, Rush Limbaugh's MC exceeds the MB he receives from welfare expenditures at all quantities beyond Q_{rl}. On the other hand, Keith Olbermann's MB exceeds his MC at every quantity up to Q_{ko}. Whatever quantity finally selected will necessarily mean that some people will experience MB > MC while others endure MC > MB.

As the diagram is drawn, the socially optimal quantity of welfare is Q_0 which results from adding, vertically, the demands or MB curves of the three voters (such a curve states the collective willingness of voters to pay for each quantity of the good) and finding the quantity at which the cost of provision is equaled by willingness to pay. Summing the demand (MB) for each voter produces the Summed Marginal Benefit (SMB) curve in Figure 5.2. Since Limbaugh's nega-tive attitudes toward welfare outweigh the positive views of the median voter and Olbermann, the SMB curve falls below Olbermann's curve for most quantities. But if all voters must share in taxes for welfare, we find that the optimal quantity, that is where MC equals the SMB, occurs at Q_0—an amount that does not cor-respond to the amount selected by anyone, including the median voter since he or she would rather have less spent on welfare. Alternatively, neither the median voter nor Limbaugh is willing to demand the same amounts as Olbermann at the prices he is willing to pay. Keith Olbermann's demand curve is much higher at all prices and at any given price he prefers more than the others.

This condition of diverse and poorly satisfied preferences for public goods is inherent and universal. Although each person is dissatisfied with the amount offered, no one is in a position to either make adjustments in personal consump-tion or alter the overall supply; unless, of course, he places so high a value on the "correct" amount that he is willing to pay the costs of political action to change the overall allocation of resources. It is not likely that many individual citizens will so decide.

Since public goods usually confer their benefits over long time spans, and the taxes levied to finance them are felt immediately and continuously, many theorists predict that the public supply of these goods will be sub-optimal. Certainly the logic is correct; the question however, is whether citizens actually perceive taxes and benefits as the theory suggests. We do not always know. Still, it makes sense to assume that variations in these expectations and perceptions should be found and that they are not trivial. Accordingly, we should hardly be surprised if attitudes toward national defense, for example, differ from those pertaining to mosquito abatement that, in turn, differ from preferences for fire protection and law and order or justice. We may, therefore, conclude that some of these public goods will be supplied in amounts (more or less) that are further away than others from the optimal quantity. Much will hinge on the degree of the good's publicness and the instruments of finance. If the degree of publicness is widely and accurately perceived and the means of financing are closely connected with the provision of the service, we should expect more optimal supplies. Conversely, the more distant the benefits and the more indirect the taxes are perceived, the greater the disparity between actual and optimal supplies. Given the problems of distant or dispersed benefits and indirect taxes, it is impossible to predict whether markets or politics will depart further from providing optimal amounts of public goods.

Providing more than optimal amounts will be encouraged by certain citizens who place higher values on having more of particular public goods, not because they enjoy consuming the goods, but because they supply resources purchased by the government to provide the goods. National defense offers the most conspicuous and costly example of the vested interest of suppliers—the armed forces, labor and management in defense industries, stockholders, and those who worry greatly about some foreign power. These citizens gain substantially by having larger defense budgets. Furthermore, they have the advantage of superior political resources for enacting larger budgets. As the suppliers of defense they can shape the demand curve for their own services to a considerable degree—a power not often granted nor obtained by private suppliers operating in private markets. Further, the coalition of interest groups, the Pentagon, and Congressional committees—what journalists and political scientists call an "iron triangle"—is able to inflate budgets and allow cost overruns that nearly defy the imagination. A nine-dollar hammer costing the government hundreds of dollars is only one of many dramatic examples of outrageous defense billing. But more important than shocking technical inefficiencies are the welfare losses, losses that go beyond the legalities of pricing and contract oversight to fundamental decisions on how much is enough defense.

Misallocation through excessive expenditures on defense is hardly the only form of waste; others include misallocation in the mix of defense programs and resources. Given pressures for increased expenditures, we should anticipate that too many people will be hired, and that they will have time on their hands. We should also expect what every veteran knows and laments—that personnel skills will not be neatly matched with job requirements. Although a powerful tendency exists to spend more on "hardware" than on salaries, positions will be upgraded and oversupplied. We have one-fifth the forces of World War II, for example, but we have many more generals. In short, citizens paying for more defense are getting less than might be desired and expected.

Even if we could eliminate incentives that exaggerate demands for public goods, we would still be faced with the persistent problem of discovering institutional arrangements that accurately aggregate individual demands into a collective choice. No matter which decision rule or institution is employed, problems will arise affecting the actual amount of the good to be offered. Regrettably, not much is known about the relationship between decision rule and output. Some analysts suggest that if simple majorities prevail, supply will tend to be excessive, and so they propose extra-majority requirements to reduce those excesses. Others contend that if elected representatives choose, they will opt for more than voters would in direct referenda. Still others maintain that although the supply of a public good may be decided by median voters, the median preference need not be optimal. There is little to suggest that voting produces rational and/or efficient outcomes. Some theorists assert that the nature of the alternatives, that is, competing amounts to be supplied, will influence the outcome. If, for example, voters must choose between some proposed amount and a much smaller amount (or nothing), the former will win, even though it may be much larger than the optimal amount.

Elementary fairness dictates recognition of the incredibly difficult problem of knowing how much is enough in the provision of public goods. What citizen can gather sufficient information to determine the efficient supply of defense, for example, information that is neither readily nor cheaply available? We simply must face the fact that we cannot ever attain fully reliable knowledge. There is a certain irreducible unpredictability in human affairs. We cannot fully understand a past we cannot remove, comprehend a confusing present, nor fully grasp a future that has yet to unfold. Of particular poignancy is the fact that preferences for public goods are not fixed as they are in the models of public choice; instead they are always in the process of being formed and reformed, often by the very public servants whose responsibility is to reflect citizen wants. So preferences for defense, roads, justice, etc., are not immaculately conceived but are the partial results of suppliers competing in a messy process.

Defense, the classic public good, would seem susceptible to rational choice, but the fact that one nation's defense rests in part on its assumptions about the conflicting choices of other nations is unsettling. Intentions and resources of possible opponents are always imponderables. Under such conditions knowing what to do, when, and with what cannot in any remotely scientific sense be regarded as certain. Faced with unpredictable responses and conditions, decision makers and citizens alike are more apt to permit their fears to reign and envisage the worst of all happenings—the Armageddon of nuclear holocaust.

Until practical means of ascertaining informed demands for public goods become available, we shall be cursed with the inherent problems of achieving optimal supplies of public goods. Short of institutions that effectively reveal demand at low cost, there is still hope that lesser gains can be realized by taking advantage of various technological improvements in pricing as well as the more extensive adoption of user-fees, privatization, and simply greater reliance on private institutions. Some of these reforms have already been accepted and found to provide significant improvements in the provision of civic services.

Technological Gains and Public Pricing

A few inventive public choice theorists have devised means that hold some promise for improving demand revelation and the supply of public goods. They are discussed below, but even more exciting than advances in theory are certain technological improvements that permit the offering of more publicly provided goods through the pricing system, enabling greater welfare gains through more efficient choices by individual citizens. There are greater welfare gains because users pay for their use rather than being able to free ride on the taxes paid by non-users. The pricing schemes are crude and subject to all the normal public choice problems one should expect in governmentally run systems. They are, however, steps toward users better revealing their demand than under a system of "free" streets and roads.

One such invention is the emergence of new methods for pricing streets and roads. Street, highway, and parking problems have long defied the pricing mechanism; that is no longer the case. The city of London began charging a flat fee of £5 in February 2003 for motorists driving in central London. The fee is charged for most private vehicles driving between 7:00 am and 6:30 pm. Drivers pay at selected stores, payment machines, by Internet, and most commonly, by cellular telephone messaging during that day. Weekly, monthly, and annual passes are available. Video cameras monitor cars and match license plate numbers with paid permits. People caught not paying are fined £80. Within the affected zone congestion has decreased and average traffic speed has increased.

The London system, as well as similar systems in Oslo, Rome, Hong Kong, and Singapore, is a flat-rate system that does not consider congestion rates at different times of the day or miles traveled, so intensity of preference based on time of use is not reflected in the price. But technology now exists to change the charge based on such considerations.

Hong Kong actually experimented with a system that measured miles traveled as well as time of day and charged accordingly. Drivers were provided price information on conveniently located electronic billboards. When costs are internalized the auto user is more likely to take account of these costs in deciding how much and when to use streets. Under such a system, traffic jams may not be eliminated but will surely be lessened, and users rather than nonusers will pay for the streets. Equity gains are likely to be substantially greater than those realized under the present crude system of differential license fees and gasoline taxes. Needless to say, the unfamiliarity of computer pricing of streets and highways shocked some people and the variable pricing system was replaced with a flat-fee system.

Variable pricing systems have been implemented on many toll roads. French toll roads to and from Paris reduced weekend peak traffic by 13 percent; Seoul's peak pricing of two toll tunnels reduced peak traffic by 24 percent. Lee County, Florida offers 50 percent off-peak discounts and peak use is down 7 percent while shoulder (the times on either side of peak times) use increased 19 percent (Poole, 2004).

As more road systems try to implement pricing systems I expect those who object most to be those who benefited from current transportation subsidies and systems of taxation. Groups will mobilize to delay and prevent further adoption of this eminently sensible means of financing a traditional public good. That was the case in London as opponents of Mayor Ken Livingstone's plan to price access to downtown London produced a website titled Sod-U-Ken (www.sod -u-ken.co.uk), and many newspapers editorialized against the plan. But given Singapore's 40 percent reduction in morning traffic and London's 20 percent overall reduction of cars, opinion is starting to change.

In the United States, congestion pricing for underutilized HOV (high occupancy vehicle) lanes has expanded greatly. On Interstate 15 near San Diego the HOV lanes have gone HOT (high occupancy toll). Single occupancy vehicles can purchase the right to ride in the HOV lanes at market prices that are adjusted every six minutes depending on the number of vehicles using the lanes. The highest rate is 50 cents per mile and the system has greatly spread out peak use. All of the tolls are collected electronically as overhead antennas scan a windshield-mounted transponder.

These advances in technology make charging for roads and even city streets far more possible. The next step is for roads and streets to be provided and financed by private markets instead of relying on governments. In actuality, and contrary to public goods theory, many roads have been provided privately for years. There are over 40,000 private roads in England and Wales. That is, the roads do not belong to a government authority and local residents maintain their road, purchase insurance, manage parking, and even prune trees (usually through an association or private company). Some of these roads are ancient and others are part of new subdivisions. This all suggests that the standard public goods argument underestimates people's ingenuity.

Advances in technology and recognition of human ingenuity suggest that many so-called public goods do not need to be provided by the government. For many ordinary citizens and especially liberal intellectuals, privatizing parks or airports is an unthinkable idea. On the other hand, proposals to turn garbage collection over to private competitors seems sensible to many citizens; so too, are fees for library use, admissions to parks, tuition fees in public colleges, etc. Where benefits are clearly personal, voters recognize the rationality of market-pricing principles in the allocation of publicly supplied services. But whenever the rent gains of keeping services publicly supplied are substantial, the political process encounters problems in gaining acceptance for privatizing institutions and laws.

Sharing the Burden of Public Goods

The discussion thus far has involved various problems encompassed by the decision of how much is enough; except for the examples of privatization, the problem of paying for whatever amounts are provided remains. Unlike the market where the dual questions of how much to consume and pay are answered simultaneously through the interaction of supply and demand forces, the polity divorces these choices. The committees of Congress that decide how much defense to provide are not the same committees that decide how to pay for defense or any other service. There is no attempt to relate who gets how much benefit from defense with payments for those benefits. It is assumed that, since all benefit from a public good, all should pay, but that leaves open the questions of who should pay how much, when, and how. The fact is there is no attempt to relate defense benefits and costs at the "consumer" level. Instead we have accepted the notion that those who receive more income should pay not only larger amounts of income tax but higher percentages of their income. The rationale for this policy is sometimes based on the idea that the better off should pay more because they have a larger stake in the system. Because we do not know the subjective worth of defense to the wealthy, that position cannot be sustained. In fact, we know that some wealthy people, including Keith Olbermann, do not like defense and view it as a negative good, much as Rush Limbaugh (Figure 5.2) views welfare expenditures as a negative good or public bad.

Many theorists suggest we would achieve more optimal supplies of public goods if we adopt what is known, after its inventor, as Lindahl prices. In effect, citizens are charged according to the marginal value they place on varying levels of provision. Since each citizen's income and tastes differ they are likely to prefer different amounts of the good, but since a single quantity is supplied to all, each will prefer to pay a different price (tax). Unlike the private goods pricing system, each citizen would be paying a different price for the same quantity of the good.

However, charging citizens different prices for the same quantity of the same good poses all sorts of ticklish and persistent problems. In the first place, the government would have to know the marginal benefit schedule of each individual taxpayer, that is, demand curve for each public good. But these schedules are not in any way directly observable and they are, in any case, non-comparable. Furthermore, the government cannot deduce marginal benefits from knowledge of income levels. Given each citizen's understandable desire to minimize taxes, there would be a powerful incentive to deceive the government. One does this by claiming less benefit from the good. Since every citizen would soon perceive this compelling free-rider possibility, total demand for the good would diminish and quite possibly everyone would consider themselves worse off.

We should also be aware of an important difference played by prices in the market and polity. Prices for private goods in markets serve to allocate resources because they determine how much is enough for each buyer. Since everyone consumes the same quantity of a public good—all of it—"tax-prices" in the polity cannot serve this same function. Once the quantity of the good has been decided, no one can be excluded. Olbermann and Limbaugh each get the same amount of national defense even though we assume they prefer different amounts. The only task tax-prices can perform is to determine how the financing of the public good might be shared among taxpayers and neither Olbermann or Limbaugh is allowed to determine what portion of their tax dollar goes to national defense or any other publicly provided good. In short, attempts to apply market pricing to efficient public good provision are confronted with challenging obstacles.

Publicness and Free Rider Arguments Questioned

This discussion shows that turning over the production of public goods to the polity is no guarantee of optimal results. Persuasive reasons were offered for this sad but necessary conclusion. Much of the wrong-headed rationale for public goods provision might have been averted had conventional analysts been somewhat more discriminating in their classifications of goods; mostly they relied upon a simple contrast of pure and public goods, failing to include some intermediate ones better described as "toll" and "common-pool" goods. Common-pool goods enable individual consumption decisions but few means of excluding non-payers, while toll goods enable exclusion but entail a good deal of joint consumption. Fish in the sea are a prime example of a common-pool good, while a rock concert may be best understood as a toll good. This discussion reminds us that the definition of pure public goods contributes to confusion because such goods are almost impossible to find in complex societies. Most so-called public goods are "impure," that is, admit of certain private good properties. For example, as more people use the good, the benefits of consumption are reduced through congestion; for example, roads and swimming pools. Consumption becomes rivalrous after some threshold of use has been reached. Second, as with private goods, the amount of consumption by individuals varies. So we can well imagine congested public goods without variability of use as well as congested public goods with variable use. These possibilities strongly suggest that financing these different combinations pose quite different problems.

While most economists will agree with these observations, some will raise other considerations. For example, Richard Musgrave (1959) coined the term "merit wants" to classify still another form of good in need of public provision. Merit wants are those items people *ought* to consume but do not or cannot when left to the whim of market provision. Such goods include, according to Musgrave, cultural events, school lunches, environmental amenities, low-cost housing, and free education. Musgrave also suggests that there are goods that ought to be discouraged, including illegal drugs. He concedes that these merit wants entail interference with consumer sovereignty and that elites will decide what is and is not meritorious. He admits, too, that the reason for public action is to "correct" individual choice. He claims that none of these goods or wants can be efficiently rationed by price so public action becomes mandatory. His examples are not all well chosen since all such goods can be, have been, and are sold in the market. Most so-called "merit wants" appear to be the wants of elite intellectuals.

Recent research and theory now demonstrate the fallacious argument that market failure provides an irrefutable rationale for government provision of public goods; the analysis is based on both faulty and incomplete reasoning. Equal access to an alleged public good may be converted into selective access by technological improvements, as in the case of London's streets.

If the elementary law of demand is applied to public goods, we have a devastating answer to Galbraith's (1958) and Downs's (1960) contention that public goods are always in short supply. Their vivid and dramatically used illustrations of shortages of public parks, education, environmental amenities, law and order, etc., are based on the assumption that citizen demand is unconstrained by price. Obviously, any rational citizen-consumer of such services will demand more when the price is arbitrarily reduced or eliminated than when they pay a market clearing price.

The conventional wisdom about free riders and public goods has difficulty accounting for some current and possibly over-supplied publicly provided goods. One reason is exaggerated demands for greater amounts of publicly provided private goods. Deception in this instance really pays off since the benefits of the private good are, by definition, confined to the few using the good while the costs may be passed on to innocent others. Worse, the costs may even be defended as legitimate sharing in the financing of a good with positive externalities—a claim often advanced in advocacy of greater welfare budgets. Since everyone, rich and poor, is supposed to benefit from fighting poverty, welfare is considered to be a public good.

Conclusion

The problem of getting free riders to contribute to providing public goods has caught the attention of and fascinated a great many political scientists, economists, and even sociologists and social psychologists. Such attention is excessive and improperly employed in normative theory and policy choice. Far too many analysts have used the free-rider problem as a means for justifying the state and extending its activities. Since the market is viewed as inadequate to the task of supplying public goods, the state must do so. I do not believe that markets and other private institutions are so helpless and, as we have seen, it is quite possible to change the nature of alleged public goods as well as make greater use of private initiatives to supply public goods. Furthermore, I have pointed out the problems political systems face in solving the alleged difficulty. Demand revelation is a universal problem whenever political processes are used to determine optimal supplies of goods. But in those instances where the polity must be used, the better decision rules can obtain different, superior results.

Bibliographical Notes

Questions involving demand and supply of public goods have been at the forefront of public choice since its beginnings. Much of the work is highly technical and probably beyond the analytical grasp of many readers, myself included. Still, the basic questions can be easily stated in simple terms and the basic principles understood in simple English. After all, we experience public goods problems in our own personal, everyday lives. But the explanations are not experienced and can, therefore, be easily misunderstood.

Virtually every modern economics text includes a chapter on public goods, if only to show that markets have difficulties stimulating their production. In any case, the single best introduction as well as classic rendition is that of Mancur Olson in his 1965 book, *The Logic of Collective Action* (Cambridge: Harvard University Press), a book available in paperback. In 1971, Norman Frohlich, Joe Oppenheimer, and Oran Young published a book based on Frohlich and Oppenheimer's joint doctoral dissertation at Princeton under the title *Political Leadership and Collective Goods* (Princeton: Princeton University Press). Their book supplied a missing element in the Olson thesis, namely, a political leader who would offer to organize the production of public goods. Just as markets require entrepreneurs to organize and distribute private goods, so, too, is the political system in need of a similar person and function. Most of the book is straightforward and easily understood.

An even earlier volume by James M. Buchanan, *The Demand and Supply of Public Goods* (now available as Volume 5 in Liberty Fund's *The Collected Works of James Buchanan*), sets forth a theory of demand but not really of supply, despite the title. The book is a bit heavy going, not because of any formal or mathematical analysis, but because of its closely reasoned argument about a seemingly abstract matter. No bedside reading here.

Another closely reasoned volume is that of Russell Hardin, a University of Chicago political theorist, entitled simply *Collective Action* (Baltimore: Johns Hopkins Press, 1982). In this book Hardin examines, critically, three different theories—public goods, the prisoner's dilemma, and game theory—to explore various collective actions. His is a philosophical critique of the ability of these three constructs to make sense of our collective existence. He is much less the economist and more the caring philosopher who sees human motives as considerably more diverse than does the typical economist working on public choice problems. The book is not only closely argued, it is very scholarly, and sometimes eloquent—a book well worth the effort to plow through.

One quite new book on public goods stands out because it describes how various wants that we normally consider to be public goods, or at least quasi-public goods, are provided privately. *The Voluntary City* (Independent Institute, 2009) by David Beito, Peter Gordon, and Alexander Tabarrok investigates the history of large scale, private provision of social services. The volume includes essays on education, transportation, crime control, park maintenance, medical care, and arbitration. In the final chapter, Tabarrok points out that the authors of *The Voluntary City* see market opportunities where theorists and practitioners see market failures. That conclusion is absolutely contrary to that of those who see public goods and externalities as justification for many kinds of government actions. One reviewer of the book suggested it could take a place of honor in the literature of cities next to Jane Jacobs's *The Death and Life of Great American Cities* (first published in 1961, now available in a Modern Library Edition). We agree. Jacobs's first chapters are extraordinary discussions about how planning for public goods goes awry. Her concluding chapters, however, promote more, just different, government actions. *The Voluntary City* provides examples of voluntary alternatives.

Another book that provides a host of evidence of people's abilities to solve public goods problems without relying on centralized governments is *Governing the Commons: The Evolution of Institution for Collective Action* (Cambridge: Cambridge University Press, 1990). The author is Elinor Ostrom, who shared the Nobel Prize in Economic Science in 2009. Ostrom has spent her career developing theory and doing detailed case studies of cooperation in common-pool situations around the world. It was odd and sad that so many economists had no idea who she was, or the importance of her work when the Nobel Prize was announced. Their ignorance says a great deal about the poverty of modern economics education.

References

Beito, David, Peter Gordon, and Alexander Tabarrok. *The Voluntary City: Choice, Community, and Civil Society.* Oakland: Independent Institute, 2009.

Buchanan, James M. *Demand and Supply of Public Goods* (Collected Works of James M. Buchanan). Indianapolis: Liberty Fund Inc., 1999.

Downs Anthony. "Why the Government Budget is Too Small in a Democracy," *World Politics* 13 (July, 1960), pp. 541–62.

Galbraith, John K. *The Affluent.* Boston: Houghton Mifflin Co., 1958, Chapter 18.

Hardin, Russell. *Collective Action.* Baltimore: John Hopkins University Press, 1999.

Hume, David. *A Treatise of Human Nature,* ed. L.A. Selby Bigge. Oxford: Clarendon Press, 1978, p. 300.

Jacobs, Jane. *The Death and Life of Great American Cities.* New York: Modern Library, 1993.

Mancur, Olson. *The Logic of Collective Action; Public Goods and the Theory of Groups.* Cambridge: Harvard University Press, 1977.

Musgrave, Richard A. *The Theory of Public Finance.* New York: McGraw-Hill Book Co., 1959, pp. 8–15.

Oppenheimer, Norman, Joe A. Young, and Oran R. Frohlich. *Political Leadership and Collective Goods.* Princeton: Princeton University Press, 1971.

Ostrom, Elinor. *Governing the Commons: The Evolution of Institutions for Collective Action* (Political Economy of Institutions and Decisions). New York: Cambridge University Press, 1990.

Poole, Robert W. Jr., 2004. "Commercializing Highways: A New Paradigm for 21st Century Roadways," http://www.ftc.state.fl.us/PDF/Presentations/Transportation _Solutions_(5–11–04).pdf.

"Sod-U-Ken." *Sod-U-Ken.* http://www.sod-u-ken.co.uk.

PART III

Understanding Property, Markets, the Firm, and the Law

THIS SECTION CONSIDERS property, markets, the firm, and the law—concepts that create the basis for the analysis underlying the case studies in Part IV. Each of these concepts is fundamental to public choice analysis, but often implicitly rather than explicitly. The chapters in this section attempt to make them explicit.

Property is a fundamental concept in any society. Once at least two people come together they have to decide how to allocate use rights to scarce resources. Those rights establish the behavioral rules that establish relationships. How well-defined those rights are and how well they are defended determines a society's success. It is impossible to develop a clear understanding of the role of government without understanding the social role of property.

Without property, markets and firms operate poorly. A basic question is why firms exist in the first place. They operate in markets yet their internal operations are hardly market-like. And if we expect producers, politicians, bureaucrats, and factions to pursue their interests, what about the people inside the firm? Shouldn't we expect them to act strategically as well?

Property, markets, and firms exist within a legal environment. So we should ask how rational people will adjust their actions to legal rules. What will be the effects of different legal rules on political and private actors? What are the implications of legal rules being produced by a political market where rent seeking is the norm?

6

Private Property and Public Choice

ECONOMISTS HAVE REDISCOVERED property rights relatively recently; meanwhile there are few political scientists focusing on what property rights are or how they function. Building on the pioneering work of Harold Demsetz (1967), economists explored how private property rights emerge and what they mean for social cooperation, organization, and coordination. We now understand how property tamed the not-so-wild, wild west (to use a phrase from Anderson and Hill, 2004); the effects of new technology; and how clearly defined, defended, and divestible property rights promote a dynamic economy. We also now know much more about the effects of politics on property holders.

Property rights, to the economist, are not rights to things; they are a set of use rights that may be asserted against others. More simply put, property rights are rules of behavior. These rules of behavior "define or identify the kinds of competition, discrimination, or behavior characteristic of society" (Alchian 1977, p. 128). To say you own a thing means that others respect your rights to certain uses of that thing. Economist Armen A. Alchian (1977, p. 130) held, "A property right, for me, means some prohibition against other people's choosing against my will one of the uses of resources, said to be 'mine.'"

This shared understanding of rights, responsibilities, and limitations creates a social contract that predates formal or civil society. Property as a social contract applies even to necessities such as food. For example,

> . . . even if a man is starving, he must buy the right to obtain food "owned" by another; indeed if the starving man is impoverished, we do not seek to improve his position by giving him the right to grab

another man's food but instead seek, in one way or another, to improve his purchasing power so that he may purchase needed products "owned" by others. By choosing this second remedy, the law attempts to resolve the property problem within an economic system in which individuals are given exclusive property rights rather than by relying on a common property system in which no man has a legal right to exclude another from the resource in question (Ackerman 1975, p. 2).

Property Rights as Behavioral Rules

The set of behavioral rules that make up our modern understanding of property are relatively simple and easily remembered as the "3 D's": defined, defendable, and divestible. To be defined means that we have a shared understanding about what you own and the extent of those rights. To be defendable means that an owner can exclude others from that property, whether it is something tangible like land or intangible like copyright. To be divestible means the use rights can be gifted, traded, or sold.

Defining property is at once simple and complex. Building a fence defines property, but only if others accept the fence. Pacific Northwest Indian clans marked the portions of streams they and others accepted as being theirs. They erected clan symbols to identify where their property began and ended. On the American grazing frontier, cattlemen created grazing associations that established rights and responsibilities to land. Miners established rules for staking mining claims and even for rights to water. These efforts to establish a social contract of shared understandings occurred ahead of formal law-making institutions and became formalized and widely recognized through time.

Today defining property often uses the force of government. Sometimes government is used to reinforce existing definitions of property such as using satellite surveys of land to better identify boundaries. But it can also include inventing new rights such as patents and copyright rules. The more controversial property rights being established through government are patents to medicines and to human genes, such as two breast cancer genes for which the U.S. Patent Office granted patents.

Defending property means that owners can exclude others from their property. The U.S. Supreme Court declared in *Kaiser Aetna v. United States* (444 U.S.

164, 1979) that, "The right to exclude others" is "one of the most essential sticks in the bundle of rights that is commonly characterized as property." Without the ability to exclude, owners cannot know if an investment will pay off because they will not be able to control the actions of non-owners. The amount of exclusivity determines a property owner's expectations about whether his decisions about the uses of his property will be effective. "The greater the probability those expectations will be upheld in one way or another (custom, social ostracism, or government punishment of violators), the stronger are his property rights" (Alchian and Allen, 1977, p. 114). When exclusivity rules are clearly defined and enforced (defended), I must gain your permission through sale, exchange, or gift in order to affect your property. I cannot trespass or use your property without your permission.

Gaining permission illustrates the third important feature of property—divisibility. Owners can transfer all or a portion of their rights to others. A property owner may sell or lease hunting rights to mule deer to one set of users, fishing rights to others, and upland game rights to still others while retaining the right to raise crops. Owners may grant general public access on designated footpaths, or not. They can sell a right to a view across their property, to not build a house taller than a certain height, or to restrict choices in paint colors. Where sunshine rights are defined and defended, as they are in Japan, owners can even sell those sunshine rights to others. Property rights are marvelously adaptive.

The ability to transfer property holds people accountable for choices about their property. If they treat their property poorly, its value decreases. If they treat it well, its value increases. An increased value means that others approve of the actions owners are taking and indicate that approval through market prices to purchase or use the property. Thus, owners have a monetary incentive to care for and improve their property's value in the market. They act as if they care for others' preferences. If, however, rules change and owners cannot charge for access to their property, they have little incentive to care about others' preferences.

Sticks and Property

In *Kaiser Aetna v. United States*, cited above, the U.S. Supreme Court used a term familiar to most economists: "sticks in the bundle of rights." The Court was referring to the idea that there are often many separable features or "sticks" to a particular property right, thus the "bundle of sticks" analogy. The property owner selling rights to mule deer, fish, and upland game all on his land is selling or renting a different stick from the bundle to different people. Patent holders do the same thing—they license some or all of the claims of a patent, all of the claims but for only a particular kind of research, all of the rights but only in certain countries, or the right to make and use but not the right to sell. Each of these sticks makes up the bundle of rights conferred by the patent.

Although each stick in a bundle of rights might be held privately, they are sometimes held communally. In the Swiss Alps, for example, villagers communally own and manage grazing pastures. A strict and enforced set of rules determines how many cows one can send to the high mountain pastures, the fees paid to the summer herders, and the distribution of milk and cheese. Each farmer has rights to graze, but only according to the rules established by the group.

Homeowners' Associations (HOA) in the United States own sticks that are normally part of a homeowner's bundle. An incomplete list of HOA rights include determining the acceptable color palette for painting homes and doors, restricting basketball hoops to the backyard instead of in the driveway, mandating the kinds of trees that may be planted and those that must be planted, whether the garage door can be left open, and determining whether on-street parking is permissible. Each of these sticks is granted to the HOA by the homeowner when he or she purchases a home in the development. Owners are, in effect, transferring rights to others in the homeowners association, while receiving a share of everyone else's rights in exchange.

The number of sticks in a bundle of rights is limited only by imagination or legal rules. Clever entrepreneurs continually recognize or invent new sticks in the traditional bundle of rights. Property owners own and can sell rights to unrestricted or partly restricted views. Online companies sell rights to view articles on the web. Software companies sell different levels of access to their products.

On the Western frontier people invented and owned brands that they burned into the hides of their livestock. It was clear that a horse or cow carrying the Rocking R brand belonged to the Rocking R ranch. Today, companies spend millions to "brand" themselves. The Coca-Cola trademark and Nike Swoosh are registered, recognized brands just as was the Rocking R. Companies license their brands to others, clothing manufacturers for example, in exchange for payment. The brand is one of the sticks in Coca-Cola's or Nike's bundle of rights.

Government prohibits many sticks in a bundle of rights from being sold, rented, or transferred. In the United States you are not allowed to break your prescription pills in half and sell the unused portion to someone else. You own the right to consume but not the right to sell. Neither can you legally sell body parts such as a kidney to someone who needs one. You can donate the kidney but accepting compensation is forbidden. You can only sell some sexual favors but not others. You may legally purchase a lap dance or massage but not intercourse. Of course, legal restrictions do not stop sales; they simply encourage rent seeking, black markets, and under-the-table rationing.

Property Types

Our hunter-gatherer ancestors owned everything and nothing. The world was a commons where no one could exclude or control others' access to resources they wanted. Once conflict developed over who got what, rules about who got what and when were developed. That is, property institutions emerged and they took three general forms—open access common property, common property, and private property.

The open access commons of early hunter-gatherer societies was the first form of property. Because there were not ways to exclude some and privilege others, the only way a person could own something was to beat everyone else to it. Thus, the only real property law was the law of capture—I keep what I capture and you keep what you capture. What I beat you to is mine and what you beat me to is yours, if I cannot hit you over the head and take it from you.

Common property is an alternative to the open-access commons. Rights to use a resource are vested in a limited set of owners of those rights within a set of defined rules recognized by users and non-users. Those rules can allow or prohibit one's rights in the common property to be sold. Common property rights have proven to be very effective at managing resources in small, well-defined communities ranging from lobster fishing communities in Maine to alpine villages in Switzerland.

The fundamental feature of common property, as with private property, is the right to exclude. Without that right, both forms of property devolve back to the open-access commons from which they emerged. And when resources are limited, desires unlimited, and exclusion impossible, overuse of an open-access commons is inevitable. The most famous statement of that inevitability is biologist Garrett Hardin's 1968 essay, "The Tragedy of the Commons," in which Hardin compared the world to an open-access commons and claimed that some form of "mutual coercion, mutually agreed upon" was the only way to save the world from ecological disaster. Common property with its rules for inclusion and exclusion gets a community out of Hardin's "tragedy."

Under private property rules, an owner possesses more of the sticks in the bundle of rights than in an open access commons or under common property. Choices are made by the owner, not by the community of users. Benefits of good choices flow to the owner. Costs of bad choices also flow to the owner.

Clear private property rights are most likely to be established when the resources to which rights are held are scarce. Where land is scarce relative to demand for food and housing, rights are most systematic and clear. There was little need for the first cattlemen in Montana to define property as each succeeding herd arriving from Texas could be pushed into the next empty valley. But more and more cows and cowboys meant that eventually there would be disputes. That is when people began to define and claim rights.

Conversely, when a resource becomes less scarce it can revert to open-access common property. The value of horses in the American West after World War I, for example, dropped dramatically as demand for cavalry mounts dried up. Owners of previously valuable horses ended up turning the horses loose on the public lands to forage for themselves. Similarly, a 2007 U.S. Fifth District Court Decision that effectively prohibits selling horses for human consumption means that many, especially older, horses are now turned loose because their economic value has been reduced below zero—it costs more to feed and care for them than their owners believe they are worth.

Well-defined and agreed-upon private property rights establish trust between strangers because the more certain I am about your right to the goods or services you will offer me tomorrow, the more I can rely on your promise to repay a favor you expect of me today. I choose the words "promise" and "favor" intentionally. When customers order books from Amazon.com, they pay today and Amazon promises to deliver the book in the near future. Paying today is a favor to Amazon. Delivering the book is honoring the promise.

Internet sales such as those on eBay take trust between strangers to fantastic levels. Trust is facilitated by secure payment services that offer buyer protection, "trust and safety teams" that work to prevent fraud and advertise seller reputations, and spoof protections. The auction houses have a property right in their reputation and work to improve and protect that reputation. Buyers and sellers trade property within these institutions with little consideration of just how amazing the levels of trust are.

I need to note that property rights can be costly to create. The costs of establishing, monitoring, and trading rights may exceed their benefits. Thus, we should not expect property rights to develop unless an entrepreneur can find ways to overcome all the transaction costs.

Property and Externalities

Our beginning chapters introduced the welfare economics view of externalities as a form of market failure. People taking legal actions may produce incidental and even unintentional byproducts that help or harm others. An unintentional benefit is a positive externality, which in some instances can be a public good. An unintentional harm is a negative externality. The problem for both kinds of externalities is that producers do not capture the benefits of positive externalities nor do they pay the costs of negative externalities. Thus, positive externalities, including public goods, are under-produced by markets and negative externalities are over-produced.

Over- and under-production are based on the assumption of a perfectly functioning private property system, one in which producers pay the value of their inputs and receive more than they pay and make a profit. If the goods are worth less than the value of the inputs, the producers lose money and switch to doing something that makes them money. In this system, goods that "should" be produced get produced and those that "should not" be produced do not get produced. Goods that "should" be produced are those that make a profit. Goods that "should not" be produced are those that make a loss.

This system only works, according to standard welfare economics analysis, if producers pay all the costs of producing their goods. But if some byproduct, pollution for example, is produced as part of the manufacturing process producers do not include that cost in their profit and loss calculations. Two kinds of inefficiencies result. One is that goods whose production costs and pollution costs are greater than the value of the good itself will get produced. The other is that although producers might be able to reduce or control the pollution and still make a profit, they do not do so. Thus, too much of the product and too little pollution control are produced.

Pollution problems and their solutions are discussed at length in Chapter 13. For the purposes of this chapter it is sufficient to note that the solutions usually proposed for solving externality problems are for government to either regulate the activities or to charge taxes to discourage the activities. Under a regulatory scheme, someone in government tells the producers what to do and even how to do it. The taxing approach assumes that government agents can identify the cost of an externality, the damage done by pollution, for example, and charge a fee sufficient to get the producers to internalize the external costs into their profit and loss calculations. Regulation relies on detection and monitoring by government. Taxes rely on the self-interest of the producers.

This analysis of externalities was once accepted by nearly all economists but was exploded by Ronald Coase in his 1960 paper, "The Problem of Social Cost." He offered an entirely new way of approaching social costs and the policies needed to deal with them. The idea underlying Coase's analysis, once understood, is fairly simple. Coase claimed markets do not cause externalities; instead, they are caused by failures to specify property rights so markets can internalize all costs and benefits. Once such rights are well, if not fully de-fined, the allocation of scarce resources is accomplished efficiently. According to Coase, the only time externalities can result in market failure, if property rights exist, is when exchange costs are high.

What happens in most pollution situations is this: someone emits costly emissions into space occupied by others who have no control over the actions of the emitter. Since the persons damaged by the pollution do not "own" the air space or waterways adjacent to their surface property, they cannot legally claim damages. If they could assert legal ownership to that space, they could either sue for damages or demand a price from the emitter in a regular market transaction. From an efficiency perspective, it makes no difference who is the initial owner of the rights so long as transactions are permitted. If the emitter is assigned the property rights, the receiver of the emissions must pay the emitter not to release emissions, while, if the receiver of the emissions is given the rights, the emitter must pay to emit. Fully informed utility maximizers will then arrange a mutually beneficial exchange and arrive at the "correct" amounts of pollution and production. Establishing property rights causes costs and benefits to be internalized and, thereby, aids in the calculation of efficient courses of action.

Coase explained that the parties to externalities could come to an agreement as to who owed what to whom if there are clear property rights. Clear property rights are what make negotiated, voluntary solutions possible. Without property rights, there are only two solutions to conflict over scarce resources: violence or politics. Violence easily leads to vigilantism, where guilt, punishment, and privilege are determined in secret and the values of the vigilantes are imposed. Politics is much the same way, as the political body imposes its values and chooses to privilege one person over another. After all, one of the famous definitions of politics is "the authoritative allocation of value." (Value can mean values as well as goods and services. America's argument over abortion is an argument as to whose values the political system will adopt and enforce.) Some will argue that war is a third solution to conflicts over scarce resources. War, however, is simply the extension of both politics and violence by other means.

Natural Rights?

The discussion about property to this point has been rather utilitarian—clearly defined and enforced property rights bring narrow personal interests into harmony with the general welfare as measured by market transactions. They promote harmony and cooperation. They establish clear expectations about rights and responsibilities. It is even possible to make a utilitarian argument that "property rights are human rights to the use of economic goods" (Alchian and Allen, 1977, p. 114). Human rights to use things, to own them exclusively, and to gift or trade them are fundamental to a well functioning society. They "eliminate destructive competition for control of economic resources. Well-defined and well-protected property rights replace competition by violence with competition by peaceful means" (Alchian, 2008). "Peaceful means" include trading, selling, gifting—all means of moving resources from lower-valued to higher-valued uses.

A moral, rather than utilitarian, understanding of property is the Lockean view that property rights are natural rights. They are the basis of human freedom. In Locke's *Second Treatise of Government* (1965, §123) he stressed, "Lives, Liberties, and Estates, which I call by the general Name, *Property*." Property rights predated government, and government's purpose is to protect those rights. Being a natural right, property was not given by any ruler nor should it be taken by any ruler.

The connection between liberty and property rights in the thought of early Americans was suggested by Supreme Court Justice William Paterson in 1795 (*Van Horne's Lessee v. Dorrance,* 2 U.S. (2 Dall.) 304, 309): "It is evident, that the right of acquiring and possessing property, and having it protected, is one of the natural, inherent, and inalienable rights of man." This notion that property is a "natural, inherent, and inalienable" right animates a modern property rights movement formed in recent years to defend private property rights from a perceived assault on private property by officials at all levels of government.

The utility-based argument for property is less powerful than the rights-based argument. If private property is primarily a means of providing social benefits, then restricting the actions of property owners can be justified if fifty percent plus one believe more social welfare can be provided. That is exactly what happened in the early nineteenth century in the United States as dams were built to use water to drive industrial machinery. Legislatures and courts decided that allowing the dams to flood private lands both upstream and downstream of the dams was allowable because of "public necessity and utility." Private property, then, became simply instrumental in serving goals of economic growth.

The rights-based argument would not allow flooding of private lands without the owners' consent regardless of claims that the public interest might be served. The justly famous *Pride of Derby* case (1953) in England illustrates. The Pride of Derby fishing club brought suit against the City of Derby, the state-run electricity board, and a commercial company because these government and private entities were discharging waste into the River Derwent, where the fishing club owned fishing rights. The pollution was described in one of the court documents as "a Blue Gray glutinous substance that lies thick on the bed of the Derwent." Rather than ask if the pollution value was greater than the value of the fishing rights, the court simply upheld the club's fishing rights. Rights rather than utility determined the outcome.

Property and Government

In the United States, at least, the utility-based justification of private property usually trumps a rights-based argument. Legislators view property as something to be taxed, regulated, and even taken for "public purposes." The battle between the individual and the state over property is over the border between what is mine and what is ours. Constitutional restrictions on government attempt to make that border clear. Under socialist governments there is not much of a border. Rights to broadcast television shows, to pump oil, to make profits are all restricted and often revoked. Taxes and regulations in democracies restrict what you can do with your property. Administrative rules and directives direct how you may and will use the state's property. I restrict my analysis of property and government to democratic states, although it applies to socialist states as well.

Economist Thomas Leonard (2004) began his review of Anderson and Hill's *The Not So Wild, Wild West: Property Rights on the Frontier* with the following discussion of property rights:

> Rival tobacco executives resolve their disputes with litigation, not with guns. The reverse isn't true for rival cocaine vendors. What explains these very different strategies for dispute resolution? Some explanations rely upon differences in the nature of the good. Other explanations appeal to differences in the nature of the seller—drug dealers are violent but cigarette sellers are peaceful. The law and economics scholar finds an explanation in differing property rights. Unlike their cousins who sell legal drugs, sellers of illegal drugs cannot lawfully possess or transfer their goods, and thus lack recourse to legal avenues for dispute resolution. There is good circumstantial evidence that violent trade disputes are the product of missing property rights. Upon the repeal of Prohibition, for example, a violent liquor industry quickly became more peaceful. The grant of legal rights to possession and transfer made many bootleggers into respectable businessmen, and hired lawyers replaced hired guns.
>
> This is not to say that those skilled in the violent arts are not drawn to the opportunities illegal markets offer them. They are. Nor does this claim that fuller rights to property will remove all opportunities for those skilled in the violent arts—gangsters still extort protection money from sellers of lawful goods. But it does claim that trade bans—the restriction of legal rights to possess and transfer—do not end trade. And, because trade bans force markets underground, they have the effect

of increasing violence, and other adverse effects, such as corruption and tainted products. So, the lawlessness of illegal markets, such as illegal drug markets, comes from the lack of law—incomplete rights to property.

Incomplete property rights produce many unintended consequences. One area where the unintended consequences are especially harmful is in the market for human organs such as kidneys. People do not object to the transfer of a healthy kidney from one person to another since a significant portion of kidney transplants come from live donors, usually relatives of the recipients. They do object to the idea that people should have transferable property rights to their bodies—to transferring a kidney from one person to another for a price. While applauding those who give kidneys, they prohibit selling them. The standard argument is that buying and selling organs degrades humankind and is morally wrong. That argument, however, does not increase the supply of kidneys. It simply lengthens the queue.

As of June 2010, nearly 100,000 Americans are on transplant lists waiting for kidneys, livers, hearts and lungs. Eighteen of those people die every day waiting in vain for a transplant. The kidney market is especially difficult as over 70,000 people are waiting and hoping for a new kidney to replace their failing ones. While waiting for one of the 11,000 cadaver kidneys or one from one of the 6,500 living donors, people spend about five years on dialysis. Half of them die still waiting.

The ethical problems are immense—who should get the next well-matched kidney? Should it go to a 40-year-old or a 70-year-old person? Is adding a few years to the life of an older person worth as much as adding many years to the life of a younger person? Should such questions be left to the United Network for Organ Sharing, a nonprofit organization overseen by the Department of Health and Human Services? Should politicians establish a national policy?

An alternative to public choices about who gets the next kidney is to allow at least some form of transferable rights in kidneys. Some have suggested amending the 1984 National Organ Transplant Act, which prohibits receiving any "valuable consideration" for donating a kidney, to at least allow some form of consideration—lifelong Medicare coverage, tax credits, tuition vouchers, even cash. Allowing even a limited market in kidneys would increase the supply and reduce the number of people dying from kidney failure in the United States from eighteen people per day.

Governments find many ways to reduce property rights that are not as controversial as restricting rights to our bodies. One example is the Endangered Species Act (ESA), which prohibits "taking" an endangered species. "Taking" as defined by the U.S. Fish and Wildlife Service includes not just killing a member of an endangered species, but modifying its habitat on both public and private lands. Supreme Court Justice Antonin Scalia describes that definition as meaning that "a forest landowner harvesting timber, a farmer plowing new ground, or developer clearing land for a shopping center [stands] in the same position as a poacher taking aim at a whooping crane" (Babbitt v. Sweet Home, 1995).

If an endangered species is found on your property or if your property is designated as endangered species habitat, you have few legal protections. You can take extra-legal actions, however. One extra-legal action is to remove habitat that might attract an endangered species. Michael Bean, formerly at the Environmental Defense Fund, as of this writing Counselor for Fish Wildlife and Parks in the U.S. Department of the Interior, believes that one overall effect of enforcing the ESA has been to create "unintended negative consequences, including antagonizing many of the landowners whose actions will ultimately determine the fate of many species." There is, he said, "increasing evidence that at least some private landowners are actively managing their land so as to avoid potential endangered species problems." He emphasized, however, that these actions are "not the result of malice toward the environment" but are instead "fairly rational decisions, motivated by a desire to avoid potentially significant economic constraints." He even said they are a "predictable response to the familiar perverse incentives that sometimes accompany regulatory programs, not just the endangered species program but others."

Two studies of systematic, widespread preemptive habitat destruction support Bean's conclusions. The first (Lueck and Michael, 2003) examines timber-harvest practices in forests occupied by red-cockaded woodpeckers and concluded that trees close to colonies of red-cockaded woodpeckers are logged prematurely. That is, the trees are not allowed to get old enough to provide nesting cavities for the birds. The authors conclude, "This evidence from two separate micro-level data sets indicates [red-cockaded woodpecker] habitat has been reduced on private land because of the ESA."

The second study (List, Margolis, and Osgood, 2006) asks how people will respond to a reduction of their property rights. It found that people respond rather quickly. The authors found that "undeveloped land fell in value by about 22 percent if it was within the critical habitat boundaries [area the government designates as necessary for the species and for which development restrictions are applied]." They also found that property owners took actions to make their property unattractive to the endangered species so that the property would be less likely to be included in the critical habitat boundaries.

Eminent Domain

In the United States, government is restricted from taking a private citizen's property by the Fifth Amendment to the Constitution which says no person shall be "deprived of life, liberty, or property without due process of law, nor shall private property be taken for public use, without just compensation." The rub is in defining "taking" and "public use."

The Fifth Amendment's concluding phrase, "nor shall private property be taken for public use without just compensation," is known as the Takings Clause. Property owners must be compensated if the title to their property is transferred to the state or when their property is physically invaded by government order. Transfer of title and physical invasion are relatively easy to interpret, especially after *Loretto v. Teleprompter Manhattan CATV Corp* (1982) in which a cable television company had to pay compensation for physically occupying less than a square meter of a private citizen's property, even though the city had granted authority to the cable television company.

When restricted from taking a person's property by constitutional rules or by limited budgets to pay for the property, politicians have another avenue—regulation. The appeal of regulation is that the owner continues to possess the land, but politicians remove some of the sticks from the property rights bundle. Regulation is far cheaper than paying compensation; in fact regulation is a relatively unlimited budget. Politicians and bureaucrats do not have to consider the opportunity costs of purchasing bird habitat here versus purchasing it there. They can simply rule that both properties are bird habitat and then look for other properties to regulate.

Taking some of the sticks from the property rights bundle through regulation, or regulatory takings, has the blessing of the U.S. Supreme Court. One of the early cases claiming a regulatory taking was *Village of Euclid v. Ambler Realty Co.* (1926) in which zoning was determined to be in the public interest and an appropriate way to control nuisance, even though zoning restricted owners' potential uses of their property. In *Penn Central Transport Co. v. New York* (1978), the Court upheld a lower court ruling that New York's Landmark Preservation Law could be used to stop Penn Central Railroad from building a fifty-plus-story addition above Penn Station in New York City. Penn Central's attorneys argued that this use of the Landmark Preservation Law violated the Fifth Amendment takings clause and that Penn Central should be compensated for their loss. The Court held New York City's denial of the permit was not a Fifth Amendment taking. The Court declared that its past taking decisions were "essentially ad hoc, factual inquiries" and established what is now known as a "balancing test" for determining when a regulation is a taking. The balancing test includes: "[t]he economic impact of the regulation on the claimant, particularly, the extent to which the regulation has interfered with distinct, investment-backed expectations," and "the character of the governmental action." In this case, the governmental action was not a taking for a purely governmental purpose and did not, therefore, violate the Fifth Amendment. Justice William J. Brennan, Jr. wrote the opinion for the court: "This is no more an appropriation of property by government for its own uses than is a zoning law prohibiting, for 'aesthetic' reasons, two or more adult theaters within a specified area."

How much value government can remove from a person's property through regulation was the focus of the 1992 case, *Lucas v. South Carolina Coastal Commission*. Lucas brought suit after purchasing two beachfront lots on a South Carolina barrier island. Before Lucas built on the lots, the Legislature enacted the South Carolina Beachfront Management Act, which prohibited Lucas from building on his lots. Lucas sued, claiming the Act made his property valueless and asking for compensation. The Court held that land-use regulations that deprived an owner of "all economically beneficial uses" of property violated the Takings Clause. Thus, *Lucas* provides a very narrow definition of a taking—"all economically beneficial uses."

That narrow definition was used in *City of Monterey v. Del Monte Dunes at Monterey, Ltd.* (1994) in which the City of Monterey's refusal to approve any of nineteen proposed site plans for developing a 37.6 acre parcel was declared to be a case of denying all economically viable use of the property. It was also part of the basis for denying a landowner compensation for the regulatory taking of the wetlands portion of his property (*Palazzolo v. Rhode Island,* 2001). The Court agreed that the owner had lost economic use of the wetlands, but because he had $200,000 in development value remaining on an upland parcel of the property he was not entitled to compensation.

Cases such as these suggest that the observant politician or bureaucrat can use the power to regulate property to extract rent. "Rent extraction" is a term coined by Fred McChesney (1997) and is the ability to threaten to regulate or tax, unless the targeted individual or industry changes in accordance with the directives of the threatening politician or bureaucrat. The politician schedules hearings, has legislation drafted, holds press conferences and later cancels the hearings or lets the legislation die in committee if he gets what he wants, which is often campaign contributions. The bureaucrat initiates studies and proposes rules until he gets what he wants, often changes in private practices or even land "donated" to the government. While rent seeking is paying money to get something from government, rent extraction is paying money to get nothing changed. It is, in McChesney's words, "money for nothing." Another public choice analyst, Richard Wagner (2002) calls rent seeking "the political cousin of bribery" and rent extraction "the political cousin of extortion."

In addition to taking a portion of the bundle of sticks in the property bundle, government sometimes just takes the whole bundle and pays the original owner "just compensation." In the *Penn Central* case, the railroad did not argue government could not take their property. They argued that the government must compensate the railroad. The Court disagreed. If New York City had simply taken the entire railroad station, they would have been required to pay.

The power to seize private property for public use while paying fair market value is known as the power of eminent domain. Cities use their eminent domain powers all the time to create road and utility corridors, build sewer plants, and construct municipal buildings. But they use eminent domain for far more than that. The Fifth Amendment states, "nor shall private property be taken for public use, without just compensation." City officials stretch the definition of "public use" to include transferring private property from one private party to another. The most visible case of such actions being upheld by the U.S. Supreme Court was in *Kelo v. New London* (2005). The Court held that a one person's home could be taken by the city and given to a developer if two conditions were met. The first condition is that the purpose must be for public use, which includes economic development. Even if the city council determined that public benefits would be indirect, the home could be taken and given to the developer. The second condition is that compensation is required.

Justices Sandra Day O'Connor and Clarence Thomas provided public choice objections in their dissents. O'Connor recognized that the politically powerful have an advantage in the takings game:

> Any property may now be taken for the benefit of another private party, but the fallout from this decision will not be random. The beneficiaries are likely to be those citizens with disproportionate influence and power in the political process, including large corporations and development firms. As for the victims, the government now has license to transfer property from those with fewer resources to those with more.

Justice Thomas worried about the effects on the poor and claimed that the previous incarnations of taking private property for development purposes, known as urban renewal, had really been a form of "Negro removal." He cited Detroit's famous Poletown case in which urban planners in Detroit, Michigan, uprooted the largely "lower-income and elderly" Poletown neighborhood for the benefit of the General Motors Corporation. He said, "Regrettably, the predictable consequence of the Court's decision will be to exacerbate these effects."

In the *Poletown* case cited by Justice Thomas, Detroit used the cover of economic development to take an entire neighborhood of 450 acres consisting of 144 businesses, 16 churches, a school and a hospital. The city also took 1,500 homes. After condemning the land, Detroit gave it to General Motors to construct a new factory. In 2004, the Michigan Supreme Court reversed its 1981 decision that allowed Detroit to take the neighborhood in the name of jobs and taxes. "We must overrule *Poletown,*" the Court wrote, "in order to vindicate our constitution, protect the people's property rights and preserve the legitimacy of the judicial branch as the expositor—not creator—of fundamental law."

When property rights are not secure, such as in central city areas that governments target for economic development projects, owners are less likely to invest in improving or protecting their property. Thus, designating an area for future "redevelopment" discourages current development. And on the margin, the more purposes for which government authorities may exercise eminent domain, the less secure private property rights will be and the more neighborhoods will deteriorate.

Property Rights in the Developing World

Although the residents of Poletown lost their fight in 1981, they did have clear title to their homes and were paid compensation. By contrast, half of the world's population live in squatter settlements and work outside the official economy—in shadow economies. More than one-third of the developing world's GDP is produced in shadow economies where the people do not own land, and do not have legal addresses, titles to their houses or their market stalls, or the ability to register their businesses. They sit on what Peruvian economist Hernando de Soto (2003) calls "dead equity," or property and assets whose value is not accessible because the property cannot be sold.

The poor's equity is dead for two simple reasons. First, there is little or no rule of law that protects and enforces property rights or contracts to sell or trade. What law does exist is time-consuming, expensive to use, and often ineffective. Former U.S. Ambassador to the United Nations Madeleine Albright, writing with Hernando de Soto (2007), explains that, "In Egypt, for example, starting a bakery takes 500 days, compliance with 315 laws, visits to 29 agencies and the financial equivalent of 27 times the monthly minimum wage." They switch to a recent study in Latin America by the Inter-American Development Bank for other examples, ". . . only 8 percent of all enterprises are legally registered and . . . close to 23 million businesses operate in the shadow economy. The proprietors of these businesses cannot get loans, enforce contracts or expand beyond a personal network of familiar customers and partners."

The second reason is that no one has clear title to property. They are squatters, not owners. Their world is one of instability and insecurity. Their property is not defined, defendable, or divestible. Albright and de Soto are working through the United Nations to "extend enforceable and fungible legal rights" to those who sit on otherwise dead capital. They face an uphill battle, in part because the Byzantine processes for starting a business or registering land provides so many opportunities for rent seeking and especially rent extraction.

Property rights sometimes emerge in the developing world. In Niger, for example, deforestation contributed to dry wells, winds carrying away topsoil, and encroaching sand dunes. Because trees were regarded as the property of the state, they were cut for firewood or construction without regard for consequences—they were an open access resource. Because farmers received no benefit from them and because they interfere with crops as they grow, saplings that appeared in a farmer's field were immediately removed. But in the mid-1980s farmers asserted and the government allowed private ownership of trees on private property. As owners of the trees, the farmers stopped clearing saplings and nurtured them instead. The owners now sell branches, pods, fruit, and bark to supplement their income. These owners have increased the number of tree-covered acres by 7.4 million acres, and satellite images and on-the-ground surveys find farmers have added millions of new trees. The ecological benefits are impressive; the social benefits are impressive as well because the tree income cushions the boom and bust cycles that are inherent in a society relying on herding and farming. All this has happened as population doubled and, contrary to conventional wisdom about the developing world, the vegetation is densest in some of the most populated regions of the country. Of course rainfall has helped, but property rights emerging where there had been none before completely changed human behavior so that trees replaced dusty, barren wastelands (Polgreen, 2007).

These examples show that when property rights emerge in the developing world they dramatically change individual and social outcomes. The trick, however, is to get the rights established well enough that they cannot be stolen by governments. In Zimbabwe, for example, a system of village rights to wildlife made substantial improvements in wildlife conservation. But district and central government politicians decided to take much of the profit from the villages and the village rights, and now wildlife are being destroyed. In Namibia, on the other hand, similar experiments are going forward without interference by governments above the village level. If those experiments continue on their current trajectory, they will improve the situation for humans and wildlife.

Conclusion

In discussing property rights I want to emphasize that while property rights are about rights to things or ideas, at a more fundamental level they are a set of behavioral rules that condition our relationships with those around us. They create incentives for us to consider others' values as we pursue our own ends. They determine whether we take care of trees or cause desertification. They determine how bargaining can resolve disputes. They are fundamental to society, so much so that they can be thought of as the basis of well-functioning societies.

Bibliographical Notes

Ronald Coase's classic essay, "The Problem of Social Cost," is a good place to start in order to understand how property functions in the service of society. You can find that essay and a companion essay, "Notes on the Problem of Social Cost," in *The Firm, the Market, and the Law*, University of Chicago Press, 1988. Coase notes in his introduction to a collection of Armen Alchian's papers (*Economic Forces at Work*, Indianapolis: Liberty Fund, 1997) that Alchian "has played the leading role in the development of property rights theory." Coase goes on, "His writing is distinguished by his ability to disentangle the essential from the trivial, and above all, by his skill in showing how the same basic economic forces are at work in a wide variety of apparently completely different social settings." I agree.

Perhaps the best and most intellectually challenging defense of property from government takings is Richard Epstein's *Takings: Private Property and the Power of Eminent Domain* (Harvard University Press, 1985). He organizes his argument around four questions: What constitutes a taking of private property? When is that taking justified without compensation under the police power? When is a taking for public use? And when is a taking compensated, in cash or in kind? He uses his answers to those questions to take on zoning, rent control, various kinds of taxes, bankruptcy, and the New Deal.

A very thorough and well-written casebook on takings that makes an excellent companion to Epstein's book is Steven J. Eagle's *Regulatory Takings*, in its fourth edition with Lexis Publishing in 2009. Eagle, a professor at the George Mason School of Law, examines how takings law has expanded at local, state, and national government levels and how that expansion clashes with Fifth Amendment rights to be compensated when property is taken. I admit to not having read all 750 pages but have used it extensively as a research guide.

Political scientists usually begin their discussions of property with the fifth chapter of John Locke's *Second Treatise of Civil Government*. Although they start with Locke, most political scientists who think about property doubt the legitimacy of private property itself. One political scientist who understands and values property rights is Elinor Ostrom, former President of the American Political Science Association. At the end of Chapter 5 I noted that she won the Nobel Prize in Economic Sciences in 2009 and suggested another of her books.

Here I recommend her volume co-edited with Nives Dolsak, *The Commons in the New Millennium: Challenges and Adaptation* (MIT Press, 2003). The emphasis is on natural resources such as fisheries and forests. One advantage of this volume over her earlier work is time—enough of it has passed for empirical data to be gathered on the effects of property rights arrangements on managing, for example, irrigation systems in the Dominican Republic, lobster fisheries in Maine and off-shore fishing rights in Iceland and New Zealand.

References

Ackerman, Bruce A. *Economic Foundations of Property Law.* Toronto: Little, Brown and Company, 1975.

Albright, Madeleine and Hernando de Soto. "Giving the Poor Their Rights." *Time Magazine.* http://www.time.com/time/magazine/article/0,9171,1640435,00.html.

Alchian, Armen A. *Economic Forces at Work.* Indianapolis: Liberty Fund, 1977.

Alchian, Armen A. "Property Rights." *The Concise Encyclopedia of Economics,* 2008. Library of Economics and Liberty. http://www.econlib.org/library/Enc/Property Rights.html.

Alchian, Armen A. and William R. Allen. *Exchange and Production: Competition, Coordination and Control.* 2nd ed. Belmont, CA: Wadsworth Publishing Company, 1977.

Anderson, Terry L. and Peter J. Hill. *The Not So Wild, Wild West: Property Rights on the Frontier.* Stanford, CA: Stanford University Press, 2004.

Babbitt v. Sweet Home Chapter of Communities for a Great Oregon (94–859), 515 U.S. 687 (1995).

Bean, Michael. "Endangered Species: Endangered Act?" *Environment* (January 1999).

Coase, Ronald. 1960. "The Problem of Social Cost." *Journal of Law and Economics* 3 (October): 1–44.

Demsetz, Harold. "Towards a Theory of Property Rights." *The American Economic Review* 57, no. 2 (May 1967): 347–59.

De Soto, Hernando. *The Mystery of Capital: Why Capitalism Triumphs in the West and Fails Everywhere Else.* New York: Basic Books, 2003.

Dolsak, Nives and Elinor Ostrom. *The Commons in the New Millennium: Challenges and Adaption.* Cambridge: MIT Press, 2003.

Eagle, Steven J. *Regulatory Takings,* 4th ed. New York: Lexis Publishing, 2009.

Epstein, Richard. 1985. *Takings: Private Property and the Power of Eminent Domain.* Cambridge: Harvard University Press.

Hardin, Garrett. "The Tragedy of the Commons." *Science* 162 (1968): 1243–248.

Kaiser Aetna v. United States, 444 U.S. 164 (1979).

Kelo v. City of New London, 545 U.S. 469 (2005).

List, John A., Michael Margolis, and Daniel E. Osgood. "Is the Endangered Species Act Endangering Species?" *National Bureau of Economic Research*, Working Paper 12777, December 2006.

Leonard, Thomas. 2005. "Review of Terry L. Anderson and Peter J. Hill, *The Not So Wild, Wild West, Constitutional Political Economy*," *Constitutional Political Economy* 17:1 (March 2006): 63–66.

Locke, John. *The Second Treatise of Government, in Two Treatises of Government*, ed. Peter Laslett. New York: Mentor, 1965.

Loretto v. Teleprompter Manhatten CATV Corp. 458 U.S. 419 (1982).

Lucas v. South Carolina Coastal Council 505 U.S. 1003 (1992).

Lueck, Dean and Jeffrey Michael. "Preemptive Habitat Destruction Under the Endangered Species Act," *The Journal of Law and Economics*, vol. 46 (2003) pp. 27–60.

McChensey, Fred. *Money for Nothing: Politicians, Rent Extraction, and Political Extortion.* Cambridge: Harvard University Press, 1997.

Monterey v. Del Monte Dunes at Monterey, Ltd. (97–1235) 526 U.S. 687 (1999).

Palazzolo v. Rhode Island, 533 U.S. 606 (2001).

Penn Central Transportation Co. v. New York City, 438 U.S. 104 (1978).

Polgreen, Lydia. "Trees and Crops Reclaim Desert in Niger." *International Herald Tribune* (February 11, 2007). http://www.iht.com/articles/2007/02/11/news/niger.php.

Stubblebine, William Craig. "On Property Rights and Institutions," in Henry Manne, ed., *The Economics of Legal Relations.* St. Paul: West Publishing, 1972.

Van Horne's Lessee v. Dorrance, 2 U.S. (2 Dall.) 304, 309 (Circuit, Pa. 1795). Quoted in Steven J. Eagle, "The Birth of the Property Rights Movement," Cato Institute Policy Analysis No. 404 (June 26, 2001), 4.

Village of Euclid, Ohio v. Ambler Realty Co., 272 U.S. 365 (1926).

Wagner, Richard E. "Property, Taxation, and the Budgetary Commons," in *Property, Taxation and the Rule of Law*, edited by Donald P. Racheter and Richard E. Wagner, Norwell, MA: Kluwer Academic Publishers, 2002, pp. 33–47.

7

Rediscovering Markets, Competition, and the Firm

THE U.S. MARKET economy came into prominence in the nineteenth century and remained relatively free until the 1930s when discovery of the redistributive potential of politics posed a potent threat to its continued workability. Of course, in some nations the market economy never developed much beyond local bazaars; in still others, notably Italy and Germany, corporate fascism allowed capitalist institutions, but the state managed them for state purposes. In still others, Russia, for example, national markets never really got started under the Czars and were for a brief time prohibited under state communism. Except for a capitalist underground economy, free markets remained illegal in the USSR until 1989–90. So the reign of capitalism has not been universal or lengthy. Where it has taken root, capitalism has always been under the threat of a redistributionist ethic and/or the power of politicians more interested in political power than in freedom and economic growth. Capitalism's intrinsic uncertainties and ambivalent moral status provided (and continues to provide) such politicians ammunition in their demands for reform, controls, and regulation.

The marketplace seemed to fail completely in the 1930s. As a consequence, socialism, public planning, and detailed regulation (the substitution of political for economic processes) gathered a new momentum that lasted more than fifty years. As wars and other governmental action seemed to rectify many economic ills, the case for the market was, all too often, left to embittered ideologues. Even Paretian welfare economics was subverted and made the technical basis for an attack on market performance.

But over time, daily experience has acquainted ordinary people and scholars with the actual workings of political and bureaucratic processes and, thus, the virtues of the marketplace have been rediscovered and its principles cast in new and promising terms. These re-discoverers include such eminent European theorists as the late Frederich A. Hayek and Ludwig von Mises, and the Americans Armen Alchian, James M. Buchanan, Milton Friedman, Douglass North, Richard Posner, George Stigler, and Vernon Smith to list but the prominent. They have provided us with new meanings of competition, monopoly, the firm, property, goods, contracts and law, and the role of supply-side considerations in both micro and macroeconomics. Truly the last seventy years have witnessed a genuine renaissance in economics, yet very little of this quiet revolution has permeated other bastions of social science. The most auspicious result has been the rethinking of public policy by economists and advisors to conservative and liberal governments. Privatizing and freeing markets are no longer unthinkable in countries that once completely rejected markets.

New View of Market Processes

But in 1945, a few years after publishing his startling *Road to Serfdom*, F.A. Hayek in a single essay, rewrote the meaning of competition for economists. Ironically, his technical understanding of the term is quite consonant with the more ambiguous terms used by laymen. In "The Use of Knowledge in Society," Hayek argued that the standard neoclassical definition of competition emphasizing equilibrium led economists astray from studying real-world behavior in markets. His point remains true for many mainstream economists who still study final equilibrium states where everything supposedly comes to a rest rather than the processes of unstable competition or as Hayek more appropriately termed it "rivalry." While Hayek did not deny equilibrating forces, he wanted more attention devoted to disequilibrium, a process endogenous to free markets where little can be controlled by any single seller or consumer. Capitalism produces a kind of partially ordered chaos, not quietly equilibrated firms and markets. Everything is in transition and doubt: knowledge, opportunities, and above all, expectations. Nothing is sacred. Wealthy one day and poor the next may be an exaggeration, but it does suggest the dynamism and uncertainty of market economies. For every competitor, there is another wishing to surpass him and while some will be tempted to employ illegal and unethical means, most improve their fortunes by improving those of others through inventions of new and better goods and services, offering lower prices, etc.

The entrepreneur and his innovations occupy an analytical role for Hayek, von Mises, and others who form the school of thought now known as Austrian economics. The entrepreneur constantly upsets routine through what another Austrian, Joseph Schumpeter, called "gales of creative destruction." That is, his innovations make old ideas, skills, technologies, methods, tools, organizations, and processes obsolete while improving standard of living. Think, for example, of computer data storage devices. From the 1970s to the late 1990s, 8-inch, then 5¼-inch, then 3½-inch floppy disk drives were the industry standard. A 3½-inch drive held 1.44 MG of data. In 1998 Apple dropped floppy drives from iMac computers, and Dell no longer included them as standard equipment on their desktop computers. By 2010, the floppy was dead except as the "save" and "save as" icon in Microsoft Word. It was replaced with USB drives that generally contain at least 8 GB of data, external hard disks that can contain a Terabyte or more, CDs, DVDs, memory cards, or Internet storage.

Entrepreneurs proceed to sell themselves and their products through advertising, product differentiation, brand names, collusion, price cutting, trial and error—perfectly natural forms of rivalry but known to many economists only as unmistakable signs of imperfect markets and in need of remedial governmental intervention. The very activities that make markets dynamic and competitive are, according to Hayek, the very activities that some economists want suppressed or regulated.

Once the idea of rivalrous flux is accepted a great many other new ideas and ideals flow forth to constitute a well-rounded paradigm of economic life. According to this view, market competition is considerably more robust than either market supporters or critics thought to be the case. That political competition cannot perform the miracles of market competition is an important corollary; lacking a "hidden hand" of prices, the political process is usually a zero-sum and sometimes negative-sum game, whereas the market is a positive-sum or unanimous transaction.

In the new learning on markets both competition and monopoly have been redefined in unexpected ways. For example, how much competition and/or monopoly exist depends on two factors: economies of scale and entry barriers.

Economies of scale are the cost advantages a firm achieves because of size. When average costs for a firm are very low, it is apt to become dominant or that market is likely to be dominated by a small number of large firms producing most of the total product. Products that are easily produced at low cost lend themselves to mass production and few firms; complex, highly individualized products or services are apt to be offered by many firms, none of which has a large share of the market. Most academic critics of modern markets emphasize the overwhelming presence of monopoly; casual public opinion affirms the same misperception. Actually, while the large firms are extremely competitive, there has been a resurgence of small, specialized firms offering unique products and services. Indeed, we should think of every rock music group in this sense. If we do, we also learn that all monopolies are very short-lived. Furthermore, there are very few monopolies in the common sense meaning of that term, that is, a seller without competition from close substitutes. Those who are inclined to question might ask the United States Steel Corporation about the mass production of aluminum, not to mention foreign steel competitors or the competition from steel substitutes. Or, one might ask the railroads about the trucking industry, the bus industry, or the airlines. Then, too, every monopolist's returns attract potential monopolists and, thereby, lower dissipation of profits.

These strictures on the nature and significance of monopoly must be qualified in one very important way, namely, the role of labor unions in a competitive economy. Labor unions have, in fact, been the most singular example of government-mandated monopoly. For decades, they have been awarded a special status in the law permitting them to benefit in ways not permitted other organizations, especially, private firms. Private firms must worry about how much demand for its products will change as prices change. Unions, however, have been able to increase their members' wages by excluding those willing to work for less. Buttressed by closed shop privileges, the union was able to exercise a degree of coercion unknown to other sellers. Many citizens seem to think that granting such power to unions benefits society. But, there is a continuing weakening of these beliefs, not only in public opinion polls but also in the decreasing membership of unions and their dramatically diminished power at the bargaining table. Union membership in the private sector has fallen so fast that there are now more unionized public-sector workers than unionized private-sector workers. Monopoly tendencies exist in the free market but the chief form of monopoly is found in government mandated labor unions, including public-sector unions. If there is a role for antitrust laws perhaps they ought to be applied to labor organizations. (Chapter 10 contains a more extended description of antitrust.)

Although the economy of scale explanation is important, the more significant aspect of monopolistic processes is a purely political phenomenon, namely, government-created barriers to entry into a market or industry. Market advantages are available and they are best obtained and most effective when granted by sovereign governments. Mercantile Europe provided a plentitude of examples, but the more relevant are found in present-day USA. Not all industries seek the same forms of protection, partly because some are irrelevant to their situation while others are considered more or less politically infeasible. And, in some instances, one form of protection actually maximizes privilege. For example, the domestic auto industry prefers quotas to tariffs. Barbers, doctors, lawyers, and others prefer to restrict entry and restrain competition through licensing, thereby imposing professional standards and administering their own industries. Patents and copyrights grant monopoly privilege to drug companies and recording artists. In some cities, the taxi industry has managed to limit competition by requiring purchase of an expensive medallion ($558,000 for private medallions and $775,000 for corporate-owned New York City medallions in 2010 [Perry 2010]). The shipping industry (high seas) has rules restricting the use of foreign vessels. Domestic content laws are highly popular among auto unions as well as domestic manufacturers of those parts. Peanut growers in the South must obtain a special "peanut allotment" to grow peanuts. Such allotments are exceedingly scarce, often inherited, or sold at astronomical prices. Administering these various barriers are dozens of regulatory commissions in Washington DC, commissions that should be better-known as cartel managers. By restricting competition, they attempt to stabilize if not increase the wealth and income of industries.

These official administrative agencies of political cartels must not be superficially thought of as captives of the industries they regulate. Consisting of self-interested members and staff, the commissions engage in exchanges with the regulated industries that are *mutually* profitable. As many analysts have noted, regulatory agencies place a high value on risk aversion—not upsetting the Congressional committee apple carts that provide budgets and oversee their operations. Security becomes a major goal because jobs, salaries, status, and power are at stake and easily lost by unfavorable events and publicity. Predictability of decisions is another value jointly esteemed by client groups as well as bureaucrats. So, there is a powerful desire to codify and proliferate administrative practices and policies. Having comfortable relationships with clients as well as the general public enables trouble-free days and provides the chief administrators more harmonious relationships with the President and Congress. A grateful industry will also discover the political talents and rent-seeking potential of retired administrators when it next considers hiring a Washington lobbyist. A cozy relationship may not be inevitable but it is certainly a strong likelihood.

Unlike the past, new firms and industries are born in an already functioning cartel arrangement closely regulated by political operatives. Entrepreneurs must not only have permission to enter business, but they must also meet diverse requirements ranging from having to pay innumerable and substantial fees and taxes to having their facilities approved, and meeting zoning restrictions.

The Business Firm: New Understandings

In rethinking and explaining basic economic processes, attention has quite naturally focused on the role of the firm—for it is the vehicle by which the profit-oriented entrepreneur combines and reallocates resources. Conventional textbook economics has always treated the firm as something of an "empty box," an artificial entity whose internal structure and decision-making are considered irrelevant in explaining market equilibrium. Because traditional price theory views the firm as but a mechanical response to market forces, purchasing inputs at fixed prices, transforming resources into products under certain technological constraints, and selling them in markets is viewed as beyond their control. In short, the typical firm has very little to decide; its decision processes are negligible; it is, indeed, an "empty box."

A newer conception has made considerable inroads. Consisting, in part, of behavioral approaches pioneered by Herbert Simon (1957), Austrian views of the market, and the rather special contributions of Alchian (1972), Coase (1937), Demsetz (1962), and Williamson (1985), a distinctly different conception has emerged to challenge more familiar images of economists. Once again, Ronald Coase led the way. He did so by raising two startlingly naive questions: Why do firms exist and why are they organized as they are?

The firm exists, he claimed, because formal organization reduces the cost of doing things through contracts, that is, the cost of production is reduced as hierarchies replace markets in which resource holders contract with one another afresh each day. Rejection of the contractual model by those who espouse market competitions is something of an anomaly. Nevertheless, entrepreneurs choose the very opposite practice for the sensible reason that individual contracting among the holders of resources would be extraordinarily complex, confusing, frustrating, and wasteful. So the typical firm is not a miniature market.

Instead, the firm is a "simple" hierarchy of owners, managers, and employees organized and coordinated by a formal division of labor. Combined, they are able to produce far more and at a lower cost than might be possible without such organization. It is also important to note that each group of members is compensated in a different manner: generally, employees receive hourly wages; managers earn salaries and bonuses; and owners hope to receive residual payments called profits. Needless to say such payments produce different interests among the team members, differences that must be resolved if the firm is to succeed.

Relationships among the firm members are governed by "long-term" rather than short-term, daily contracts, because such contracts enable reductions in contracting costs and increase stability of mutual expectations and performance. Such contracts also provide a more efficient means for controlling the behavior of members. In every team effort, there are members tempted by the possibilities of free-riding, shirking, or gaining at the expense of others. In large, complex, and impersonal organizations the temptation is notably increased by both the greater probabilities of not being detected and the weakened ethical ties found among strangers. Since assessing contributions in a complex division of labor is difficult, the incentive for employees to gain by avoiding or neglecting work (shirking) is further enhanced. Put another way, the lower the cost of shirking the more shirking will be "demanded" or practiced. Bosses or monitors are required to keep employees honest and sharing in the work.

Communal organizations face this problem in a peculiarly wrenching way because the assumption is that no one is tempted to shirk responsibilities; but personal accounts of former commune members and social research has shown that to be a myth. And, even when members of a commune do not shirk, they bring different skills, abilities, and motivation to the work. How shall they be paid? The shirker, of course, increases the social costs for colleagues who must make up for the reduced contributions of shirkers.

As in large polities, monitors in the firm bear scrutiny. Managers of large and small corporations alike have interests of their own that may be satisfied at the expense of employees and/or owners, owners whose very absenteeism increases the possibilities of exploitation. The capitalist way of meeting this problem is to offer the bosses a bonus for doing a good job of monitoring. Possible gain accompanied by the ever-present possibility of failing to increase production may lead to being fired; again, dual incentives perform marvelous results, especially for consumers.

In earlier chapters I observed that private firms and public bureaucracies are financed in quite different ways; because the consequences are so critical the point is worth repetition and further examination. Government bureaus obtain annual budgets from a legislature to finance operations for set periods of time. Unlike the firm they do not depend on uncertain investments and market sales. Since the latter revenues are unpredictable the firm must find investors willing to confront uncertainty. Some may invest because they enjoy risky situations, but most people will invest only because the future payment is sufficiently large to overcome their aversion to risk. As a reward for bearing the risks of losing their wealth they are offered interest payments or the possibility of a profit and held responsible for only limited liability. The greater the risk, the greater the potential reward necessary to obtain the resources. While there is an unknown personality element in explaining risk-taking, economists generally prefer to assume that risk-taking is dependent upon one's wealth while deciding among investment options. In other words, money may have diminishing marginal utility; those who have a great deal can easily afford to take the risk and will demand a smaller reward while those with fewer dollars must be offered more to overcome their greater aversion to similar risk. So owners are the specialized carriers of risk who provide the investment capital needed to finance capitalist firms. Investments are assembled by spreading and reducing risks among the many whose personal funds are limited. Not so ironically, American trade unions have become substantial investors in the very companies for whom their members work.

This exegesis on the new theory of the firm helps us to understand better how the firm operates in actual market processes. Various firms have different degrees of autonomy in the market; in some they are but "price-takers" (they do not have enough market power to affect prices), while in others some control is exercised over prices thus the expression "price-searchers" looking for optimal prices to charge buyers. In an older jargon I am describing the competitiveness of markets. Everyone knows that some markets have more competitors than others and that the "degree" or intensity of competition varies greatly. Both are important characteristics with number of competitors being more critical in price-taker markets and intensity of competition the critical factor in price-searching markets.

What is most significant in both markets, however, is the effort put forth by firms to produce goods that persuade buyers to make purchases. Demand does not exist in noble isolation from the advertising efforts of businesses. Wants are created by firms inventing products and convincing customers of new needs. In that sense, supply precedes demand. Of course, once a demand has been created firms must take account of it, but demand is neither universal nor permanent; improvements, refinements, and, above all, new products constantly alter patterns of consumption. And, price searchers must engage in a never-ending search for the "right" price. That they do is observed by anyone who visits markets on a regular basis, for the prices of everything are in constant flux affording both unexpected gains and losses for all buyers and, of course, sellers. Unexpected gains and losses are far more commonplace for the harried businessman than are the stable expectations depicted in neat diagrams of a conventional economics textbook. Those diagrams do not consider the uncertainties of something as seemingly simple as beverage flavors—Japanese companies trying to stay ahead of each other introduce 1,000 new flavors each year! Life on the supply side is never dull.

Price searchers cannot set prices at will. The market power needed to do that simply does not exist; if it does, perhaps domestic auto companies lost billions of dollars during the 2000s for diabolical reasons. These supposedly powerful corporations did not observe certain market realities while their competitors did. Growth in firms stems from superior production and marketing strategies and not from some brutal tactic of size and monopoly power. The concentration, we observe, in some industries is the result of superior performance measured by satisfied consumers. We should note that the shares of the market held by large firms in the same industry tend to change over time. Ford was once the giant of the auto industry; then it was General Motors; in 2010 it was Toyota. In the *Business Week /Interbrand* ranking of most valuable global brands, only Ford made the list from the United States coming in at number 49. Toyota was ranked 8th, while Honda was ranked 18th and South Korea's Hyundai was listed at number 69. Neither Japanese company nor Hyundai was producing automobiles when Ford was king. The only thing that is sure is that in ten years the rankings will be entirely different and there may even be new players in the automotive game.

Perhaps the most visible activity of the modern large business is its advertising—an activity that draws especially moralistic condemnation from radicals and liberals with an aesthetic sensitivity. Even the mainstream economist is inclined to view advertising as a wasteful expenditure, a view based on the traditional assumption that buyers are fully informed and, therefore, not in need of additional information. Buyers are not and cannot be fully informed about more than a few products; instead, in a world of constantly new products and services they remain ignorant until someone is willing and able to provide relevant information. That someone is the firm, and especially the new firm struggling to introduce whatever it has to offer. With literally billions of competing goods the effort to catch the fleeting attention of the consumer becomes not wasteful but imperative. An average grocery store now stocks 45,000 different items. Since individual attention and loyalties are costly to alter, advertisers must be either skillful and/or lucky in being able to divert consumers from one product to another. Advertising, itself, is subject to diminishing returns.

Many of the so-called excesses so disturbing to liberal thinkers are based on the false assumption that advertising is extremely effective; it may be under highly restrictive conditions. Still, it is a perfectly understandable tactic on the part of the advertiser. Attention is sought and gained but sales of the product hinge, in the long run, on the ability of the product to satisfy consumers, not on the advertising. Advertising, in fact, conveys information, any information sellers think will be meaningful to buyers. If it isn't, they search for other themes. And, we the buyers should be "grateful" for the information and the low cost at which it is, in fact, supplied. Just how socialists should and would provide consumers with information are issues they never seem to address. Perhaps, because the variety of goods and services would be so reduced and the homogeneity of products so increased, choice would become superfluous. Only superior goods fulfilling "real" needs would be offered. The alleged frivolousness of modern capitalist consumption would be a thing of the past. With Spartan consumption the ideal, one wonders what might happen to classified ads.

Virtues Reclaimed

Because markets change incessantly, trial and error provides a superb means for the achievement of individual and collective rationality in the production and distribution of private goods. The use of money and prices enables a highly decentralized decision-making system to function in responsive and responsible ways to changing demands and productive innovations. The market is a highly decentralized decision-making system that enables limited minds, possessing limited information, to make more intelligent choices than could possibly be made by a board of dispassionate experts sitting miles away from the sites of action. Not only is much of the information provided by markets quantitative and, therefore, easily understood and economically used by untrained individuals, but it is relevant to the immediate decision. As Adam Smith argued, the market also provides a powerful motivational system through the incentives of profit and loss, the carrot and stick, so to speak. Those who do not like what is provided in one market can usually give voice to their complaints and be heard by a responsive seller; those who prefer to vote with their feet may leave the store and try a competitor who is all too willing to have more business. The disaffected have options to a degree unheard of in history or in any contemporary society with a command economy and polity.

A number of themes emerge from this discussion. In the first place, markets, even the imperfectly competitive, achieve an extraordinary efficiency. Market economies have attained the highest GDPs in history because they not only provide incentives, but individual preferences are more accurately and quickly honored. The costly calculation of the welfare of others is minimized. Buyers, sellers, and entrepreneurs need only the information provided by price signals to make rational allocations. Operating within a decentralized authority system, they are able to coordinate their respective wishes rather than struggle with one another over fixed shares. As a result, economic dilemmas are handled with impersonality, efficiency, and a minimum of coercion. At the same time the system penalizes incompetence, miscalculation, and dishonesty while rewarding effort, ability, foresight, and probity.

While true, these abstract arguments do not in any way capture the extraordinary capacity of the market to simplify problems of allocation and thereby provide ready solutions that contribute to the welfare of the many. The rediscovery of the market has been enhanced by observation of the clumsy ways by which government regulators and central planners attempt to substitute themselves for the market. Although the airlines industry, for example, has been substantially deregulated, the Federal Aviation Agency (FAA) continues to attempt to impose its bureaucratic ways on an industry facing an overcrowding problem in major airports. Too many planes attempt to take off and land at peak hours on certain days of the week. This costly and annoying problem can be reduced by employing market principles to the problems. Increasing the cost of landing and taking off at busy hours will soon equate supply of slots and demand for flights at the appropriate quantity and price. Those who value certain flights most should be permitted the opportunity to put their money where their values reside. Those who value these flights less should be permitted the chance to purchase tickets for other less convenient flights at lower prices. But, the uninformed public, professional regulators and politicians will blame the airlines and argue that only the government can devise rules for the allocation of scarce time and runway space. But imagine the immensity of the problem if "solved" by rational discussion around the conference table. Whose time is more valuable? And by how much? These questions are answered by the market without any discussion over eternal ethical principles. The existence of overbooked seats and, now, overbooked runways is not evidence of market failure, but political failure. A market would solve the problem of under-pricing by increasing the price of certain uses of the airport. Peak hour use of privately held property elicits higher prices, while other less-valued times produce lower prices. Hotels offer weekend rates distinctly lower than those in force during the week. Restaurants offer off-peak discounts as do some electric companies and private toll road operators. These sensible decisions come about because these companies are unregulated in these regards. But, the spectacle of jammed flights and runways somehow seems to require collective solutions since it is assumed that markets created the problem in the first place.

The rediscovery of the market and the better understandings we now have of its workings enable us to understand the real source of such problems as those confronting airlines and how they can be readily resolved at low cost. Agonizing ethical discussions and selfish politicking over transportation are not only unnecessary but also wasteful.

A system of market choice seemingly encourages innovation beyond that known in any other economy. Discovery cannot be planned; it can only be facilitated by competitive markets. While inventors may ruin the careers of others they also create new, more, and better careers, and they benefit the consumers. And remember that the whole point of competition is not to decide what to do at a point in time but to introduce new products and new methods of distribution.

To Adam Smith's great credit it was he who first understood how markets could produce a collective good from diverse self-interests. A price mechanism performs the task with efficiency unattainable by any board of planners equipped with the latest computers. Still, many concerned social scientists find it hard to believe that much general good can emerge from "base" self-interests, but that is because they fail to grasp the simple workings of the market. Nor can they grasp the operations of a political process which is unable, despite their fervent beliefs, to convert competitive self-interest into public good.

Bibliographical Notes

Although the rediscovery of markets, competition, and business firms has been underway for at least sixty years, the new learning has been developed and disseminated in a highly decentralized way. As a result, one confronts several different bodies of thought whose progenitors are often seemingly unaware of one another's existence. For example, the literature on firms has taken place within conventional economics and reflects that fact, that is, the material is often presented in technical terms. On the one hand, much of the reinterpretation of markets and competition is the work of "Austrian" economists (many of whom are Americans) and is written in a non-mathematical manner. On the other hand, Chicago economists have reinterpreted monopoly. Some of the new learning about the private property, profit-seeking economy has been offered by legal thinkers and economic historians attempting to explain western development. So, while these literatures are highly complementary, they are diverse and written in distinctive languages.

Perhaps the best place to begin is if you can find a copy of the now out-of-print extraordinary economics text, *University Economics* (Belmont: Wadsworth Publishing Co., 1964) by Armen Alchian and William Allen. Get any edition you can find—it was renamed *Exchange and Production: Competition, Coordination, and Control* in later editions. This remarkable book is both an undergraduate text and a treatise—a highly original one. It does not just summarize and organize the new thinking, it actually aided in developing that thought. Like Marshall's classic, both undergraduates and advanced thinkers can profit from the ideas set forth and above all, from their unique and original application of economics in both market and non-market settings. It is truly a great book.

One should also consult the work of a scholar already mentioned in previous chapters, namely Ronald H. Coase, whose major essays including the one on the firm are now available in paperback: *The Firm, the Market, and the Law* (Chicago: University of Chicago Press, 1990). This small volume clearly demonstrates why Coase has been one of the great economists of our time.

Douglass North revolutionized the study of markets and politics with his *Institutions, Institutional Change and Economic Performance* (Cambridge University Press, 1990), and his analysis dominated the work of anyone interested in how political and economic institutions interact throughout the 1990s. In *Understanding the Process of Economic Change,* Princeton University Press, 2010) he pushes social scientists to move beyond static and mechanistic models of how societies work and develop tools for analyzing dynamic situations. His book is about adaptive efficiency, "an ongoing condition in which the society continues to modify or create new institutions as problems evolve."

I would be remiss if I did not cite at least one book by Israel M. Kirzner, the leading American "Austrian." I note but one of his writings: *Competition and Entrepreneurship* (Chicago: University of Chicago Press, 1978). This productive scholar long promulgated Austrian ideas to an indifferent conventional audience in American economics. Only in recent years have his writings gotten their deserved recognition as important critiques of contemporary price theory and extensions of the work of Mises and Hayek. Their work and the better-known works of Schumpeter are finally being incorporated into the orthodox tradition and making it a far sounder body of analysis. I expect this healthy trend to continue.

Possibly the best introductory book on Austrian economics is Gene Callahan's *Economics for Real People: An Introduction to the Austrian School* (Ludwig von Mises Institute, 2002). The style is witty enough to remind readers of Murray Rothbard. Callahan avoids jargon so well that non-economists will find the book easily accessible.

References

Alchian, Armen and Harold Demsetz. "Production, Information Costs, and Economic Organization," *American Economic Review,* 62 (December, 1972), pp. 775–95.

Alchian, Armen A. and William R. Allen. *Exchange and Production: Competition, Coordination, and Control.* 3 Sub ed. Belmont: Wadsworth Pub. Co., 1983.

Callahan, Gene. *Economics for Real People: An Introduction to the Austrian School.* Auburn, Alabama: Ludwig von Mises Institute, 2002.

Coase, Ronald H. *The Firm, the Market, and the Law.* Chicago: University of Chicago Press, 1990.

Coase, Ronald H. "The Nature of the Firm," *Economica,* 4 (November, 1937), pp. 386–405.

Demsetz, H. "Production, Information Costs, and the Economic Organization." *American Economic Review,* 62 (1962) pp. 777–95.

Hayek, F. A. *The Road to Serfdom: Text and Documents.* New ed. Chicago: University of Chicago Press, 2007.

Hayek, F.A. "The Use of Knowledge in Society," *American Economic Review,* 35 (September, 1945), pp. 519–30.

Kirzner, Israel M. *Competition and Entrepreneurship.* New ed. Chicago: University of Chicago Press, 1978.

North, Douglass C. *Institutions, Institutional Change and Economic Performance.* New York: Cambridge University Press, 1990.

North, Douglass C. *Understanding the Process of Economic Change.* Princeton: Princeton University Press, 2010.

Perry, Mark J. "Update on the NYC 'Taxi Cartel'; Medallion Prices Reach Record Highs in 2010 of $588k and $779k." *CARPE DIEM.* http://mjperry.blogspot.com/2010/03/update-on-nyc-taxi-cartel.html.

Schumpeter, Joseph A. *Capitalism, Socialism, and Democracy.* New York: Harper Perennial Modern Classics, 2008.

Simon, Herbert. *Models of Man.* New York: John Wiley & Sons, 1957.

Williamson, Oliver E. *The Economic Institutions of Capitalism: Firms, Markets, Relational Contracting.* New York: Free Press, 1985.

8

Public Choice and the Law

AS PUBLIC CHOICE was developing as a discipline where economic reasoning was applied to politics, economists and lawyers began applying economic reasoning to the law. As with public choice, the conclusions of the sub-discipline now called law and economics are sometimes commonsensical, sometimes counterintuitive, and sometimes seemingly outrageous.

Law and economics asks the simple question of how rational people will adjust their actions to legal rules. Thus, "rational actors" replace the standard legal presumption of "reasonable actors," who are presumed to act based on claimed social conventions. Law's purpose, then, is to alter incentives. Unlike ethicists or politicians who claim people "should" act in a certain way, the economic approach asks "how" people will act. David Friedman (2000, p. 8) provides an example:

> You live in a state where the most severe criminal punishment is life imprisonment. Someone proposes that since armed robbery is a very serious crime, armed robbers should get a life sentence. A constitutional lawyer asks whether that is consistent with the prohibition on cruel and unusual punishment. A legal philosopher asks whether it is just.
>
> An economist points out that if the punishments for armed robbery and for armed robbery plus murder are the same, the additional punishment for murder is zero—and asks whether you really want to make it in the interest of robbers to murder their victims.

It appears, once again, that incentives matter and that the law of unintended consequences cannot be avoided.

Ronald Coase (1961) and Guido Calabresi (1967, 1970) were among the first moderns to apply an economic analysis to law. Coase's paper on the problem of social costs attempted to correct Pigouvian orthodoxy about externalities. Chapter 6 contained a discussion of Coase's analysis of externalities, so I will not repeat it here. The article's importance for law and economics was that it helped explain that contracts, laws, and institutions had emerged to economize on transactions costs.

Calabresi, who became Dean of the Yale Law School and was appointed to the federal bench by President Clinton, introduced the idea that promoting efficiency in tort law (torts are civil wrongs as opposed to criminal wrongs) requires placing liability on the party who can avoid accidents at the least cost; the "least cost avoider." Thus, if your neighbor builds a swimming pool he is required to fence the pool to keep the neighborhood children out even though other legal rules might suggest parents are responsible for controlling their children. It is easier for the pool owner to control access to his pool than for all parents to watch their children all the time. The pool owner is the least cost avoider.

Calabresi later reformulated his rule to say that promoting efficiency requires a rule that minimizes the sum of precaution costs, accident costs, and administrative costs. Under this reformulation the pool owner is still required to fence his pool.

Gary Becker, George Stigler, and Richard Posner brought the ideas to a broad audience. Becker, Stigler, and others developed economic analysis of law and law enforcement. Becker (1968), for example, asked . . . how many resources and how much punishment should be used to enforce different kinds of legislation? Put equivalently, although more strangely, how many offenses *should* be permitted and how many offenders should go unpunished?

Critics might claim that only an economist would worry about the optimal or efficient amount of punishment. But, it is not an inconsequential worry because it leads to questions about the appropriate standard of proof. Should the standard of proof be higher in criminal cases than in civil cases? Why? What are the consequences? Should Blackstone's rule that it is better for ten guilty men to go free than for one innocent person to be convicted be used?

Richard Posner (2007), now a U.S. District Court judge, argues that law should strive for efficiency and that the common law is especially efficient. Thus Posner would make efficiency claims about the differences in standard of proof rules. In the United States and many other systems the standard of proof for finding someone guilty of a criminal offense is "beyond a reasonable doubt," while the standard of proof in a civil case requires just a "preponderance of the evidence." The efficiency explanation of this difference is that in civil cases there is no net societal loss as a result of the judgment, there is simply a transfer of money from the loser to the winner. In a criminal case, however, the penalty for losing is imprisonment or even execution. The punishment is a net cost in this case. Thus, efficiency demands that legal systems be surer when imposing a net cost than when imposing a simple transfer.

Judging Legal Rules

When a case comes to court the defendant's lawyer asks the jury to look into the past—when the alleged crime was committed and when relevant past cases were decided. An economist asks the jury and judge to look to the future and ask what incentives will be created by the verdict. Will people alter their behavior as a result of this decision? Will there be more or less of a desired or undesired behavior as a result?

Well-meaning legislators are often tempted to impose liability on people who fail to assist a stranger in distress. The issue makes for lively social commentary and was even the topic of the final episode of the television sitcom *Seinfeld*. In that episode Jerry, George, Kramer, and Elaine witness a person being robbed. During the robbery they mock the person being robbed and Kramer films the event. They are arrested under the town's Good Samaritan law, found guilty, and sentenced to a year in jail. The economist will ask how the law will affect future actions.

Landes and Posner consider the question of Good Samaritan laws in their 1987 book, *The Economic Structure of Tort Law* and ask about the consequences of passing a law imposing "liability for failure to assist a stranger in distress no matter how low the costs of assistance would be or how great its benefits." They conclude that the consequences of Good Samaritan laws are actually negative because of the effects on future, potential rescuers. That is, if people have a legal obligation to help others in distress, many people will avoid situations where they might encounter this "duty" to rescue. For example, eyes on the street, to use a term Jane Jacobs used in her book *The Death and Life of Great American Cities* (1961), often deter crime. But if I am required by the law to do more—to actually come to someone's assistance—I may stop watching the street at all. Imposing liability may actually cause less rescuing and more crime.

When someone with no prior misconduct commits a crime should the judge take into consideration the person's standing in the community, the likelihood she will commit a crime again, or her apparent remorse? The economist says these are the wrong questions and wrong focus. Instead of focusing on this case, focus on the future. Instead of questioning this defendant, hypothetically question other rational beings and ask how they will respond to the incentives created by this case. If the court lets one person off with a light sentence it is announcing to others in similar situations that the costs of getting caught are low. Thus, the important question is "will this decision deter others from taking similar actions?"

Note that this question seems to assume that the demand for committing offenses is elastic. That is, as the expected cost of committing an offense increases there will be fewer offenses committed. But for some people the demand for offenses may be inelastic. Insane people, for example, are probably not deterred by threats of punishment. Put another way, the marginal cost of deterring them will be so high that deterrence is not a practical option. Committing the criminally insane to a prison or other institution does not deter others; it simply keeps those locked up from committing more crimes.

Suggesting that different groups of people might have different elasticities of demand for crime raises the question of the rich and the poor. Will a $100 fine deter the rich person as easily as it does a poor person? It depends on the action. A rich person and a poor person may place the same dollar benefit on $100, but on average rich people value time more highly (they are willing to pay more) than poor people. This logic suggests that because rich people value the time they save by speeding more than poor people do, deterring the rich from speeding requires a higher fine.

Richer criminals, then, require a greater fine when the payoff for the crime is in time or pleasure, but where the payoff is money the same punishment may equally deter rich and poor people. Does "equal before the law" mean rich and poor receive the same sentence or does it mean they receive different sentences based on their value of time or money? The trick is whether it is efficient to attempt to apply different punishments and whether any lawmaker, judge, or jury could decide the most efficient or just approach.

Cost is a constraint on punishment. Politicians like to pass laws, moralists urge them to pass the laws, and constituents hear how their legislators have gotten tough on crime, but few people ask about the costs of punishment. The range of relevant costs includes the cost of catching the criminals, the cost of prosecuting, and the cost of being defended. Once someone is convicted there are costs to housing that person in a jail or prison.

There are opportunity costs as well. Police must allocate their time to crimes most highly ranked by legislators, not necessarily those the citizens might rank as the highest priority. Thus, time and money spent on politically designated priorities are time and money not available for more important crimes. Politicians in the United States, for example, are so fixated with outlawed drugs that they created a drug czar to direct the "war on drugs."

In March of 2005, Gary Becker estimated on his blog that the war on drugs is costing the U.S. well over $100 billion per year. That is a relatively large cost, yet it does not include "important intangibles, such as the destructive effects on many inner city neighborhoods, the use of the American military to fight drug lords and farmers in Colombia and other nations, or the corrupting influence of drugs on many governments."

Although there may be good intentions among the politicians who fund the war or the agencies that carry it out, all their good intentions, the arrests, and the incarcerations are not buying much. Street drugs are more prevalent than ever even though the United States locks up more citizens today than the Soviet Union did during the height of its powers. Consider Utah as an example. People incarcerated for drug and alcohol offenses have increased from a historical rate of 9 percent of the prison population to more than 20 percent. Even given increased incarceration rates, drugs of all types are more easily purchased than they were in the past, which suggests that Utah law fails to deter, possibly because of a rather inelastic demand. Utah treats drug offenders as first-, second-, and third-degree felons. Third-degree felons are those arrested for possession and they get 0–5 years in prison. Second-degree felons are those arrested for distributing drugs and they receive 1–15 years. First-degree felons are producers, such as those who run methamphetamine (meth) laboratories. They receive five years to life. Third-degree felons are often those already on the margins of society whose family relationships break up entirely while they are in prison and who will find it nearly impossible to return to the workforce with a felony conviction. A third-degree felon whose wife has left him often intentionally does something as his parole date approaches so that he will be denied parole, since he has little to return to life outside the prison. Many of these third-degree felons were convicted of "internal possession"—they were caught by a urine test not while carrying out any illegal activity. A third-degree drug offender spends an average of 14 months in prison at an annual cost to taxpayers of more than $30,000 (2009 dollars).

If these offenses were each decreased by one degree, third-degree to a misdemeanor, second-degree to 0–5 years, and first-degree to 1–15 years, Utah's prisons could immediately release over 500 nonviolent male inmates (10 percent of the male inmate population) and over 100 nonviolent female inmates (33 percent of the female inmate population. The state would save about $18 million and that would not include savings from reducing future prosecution costs or parole supervision costs. The problem is getting policy makers and citizens to support such a proposal because legislators often value symbolism (harsh penalties) over the reality (breaking up families, reducing earning potential) for third-degree offenders.

This discussion about rich and poor, sane and insane, the efficient amount of punishment, and opportunity costs does not make assumptions about right and wrong. It simply assumes people have objectives and attempt to achieve them. But the discussion leads to conclusions about how the goal of economic efficiency produces something that might be called ethical rules. To the economist theft is inefficient; it leads to expenditures to deter theft and misallocates resources. To the ethicist theft is wrong or wicked. Both the economist and ethicist can agree on the rule "thou shalt not steal." They will likely disagree on the appropriate punishment for stealing.

The Common Law

The Anglo-Saxon world has been guided for centuries by a traditional, unwritten law, known as the common law. This body of law is based on custom, usage, and precedent. Blackstone's 1769 *Commentaries on the Laws of England* was the basic source book for American lawyers and even for literate cowboys according to novelist Louis L'Amour.

The common law performs the role of expert witness in the court as it guides judges about how similar cases were decided in the past. Judges do not really know all the circumstances of past cases, just the general rules that have survived through centuries of trial and error. It may even be possible to consider the common law to be the law's analogue to prices. Prices are condensed information about scarcity, values, and substitutes. The common law is condensed information about cases, incentives, and outcomes.

Not only is the common law condensed information, but also it promotes economic efficiency. The continual interaction between judicial actors, lawyers, and litigants has produced effective and efficient rules. The current legal rules regarding contract, property, and tort are the result of that interaction through time. Inefficient rules were dropped as litigants fought against them or found ways around them. According to this perspective, it is as if the market has produced the efficient rules that define it. This is indeed the case described in the textbooks of Posner (2007) and Cooter and Ulen (2007).

Efficient rules emerging through time is an example of what Hayek called "spontaneous order" (see, for example, *The Fatal Conceit*, University of Chicago Press, 1991). He meant that no one is in charge, that the order we see around us is spontaneous and organic rather than planned and controlled. A better term might be the one economist Russell Roberts uses, "emergent order." Spontaneous suggests sudden, while emergent suggests the kind of process Posner and Cooter and Ulen describe.

Statutory Law

The statutory law and its resulting regulations are sometimes simply a codification of the common law, but in many cases they exist to shield someone from the common law and this is one area where students of law and economics need to apply their economics tools more broadly—to do some public choice. One reason for the efficiency of the common law is that no one lawyer or case or judge determines it. Common law is a slow, ongoing process. Statutory law, however, seldom emerges from slow, careful, thoughtful debate. It is far more likely to be the result of emotions, rent seeking, and political debts. Regulations are sometimes created by thoughtful bureaucrats applying their training, but they are also created by political pressure and sometimes result from compromise, ideology, and expediency.

Environmental laws and regulations, for example, are produced by dedicated environmentalists, but they are only part of the grand coalition. They are joined by anti-development groups who see environmental laws as a way to slow down or stop development, bureaucrats who understand it is better to be part of a growing than a stagnating or shrinking agency, politicians seeking votes, and industries who see new regulations as a way to reduce competition in their industry. Economist Bruce Yandle (1998) explains the results:

> What do we have? Rules that limit the emissions of sulfur dioxide to fight acid rain, even though the scientists who studied the issue said there was no acid-rain problem. Rules that give a black eye to industries that must publicize emissions of more than 600 chemicals, in pounds, even though all industry taken together produces just 17 percent of the total emissions. Rules that set stricter controls on new and expanding plants while grandfathering older ones. Regulations that favor one fuel over others. Endangered-species protection that limits timber-cutting on government land, raising the price of timber and the profits of firms that cut on their own land. The list could go on.

Yandle's analysis suggests that there are few concerns for efficiency in the statutory law.

Statutory law is especially inefficient when dealing with safety regulation. Efficient safety regulation would focus on accidents, after all that is what we assume safety regulation should be about. Legislators, however, emphasize safety. Safety glasses, guards on machines, and other safety practices are mandated and any employer failing to have the required safety devices faces criminal prosecution. Rather than penalizing harm as would happen under the common law, legislation requires safety inputs. Compliance to safety standards is required even if the standards do not make the workplace safer. Because firms are only accountable for having prescribed safety procedures in place they do not search for ways to reduce injuries.

As we might expect, statutory regulations focus on visible, easily regulated issues, rather than those that might be the least safe. Standards that focus on machinery accidents, for example, require myriads of safety devices even though most factory accidents involve slipping, falling, or mishandling objects. Workplaces have more safety regulations, the regulations are enthusiastically enforced, safer approaches are ignored, and companies substitute compliance for real safety. Safety engineers are replaced by lawyers, compliance costs increase, and accidents are not reduced.

Laws are often intentionally written ambiguously (see the discussion in Chapter 4 about symbolism). If the language is not clear, courts in the United States turn to the legislative record in an attempt to discern the legislature's intent. There are at least two problems with using legislative intent. The first is that the winners write legislative histories. After a bill passes the staffers whose bosses sponsored the bill write a history of the process the bill went through and identify the bill's intent. Histories written by winners tend to emphasize the winner's perspectives and downplay others. The process offers staffers a chance to highlight, embellish, and even add to the committee discussion. Although the bill may only say X, the staff can claim that the intent was to say X, Y, and Z. Thus, the diligent judge searching the record can add Y and Z to her interpretation of the law.

The second problem with legislative intent is that judges can mold the law according to their objectives. Justice Scalia (1997, pp. 17–18) argues that:

> The practical threat is that, under the guise of even the self-delusion of pursuing unexpressed legislative intents, common-law judges will in fact pursue their own objectives and desires, extending their lawmaking proclivities from the common law to the statutory field.

Legislative intent, then, can provide cover for judges to pursue their own agendas.

Judges

A category of political actor who has generally escaped the attention of public choice scholars is the judge. What motivates judges? How are their excesses controlled? Do they act differently than other political actors?

Judges surround themselves with myth. Their black robes emphasize the solemnity of the office. They sit at a raised platform and look down on the courtroom. They are called "Your Honor." They require a church-like atmosphere of attentiveness, dignity, and respect. The process, physical setting, and required demeanor suggest that judges seek Truth and dispense Justice.

A consistent analysis of political actors, however, requires looking beyond the trappings of the courtroom. We ought to assume that judges are rational actors who have personal policy preferences; that they may seek justice but that they may also seek fame, honor, respect, or glory. This suggests that judges will angle for higher office (from a lower court to a higher court), play to the writers of law review articles, try to help lawyers whose arguments the judges agree with even if they are outside the existing law, and strategically accept or decide cases to promote a particular point of view.

Judges are reluctant to talk about self-promotion or reputation. Politicians talk about getting reelected but judges, especially those appointed for life, talk about the search for justice and the majesty of the law. They do not discuss how the search for justice might conflict with getting along with colleagues, gaining esteem from other judges, having their decisions favorably discussed in law review articles, or treatment by the news media. Judges are clearly playing in a mixed-motive game, which makes predictions about their positions on particular issues difficult. Even those judges appointed for life, presumably so that they can more freely search for justice, are motivated by a mix of goals that may dominate justice.

As long as judges saw their role as clarifying the law and preserving a system where people could have consistent expectations about outcomes, any judge-made changes to the law were gradual and at the margin—just as discussed above about the common law. But as common law has been supplanted with statutory and administrative law, judges have been freed to use their position on the bench to pursue their self-interest: to expand their reach, status, and power.

We should assume that judges, like politicians and bureaucrats, are attracted to their profession in part by a desire to promote their ideological worldview. A large literature shows rather conclusively that judges do make decisions not just consistent with, but in furtherance of their ideological leanings (see, for example, Cross, 2007 and Revesz, 1997). The judges freest to pursue their ideological preferences are appointed judges. But even elected judges are more able to promote their worldview than politicians or bureaucrats.

A judge who uses her position on the bench strategically can increase her power both relatively and absolutely. She can increase her power relative to legislative and executive branches of government and to other judges and she can increase her power over society at large. The best way to increase power over other branches of government is to extend the reach of the law and nowhere is this more visible than in tort law where judges have taken over many of the regulatory functions of the executive branch. Judges force the redesign of everyday tools and airplanes. They decide if surgeons in operating rooms were acting appropriately or if CEOs ran their financial firms appropriately. They are the most powerful regulators in the American system. And with each new, groundbreaking decision a judge's status in the legal, media, and academic communities increases.

About half of the United States population elects at least some of their judges. From what we know about elections we might expect that just as normal, political elections are not necessarily about electing the candidate who best represents the people's wishes (if that were even possible), judicial elections are not likely to be about justice. Large portions of the campaign contributions in judicial elections come from the lawyers who expect to plead cases before the judges. The Florida Bar Association found that Florida's elected judges get 80 percent of their campaign contributions from lawyers (Helland and Tabarrok, 2000, 22). Although the Florida percentage is higher than in most studies, it is similar to the pattern in other states—lawyers who plan to argue cases before judges contribute to those judges' campaigns.

Elected judges respond to the incentives of facing voters. The most visible response is how they treat in-state plaintiffs and out-of-state defendants. Retired West Virginia Supreme Court Justice Richard Neely (1988) called redistributing wealth from an out-of-state company to a West Virginia plaintiff "a judge's way of providing constituency service." After all, he pointed out, the out-of-state corporation did not vote for the judge nor was it a reliable source of campaign contributions. Helland and Tabarrok (2000) conclude that a large part of the dramatic increase in tort judgments in the last several years is based in elected state judges transferring wealth from out-of-state corporations to the judges' constituents. They also note that judges elected in partisan elections grant higher awards than do those elected in non-partisan elections.

Elected judges also discriminate between in-state and out-of-state defendants. Judges elected on non-partisan ballots, in Helland and Tabarrok's study, charged out-of-state defendants an average of $384,540 while charging in-state defendants $207,957. Judges elected on partisan ballots charged the out-of-state defendants an average of $652,720 while charging in-state defendants $276,320. The authors note that this difference disappeared if the cases were heard in federal court.

This discussion of judges and their responses to incentives suggests rent-seeking possibilities beyond those discussed in earlier chapters. Groups that are unable to seek rents through legislative avenues, possibly because they lack organization, political power, or funds, can use the judiciary. Effective groups of this sort shop for the right judge in the right jurisdiction and offer him or her new opportunities for ideological voting. If those opportunities are accompanied with enhanced status, so much the better.

It becomes clear then, why environmental groups from local, nearly penniless groups to large, rich, international groups have been so effective in the courts. Their issues provide judges opportunities to enhance their status and promote an ideological agenda, an agenda often at odds with that of a majority of elected officials. That is why so many big social issues from abortion to endangered species are so often successful in the courts when they would have failed in the legislatures.

Lawyers

Legislators make law; judges interpret, extend, and invent law; and lawyers practice law. As they practice law they also shape the law and the legal system. Let's begin with the assumption that lawyers, like most of us, want to increase their wealth. As for any producer of a good or service, lawyers can reduce the supply of their product (legal services) or increase the demand. Reducing or controlling the supply of legal services is accomplished through each state's bar association, which administers the bar exam and oversees professional standards and practices. The bar association provides partly effective barriers to entry—requiring graduation from (usually accredited) law schools, and passing the bar exam with a certain score. But there are still a lot of lawyers, more than most other lawyers would prefer.

The answer to oversupply is increased demand. Thus, lawyers have a strong incentive to increase the amount and value of litigation of all kinds. In tort litigation, for example, both plaintiff and defense lawyers have a strong incentive to encourage judges to increase liability for defendants. Given the size of potential losses from expanded liability and increased judgment amounts, defense lawyers become more valuable as do plaintiffs' lawyers. They have similar incentives to promote the number and complexity of rules established by regulatory agencies and legislative bodies. Increased legal complexity increases demand for legal complexity specialists. Increased complexity also increases judges' discretion and, therefore, opportunities to increase status and power. Lawyers and judges have a mutual interest in making the law more complex and cumbersome.

Conclusions

Rather than believe law and regulations are guided by efficiency, students of the law should recognize that legislated, administrative, and sometimes even common law are outcomes of a political/legal market in which groups seek private objectives by governmental means. In addition to the interest groups, bureaucrats, and politicians in the regular political market, this market includes self-interested judges and lawyers.

As we will learn from the discussion of rent seeking in Chapter 9, a group's willingness to spend money to get a law or regulation it wants is determined by the value of the outcome and on the group's ability to overcome the free-rider problem. The nature of the issue will also determine the group's income—fear of losing something generates more funds from dispersed groups than will the desire to gain something. The imprecision of the vote as a measure of intensity of preferences adds to the problem as does the inherent problem with deciding how much of a public good to provide or purchase. Thus, the political market will seldom reflect people's real preferences for law, regulation, or enforcement. Inefficient laws result as the injury to the losers is greater than the gain to the winners. And efficient laws may well fail. The economics of law leads to the familiar conclusion that laws will tend to favor concentrated interests at the expense of dispersed interests, but it also leads to the conclusion that some legal institutions are better than others.

The practitioners of the law exhibit an amazing hubris, one consistent with that shown by politicians and bureaucrats. Judges have turned themselves into social engineers, economic planners, and regulators whose reach is the envy of the most ambitious bureaucratic regulator. They act as if they know how markets should work, how risk should be allocated, how much safety should be imposed regardless of demand, and how schools should be run. Some appear to have chosen themselves to correct social injustices. They do all this without the benefit of the features that make markets work—information in the form of prices, feedback, correction, competition, profit, and loss.

Bibliographical Notes

There is probably no better place to begin reading about law and economics than Richard Posner's *Economic Analysis of Law* (Aspen Publishers, 2010), currently in its 8th edition. It is easily the most influential work in law and economics. His writing is lively and his topics are wide ranging. While covering the standard topics of property, torts, contract, and criminal procedure, he considers such topics as sex and marriage (he wrote another book titled *Sex and Reason* (Harvard University Press, 1994), marijuana legalization, markets in human organs, rent control, and intellectual property. If his conclusions seem wrong-headed or simple-minded, read more carefully. Posner is seldom wrong and never simple-minded. It is possible to keep up with Posner on current topics by reading his blog with Gary Becker (http://www.becker-posner-blog.com/). Sometimes they agree and sometimes disagree, but reading the ideas of two of Chicago's most brilliant economists is always a treat.

After getting a taste of Becker on the blog, find a copy of his *The Economic Approach to Human Behavior* (University of Chicago Press, 1976). It is dated but delightful. Becker's work epitomizes the law and economics approach even though his focus is not the law.

David D. Friedman's *Laws Order: What Economics Has to Do with Law and Why it Matters* (Princeton University Press, 2001) is one of the best. His is a fertile, brilliant, and fully engaged mind. The book is more clearly written than anything else I have read in Law and Economics. His chapter subtitles—"Buying Babies," "Of Burning Houses and Coke Bottles," and "Why Not Hang Them All?"—are inventive and provocative. His spaghetti diagram of the Coase Theorem is especially useful. His examples are fun and challenging.

By far the best book on applying public choice analysis to law is by Maxwell L. Stearns and Todd J. Zywicki, *Public Choice and Applications in Law* (2009). The authors introduce public choice very well and evaluate how public choice analysis can be applied to law. They show how behavior in the legal profession is often just as self-interested as that of politicians and other political actors.

Another important book on the law is Bruce Benson's *The Enterprise of Law: Justice Without the State* (Pacific Research Institute, 1990). Benson destroys the claim that law is created by government, arguing instead that law emerges from people's daily interaction with each other and precedes the state. The book is historical as well as theoretical and contains an excellent public-choice analysis of the political market for law. Possibly most importantly, Benson asks why government, which suffers from all the problems identified in our earlier chapters, should be expected to administer justice fairly. His answer is that systems of private law are fairer, more humane, and more efficient.

Bibliography

Becker, Gary S. "Crime and Punishment: An Economic Approach," *Journal of Political Economy*, (1968) 76: 167–217.

Becker, Gary S. *The Economic Approach to Human Behavior*. New ed. Chicago: University of Chicago Press, 1978.

Becker, Gary S. "The Failure of the War on Drugs," *The Becker-Posner Blog*, March 20, 2005. http://www.becker-posner-blog.com/archives/2005/03/the_failure_of.html.

"The Becker-Posner Blog." The Becker-Posner Blog. http://www.becker-posner-blog .com/.

Benson, Bruce L. *The Enterprise of Law: Justice Without the State*. San Francisco: Pacific Research Institute, 1990.

Blackstone, William. *Commentaries on the Laws of England: A Facsimile of the First Edition of 1765–1769*, Vol. 1. Facsimile ed. Chicago: University of Chicago Press, 1979.

Calabresi, Guido. "Some Thoughts on Risk Distribution and the Law of Torts," *Yale Law Journal*, 1967, 70:499–553.

Calabresi, Guido, *The Costs of Accidents: A Legal and Economic Analysis*. New Haven: Yale University Press, 1970.

Coase, Ronald. "The Problem of Social Cost," *Journal of Law and Economics* (1960) 3:1–44.

Cooter, Bob and Bob Ulen. *Law and Economics*, 6th ed., Saddle River, NJ: Prentice Hall, 2011.

Cross, Frank B. and Stefanie A. Lindquist. "The Scientific Study of Judicial Activism," *Minnesota Law Review* 91 (2007) 1752.

Friedman, David D. *Law's Order: What Economics Has To Do with the Law and Why It Matters*, Princeton: Princeton University Press, 2001.

Hayek, Friedrich, *The Fatal Conceit*. Chicago: University of Chicago Press, 1991.

Helland, Eric, and Alexander Tabarrok. "Exporting Tort Awards." *Regulation* 23, no. 2 (2000): 21–26.

Helland, Eric, and Alexander Tabarrok. *Judge and Jury: American Tort Law on Trial*. Oakland: The Independent Institute, 2006.

Jacobs, Jane. *The Death and Life of Great American Cities*. New York: Modern Library, 1993.

Landes, William M. and Richard A. Posner. *The Economic Structure of Tort Law*. First ed. Cambridge: Harvard University Press, 1987.

McGinnis, John O. and Ilya Simon. Democracy and International Human Rights Law. *Notre Dame Law Review*, Vol. 84, No. 4 (July 2009) 1739–798.

McGinnis, John O. and Ilya Simon. Northwestern Public Law Research Paper No. 08–08; George Mason Law & Economics Research Paper No. 08–19. May 2009. http://ssrn .com/abstract=1116406.

McGinnis, John O. and Ilya Simon. "Should International Law Be Part of Our Law?" *Stanford Law Review*, Vol. 59, No. 5 (March 2007) 1175–247. George Mason Law & Economics Research Paper No. 06–46; Northwestern Public Law Research Paper No. 07–01. http://ssrn.com/abstract=929174.

Neely, Richard. *The Product Liability Mess: How Business Can Be Rescued from the Politics of State Courts*. First Printing ed. New York City: Free Press, 1988.

Posner, Richard A. *Sex and Reason*. Cambridge: Harvard University Press, 1992.

Posner, Richard, *Economic Analysis of the Law*, 7th ed. Aspen Publishers, 2007.

Revesz, Richard L. "Environmental Regulation, Ideology, and the D.C. Circuit," *Va. L. Rev.* 83 (1997) 1751.

Roberts, Russell. *The Price of Everything: A Parable of Possibility and Prosperity*. Princeton: Princeton University Press, 2009.

Scalia, Antonin. "Common-Law Courts in a Civil Law System." In Gutmann, Amy, ed. 1997. *A Matter of Interpretation: Federal Courts and the Law*. Princeton: Princeton University Press, 1997.

Sokol, D. Daniel. "Explaining the Importance of Public Choice for Law." *Michigan Law Review*, Vol. 109, 2011. June 14, 2010. http://ssrn.com/abstract=1624956.

Stearns, Maxwell L. and Todd J. Zywicki. *Public Choice Concepts and Applications in Law*. 1st ed. Eagan, MN: West Publishing, 2009.

Yandle, Bruce, "The Golden Age at Risk," *The Freeman*, The Foundation for Economic Education, Inc., Volume 48, Number 12 (December 1998).

Zywicki, Todd J. "Public Choice and Tort Reform." George Mason University Law & Economics Research Paper No. 00-36 October 2000). Available at SSRN: http:// ssrn.com/abstract=244658 or doi:10.2139/ssrn.244658

PART IV

Case Studies in the Anatomy of Government Failure

PROTECTING CONSUMERS, the environment, the poor, and the exploited has become accepted as normal democratic politics. In addition, government protects businesses, controls quality, subsidizes research and development, regulates workplace safety and hours, provides government schools, and suppresses foreign competition. Risks of fire, drought, and flood are covered, medical care is subsidized, income is redistributed, and striking workers are protected from losing income. But at what cost and to what effect does government undertake all these activities? Part IV suggests that the costs often exceed the benefits and that the effects are perverse.

Public goods are not easily supplied by government; in fact, private entrepreneurs are far more capable than many theorists have thought at providing what we often consider to be public goods. Democratic politics has become, in large part, the political pursuit of private gain by voters, politicians, bureaucrats, and organized interests.

9

Political Pursuit of Private Gain

Producer-Rigged Markets

THIS CHAPTER BEGINS a set of seven chapters that might be thought of as applied public choice. Let's begin with the role of profit seeking and how it easily moves from market-based competition to using the power of government to reduce competition. That is, let's examine how producers use government to rig markets in their favor.

Profit seeking is a perfectly normal activity in markets; in fact it provides the motive power of the capitalist order. Since those who earn profits unintentionally attract competitors for those profits and those who lose money go out of business, society benefits from the more efficient use of resources and increased productivity.

This benign portrait is not without blemishes, however. Some producers will note that they could be better off if competition were moderated or eliminated. Such a move could be accomplished through private collusive activity; that is, by the relevant sellers agreeing to restrain production, increase prices, and thereby enjoy higher than normal earnings. The costs of cartels include social welfare losses engendered by the lost production and the transfer from the cheated consumers to members of the cartel. All this is depicted in Figure 9.1.

The restriction in production (Q_r) and the increase in price (P_r) the producers are able to extract from consumers creates the rectangle labeled "transfer." Because of the transfer the consumers' surplus has been reduced from the large triangle (P_cP_a) to the smaller one (SWL). In addition, lost production imposes a cost signified by the SWL triangle, that is, the lost production that consumers would have purchased at the competitive price (P_c). The original consumer surplus—the larger triangle—has now been reduced to the smaller one by the sum of the transfer and the social welfare loss.

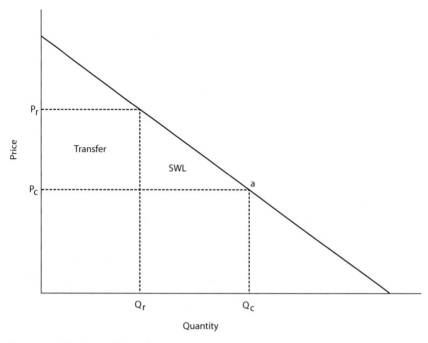

Figure 9.1 The Cost of Cartels

All this has been known for some time; what has not been generally recognized is that a good deal of the transfer from consumer to producer is dissipated by the costs of creating and maintaining the cartel. The cartel members must agree on how much each firm is to reduce output. Should large firms reduce output by a larger portion than small firms, for example? And since producers are tempted, like all of us, to free ride, private agreements among profit maximizers are costly to forge and maintain and, indeed, may be impossible to implement. Market critics who assume that businesses have no problems with free riders might consult the coffee cartel, OPEC, and other such attempted but ineffectual collusions. Self-discipline is costly. Perceptive cartelists will quickly learn, however, that discipline can be achieved if the cartel simply persuades the government to become the cartel administrator or enforcer. And, the government will be eager to provide the service, for a reward. So there are costs to seeking the services of government and those costs must come out of the expected profits. Persuading the government to adopt the correct policies to restrict production takes time, energy, and other resources. In addition, opposition to the cartel adds to the costs. Then, too, the politicians and bureaucrats must be continually monitored and "compensated."

Once some producers have obtained privileges others are, of necessity, forced to participate in the rent game as well. The Center for Responsive Politics (opensecrets.org) tracks the amount spent in the Washington DC rent game. They reported that $3.49 billion was spent in 2009 on lobbying members of Congress and about 14,000 lobbyists were employed, or roughly 26 for each member of Congress. The total number of lobbyists stayed about the same from 2005 through 2009, while the total dollars spent increased by about $1 billion, in nominal terms. The chief executives of our leading corporations now spend several days each month visiting the nation's capital. And they do not visit monuments or museums. They are rent seekers and protectors. They have become so because simple majority rule enables and encourages exploitation. From this rule stems logrolling and thence a transfer society in which short-run gains prevail over long-run general losses.

Welfare Losses from Rent Seeking

Although economists have worked out the theoretical underpinnings of rent seeking, they have been less successful in providing reliable estimates of actual welfare costs. This is particularly vexing with respect to the aggregate costs of protectionism and the like for an entire society. Still some fairly good estimates are available for particular programs during specific years. The figures are disturbing, to say the least, and an overall "guesstimate" would be mind-boggling.

Losses from Protection

Take the case of tariffs. Adam Smith laid out the basic argument that a country imposing tariffs made itself poorer. The question is "How much poorer?" It depends on a host of variables but Arvind Panagariya (2002) concluded that the welfare costs of protective tariffs generally range from one to ten percent of GNP, translating into tens of billions each year. Some of the costs economists identify are transfers from consumers to producers but other costs are, when the long run is considered, deadweight. They include fewer jobs, lower profits, reduced innovation, reduced investment and growth. Economists' models generally do not include the growing instability of the world economic order from protective tariffs—an instability that may move from trade wars to shooting wars. And, of course, protectionism leads to serious misallocation of scarce resources not only within, but between nations.

Although estimates are tricky, there is some solid evidence not only on amounts devoted to particular subsidies but the entire subsidy effort. The World Bank estimates the global economy would grow $830 billion by 2015 if all barriers to trade were eliminated (U.S. Agency for International Development, 2008). One reason for the extensive economic growth is that a tariff harms the economy of the country it targets and also the economy of the country imposing the tariff.

It is easy to understand how the targeted country's economy is harmed; less trade means less income. But what about the country imposing the tariff? The protected industry can now expand production, jobs, and prices. As prices increase, consumers buy less of that good or less of another good. Tariff increases can be thought of as reducing consumer income or as raising consumer prices. A protected few benefit while costs are dispersed, and almost always the costs to the many greatly outweigh the benefits to the few.

Protecting jobs in the steel industry is a simple example. In 2002 President Bush imposed tariffs of between 15 and 30 percent on steel products the International Trade Commission found were injuring the domestic steel industry. The portions of the steel industry protected by the tariffs claimed they would raise U.S. steel prices and output, which would protect jobs and allow the U.S. steel industry to become competitive. Most economists disagreed. Robert W. Crandall (2002), of the Brookings Institution, for example, estimated the cost to U.S. consumers and producers of saving 6,000 steel jobs was between $800,000 and $1.1 million per job saved. This, according to Crandall, "is equivalent to the price of 5 new houses or 40 automobiles for each and every steel job protected."

As illustrated by the example of U.S. steel tariffs, one of the factors influencing per capita income is how open a country is to trade. Restricted economies are just that—restricted. Trade increases wealth and restrictions on trade decrease wealth. Again, estimates are difficult but one study of 131 developed and developing countries concluded that 1 percent decrease in trade restrictiveness leads to an approximately 0.3 percent increase in income per capita (Manole and Spatareanu, 2009). The public choice scholar will immediately point out that the losses are spread among the population while the gains are captured by the few.

Subsidies act much like tariffs in that they transfer wealth from some one, usually dispersed group, to another, usually concentrated, group often with negative effects for third groups. Agriculture subsidies are a prime example. Our farm policies provide a particularly poignant lesson in the perversity of governmental efforts to control markets and stabilize income (Pasour et al., 2005). As is well known, farm crops such as wheat, cotton, feed grain, tobacco, peanuts, dairy products, and others have long been subject to price controls and supports. Price supports, intended to both increase and stabilize farm income, have come at a high price to consumers and taxpayers. Not only are consumer prices higher but so too are our taxes, which provide a substantial portion of farm income. To these increases must be added costs of transportation and storage of surpluses. And lest we forget, in a free market consumers would consume vastly more of the subsidized crops if lower market prices prevailed. These higher costs do not include the high cost of storage and waste resulting from perishable commodities.

Since surpluses pose a number of difficulties, government farm experts decided that the way to resolve them was to place restrictions on output. Doing so, however, soon created a new set of economic and political problems. While it is true that reduced surpluses can be achieved at less cost by acreage limitations than by price controls alone, there remains the problem of farmer responses to acreage controls. A farmer confronted by an acreage restriction can meet the restriction *and produce more* by applying more fertilizer and labor to the reduced acreage. If a single farmer were to do this he could earn more market income as well as receive government subsidies for honoring the acreage limitation. Since every farmer applies the same logic, acreage is reduced but total production is not reduced proportionately. And worse, the cost of producing this additional supply has come at a higher price than if the restrictions were not in effect. The farmers are encouraged by government policy to employ their resources too intensively; in other words, we have another government-sponsored inefficiency.

Compounding the farm tragedy are the seemingly intractable perversities of redistribution. The vast sums spent on only one percent of the population solve neither the productive problems nor improve the situation of less well-off farmers. Countless government reports and scholarly studies have repeatedly documented the skewed distribution of agricultural subsidies. From 1995 to

2009, 74 percent of all farm subsidies went to the wealthiest ten percent of farm program recipients. These recipients are not the small family farmer that we might think of when we think of farm subsidies. They are giants in the industry, some of whom have corporate offices in Washington DC. A Washington DC office is important for farming the halls of Congress, since in 2009, 60 percent of farm subsidies went to states represented by senators serving on the Senate Committee on Agriculture, Nutrition, and Forestry (Environmental Working Group).

One of the major effects of agricultural subsidies is the unintended devastation wrought on farmers by the capitalization of valuable subsidies into the prices of farmland and buildings. Because potential subsidies are so large, those who wish to sell their farms can command far higher prices. But young farmers hoping to purchase a farm or additional land find themselves unable to command the necessary funds. With higher interest rates added on, the future is a bleak one. Originally designed to assist the less well-off, subsidies leave the poor farmer still poorer and the better-off still better-off. While the traditional family farm was likely to become increasingly obsolete, subsidy programs have expedited the process and made corporate farming the dominant production system.

Political Losses

The Federal Election Commission reports that more than 4,000 Political Action Committees (PACs) now ply the legislative halls of the U.S. federal government seeking influence over policy and government personnel. Because the average U.S. senator must raise around $10,000 per week for campaign expenditures for each week of his six-year term we can readily appreciate the importance money and PACs have in politics.

Even at the state level the figures are impressive. In 2004, the 42 states that monitor lobbyist spending reported nearly $1 billion was spent. Nearly 47,000 interests hired more than 38,000 lobbyists—about five lobbyists per legislator— and spent about $130,000 per legislator. In the state of Oregon, for example, a small state with about 3 million citizens and 90 legislators, nearly $25 million were spent on lobbying activities, or $277,000 per legislator. By comparison, about $12 million were spent by Oregon candidates in their election campaigns (Gordon, 2005).

These few mundane examples serve to make the big point: vast sums are spent in the political process because it is now an unavoidable cost of doing business just as purchasing raw materials and paying employees are regular costs of running an enterprise. It is regrettable that so many scarce resources are thus devoted, but it is understandable once the rent game begins. Those who do not participate fail to reduce the scope of the game but pay the costs of not protecting themselves. Instead of hearing applause, they are deemed suckers because they must pay for the gains of those who do play. In any event, tens of thousands of lawyers and others devote their time to shifting money from one pocket to another and make a good living doing so.

Rent Seeking: A Precarious Future?

The thrust of this analysis is clear: rent-seeking interests are exceedingly powerful and rent seeking is costly to society. Nevertheless, all is not hopeless. As in all economic situations, there are contending forces that change and erode gains. When I emphasized the power of various protectionist interests, I indicated that for every dollar gained by such groups, others suffer and the burdens are not confined to helpless consumers. When the steel industry is protected from foreign competition, domestic automobile, washing machine, and other producers who use steel in their manufacturing processes pay higher prices for steel and are thereby disadvantaged in their competition with foreign manufacturers. Of course, as cost minimizers, the domestic producers seek to reduce their consumption of steel by substituting other less expensive metals and plastics. In the long run, protecting the steel industry most likely will have perverse effects—reductions in steel consumption and revenues.

Protectionists everywhere confront consumers whose interests are opposed; fortunately, many of these consumers are big and powerful industrial organizations that push back when pushed against. In addition to the obviously powerful consumers of goods from protected industries are industries dependent on exports whose own competitive capabilities are vitally reduced by protectionist prices. American agriculture must export its products but if its production costs are increased by a protected steel industry, farmers lose sales. And the same can be said for the internationally competitive airlines and producers of electric power machinery, precision instruments, pharmaceuticals, photographic supplies, telecommunications, and other highly specialized, high technology products. Fearful of their reduced competitive capacity they also fear that trade wars may be initiated by other countries.

Labor unions in adversely affected industries quickly identify their own security with that of employers and join in political action designed to minimize damages. At the same time, free trade has its own less self-interested, but no less ideological supporters including economists, politicians, and State Department bureaucrats worried about America's foreign policies. A Department of Treasury concerned with our trade position overall, and the impact of that trade on domestic money markets must also be considered an ally of free trade. Clearly, there is no monolithic business interest dictating government policies. Many Reagan and George H. W. Bush administration actions, while far more protectionist than Reagan's free trade speeches, nevertheless, showed a certain sensitivity to the complexity of contending interests. The Clinton administration may have been more pro-free trade than the Reagan, George H.W. Bush, or George W. Bush administrations. Providing some protection for selected industries, these administrations reduced subsidies for others, and reshaped the support programs in still others. Not all industries will get all they want, or have grown accustomed to receiving. Politicians cannot simply grant unlimited protection to everyone; a dollar gain for one costs more or less than a dollar for others.

Although self-interest can provide a check on others' self-interest, there are numerous occasions when it does not. In markets, some interests may gang up into bilateral monopolies and take advantage of third parties. And, lest we forget, in legislatures operating under majority rule without a balanced budget constraint, log-rollers honor rather than resist one another's subsidies and one business supports another out of fear of retaliation. The political constraints on these ever-present and powerful incentives stem from the facts noted above, namely, differential political power among industries. One of the Obama administration's earliest actions was to impose tariffs on Chinese tires, at the request of the United Steelworkers (USW), the union representing steel, tire, and chemical workers. The union is the largest in the United States and had endorsed Obama early in the campaign. The copper industry did not get similar protection. The USW, apparently, either outnumbered copper workers or was better organized.

One new challenge to politically created cartels is from public interest groups who, unlike the better known "consumer protection groups," argue for economic liberty. One such group is the Washington DC-based Institute for Justice, which regularly challenges state and local laws that create cartels and even monopolies. The Institute for Justice challenged Tennessee's law granting licensed funeral directors' an exclusive right to sell caskets. Because of the government-protected cartel, caskets sold in funeral homes cost were typically marked up 250 to 400 percent, occasionally as much as 600 percent. A Chattanooga Pastor interested in helping his poor parishioners began selling caskets, as did a store in Knoxville. Neither of these retailers had a funeral director's license or any embalming training. But, they did not handle bodies or perform funerals—they just sold caskets and delivered the casket to the funeral home. The state ordered the casket retailers to stop selling caskets or they would be criminally prosecuted. The Institute for Justice filed suit on behalf of the casket retailers and in December 2002 the 6th Circuit Court of Appeals unanimously declared that the government-imposed cartel was invalid (*Craigmiles, et al. v. Giles, et al.*). Tennessee did not appeal to the U.S. Supreme Court. Judge Danny Boggs, writing for the court, said, "Tennessee's justifications for the [law] come close to striking us with 'the force of a five-week-old, unrefrigerated dead fish.'" He further found that Tennessee's law was a "naked attempt to raise a fortress protecting the monopoly rents that funeral directors extract from consumers." Finally, Judge Boggs stated, "This measure to privilege certain businessmen over others at the expense of consumers is not animated by a legitimate governmental purpose and cannot survive even a rational basis review."

The Institute for Justice has successfully challenged laws requiring African-American hair braiders to have a cosmetology license, even though cosmetology schools do not teach hair braiding; Las Vegas rules restricting limousine operating licenses; Denver laws and regulations restricting new cab companies; Minneapolis laws limiting taxi numbers; and New York regulations forbidding jitney van owners from operating on any New York street served by a city bus and from picking up passengers except by "pre-arrangement." Such challenges to rent seeking behavior may become more effective and prevalent over time. George

Will (2007, B07), writing about Ecuadorean-born Luis Paucar's challenge of the Minneapolis taxi restriction made the following point about rent seeking:

> By challenging his adopted country to honor its principles of economic liberty and limited government, Paucar, assisted by the local chapter of the libertarian Institute for Justice, is giving a timely demonstration of this fact: Some immigrants, with their acute understanding of why America beckons, refresh our national vigor. It would be wonderful if every time someone like Paucar comes to America, a native-born American rent-seeker who has been corrupted by today's entitlement mentality would leave.

Conclusions

Let's also note that the more cartels and collusive action are difficult to establish and maintain, the larger the number of sellers. Likewise, those who produce a non-homogenous product also experience difficulty in maintaining collusion. There also seem to be greater costs involved in maintaining collusions among industries with excess capacity, which means mostly the older, stagnant ones. Since much of the U.S. industrial sector is not terribly old and without excess capacity that bodes well, at least for the short run. These several conditions suggest that collusion is both costly and unstable; they do not suggest that it is impossible. Indeed, as this chapter has shown, the existence of such conditions only encourages industrialists to seek the aid of government as the most effective way of dealing with their persistent market problems.

Finally, some economists maintain that while rent seeking is, from a social perspective, largely inefficient, there are political forces at work serving to encourage legislators to opt for the less inefficient policies. As yet, this theory has not been adequately tested. But it does have some logic.

Bibliographical Notes

The brevity of this chapter is not a product of scarcity of materials; quite the contrary, the enterprise of interest group scholarship is not only large but also burgeoning. One might well contend that it is the main focus of current public choice. The basic article is by Gordon Tullock who, in 1967, published

"The Welfare Costs of Tariffs, Monopolies, and Theft" in *Western Economic Journal* 5 (June, 1967). It is a truly landmark piece. Tullock developed his insight in subsequent investigations, many of which are found in the volume edited by James Buchanan, Robert D. Tollison, and Gordon Tullock, *Toward a Theory of the Rent Seeking Society* (College Station: Texas A & M University Press, 1980). Some twenty-one papers by a variety of scholars are also printed in that volume. Some of the best are by Posner, Krueger, Lee and Orr, Demsetz, and Browning. Another outstanding collection is the two-volume set titled *40 Years of Rent Seeking* (Springer, 2008) and edited by Roger D. Congleton, Ayre L. Hillman, and Kai A. Konrad. The collection contains some of the foundational papers in the volumes cited above as well as recent work both in theory and application. Especially useful are the broad surveys of the literature provided by the editors at the beginning of each volume.

Another book worth reading has an intriguing title—*Money for Nothing: Politicians, Rent Extraction, and Political Extortion* (Harvard University Press, 1997). In this book Fred McChesney shows that rent seeking provides only a partial understanding of the interactions between producers and politicians. He makes a powerful case that rent seekers get exploited by politicians who threaten political disfavors. The politicians extract rents from producers not for passing legislation the producer wants, but by threatening to pass legislation the producer does not want.

Chapter 51 of Murray Rothbard's book *Making Economic Sense* (Ludwig von Mises Institute, 2nd edition, 2006) reminds the reader that "the point of much of Big Government is precisely to set up such 'partnerships' for the benefit of both government and business, or rather, of certain business firms and groups that happen to be in political favor." Read the whole book as it is a compilation of Rothbard's commentary on economic issues from 1982 to 1995. Almost all of the issues presented are still with us.

Plowshares and Pork Barrels: The Political Economy of Agriculture (Independent Institute, 2005) by E.C. Pasour and Randall R. Rucker is an informative and well-written case study of rent seeking in a specific industry—farming. It is an extended illustration of much of what we have claimed in a more general way. I commend the book not only because of these virtues, but also because of its explicit use of public choice models. They are appropriately and skillfully employed by the authors.

References

Center for Responsive Politics. "Lobbying Database." OpenSecrets.org. http://www.opensecrets.org/lobby/index.php.

Craigmiles, et al. v. Giles, et al. 312 F.3d 220 (6th Cir. 2002).

Crandall, Robert. *The Futility of Steel Trade Protection.* Washington DC: Criterion Economics, January 2002.

Congleton, Roger D., Ayre L. Hillman, and Kai A. Konrad. *40 Years of Research on Rent Seeking.* 1st ed. New York: Springer, 2008.

Environmental Working Group, "Farm Subsidy Database. http://farm.ewg.org/summary.php

Federal Election Commission. "PAC Count 2008A." Federal Election Commission Home Page. http://www.fec.gov/press/press2008/20080117paccount.shtml.

Gordon, Neil. "State Lobbyists Near the $1 Billion Mark," The Center for Public Integrity. http://www.publicintegrity.com/hiredguns/report.aspx?aid=728.

Manole, Vlad and Mariana Spatareanu. 2009. "Trade Openness and Income—A re-examination," *Economics Letters,* Vol. 6, Issue 1, pp. 1–3.

McChesney, Fred S. *Money for Nothing: Politicians, Rent Extraction, and Political Extortion.* Cambridge: Harvard University Press, 1997.

Panagariya, Arvind. "Cost of Protection: Where Do We Stand," *American Economic Review.* Volume 92, Number 2. (May 2002).

Pasour, E. C. and Randall R. Rucker. *Plowshares and Pork Barrels: The Political Economy of Agriculture,* Oakland, CA: The Independent Institute, 2005.

Rothbard, Murray N. "Government—Business Partnerships." *In Making Economic Sense.* 2nd ed. Auburn, AL: Ludwig von Mises Institute, 2006.

Tollison, Robert and Gordon Tullock. *Toward a Theory of the Rent-Seeking Society.* Austin: Texas A & M University Press, 1980.

Tullock, Gordon. "The Welfare Costs of Tariffs, Monopolies, and Theft." *Western Economic Journal* 5, no. 3 (1967): 224–32.

U.S. Agency for International Development. "The United States Commitment to the Millennium Development Goals." (Washington: GPO, 2008), 1–13.

Will, George F. "Cabs and Cupidity: Luis Paucar Tackles a Twister Sense of Entitlement," *Washington Post* (Sunday, May 27, 2007, p. B07).

10

Political Pursuit of Private Gain
Consumer Protection

CONSUMERS AND WORKERS attempting to use the power of government to advance their interests is the topic of this chapter. Before we can make much sense of the new learning in this area, we must expand the discussion in Chapter 1 about how not only theorists but also ordinary people view markets. Strangely, the market is subject to some unusual stereotyping; great myths have arisen that are exceedingly difficult to dislodge. We might call it agoraphobia—a fear of the marketplace.

Agoraphobia

As buyers and sellers, we participate in markets virtually every day, but our knowledge of their operations and interpretations of their meaning are neither profound nor consistent. Part of the reason is that attending to the details of price, quantity, and quality has distinct payoffs while obtaining an intellectual grasp of the overall economy does not; worse, gaining an intellectual grasp is costly since disciplined thinking and reliable information are prerequisites. One consistent interpretation by average consumers and workers, however, is that market exchanges are what the jargon of game theory calls "zero-sum games" in which the gain of one person necessarily is matched by the loss of another; in other words, gains equal losses. Several implications are thought to follow from this basic view, implications both widely and deeply held: whatever competition prevails is cutthroat; most prices are too high; the seller has all the advantages; labor is weak, exploited, and even impoverished; monopolies pervade the economy; profits are unconscionable; markets are impersonal and unforgiving; advertising is all-powerful but wasteful; and, the consumer is helpless. Given these widespread opinions and beliefs there is little wonder so many call upon government to protect consumers and workers.

This portrayal of the market is decidedly one-sided in that it conveys the views of only the consumer and worker. They are not the only citizens fearing competition in the market and who, therefore, seek shelter from its vicissitudes; capitalists, managers, and producers, more generally, have solid rational reasons for fearing competition. They, too, can entertain the possibility of greater gains by reducing or restraining competition and "stabilizing" market forces. In short, markets impose a powerful and unremitting discipline on sellers. While everyone has a vested interest in maintaining rivalry among their suppliers (a public good), no supplier desires greater competition among his competitors (a public bad to existing suppliers). Recognition of this dual nature of the market led Milton Friedman to complain for fifty years that he was not a friend of business; instead, he maintained a consistent *pro-market* "bias"—a fundamental distinction not widely understood nor appreciated.

Since markets are neither well understood nor appreciated it is nothing less than remarkable that they survive and even prosper. The dilemma is that while everyone gains from markets, everyone is also tempted by a powerful short-run motive to engage in actions that in the long run make them worse off. In seeking greater security everyone is led to seek special protection and gain through politics. We must, therefore, be suspicious of and opposed to claims for safety nets and other protectionist policies that reduce efficient market competition but necessarily increase inefficient political competition.

The Market as a Positive Sum Game

In modern market economies, markets of all sorts exist and competitors come and go as do new products. Creative destruction, as noted in Chapter 7, is the basic fact of market life. But the main point is simple: markets, even those possessing some monopoly power, offer all participants the possibility of making *mutual* gains. A buyer goes into a market to obtain a good but must make some sort of payment for that good. While the seller wishes to maximize that payment, the buyer not only has power to resist but also usually ends up with the product. I have known many highly educated academics who complain about "plastic societies," materialism, inequality, "obscene" profits, and monopoly while somehow managing to purchase the latest electronic equipment, sports cars, outdoor recreational gear, cameras, and so on—possessions evidently cherished. Still, they believe consumers are usually "taken." If consumers are taken, why return to be taken again and again? My academic friends refuse steadfastly to acknowledge the ability of capitalism to provide us with a steady flow of pleasurable and useful material goods and a high and increasing standard of living. All of that is taken for granted and need not be explained. Like many people, they want everything at a lower price. They confuse relative gain with their personal notion of a "just" price. Judged by these contradictory criteria no transaction can possibly be good for both parties. Dissatisfaction with market results would seem then to be based on the belief that everyone but sellers should gain absolutely from exchanges but that they should also gain relative to others. We cannot have it both ways.

On the basis of these fundamental ideological commitments, some people choose to believe that monopolies pervade the economy, that the only way workers can protect themselves is through powerful unions and that consumers require the continual guidance and assistance of a benevolent government. Oddly, the alleged monopolists and oligopolists must constantly advertise to create demand for their offerings. When their power to compel consumption is so great, one is led to wonder why. This constrained but widespread view is at glaring odds with economic reality. Unfortunately, much of the analysis in this book is counterintuitive as, indeed, is an appreciative understanding of the beneficial workings of the market-economy.

Monopoly: Sources, Power, and Welfare Losses

If the term monopoly means "sole seller" there are no monopolies in the United States except the government itself. All sellers face downward sloping demand curves they cannot control, and while they may be price-searchers, they must still pay attention to supply constraints (costs) and demand because in neither case can they simply impose their own preferred demand and supply curves. Close substitutes are always available or becoming so. Bus companies compete with one another but their major source of competition comes from automobiles, trains, airlines, and even bicycles and, yes, walking. Paint manufacturers must compete not only with other paint producers but suppliers of wallpaper and pre-colored exterior stucco. Wine competes with other wine brands as well as with wine coolers, hard liquor, soft drinks, beer, water, and drugs. The potential monopolist has a hard row to hoe. Monopolies in unregulated markets tend to erode rather rapidly and usually persist only when protected by government.

Without the coercive power of government, monopolies cannot survive. In fact, monopolies generally cannot be formed without political assistance. The one exception seems to be those industries such as utilities in which long-run average cost continues to decrease over substantial ranges of production. And, then, of course, public ownership or regulations are the preferred political modes of control. Finally, monopoly profits attract outside competitors who expand production and thereby lower prices and dissipate profits; the monopolist can win, but not for long. Hardly any of this year's "Fortune 500" largest corporations even existed 50–75 years ago. What happened to 1920's "Fortune 500"?

Of far greater importance than outright monopoly are industrial cartels created and administered by government. Because of the free-rider problem, few private cartels survive for protracted periods. Without an enforcement agent, cartels are doomed to a short existence. This, incidentally, is one of those occasions in which the free riders are to be commended for they advance the cause of competition and the welfare of the consumer. But even if the free rider could be controlled it would have to be by court decree and courts are reluctant to uphold collusive contracts. But democratic governments will gladly maintain cartels and justify them as promoting the public welfare.

Collusive regulation is something that Adam Smith knew more than 200 years ago. He explained:

The interest of the dealers, however, in any particular branch of trade or manufactures, is always in some respects different from, and even opposite to, that of the public. To widen the market and to narrow the competition, is always the interest of the dealers. To widen the market may frequently be agreeable enough to the interest of the public; but to narrow the competition must always be against it, and can serve only to enable the dealers, by raising their profits above what they naturally would be, to levy, for their own benefit, an absurd tax upon the rest of their fellow-citizens. The proposal of any new law or regulation of commerce which comes from this order, ought always to be listened to with great precaution, and ought never to be adopted till after having been long and carefully examined, not only with the most scrupulous, but with the most suspicious attention. It comes from an order of men, whose interest is never exactly the same with that of the public, who have generally an interest to deceive and even to oppress the public, and who accordingly have, upon many occasions, both deceived and oppressed it (Smith, 1776, 264).

As Smith worried, cartel management or as it is better known, "regulation," comes about as a result of demand on the part of producers to reduce and manage their own competition and the willingness of politicians to supply appropriate regulation. The interaction of economic demand and political supply sets the "price" that must be paid for mutual gains to be realized. Producers demanding regulation want competition made more livable, that is, they want entry to their market strictly controlled so that the market is stabilized for the fortunate few in the industry. Detailed regulation of supplies, prices, quality, and entry are all-important ingredients of cartel management and success.

The politicians and bureaucrats who provide the supply of regulation collude because of tangible and substantial gains provided to them by the industry. Regulators gain more positions with more authority, higher salaries and more status, while the politicians gain votes, campaign monies, possible positions in the regulated industry once they retire or resign, income from the industry lecture circuit or, perhaps, bribes. Obviously, the consuming public loses from all these cozy arrangements: reduced supplies, increased prices, and higher taxes.

In fact, regulation itself may be considered a form of taxation—the cross-subsidies some consumers gain, as they did under regulated airline and telephone services, are paid for by still other consumers whose fares and prices are increased. The airlines were permitted to charge higher-than-cost prices on long-distance flights in order to finance the below-cost tickets on short hauls to Podunk. First-class postage has usually subsidized third-class mail, and long-distance telephone charges made up for unlimited local service. In other words, those who paid the higher charges were being taxed to support services to those paying below-cost prices. "Cross-subsidies" is one name for this practice; regulation as taxation is another. The regulated firms complain publicly about all these practices but regulation is the price they pay for greater stability and profits in the industry. Remember that the airlines and AT&T did not ask to be deregulated. Apparently, regulated companies have been willing to pay since few have shown any ardor to be deregulated, and those few who have, clamor to regain the benefits they once knew. Cartels cannot be maintained without firm control and government offers industry the best, if not the only, legal deal.

The story gets worse. Not only do producers and politicians collude, but producers also collude with their "natural" enemies as Bruce Yandle (1983) explained in his theory of regulation he calls Bootleggers and Baptists. Both Bootleggers and Baptists want to ban Sunday liquor sales but their incentives are very different. Bootleggers wish to be the only sellers on Sundays. Baptists wish to protect consumers from their own evil desires. Politicians want to appear to be on the side of angels—in this case the Baptists who provide cover for the self-interested Bootleggers.

Russell Roberts (2007), one of the two contributors to the blog "Café Hayek" explains the Bootleggers and Baptists dynamics:

> The altruists often inspire the general public to encourage politicians to "do something." But they lose interest in the details of the legislation. The bootleggers, the self-interested folk, spend a lot of time on those details making sure that the legislation is structured to line their pockets. So the tobacco settlement got public support—everyone's in favor of good health and protecting the children. But the legislation is structured to enrich tobacco companies and lawyers. Very few are paying attention when the details are hammered out. The noble Clean Air Act's benefits are mitigated because it encourages the use of dirtier West Virginia coal and enriches politically connected coal producers at the expense of clean air for the rest of us.

Welfare losses from monopoly and politically manipulated competition are relatively easy, in theory, to identify and measure but exceedingly difficult to estimate in practice. They are particularly easy to describe in graphical terms if one deals with the short-run. Figure 10.1 depicts the situation in typical textbook fashion. The triangle ABC constitutes the welfare loss to society while the box $P_r P_c$ BA indicates the magnitude of the transfer of income from consumers to the monopolist or cartel.

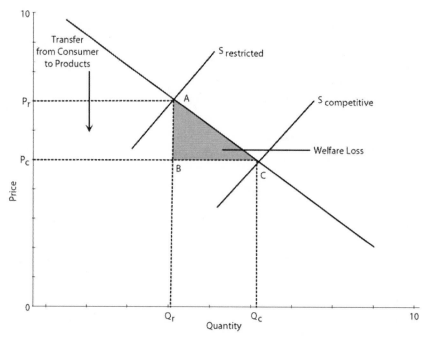

Figure 10.1 Welfare Losses from Monopoly

As we will learn below, this rectangle is not simply a zero-sum transfer but creates additional social loss because some portion if not all may go to payments incurred in privilege or rent seeking. In fact, rent seeking is a billion-dollar growth industry. The total loss to society, then, may approach the entire area of the trapezoid. When the long run is introduced, measurement is dubious. Welfare losses are manifested in less than optimal supplies and temporarily higher prices, but since monopolies do not exist for a protracted time, losses have been estimated at not more than 3 percent of annual GNP to about 12 percent. On the other hand, some analysts have contended that monopoly may even confer some long-term benefits. The less perfectly competitive firms are also thought to confer similar gains in the form of greater willingness to innovate, although other theorists have suggested that the monopolist wishes nothing more than quietude.

Government-sponsored cartels are everywhere; in agriculture, the professions, some transportation, and even local trades such as barbering, building, communications, and public utilities. Our losses would not be great or at least tolerable if but one or two industries were regulated but when all are, costs mount rapidly. At best, rent-based regulation is a poor substitute for market competition. Much regulation not only favors the regulated, but is also costly in and of itself. In the first place, regulation is inherently difficult even in the hands of "experts" and moralists. The purposes of regulation may be vague or contradictory and every situation in regulation is in some respect unique. Every violation of the regulation calls for another more detailed regulation, and regulation is expensive. Some estimates of regulatory costs in 2010 range in the neighborhood of $50 billion, annually, for administration and about $1.2 trillion in compliance costs (Crews, 2010). By comparison, Canada's 2009 GDP was $1.32 billion. And it is unlikely that we are better off for having made these expenditures.

These obvious costs entailing sacrificed welfare for society and costly administration constitute but a portion of the total losses. While technically not a welfare cost, there is substantial transfer of gains from consumers to producers in the form of artificially high profits. Society may not lose but the consumers do while producers fortunate enough to have monopoly advantages gain. Perhaps, more important are the rent seeking costs paid by producers for governmentally mandated privileges. The cost of obtaining political advantages is a deadweight cost; interest group efforts to gain the benefits generate social waste rather than welfare. Otherwise productive resources are employed in an attempt to gain rights to governmentally created scarcity. And once a costly political gain has been realized, it must be maintained against the competing efforts of others to share in the profits as well as those who may wish to do away with the rights. Eternal vigilance is the price of rent seeking.

Even though the strictly based welfare costs may be as low as several Chicago economists maintain, these costs are a serious under-estimate of the total costs of monopoly. Less output and higher prices reduce consumer surplus, but the greatest loss may well be in the enormous rent-seeking costs engendered by the political search for gain. Once more, take note of the curious fact that while market competition leads to inadvertent social welfare, political competition generally leads to social waste.

In dealing with rent seekers and monopoly there are but six options: live with them; buy back from the holders; auction off monopoly rights for a specified term to the lowest bidder; slowly dissolve rents; regulate; or, finally, reduce governmental intervention in markets. At various times we seem to have practiced all, except perhaps, the second and third options. Antitrust laws have had some effect on industry but the consequences of its enforcement have been mostly bad for the general public. Such protection has been mostly redundant and, therefore, wasteful. And sometimes it has been perverse. The market is far more demanding and resilient than the trustbusters ever dreamed. Living with temporary market-based monopolies is a small price to pay for maintaining market institutions. Far more consequential would be a policy of buying back monopoly privileges. Compensation seems in order for those, who like the cab drivers of New York City have had to invest up to $950,000 for a corporate license to operate a single cab. Since the government in collusion with the original industry imposed this requirement on drivers who did not create the restrictive practice I think that medallion holders should be compensated for the inevitable losses of allowing competitors to freely enter the cab industry. In other industries, I am less sure that compensation should be given, mostly because the current holders of privilege (such as doctors and peanut growers) may be able to make the transition with less sacrifice than cab drivers. In any event, antitrust laws ought to be eliminated and more industries deregulated. Let us deny exclusive franchises that create barriers to entry and legal monopolies. Let us reduce regulation so that the regulated will not be forced to seek control of their regulators.

Consumer Protection: How Much Is Enough?

Until the age of Ralph Nader, a common myth was that consumers and workers either did not care about their own safety or were forced by monopolists and oligopolists to accept defective products and hazardous work situations. While this view is mostly false, it is true that both workers and consumers have become increasingly conscious of safety during the past decade or two. Just why preferences on these matters have altered is not a simple question with a simple answer. Regardless of the answers the fact is that while safety is now more highly valued it is still not thoroughly nor widely understood. One result has been a rash of crisis legislation mandating immediate action; OSHA is but one manifestation. Ironically, government first creates monopolies and is then forced to protect consumers from monopoly abuses.

Safety, whether in automobiles, kiddy-cars, ladders, prescription drugs, or on-the-job, is an attribute that affects demand. In a sense, then, safety is no different from any other object of demand; it comes at a price, is subject to individual preferences, and has a market. Accordingly, we can best understand consumer protection if we apply the laws of supply and demand as in Figure 10.2.

Individual demand varies as benefits and costs change. Accordingly, some people will prefer—all else remaining equal—to have more safety while others prefer less safety and some even a good deal less. As price varies so our demand varies, inversely. Both of these choices are illustrated in Figure 10.2 by different downward-sloping demand curves for consumers preferring more and less safety. For any given quantity of safety the risk-avoider is willing to pay more than would the risk-taker. At the same price the risk-taker prefers less safety than does the risk-avoider.

As the diagram is drawn, the two consumers show preferences such that the risk-avoider will buy more safety and pay more for it than will the risk-taker. For example, some auto purchasers buy Volvos because they are thought to offer more safety or protection than other cars, and such buyers do in fact pay more for their Volvo. The owner of a Volvo is not necessarily more rational than the buyer of a much cheaper automobile. Given their respective incomes,

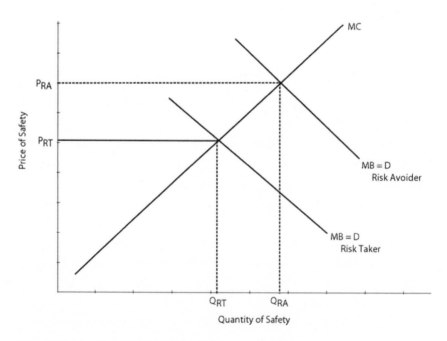

Figure 10.2 Supply and Demand for Safety

prices of the autos, tastes for other features in cars, and, of course, differing preferences for safety, the chooser of a Hyundai is every bit as rational as the Volvo fancier. The nice thing about competitive markets is that both buyers can be satisfied. The problem with government mandated safety or protection is that fixed types and amounts of protection must be enacted, thereby, violating consumer preferences. A seat belt or air bag not only costs money to build and install but either or both may confer, at given prices, more or less safety than a particular driver prefers.

The example of auto safety is worth pursuing further. Depending on the car make and model, an air bag, the sensor that tells the bag to inflate, the computer to control its activation, and the gas that inflates the bag cost somewhere between $1,200 and $2,500 in 2010 dollars. This is a significant addition to the cost of an auto even at today's prices. If airbags are mandated, it is entirely possible that some buyers will not purchase new autos and instead opt for second-hand cars without air bags, a somewhat perverse result. Other rational responses might include the purchase of still less safe modes of transportation such as motorcycles, and bicycles; at a less dramatic level one can understand why consumers might choose an entire array of less costly, presumably less safe products.

Even when a good case can be made for increased safety, we must always recognize that some distinction must be made between safe products and work situations and product use by users. Users' choices, as police and insurance people know so well, may leave much to be desired. Young male drivers have notably greater accident rates than other drivers. Many people insist on climbing mountains, some without proper training or equipment; some people pilot motorboats without knowledge of boats and/or water and its dangers; and, some people insist on flying hang-gliders without formal training. I feel that everyone should have the right to endanger themselves but not at your cost or mine. Improving the safety features of autos, boats, and table saws rarely compensates for recklessness. In fact, as research has shown, added safety not only complicates product use but also all too often emboldens users to further risk, a phenomenon known as a "moral hazard." Moral hazards are not fictions conjured up by the greedy insurance men. Better tires, auto bodies, safety belts and highways make some drivers willing to assume greater risks because these features appear to lower the cost of risk. And, indeed, they do when cost is socialized among the innocent.

Analyzing the demand for consumer protection does not provide all the answers to our problems. Polemicists of consumer protection usually claim or imply that business will not provide safety because it is costly and reduces their profits. The logic is no better than the historical record assumed in such arguments. The fact of the matter is that sellers invent and adopt safety features as a means of creating and increasing demand. Long before the modern consumer protection groups were organized, U.S. automakers continuously offered automobiles that were safer than previous makes. Consumer protectionists did not invent or mandate more reliable engines, radial tires, better lights and air circulation, better brakes, more reliable windshield wipers, rear-view mirrors, door locks, steering mechanisms, shatterproof glass, roll bars, etc. Competing oligopolists marketed these improvements without the force of law. They not only responded to changing demand but invented new means of safety as a method of competition. One must assume that in the absence of regulation automakers would have continued these profit making activities.

Not all consumers will choose all of these or other auto safety improvements but many will. Not all parents need to be coerced into protecting their own precious children. We all make mistakes and no life can be completely risk-free. Recognizing these truths should enable us to better understand why much legislated airline safety is redundant. Neither passengers nor airline employees want to risk their own limbs and lives unnecessarily. Few if any pilots can be coerced into flying planes carrying hundreds of people knowing full well that a safe journey is not very probable. Stunt and test pilots may fly themselves around at greater risk but that is their own private concern. Any airline that gained a reputation for unsafe flying would soon be out of business. A prescription drug company faces the same fate if its products are deemed unsafe.

It seems odd, indeed, that consumers of private goods are assumed by consumer activists to be incapable of assessing their own risks but highly capable of voting the right people into public office who can assess those risks for others. Of course, consumers need information about product safety, but that, too, comes at a price. Do not overlook the many private sources of information available to users. Consumer guides are available at low prices or at no charge on the Internet. And, while we may choose to socialize risk, the best way seems not to coerce individuals into purchases they do not want but to supply them with relevant information and allow them to make a more informed choice. If they choose not to be informed, and many will, there is a limit to what the protective state should do, and indeed, can do, to protect people against themselves. As cartoonist Walt Kelly's character, Pogo, said, "We have met the enemy and he is us."

How much safety is enough is best decided by the person most interested in the question—the buyer. In the case of children, some of the aged, those who are senile, and mentally retarded, responsibility seems best left in the hands of their families and other private protectors. Where none are to be found, then obviously some private organization and/or the state must assume some responsibility.

Perverse Regulation: Quotas and Standards

An automobile-related case that will give pause to those who rely on the government to protect consumers is the Corporate Average Fuel Economy (CAFE) standards. The National Highway Traffic Safety Administration, at the direction of Congress, sets fuel economy rules for automobiles. These standards were initially created in 1975 to reduce demand for oil and gas. Regulations were keeping the price of oil and gas artificially low, and Congress attempted to offset those incorrect market signals with regulations to improve fuel economy (simply removing the price restrictions would have allowed markets to solve the demand "problem").

The simplest way to meet CAFE standards is to build smaller, lighter-weight cars, which are less safe than larger, heavier cars. Small, light cars kill people. Ralph Nader used to understand this simple fact as he co-authored a 1972 book called *Small on Safety: A Critique of the Volkswagen Beetle* in which he claimed, "Small size and light weight impose inherent limitations on the degree of safety that can be built into a vehicle." So how many people are killed by CAFE standards that cause small cars to be built? A 2001 report from the National Academy of Sciences estimated that CAFE contributes to between 1,300 and 2,600 traffic deaths per year, plus ten times as many serious injuries. The study is consistent with the 1999 *USA Today* study finding over 40,000 deaths from CAFE since the standards were first created (Healey, 1999).

CAFE standards are an excellent example of symbolic politics. Voters and politicians are attracted to it because they believe it will solve global warming or provide energy security or reduce pollution or reduce congestion. They also believe CAFE standards will prohibit their neighbors from purchasing a huge Sport Utility Vehicle. But it will accomplish none of these solutions except maybe the last, because CAFE only targets automobiles instead of all energy uses that consume carbon-based fuels. It also has no effect on older cars or on cars that are poorly tuned. It costs billions of dollars per year in lost consumer surplus. Worst of all, it kills and maims thousands of people year after year.

Governmental protection is a two-way street or, to mix metaphors, a two-edged sword. Consumers ought to be wary of their benefactor.

Vehicle Safety Inspection Laws

In a comprehensive examination of federally mandated vehicle safety inspection programs administered by states, W. Mark Crain (1980) discovered that such programs have had no discernible effect on highway safety. Through the use of standard statistical analyses comparing states with and without such systems he was able to demonstrate quite convincingly that in view of the costs and the relative lack of benefits the programs ought to be reevaluated and perhaps terminated. He compared different inspections, frequency of inspection, inspection by state-owned and privately operated systems, spot and periodic checks, etc. The dead weight welfare costs were estimated to be in excess of $300 million in 1976 when 76 million vehicles were inspected. In addition, the rent seeking costs of obtaining an inspection license were estimated to approach $200 million annually.

Crain claimed that this highly inefficient program of safety is actually a rent seeking operation by the operators of inspection stations and the auto parts industry that manufactures and distributes vehicle parts and accessories. The rent-seeking conclusion is certainly plausible for getting such programs established. The programs may continue to exist out of continued rent seeking behavior, because it is in no one's interest to challenge them, or because of political transaction costs. It may also be that this is one more example of Bootleggers and Baptists—a coalition of interest groups benefiting from the mandatory inspections and safety groups making a consumer protection argument—even though there are no data supporting claims that compulsory, periodic inspection schemes provide little, if any, benefit.

Protecting Citizen-Consumers:
The Case of Government Goods

People who worry about private monopolies seldom seem equally concerned over the real monopolists, our 80,000 governments (federal, state, county, city, special districts, school boards, and so on) that simultaneously over-supply some services and fail to provide many other important daily wants. Each day, drivers traverse poorly designed and maintained highways and streets. Each day, we must deal with an inefficient postal service, slow moving bureaucracies, and ineffectual schools. We use poorly maintained parks and other public facilities, not to mention a questionable national defense. While increasing numbers of retired people find the Social Security system a bad deal, each payday young workers discover increasing payroll taxes to maintain the Social Security program—possibly the world's largest Ponzi scheme. Every year we confront an increased property tax—a tax most taxpayers regard as excessive and unfairly allocated. Governmentally supplied services generate many of our most critical current concerns as consumers. And, if we wish to sue government for unkept promises, poor service, or damages, we must await its approval; government, it seems, does not readily honor consumer sovereignty.

Alcoholic Beverages: State Liquor Stores

One particular instance may serve to illustrate the continuing failure of government in its relationships with citizens—state-operated distilled spirits distribution systems. When Prohibition ended in 1933, seventeen states decided to get into the liquor distribution business by creating state agencies with monopoly rights in the distribution of alcoholic beverages. One of those states is Oregon, which operates the Oregon Liquor Control Commission (OLCC). In Oregon, wine and beer are sold by private wholesalers, wine stores, and, of course, privately operated nightclubs, bars, and restaurants. Hard liquor is sold by state-owned but privately operated liquor stores. The Commission makes all the critical decisions concerning the number of retail stores (it has a population formula to guide its choices), who may operate a retail outlet, how many days the owner may be absent from the store (only three days!) the location of stores, exterior signage, interior design, business hours, prices, displays, and brands offered for sale. In short, they make all the decisions and most if not all work against the consumer unless, of course, one is a teetotaler.

The stores are few in number, inconveniently located, and have highly inconvenient hours. The prices on nearly all brands are among the highest in the country. Consumers with special tastes must place orders for their preferred brands and they must usually purchase a minimum of an entire case and then wait several weeks for delivery. While the Commission has loosened some of its practices during recent years, the business is not run as a competitive industry might and does in other states. Clearly, the Commission wishes to maximize two partially conflicting goals: discourage drinking and make exorbitant profits, profits that are used, in part, to finance alcohol treatment programs. In one sense, the Commission is quite rational in that the high real costs endured by drinkers tend to discourage consumption and high bottle prices do provide large sums for the treatment of alcoholics. On the other hand, changes in drug as well as liquor prices have led many young people to greater consumption of substitutes—beer and wine as well as pot, speed, and crack, for example. It is clear that the Commission monopoly does not honor consumer sovereignty. Unfortunately, like many appointed governmental bodies, the Commission is not terribly responsive to changing public preferences.

Oregon's state liquor monopoly has had another perverse consequence, namely encouraging Oregonians to illegally import substantial quantities from California where prices (despite a stiff sales tax) are much lower. In addition, a few moonshiners still operate in the Oregon hills providing not only private drinkers but also private taverns with sometimes lethal booze. Bars have been known to mix the cheaper home brew with the commercial product thereby enhancing profit margins. Home breweries are also gaining in popularity even though they are illegal. Typically the home still is hidden in a garage and makes only about a gallon at a time. Home distillers are urged to avoid the methanol "head" produced by the still and to be careful of explosions as purified ethanol is highly flammable (sometimes 96 percent pure alcohol) and is produced with an open flame under the still. Again, governmental action leads to unintended results including greater immorality, cynicism, and bodily damage. Higher prices have not reduced consumption by addicts; instead, moderate users are penalized.

Conclusions

Consumer protection is an expanding arena for bureaucrats, politicians, and interest groups who want to get into the nanny business. The Phoenix City Council banned churches from feeding the homeless in an area not zoned for restaurants. Minnesota's Department of Human Rights banned special deals on drinks and cover charges for women—no more ladies night, it discriminates against men! Some states want to ban baggy pants and the Los Angeles City Council forbids people dressed as super heroes who take pictures with tourists on Hollywood Boulevard. California banned trans fats. Some want to regulate salt intake, sodas, and school bake sales. Whatever happened to the right to choose? As some wag put it, "I support a woman's right to choose. . . . salt!"

Bibliographical Notes

Most of the better work on consumer protection is found not in books but in journal articles and specialized monographs. Much of that literature is treated under the label of "regulation," meaning regulation of producers including drug manufacturers, airlines, automobile companies, providers of medical services, etc. But very little deals with the government as producer of consumer goods and services, except, of course, education, about which far too much has been written.

One classic paper that should be read by serious students is George Akerlof's "The Market for 'Lemons': Quality Uncertainty and the Market Mechanism," printed in *Quarterly Journal of Economics,* 84 (August, 1970), 448–500. This is another of those germinal articles that begins with some simple observations of the real world and comes to some non-obvious implications. Read it.

Bruce Yandle's "Bootleggers and Baptists: The Education of a Regulatory Economist" (*Regulation,* Viewpoint column, 1983) is a classic, enough so that he was enticed to write a retrospective ("Bootleggers and Baptists in Retrospective," *Regulation,* 1999. Vol. 22, Issue 3). Yandle believes that the story of bootleggers and Baptists each supporting a ban on Sunday alcohol sales explains why and how two seemingly incompatible groups join forces to achieve the same political goal. One group (Baptists, environmental groups, Al Gore) provides a public argument with moral appeal. The other group (bootleggers, coal producers and users, industry) has an economic interest and gives inconspicuous support to the cause. Yandle uses the example of the Kyoto protocol to show how some energy producers were able to raise competitors' costs and how some countries were able to gain a trading advantage, all in the name of reducing carbon emissions.

On the matter of governmentally provided goods we recommend Marc Reisner's *Cadillac Desert: The American West and Its Disappearing Water* (Penguin Books, 1993). This volume documents the inter-bureau conflicts between the Bureau of Reclamation and the U.S. Army Corps of Engineers as well as their respective client allies. One result has been the over-building of dams and, worse, the waste of water resources. The pork-barrel, logrolling processes of Congress are shown in dismaying detail. This book is a stunner.

A rather complete discussion of state alcohol laws is provided by Douglas Glen Whitman in *Strange Brew: Alcohol and Government Monopoly* (Oakland, CA: The Independent Institute, 2003). He explains that franchise termination laws make it difficult for alcoholic suppliers to terminate their contracts with beverage wholesalers and how that turns wholesalers into virtual monopolies. The laws protect wholesalers from competition and consumer demands. Consumers are the ultimate losers from these politically created and maintained monopolies.

References

Akerlof, George. "The Market for 'Lemons': Quality Uncertainty and the Market Mechanism." *Quarterly Journal of Economics* 84 (1970): 448–500.

Center for Auto Safety. *Small—on Safety: The Designed-In Dangers of the Volkswagen.* New York: Grossman Publishers, 1972.

Crain, W. Mark. *Vehicle Inspection Systems.* Washington, DC: American Enterprise Institute, 1980.

Crandall, Robert. "Assessing the Impacts of the Automobile Voluntary Export Restraints upon U.S. Automobile Prices," paper delivered to the Society of Government Economists, New York, December 1985.

Crews, Clyde Wayne. *Ten Thousand Commandments: An Annual Snapshot of the Federal Regulatory State.* Washington, DC: Competitive Enterprise Institute, Washington, DC, 2010. http://cei.org/issue-analysis/2010/04/15/ten-thousand-commandments-2010.

Healey, James R. "Death By the Gallon." *USA Today* (July 2, 1999).

Insurance Institute for Highway Safety. "IIHS-HLDI: Crash Testing & Highway Safety." Insurance Institute for Highway Safety. http://www.iihs.org.

Nader, Ralph, Lowell Dodge, and Ralf Hotchkiss. *What to Do with Your Bad Car: An Action Manual for Lemon Owners.* New York: Grossman, 1970.

National Academy of Sciences. *Effectiveness and Impact of Corporate Average Fuel Economy (CAFE) Standards.* Washington: National Academy Press, 2001, 13–30.

Pelzman, Sam. "The Effects of Automobile Safety Regulation." *The Journal of Political Economy,* 83: 4 (1975) pp. 677–726.

Reisner, Marc. *Cadillac Desert: The American West and Its Disappearing Water.* New York: Penguin, 1993.

Roberts, Russell, "Free Markets and Business." http://cafehayek.typepad.com/hayek/2007/05/free_markets_vs.html

Smith, Adam. *An Inquiry into the Nature and Causes of the Wealth of Nations.* Library of Economics and Liberty. http://www.econlib.org/library/Smith/smWN5.html

Whitman, Douglas G. *Strange Brew: Alcohol and Government Monopoly.* Oakland, CA: The Independent Institute, 2003.

Yandle, Bruce. "Bootleggers and Baptists: The Education of a Regulatory Economist." *Regulation* 7, no. 3 (1983): 12–16.

Yandle, Bruce. "Bootleggers and Baptists in Retrospect." *Regulation* 22, no. 3 (1999): 5–7.

11

Political Pursuit of Private Gain
Government Exploitation

AS NOTED IN the previous two chapters, producers, including virulent free traders and believers in market competition, are among our primary and most successful rent-seekers. Their protectionism is, however, supposed to be mitigated by the policies of an objective government, a government not unlike that described in Chapter 2, the idealized liberal state. As also seen in Part I, there is no such state. Worse, the state, itself, may be counted among the rent seekers. Its members not only take sides in policy disputes among interest groups, but pursue their own interests and perspectives as, indeed, one should expect. These perspectives on the political world and the interests policy makers and administrators possess are unique and not to be solely identified with those of other rent-seekers. In brief, we must consider officials in the same terms employed to explain the actions of private individuals and organizations.

Governments may not be and are not all-powerful, but they are surely the single most powerful agency in society. Accordingly, they are protective of their positions, wealth, status and income. The larger the budget, the greater the power of the officials.

The following case studies document how politicians and non-elected officials are able to exploit the citizenry. It is possible, in the abstract, if not empirically, to not only identify the exploiters or rent seekers, but whom they exploit, how much they gain, and, of course, explain their ability to accomplish this task.

Exploitation Defined

To exploit, in everyday terms, means to take advantage of someone. Political exploitation occurs whenever purposive political or rent-seeking efforts increase one's wealth and/or income at the expense of others. It is important to further qualify this definition by stressing the fact that the exploited have not consented to the deal. Governments and officials may well rest their authority on the premise that since they are elected or otherwise chosen by constitutional rule no one is being coerced or taken advantage of. But that is a weak formality. The more important point is that citizens can be exploited by their governments because of two highly important factors. First, decisions can and are made with less than unanimity, meaning that majorities (including those constituted by transient log-roll deals) are enabled to exploit minorities. There are, then, winners and losers. Second, opportunistic behavior is difficult to counter because the costs of organizing collective action against political opportunists is costly, as is exiting a political jurisdiction. We usually have to accept our political fates if not in the long run, at least the short run.

Rent seeking and exploitation can, of course, occur within the private sector. But in the private sector rent really does dissipate and profit making generates social welfare; political profit making does not. Overpaying public employees, for example, should be regarded as rent inasmuch as it is a payment higher than would be necessary to attract the requisite quantity and quality of labor to the public sector. More on this below.

Finally, what makes rent seeking by politicians and bureaucrats so insidious is the fact that, unlike the private economy, the gainers can camouflage and rationalize their gains with the flag and some purported national interest. The exploiters speak not for themselves, but others whose roles are easily defended in the national interest. Then, too, one's exploiter in the economy is much more readily known than in politics. The widespread ignorance of consequences is the culprit. Those who often benefit from any specific policy are rarely those who have fought for it while those who are injured are rarely those who know or oppose it. And, of course, the unborn cannot possibly oppose their masters.

Let's begin with the most fundamental coercive act of government: taxation.

Official Exploitation of Citizens: Taxation

The work of the New Institutional Economics shows that property rights, transaction costs, and institutional infrastructure are fundamental determinants of economic growth (see, e.g. North, 1990, 1993, 2005). As states shape the basic rules (including property) of society, they affect economic growth and, thereby, assist in determining the distribution of income, allocation of resources, and of course, political power, itself. Since predatory behavior has been a prominent aspect of the historical development of the state, that fact is prominent in much of this literature. Some analysts, including North (1981) and Levi (1988), have maintained that even non-democratic states develop constraints on the state's capacity to exploit (see also Charap and Harm, 2000; and Abed and Gupta, 2002). Rational rulers concerned with maximizing their revenues from taxpayers pay due attention to incentive effects. Tax rates have important effects on the GDP and if they adopt too high a rate they run the risk of destroying the tax base, whereas adopting a lower rate enables not only a stable tax base but also a larger GDP and, therefore, an expanded tax base for the next period.

Nevertheless, short-term exploitation even by democratic states is a distinct possibility because politicians tend to be myopic in their pursuit of votes and reelection. In Figure 11.1 this possibility is shown by the dotted line, which may be termed a short-run as distinct from a long-run Laffer curve. Since private economic agents, particularly investors, are unable to adjust their behavior rapidly

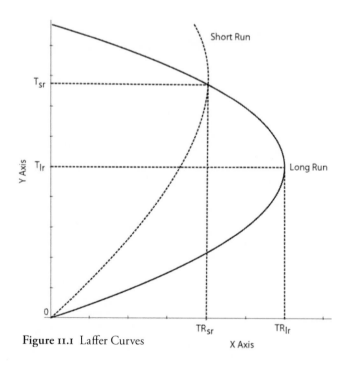

Figure 11.1 Laffer Curves

it is possible for the politicians to enact higher tax rates that generate higher revenues in the short-run even though in the long-run the negative incentive effects dominate and the state's revenues diminish. Even in the short-run there is some constraint on tax rates and, therefore, on the amount of exploitation.

Once at point A, politicians are caught in a dilemma; they can understand that a rate reduction will produce more revenue, but only in the long run. They can also perceive that a rate reduction will cut into current revenues and that will mean either a reduction in social programs and/or an increase in deficits. Vote-maximizing politicians resolve the dilemma by opting for short-run choices and camouflaging them as best they can. In any event, helpless future citizens are exploited in the interests of the current generation. The U.S. Social Security program may be viewed within this context.

Bureaucracies Exploiting Citizens

Practically everyone has horror stories to relate about bureaucracies; some become novels while others become sociological treatises. Economists working within the public choice framework have detailed the fiscal activities of bureaucrats to show that budgets are likely to be excessive; that wage costs are too high; that too much of a "good thing" is produced; that perks are magnified; and that all this waste drastically reduces the size of the citizens' welfare. We also learn that bureaucracies have preferences regarding their own mixes of equipment and personnel and that these mixes do not necessarily make the citizen clients better off.

The best known of the bureaucracy models is still Niskanen's (1971). His concern was to demonstrate that the typical bureau could opt for and probably receive an outsized or excessive budget. On the assumption that total costs must be covered by total benefits the bureau opts to maximize its budget at that point rather than at the smaller one in which marginal costs are equated with marginal benefits. What Niskanen accomplished so neatly was to show the limits of the bureau's budget, and therefore, the inefficiency or exploitation. The limit was determined by the size of the consumer surplus under competitive conditions as shown in Figure 11.2.

Once the agency knows the sponsor's demand and its own cost curve, it is able to calculate the size of the sponsor's "consumer surplus" and that informa-

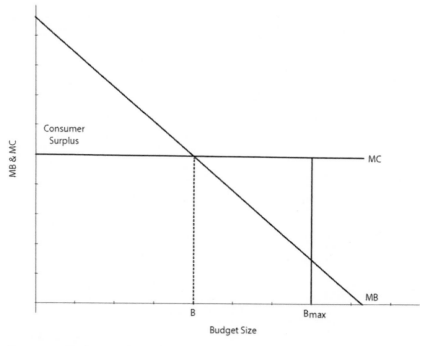

Figure 11.2 Exploitation by Niskanen Bureau

tion enables them to decide the maximal size budget that can gain the sponsor's approval. In the diagram the triangle beneath the MC must not exceed the size of the consumer surplus area located above the cost line. The added budget and production of services amounts to "too much of a good thing" thus wasting the tax dollars of the taxpayers but increasing the returns of the agency and its clientele.

Niskanen explained inefficient budgets in terms of an asymmetric information relationship between the legislative sponsor and bureau with the latter having most of the advantages. Citizen-taxpayers are in an even worse position and can, therefore, be readily taken advantage of or exploited. While bureaucrats continue to benefit from too much of a good thing, taxpayers incur a net loss. The opportunity costs of their taxation or excess burdens are not inconsiderable. They could enjoy having their taxes reduced and/or having the excessive budget spent on other more preferred public programs. But, neither option is likely to be adopted and to the extent that it is not taxpayers are taken advantage of. Voting with one's feet or exit as a response is usually too costly and protest is both costly and unlikely to succeed. Because of this situation affected citizens are exploited. In the long-run, they may obtain some relief from competition among bureaus, that is, competition over shares of the budget. Unfortunately, bureaus and the budget-writing legislators can choose to logroll rather than compete over a fixed-sized budget.

Although not derived directly from Niskanen's theory of the bureau, a good deal of research on the wages of public employees supports his main contentions. By 2008, for example, the average total compensation for U.S. federal workers was about twice the average in the private sector ($119,982 vs. $59,909, Edwards 2010a) and the average total compensation for state and local government employees was 1.45 times the average in the private sector (Edwards, 2010b). Overpayment of such employees seems well documented. Such overpayment has a variety of consequences—all costly—for society. For example, generous rewards have attracted a surplus of applicants seeking public employment. This being the case, some way must be found to choose among them. In the real world a surplus would lead to a lower wage and reduction in job seekers; not so in the public sector. One frequently used allocative device is the civil service exam. Since the examination is often a general, not job-specific test it selects over-qualified applicants for the jobs to be performed. One result is that at the margin rents have been competed away; in other words, individual public employees obtain no higher returns than they could in the private sector, given their education or other training. That is in fact what has happened since 1970 as salaries of statistically comparable workers in the U.S. private and federal government sector converged (Borjas, 2002). At the same time, public employees as a class are overpaid for the type of work they do in the bureaucracy.

Research on wages in the private and public sectors provide mixed results. Some show that federal workers are underpaid and others find they are overpaid. But most comparison studies consider wages and not total compensation, including job security. In comparison to private workers, government employees have better retirement and health benefits, pension plans with inflation buffers, and generous matched retirement plans. They also have more generous vacation schedules, incentive rewards, and disability benefits. They have these benefits because, unlike private employers, politicians are able to increase benefits without unduly disturbing taxpayers. The political cost of increases in fringe benefits is less than those attached to direct wage increases. Furthermore, government employees have had considerably more security than their private counterparts. Their lower quit rates reflect this particular job attraction—the rate of voluntary and involuntary separations for U.S. federal government employees is about one-quarter of the rate in the private sector. At current wage rates there is a persistent queue of qualified applicants suggesting not a chronic shortage but a surplus. Obviously, there cannot be underpayment.

The public bureaucracy is overmanned, overpaid, overqualified, and well protected. Much of it also enjoys and wields far more power than would seem desirable. While many bureaucrats are highly dedicated and work hard, the bureaucracy within which they labor does not work well. Without the guidance and constraint of the competitive market it could hardly be otherwise.

Manipulating Median Voters: Agenda Control

Little did Downs know that his median voter theorem would lend itself to explaining exploitation of voter-taxpayers by government officials. Romer and Rosenthal (1978) surely demonstrated that possibility in their justly famous model based on Oregon school district referenda.

They consider a simple situation in which bureaucrats prepare a proposed budget that is to be placed before the voters for approval or rejection by a simple majority vote. If the proposed budget does not pass, a "reversion" budget will be adopted. The reversion level is set ahead of the election by some means exogenous to or outside the model; that is, it is simply assumed by Romer and Rosenthal.

The bureaucrats must offer a proposal they think will be acceptable, and it must be understood by voters in comparison with the reversion budget level. Clearly, some strategic thinking by the school board and voter information is involved. Aside from the empirical details the model can be set forth in the forms shown in Figure 11.3A and B.

Figure 11.3A depicts a representative voter whose choices between a private good Y and the bureau's budget (X) are shown as being optimal at budget X. The budget line represents the voter's tradeoff between X and Y and its slope is the negative of the taxpayer's tax-price for X as determined by the financing plan in effect. If the reversion level is X_r then clearly that voter prefers a larger budget because the reversion level places him on a lower indifference curve. The question is how much larger a budget will that voter accept rather than be

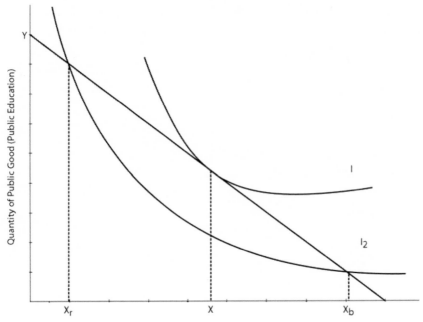

Figure 11.3A   Quantity of Private Good (Private Education)

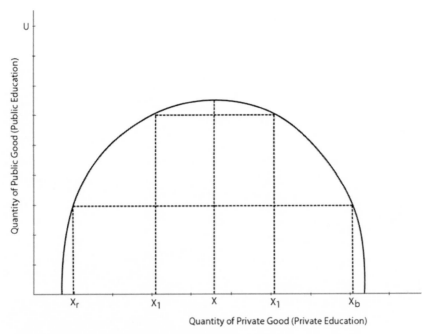

Figure 11.3B   Romer-Rosenthal Exploiters

forced to live with the reversion level. The answer is simple: she will, despite her preference for X accept budgets beyond that level up to one which generates the same utility as the reversion level and that is X_b on the same indifference curve. The same analysis is set forth in Figure 11.3B which shows a utility curve for the voter and the range of choices as the reversion level differs. Ironically, the lower the reversion level, the larger the budget the officials can extract from voters. Avoiding the lower reversion level comes at a high cost. Of course, if the reversion level is less threatening, the capacity of the bureaucrats to increase their budgets is considerably reduced. Contrast X_r with X_I.

Even if the reversion level is above that of the median voter's, the bureaucrats could still prevail and obtain the higher levels of expenditure. Apparently, the best situation for the bureaucrats is a reversion level of zero since virtually all voters will prefer an excessive budget to none at all. Again, it appears that the officials have a superior strategic position to that of voters. However, one must also know how the reversion level is chosen. In the Romer-Rosenthal model it is a given.

It is clear that the reversion level is all-important but whether and how much exploitation takes place is dependent on whether the median voters' preferred supply is itself, efficient. And, that may not always be the case. However, if the median voter's preferred level of expenditure is greater than the optimal level, then the outcome will be even more inefficiently high and bureaucratic exploitation of taxpayers still greater.

Limits on Exploitation

The power of states and various groups within them cannot be easily exaggerated. In the first place, whenever a state emerges to offer public goods such as law and order or defense, it is a natural monopoly and possesses all the market advantages of such systems. One is the monopoly over violence. If successful in providing these goods, the state gains credence and a position enabling it to discourage competitors.

While the state has a monopoly of force its power is not unlimited as we are now learning more about "totalitarian" societies. As with all monopolies an increased rate of exploitation will lead, eventually, to a decrease in the number of consumers. Demand curves, it should be remembered, slope downward and to the right for private and public monopolies (Brough and Kemenyi, 1986; Bloch, 1986).

Exploitation is limited in the first place by the self-interests of the exploiters since optimal tax rates can be low. This same self interest on the part of officials may serve to alert them to the possibilities that their subjects can, under majority rule, supplant them. Subjects may also emigrate or vote with their feet in federal systems. More likely, citizens will engage in various forms of cheating the government through tax evasion and resistance. They may also enact more limitations on the taxing power than the officials would prefer (Brennan and Buchanan, 1980). Although exploitation cannot be eliminated it can be countered in democracies but only with a realistic understanding of the advantages possessed by government.

Bibliographical Notes

Five books provide these notes on the state as an exploiter. The first and most technical is *The State as a Firm* (Boston: Martinus Nijhoff, 1979) by Richard Auster and Morris Silver, two economists with a firm grip on both economics and the nature of politics. The authors are able to cast new light on the state by viewing it as a special type of business firm and then comparing it with how real firms operate. A far more eloquent and, perhaps, profound study is that of Anthony de Jasay, *The State* (London: Basil Blackwell, 1985), a rare treatise both highly original and wise. The book is a beautifully written, genuine masterpiece. His insights come from an original if simple question: "What would you do if you were the State?" I will not answer the question; instead, I will let you the reader, discover the answers as you read along.

I also suggest one of the many books written by Murray N. Rothbard, a prominent Libertarian. In paperback it is titled *Power and Market: Government and the Economy* and was published in 1970 by the Institute for Humane Studies, an organization that is presently located at George Mason University in Virginia. Rothbard pulls no punches in his characterization of the state as an exploiter. He deals with state expenditures and taxation as well as regulation or intervention in the marketplace. If you like forthright language, try this book. It is also logically argued and clearly stated.

James Bovard, who has been called by the *Wall Street Journal,* "America's roving inspector general," is author of *Lost Rights: The Destruction of American*

Liberty (Palgrave Macmillan, 1995). This paragraph from the introduction is an excellent summary of the book, one I strongly recommend:

> The attack on individual rights has reached the point where a citizen has no right to use his own land if a government inspector discovers a wet area on it, no right to the money in his bank account if an IRS agent decides he might have dodged taxes, and no right to the cash in his wallet if a DEA dog sniffs at his pants. A man's home is his castle, except if a politician covets the land the house is built on, or if his house is more than fifty years old, or if he has too many relatives living with him, or if he has old cars parked in his driveway, or if he wants to add a porch or deck. Nowadays, a citizen's use of his own property is presumed illegal until approved by multiple zoning and planning commissions. Government redevelopment officials confiscate large chunks of cities, evicting owners from their homes and giving the land to other private citizens to allow them to reap a windfall profit. Since 1985, federal, state, and local governments have seized the property of over 200,000 Americans under asset forfeiture laws, often with no more evidence of wrongdoing than an unsubstantiated assertion made by an anonymous government informant.

One of the best descriptions of how America's government has evolved from a nation based on liberty to one where democratic destruction of individual rights is increasingly the norm, is Randall Holcombe's *From Liberty to Democracy: the Transformation of American Government* (University of Michigan Press, 2002). Using public choice analysis, Holcombe explains how government continues to grow larger and more involved in what were previously individual choices. Think of the book as an exercise in looking at American political history through the eyes of a very good economist.

References

Abed, George T. and Sanjeev Gupta, eds. *Governance, Corruption, and Economic Performance.* Washington, DC: International Monetary Fund, 2002.

Auster, Richard D. and Morris Silver. *The State as a Firm: Economic Forces in Political Development.* 1st ed. New York: Springer, 1979.

Bloch, Peter C. "The Politico-economic Behavior of Authoritarian Governments," *Public Choice,* 51 (1986), pp. 117–28.

Borjas, G. J. "Wage Determination in the Federal Government: the Role of Constituents and Bureaucrats," *Journal of Political Economy,* 88 (Dec. 1988), pp. 1110–147.

Borjas, G. J. "The Wage Structure and the Sorting of Workers into the Public Sector," NBER Working Papers 9313, National Bureau of Economic Research, 2002.

Bovard, James. *Lost Rights: The Destruction of American Liberty.* New York: Palgrave Macmillan, 1995.

Brennan, Geoffrey and James M. Buchanan. *The Power to Tax: Analytical Foundations of a Fiscal Constitution.* Cambridge: Cambridge University Press, 1980.

Brough, Wayne T. and Mwangi S. Kemenyi. "On the Inefficient Extraction of Rents by Dictators," *Public Choice,* 48 (1986), pp. 37–48.

Charap, Joshua and Christian Harm. "Institutionalized Corruption and the Kleptocratic State," in Ménard, Claude, ed. *Institutions, Contracts and Organizations: Perspectives from New Institutional Economics.* Cheltingham, UK: Edward Elgar, 2000.

Edwards, Chris. "Employee Compensation in State and Local Governments," Cato Institute Tax and Budget Bulletin, No. 59, January 2010. http://www.cato.org/pubs/tbb/tbb-59.pdf.

Edwards, Chris. "Overpaid Federal Workers," Cato Institute. http://www.downsizing government.org/overpaid-federal-workers.

Holcombe, Randall G. *From Liberty to Democracy: The Transformation of American Government: Economics, Cognition, and Society.* Ann Arbor: University of Michigan Press, 2002.

Jasay, Anthony de. *The State.* Indianapolis: Liberty Fund Inc., 2009.

Niskanen, William A. *Bureaucracy and Representative Government.* Chicago: Aldine-Atherton, 1971.

North, Douglass C. *Institutions, Institutional Change, and Economic Performance.* Cambridge: Cambridge University Press, 1990.

North, Douglass C. *Structure and Change in Economic History.* New York: W.W. Norton & Co., 1981.

North, Douglass C. *Understanding the Process of Economic Change.* Princeton: Princeton University Press, 2005.

Romer, T. and H. Rosenthal. "Political Resource Allocation, Controlled Agendas, and the Status Quo," *Public Choice,* 33 (Winter, 1978), pp. 27–43.

Rothbard, Murray N. *Power and Market: Government and the Economy.* Fairfax: VA Institute for Humane Studies, 1970.

12

Political Pursuit of Private Gain
Government Schools and Mediocrity

STATE LEGISLATORS ARE told at every legislative session that education at all levels is in short supply because it is a good with positive externalities verging on being a genuine public good. The important policy implication is the need for political action and public schools. Since all benefits beyond those going to the student are underestimated by the market, some means must be adopted that permit the extra gains to be reflected in the prices and quantities of education supplied. The means can range all the way from educational subsidies to outright government ownership and control. The latter is better known as public education. A more accurate designation is "government schools."

Those who worry about the alleged shortage of education are apt to ignore the thousands of private schools that offer instruction in everything from aviation mechanics to the training of gourmet chefs and ballroom dancing. They also ignore the great private institutions like Harvard, Yale, Princeton, Chicago and Stanford, possibly because of the high cost of tuition. Many supporters of government schools attended private schools and sacrifice greatly to enroll their own children in the leading private secondary schools and colleges. But the more important point is that, while education has external benefits, its primary ones return to the advantaged and usually are better provided by highly competitive, private suppliers.

The value of competition in providing education is only now being appreciated by ordinary people who, in increasing numbers, are demanding either an end to the government school monopoly or that it be broken up into competing components through vouchers or charter schools. Polls now show, for example, that a solid majority of Americans favor allowing parents a choice of where to send their children to school. And, interesting but hardly surprising, is the fact that this demand is emanating mostly from lower-income families. They are the ones who suffer the failures of government schools. Higher income groups have access to the best of the public schools and, when good public schools are not good enough, they send their offspring to the expensive private schools. Less affluent academics living in college towns make certain that they reside in that portion of town having the best schools.

State Systems of Primary and Secondary Education

"Free" Education

Government schools in most parts of the world provide a "free" elementary and secondary education. That is, the students and their parents are not charged directly for schooling. Although schooling is provided to consumers free of charge there is little freedom of education such as the freedoms to establish schools; to establish and follow principles based on educational, religion, or ideology regardless of the beliefs of the state; and to determine teaching methods. Government establishes the rules, decides on principles—no Christmas songs at Christmas or witches at Halloween, for example—and core requirements and teaching methods. Homogeneity is encouraged. Experimentation is discouraged.

Creating government school systems violates basic principles of economics. First, it violates the notion of consumer sovereignty. Parents are told where their children are to go to school, what the curriculum will be, how many days the child must attend school each year, and which holidays will be observed. The unit of society patronized by government is the school, not the consumers of education. Schooling may be "free" but parents are not free to choose. That may explain in part why parents of government school children have lower levels of participation, enthusiasm, or interest than parents of private school children.

Second, government schools are state-supported monopolies. Thus, competition's dynamism, which lowers costs, increases quality, and innovates is absent. In place of competition, government school systems have administrators, legislative mandates, standardized tests, and enforcement costs. Of course none of these systems is as effective as a little competition at sharpening up the offerings of the competitors.

Supporting consumer sovereignty and ending the government school monopoly can be accomplished by decentralizing government schools and increasing privatization. Decentralization enables a greater variety of choice while privatization encourages competition among suppliers, thus widening choice as well as serving to reduce costs. To the extent that education is considered a public good it seems clear that public financing is desirable, but at least the consumption of education should be viewed as a private good. Under present arrangements far too many citizens are denied their preferences as to quantity and type of education, which is an argument to oppose further the consolidation of school districts. It is also an argument for school vouchers, tax reductions for those attending private schools, privatizing the government school system, or permitting parents to send children across public school district lines.

Our large, consolidated, monopolistic districts frustrate all those families who wish for other types of education as well as those who, despite approving the education their children receive, must finance amounts higher than they prefer. The latter situation is depicted in Panel A of Figure 12.1 in which nine voters who have quite diverse preferences for quantities of education must accept the choice of the median voter (Q_B). More preferred amounts could be gained by

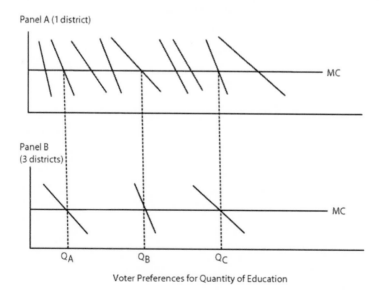

Figure 12.1 School District Realignment

all if the district were reorganized into three districts consisting of three groups of voters whose preferences are less divergent. This resolution of the problem is shown in Panel B of Figure 12.1. Voters in District B face an unchanged situation but those in Districts A and C now obtain education that is much closer to their most preferred quantities. That would seem highly desirable. Note that such differences among school districts are only possible if state legislatures and state boards of education allow the districts to respond to the preferences of voters.

Vouchers, Competition, and Choice

An alternative to choosing among school districts is allowing students and parents to choose among individual schools. The easiest method is to simply fund the students just as the GI Bill funded veterans who went to college after World War II. Because of fears that students will choose to attend private schools or will choose a school for racial or religious reasons, outright vouchers or even tuition tax credits have been slow to gain acceptance from legislators. But there have been some advances in the United States where voucher programs in Cleveland, Milwaukee, Florida, and Washington DC have been enacted (the Obama administration ended the Washington DC program). In these school systems students who use the voucher to switch to a private school show significant improvement. The results are particularly strong for African-American students.

Manhattan Institute researchers Jay Greene and Greg Forster (2003) examined whether vouchers hurt the students remaining in the public schools, since critics often claim private schools will just "skim the cream" and leave the less academically gifted students for the public schools to educate. They examined school districts in Milwaukee and San Antonio that had significant competition from voucher programs. They found that test scores in the public schools actually increased and attributed the increased scores to the effects of competition between the public and private schools.

Greene and Winters (2003) evaluated the effects of vouchers on Florida public school achievement and found similar results. Specifically, they found that "Florida's low-performing schools are improving in direct proportion to the challenge they face from voucher competition."

Government schools in developing countries provide low-quality education, especially to the poor (Rauch and Evans, 2000). One group of researchers, for example, visited Indian schools and failed to find the headmaster at the school in one-third of the visits (PROBE team, 1999). Kenyan teachers were absent 28 percent of the time in another study (Glewwe et al., 2000). No wonder people throughout the developing world including Colombia, Chile, Bangladesh, Guatemala, Belize, and Lesotho have been experimenting with alternative ways to make education available.

One of the largest school voucher programs conducted anywhere is in Colombia. The government awarded renewable vouchers covering more than half the cost of private secondary school to more than 125,000 students. Renewal required satisfactory educational performance. The vouchers were awarded by lottery, which allowed researchers to carefully consider the effects of the vouchers. The results of the research show secondary school completion rates increased by 15–20 percent and test scores increased significantly (Angrist, Bettinger, and Kremer, 2004; Angrist et al., 2002).

One thousand private schools entered Chile's education market, and private school enrollment increased by twenty percentage points after vouchers were introduced in 1987. Studies of the Chilean system do not provide a clear picture of success as one study found no evidence of improved graduation rates or test scores (Hsieh and Urquiola, 2003). Another study (Gallego, 2004) found significant increases in test scores and school productivity.

The theory behind school vouchers has been around at least since 1955 when Milton Friedman proposed them in an article titled "The Role of Government in Education." Since then, economists have promoted the idea and there have been several experiments. But intense and emotional opposition has also arisen. Much of the opposition is a form of rent seeking as teachers, administrators, and others try to protect government schools' near-monopoly status. Part of that status includes teachers and schools being relatively free from accountability. Having much to lose, they will not surrender gracefully. Instead, they contend that the federal government must take a more active role, controlling more and financing it by taxing the wealthier. "Social justice" will dictate the solution. Nevertheless, the citizens of thirty American states have adopted various school choice policies that serve to decentralize schools and make them more responsible to the students and their parents. If the schools produce mediocrity at least it will be by the explicit choice of informed citizens. More likely, parents will demand a higher quality education.

Competition is one means of increasing accountability, and teacher unions are opposed to competition in education. They claim, "We are educators, not competitors." Thus, they oppose merit pay increases and programs that attempt to highlight one teacher's accomplishments over another's. For example, in a school district I know, the local, private education foundation attempted to award $500 prizes to the outstanding teacher in each school in the distrlct. The school principals turned down the offer because it might promote ill feelings by singling out one teacher's performance. They wanted to promote a spirit of cooperation in their schools and recognizing one teacher's performance instead of the teachers as a group was considered a bad thing. The language of cooperation is so ingrained in the government schools that teachers who supervise student teachers are no longer called "Supervising Teachers." They are "Cooperating Teachers."

One of my favorite bloggers, Don Boudreaux at the blog Café Hayek, responded to the Maryland Teachers Association president's opposition to pay increases based on improvements in student performance. Boudreaux (2010) wrote:

> One of your organization's spokeswomen (speaking today on WTOP radio) explained that performance-based pay for teachers is "unfair" to teachers. The proffered reason is that so much of a child's intellectual development is affected by home environment, neighborhood influences, and other factors outside of teachers' control that it is impossible to determine each teacher's success or failure simply by measuring changes over time in the academic abilities of that teacher's students.
>
> Fair point. But if it's true that teachers have so little influence over their students' learning that it's "unfair" to tie teacher pay to the measured academic performance of their students, then what's the use of public schooling? If what students learn or don't learn is largely outside of the influence of their schoolteachers, why spend all of these resources, year after year, on government schools? Why continue to fund schools if children are so impervious to the fruits of formal education that any amount of knowledge that might actually take hold in their minds as a result of their schooling is too small to be measured?
>
> In short, *if* your spokeswoman is correct, not only should pleas for performance-based pay for teachers be tossed into history's dustbin,

so, too, should government schooling itself be abandoned—for we can have no reliable evidence that it is serving its stated purpose of educating children.

Statements like that from the Maryland Teachers Association raise the question of whether teachers unions are more interested in protecting the status quo than they are in improving the quality of education. Protecting the status quo is expressly manifest in the claims that vouchers will take money from failing government schools. That claim depends, of course, on the amount of the voucher (most are only for a portion of the per-pupil amount granted to schools) and on the demand for the vouchers. In most cases, vouchers actually leave the schools with more money per pupil than before the voucher system was instituted. For example, voucher students in the Milwaukee Parental Choice Program saved the government school system $2,640 each in 2008 for an estimated total savings to the government school system of $31.9 million (Costrell, 2008). Despite such demonstrated savings, the fear of losing money dominates discussions about voucher systems. Can it be that voucher opponents are really afraid that the government schools cannot compete with the private schools and they do not want government schools to lose their favored position?

Administrators attempt to protect their monopoly by claiming that parents should not be allowed to choose their children's schools. Education, they claim, is not like other goods traded in markets and must be managed, allocated, and designed by professionals. Children and their parents should not, therefore, be allowed to act like sovereign consumers.

Politicians promote myths about the great virtues of government schools while sending their own children to private schools where they join the children of many public school teachers. A 2004 study by the Thomas B. Fordham Institute (Doyle, Diepold, and DeSchryver) found that 44 percent of Philadelphia's public school teachers, 41 percent of Cincinnati's, 39 percent of Chicago's, and 34 percent of San Francisco's sent their children to private schools. In the meantime government schools, especially those where the students are poor, continue to act like cartels by providing a substandard product to a population with few other options.

One effect of the opposition to school vouchers is that few school choice programs have actually been anything like a free market in education. Although many American states theoretically allow students to move freely between public schools, the money from students moving from one school to another within a school district does not reduce the budget from the old school and increase the budget of the new school. Thus, there is no monetary incentive for the new school to take the student. The rational school administrator, therefore, creates barriers that make moving from one school to another highly difficult.

Voucher programs are similarly designed to have little effect on the government schools. Vouchers have left the existing government schools, their funding systems, and therefore, their monopoly intact. I should note that although there are hundreds of government school districts and thousands of schools, the number of suppliers in this market is not what determines monopoly. The key determinant in this case is the difficulty of entry by new producers and whether they can gain significant shares of the education market (Merrifield, 2002). Few of the voucher systems adopted so far in the United States do much to break up that kind of monopoly. They are too small and too restricted to effectively create a market in education. We should be surprised, therefore, when any of the voucher experiments produce positive results. After all, in order to pass political muster they had to be designed to have little if any real effect on education.

In fact, some studies show no significant difference between student performance in public schools and schools chosen by voucher recipients. The competing studies and contradictory findings suggest there is still a lot to learn about the education market. And as we have just noted, given the design of voucher systems, we should be surprised to see any differences. But maybe scholastic performance is not the only education product parents wish to purchase. Those products can include discipline, religious orientation, location, safety, uniforms or other dress codes, before- and after-school programs, or just the desire to be allowed to choose.

Even More Choices

The charter school movement in the United States has arisen in response to parents wanting more choices. Over the objections of the education establishment, state legislatures have allowed private individuals to put together a plan and an organization and use public funds to run a publicly funded school under a charter from the state. The private organizations are, in effect, bidding to provide education and they often do it at half of what regular government schools cost. Here is how Mike Munger (2008), department head of political science at Duke University and 2008 Libertarian Party candidate for governor of North Carolina describes the charter school his sons attended, a charter school that ranks ninth in the United States among all public high schools:

> Even though Raleigh Charter is one of the top ten high schools in the nation, its cost per student is less than half that of the average for NC high schools. Facilities costs are less, administrative costs are less, and janitorial services are either provided by the students (they take out their own trash), or by contracting out to private firms that clean the bathrooms and mop the floors. In spite of only spending 50 cents on the dollar compared to traditional state-run schools, students are still better off because they had a choice.

Of course not all charter schools are as good as Raleigh Charter and some of them even fail to continue to attract students and end up closing. But the fact is that they can fail and close, unlike more traditional government schools that continue to be funded regardless of the quality of the educational product they produce.

I would prefer that government education policy respected consumer sovereignty by allowing and even promoting choice. Voucher programs and charter schools are huge steps in the right direction, but they are continually opposed by teachers' unions and government school administrators who have a stake in perpetuating the government school monopoly.

For many parents whose children are in failing or mediocre schools, the only choice is to drop out of the government system entirely and educate their children at home. That is the choice being made by increasing numbers of parents. In 2007, for example, there were 1.5 million home-schooled students in the United States and the number of students being schooled at home grew about 8 percent per year between 2007 and 2010. Contrary to popular perceptions, home-schooled children are not being raised by religious or survivalist kooks. They live primarily in households headed by a married couple with an annual median income of nearly $80,000 per year. What is more, home-school parents have more formal education than the parents of their children's government school counterparts. Home schooling gives new meaning to the term "drop out." In this case, the students and their parents drop out of the government system and accept responsibility for education, possibly recognizing that education is far more a private than a public good.

State Systems of Higher Education

Rent Seeking in the Academy

Thus far, I have concentrated on failures of government education at the primary and secondary levels, ignoring the vast state college and university system consisting of nearly 2,000 institutions. These criticisms of this enterprise are voiced with the knowledge that the system is, without any question, the finest in the world. Scholars and students alike seek to enter it by the tens of thousands. But the fact that it is the best serves to remind us that the others represent an advanced case of inefficient state ownership and control as well as rent seeking (Steindel, 1990). We should not wish to emulate others.

A state institution of higher learning is an organization and, like most others, it is bureaucratic and complex in its ways. It produces goods and services and is financed by means other than the market. It must deal in markets but it is not a firm. Its property rights structure is quite different from those seeking profits. Following Buchanan and Devletoglou (1970), one might say that it combines students as consumers who do not buy with faculties as producers who do not sell, and taxpayers as owners who do not control. With this peculiar structure one obtains behavior that is quite rational on the part of all participants, but irrational in outcomes and permitting of a great deal of rent seeking—successful rent seeking—on the part of both faculty and administrators.

Although professors and administrators are fond of claiming they are paid less than other professions and much less than they are "worth," the facts are that they do quite well. On average, doctors and lawyers are better paid but both professions put in far longer hours and have far less freedom to allocate their time and energies. And the consequences of their work are far more serious. Tenured professors usually teach but a few hours a week at times of their own choosing. They can quite literally work but five hours a week in the classroom and do that for but a total of 28–30 weeks of the year for a grand total of, say, 150 hours. Add to that the time required to grade examinations and the total is, depending on type of examination and number of students, another 50 hours. Then add a few hours of departmental committee work and one can work just over 200 hours per year, or a little more than one month. Obviously, a great many academics work much longer and harder than these casual estimates suggest, but such work is chosen by the professor, not imposed by the job's requirements. In addition to these basic considerations, the academic profession affords considerable social status and a more or less monopolistic position within one's department and certainly in the classroom.

What enables all these achievements? Not so ironically, this favored profession has been the product of highly successful rent seeking. Figure 12.2 is helpful in understanding the process. If universities were genuine competitors in a free market, enrollment would be S_c and the price paid by students would be P_c. State universities, however, do not participate in free markets (although they do compete); instead, state schools offer highly subsidized educations paid by taxpayers and controlled by state officials. Typically, the student pays but one-fourth to one-third the cost of her education, unless, of course, the student is a nonresident,

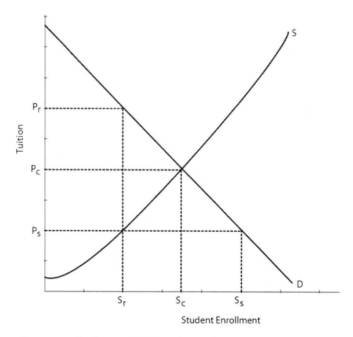

Figure 12.2 Profscam at Universities

in which case she bears nearly all of the cost. The fact that students pay less than the full cost means demand for admission exceeds the supply of "seats."

As is true of any price-controlled good, holding down the price enables the suppliers to decide who will obtain the good. And thus we have the beginning of exploitation. Universities are now in a better position to decide whom they will admit. Their choices are valuable and much sought after, thus enabling universities to impose more stringent entrance and graduation requirements. Such institutions will select those students who appear to be easiest to teach and least likely to disturb the professors' daily lives. In fact, they will select those able and compliant applicants who can further the careers of the professors thus enabling a certain amount of exploitation, particularly at the graduate level (Steindel, 1990).

In Figure 12.2, an enrollment of S_r enables rent amounting to the difference between P_S and P_r. This is so because the students are willing to pay up to the higher price rather than go without the education. Ironically, the lower the tuition fee the greater the rent for professors. The difference between the two prices consists not of money exchanges but of real costs paid by the students to the chief beneficiaries—the faculty. The students pay in the form of having to meet standards set by the professors, of deference to be shown, of willing-ness to accept the monopolist role of the professor in the classroom, having to take exams and perform menial but important work for faculty. Again, ironi-cally, if the free market prevailed the money cost of tuition would be higher but the amount of rent lower. In Figure 12.2, contrast P_C with P_r and P_S the amount of rent is cut by half.

Since the slope of the demand curve is all important in determining the amount of rent we can readily appreciate why rents are higher in Ivy League institutions than in state universities thus indicating substantially greater op-portunities for the professorate to exploit their situation. A more elastic curve discourages and limits exploitative tendencies.

This analysis also enables us to better understand the connection between rent seeking and the numbers game played on most campuses. Since univer-sity budgets are set by politicians attuned to voters, most of whom are more interested in teaching than in research achievements, the legislators tend to tie budgets to enrollment. So, although the professors would like to limit enroll-ment to the better students the legislative preference must be honored. But how?

The answer is simple. The professors counter the increased demand for their teaching time by providing "guts" for the less motivated and able students, courses to be taught by obliging teachers and/or poorly paid graduate students. The easy courses and requirements are not aberrations; they follow logically from the professorate's desire to expend as little time and energy in classroom as possible. And so the tenured professor has his precious little seminar of three students, his kind, while the untenured teach the mass "mickies" or "gut" courses.

The discussion, thus far, suggests that academic rent comes in the form of real benefits rather than monetary returns. While much of the rent assumes these real forms, some of it is pure income. Given the fact that professors' salaries are determined within a bureaucratic-political process and the fact, alluded to, that the output of the university makes marginal productivity measurement difficult, salaries may all be excessive, that is, more than necessary to retain the services of the professors. Even the salary of the least able faculty member may be higher than the salary he would earn in his next best employment possibility.

Given the fact that salaries vary and that the politics of salary determination enable a great deal of discretionary behavior on the part of authorities it is quite possible, and indeed, highly likely that competition among faculty for rents will ensue. It is also possible and quite probable that the less able professors gain the most rent (Frank, 1985). This leveling tendency is abetted by the practice of state legislators and university administrators to authorize across-the-board salary increases. Those who remain at the same institution for lengthy periods increase the base of future increments beyond what they would earn if salaries were determined in a competitive market. Those who have the lowest reservation prices—would work for the least income—have the greatest rents while those whose professional status are highest usually earn more but obtain less rent (Brennan and Tollison, 1980).

Less able faculty also have a distinct advantage, in the fact that the replacement costs of obtaining a superior person can be high, not only in additional salary but also in the uncertainties that inevitably accompany hiring a new person. Even those with well-known reputations can turn out quite differently, once installed in new positions. Dealing with a known liability may be preferable to an unknown potential. Finally, the employment of a "star" may also generate invidious comparisons and upset existing, but acceptable inequities.

Thus, rents exist and are unequally divided among the academy members. Nevertheless, opportunity costs paid by the professors are relatively low since most would rather work in the halls of ivy than apply their skills elsewhere. In fact, many professors could not offer much in the labor market. Their intellectual assets are not readily transferable, nor of much value to the average employer. Their social skills may be even less valuable. From the point of view of the academic, alternative positions are not very attractive. One might therefore conclude that professors are in a weak bargaining position vis-à-vis the administrators and indeed that is probably true.

Professors whose opportunity costs are high, such as law, engineering, and accounting professors are exceptions. Their skills are in high demand among non-academic employers and accordingly, command much higher salaries. Among social scientists only the economists appear to have that advantage.

Tenure as Monopoly

One form of rent needs some elaboration: tenure. This lifetime guarantee has enormous benefits for the professor holding it, but at a great cost to students, younger faculty, and society. Tenure enables monopolistic power that, in turn, means that positions for others, possibly more talented, are reduced. Tenured professors have a power over students that could not be maintained in a continuously competitive market for teaching. The tenured person is simply beyond the control of the students and taxpayers. And, if desired, the tenured professor can become the ultimate free rider in his department. What is taught, how it is taught, when, and under what conditions is decided by the professor-monopolist. Although dedicated, student-oriented, humane, etc., the professor remains a monopolist and potential free rider. Unlike regular consumers, students have little sovereignty and few rights, except to vote with their feet. Exiting from one class means moving into another monopolist's classroom.

A last word on tenure. Whereas this venerable practice once protected the deviant intellectual or, at least, was supposed to do so, it has had that purpose subverted as the tenured now use it as an instrument to keep the deviants from being hired in the first place. Thus, the tenured enhance the scholarly environment within which they work; they now have amiable colleagues instead of challenging but possibly abrasive individuals who are unsettling, to say the least. Tenure should be abolished and replaced with, say, five-year renewable contracts.

College Price Fixing and Discrimination

This discussion of the academic as a rent seeker ends by noting, but not fully developing, an analysis of college price-behavior including price fixing and discrimination, both examples of collusion and monopoly in America. The Department of Justice investigated the practice of price fixing among forty of America's most prestigious institutions of higher learning and identified twenty-three colleges and universities that met each spring to share information and make agreements on tuition and other costs. They were clearly fixing prices, and as the Department of Justice claimed those meetings and agreements actions violated the Sherman Antitrust Act. I do not accept the Sherman Antitrust Act as good policy and only invoke this example to demonstrate collusion among institutions of higher education.

Universities engage in a number of other anti-competitive practices including mandatory room and board contracts for non-local freshmen, and of course, the cartel behavior of the NCAA in suppressing wages (Becker, 1989). As one study explains,

> The NCAA operates behind a veil of amateurism as its members generate revenues comparable to professional sports, practice and play in facilities that rival those found in professional sports, and pay their top coaches salaries comparable to those paid to coaches of professional teams. Only the student athletes are bound by amateur status and restricted in their ability to share in the bounty generated by their play (Fizel and Fort, 2004).

Academic regulation of sports is indeed unsavory.

Perhaps the most pervasive and well-known but least-objected-to form of price fixing concerns tuition, that is, the practice of discrimination between in-state (i-s) and out-of-state (o-s) residents. The latter are charged far higher rates because they have a less elastic demand than in-state residents. As shown in Figure 12.3, price discrimination maximizes profit for the university. The same may be said about the common practice of charging the same tuition to students

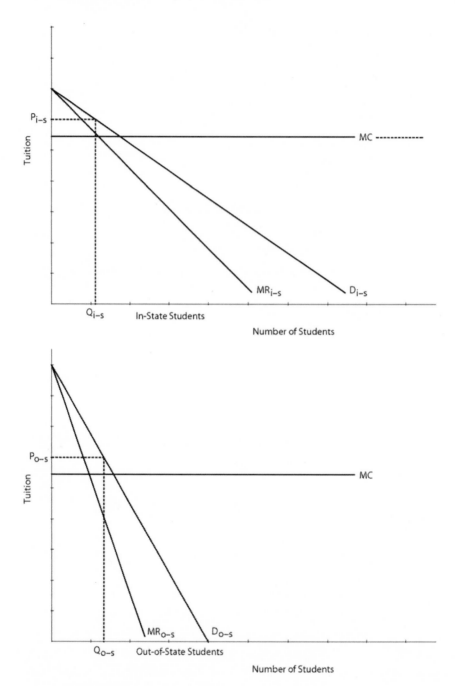

Figure 12.3 Price Discrimination at the University

majoring in different disciplines. In this case, cross-subsidies are involved as students in the non-sciences subsidize those in the sciences. Surely the cost of educating a political science major is less than that of training a science major who must use expensive equipment and facilities. Yet both pay the same tuition.

Students as Consumers—Not

Within our system, students—as consumers—get much less than they might were institutional arrangements different. Some consumer protection is desirable but that protection is best provided by applying market principles in the provision of education.

Insofar as education may be considered a "good" and students as consumers of that good it is clear that they are not treated as sovereign consumers. In part, of course, this limitation stems from the institutions of choice presented students. Students are treated as immature, uninformed, and in need of considerable guidance. Thus, many of their course requirements are prescribed within whatever professors deem essential or find convenient to teach. The typical university catalog is replete with exotic courses, duplication, and minute requirements that the average professor does not even pretend to know. Four years of study are imposed when a carefully thought-out curriculum would surely not require more than three. Students are required to take esoteric topics and learn tools of thought having little relevance in the real world.

As rational humans, students soon learn how to survive and flourish within the educational system. They learn all the shortcuts, both ethical and unethical. They learn not to attend class in those courses in which attendance has little bearing on the decision to pass. They learn how to write exams that will pass. They learn how much reading is necessary in order to pass in each class. In short, they learn that scholarship is secondary to learning how to work the system. For many, the most valuable learning in college comes not from the intended lessons of the professors but from the unintended experiences of having to associate with all sorts of people on campus. There they learn about sex, sharing living quarters, paying rent each month, having fun, meeting a few deadlines, and so on. Much of the academic knowledge they pick up lasts but a short time and is promptly forgotten, and deservedly so.

Students do not typically complain a great deal and for two simple reasons: one, they do not know what education could be and, two, since they pay such a small portion of the total costs of their formal education the cost of inefficiency is low. But if they had to bear 100 percent of the formal costs of education they might think more carefully about whether they get their money's worth. At the average state university the student pays but one-fourth to one-third the costs of her education, unless, of course, the student is a non-resident. No wonder so little value is attached to the classes, work assignments, etc. No wonder there is so little complaint about having to stay four years. No wonder the students demand so little from their teachers.

Conclusion

Higher education will become more responsible and responsive only when its monopoly powers have been diminished and its officials and professors are required to behave in more market-like settings. That might be accomplished by a more thorough use of the pricing mechanism throughout academia; that is, complete elimination of subsidized education, greater use of variable prices for different courses, greater use of charges for use of facilities including payment of rent by professors for their offices and laboratories. Only with the use of campus pricing will efficiency be improved. We believe, also, that when this is accomplished, resources will be rationally allocated. The overall price of education will decrease as waste is eliminated.

If the voters wish to subsidize certain groups they should do so with vouchers or straightforward grants to students rather than granting the money to administrators. Vouchers would provide the low-income but able student with educational funds that can be used anywhere his qualifications permit. Pricing would also revolutionize teaching practices and reward the able teachers, something that is not currently done. Professors would learn, like enterprisers, to respect consumer sovereignty or find another trade in which to ply their wares.

All these reforms will be resisted bitterly because much is at stake. The monopoly position of the traditional academic will be threatened as never before. Professors will have to sell, a task most regard as crass and demeaning to their self-image as selfless, sophisticated, dedicated seekers of truth and bearers of culture. I envisage a new academy resembling the real world of diversity not only on individual, privately-owned campuses, but across all campuses. Liberty will be genuine and liberals will have to compete with conservatives and libertarians and not enjoy the monopolistic hold they have enjoyed over the past sixty years. Universities will no longer be enclaves designed to advance and protect the privileges of the tweedy class. Our age-old depiction of the university as a hallowed, disinterested searcher for truth and exemplar of altruistic values must be subject to the same careful analysis we accord business firms, political parties, and interest groups.

Bibliographical Notes

With respect to education, a major activity and service of our governments, one of the better books is that of James M. Buchanan and Nicos E. Devletoglou, *Academia in Anarchy: An Economic Diagnosis* (New York: Basic Books, 1970). They are the source of my claim in this chapter that students are treated as consumers who do not pay; faculties as producers who do not sell, while taxpayers are owners who do not control. It is a most revealing analysis. A more recent book is one by Ryan C. Amacher and Roger E. Meiners, *Faulty Towers: Tenure and the Structure of Higher Education* (2004). They focus on far more than the problem of tenure and suggest that tenure is often the scapegoat for problems generated by universities not treating their students as consumers.

Still another excellent but different sort of book on education is *PROF-SCAM: Professors and the Demise of Higher Education* (1988) by Charles J. Sykes, a son of a professor. Regnery Gateway of Washington DC is the publisher. Unlike the previously mentioned authors, Sykes devotes most of his words to documenting the demise of higher education and rather less to gaining an understanding of why the demise has occurred. If this book is read along with the Buchanan/Devletoglou and Amacher/Meiners volumes, the documentation makes considerable sense. The sources of the problems are the institutional arrangements that do not permit costs and benefits to be internalized in the decision makers, a point we may have pounded into the ground. Anyway, repetition is the foundation of pedagogy.

There is now a compendium of studies on school choice titled, *School Choice: The Findings* by Herbert J. Wahlberg (Cato Institute, 2007). In just over 100 pages, Wahlberg surveys and summarizes the research on charter schools, vouchers, and public versus private school effectiveness. His distillation of the evidence shows that charter schools and vouchers consistently improve student performance. As a bonus, he reveals the flaws in the studies commissioned by the government education establishment.

References

Amacher, Ryan C. and Roger E. Meiners. *Faulty Towers: Tenure and the Structure of Higher Education* (Oakland, CA: The Independent Institute, 2004).

Angrist, Joshua, Eric Bettinger, Erik Bloom, Elizabeth King, and Michael Kremer, "Vouchers for Private Schooling in Colombia: Evidence from a Randomized Experiment." *The American Economic Review,* December 2002, 92(5) pp. 1535–558.

Angrist, Joshua, Eric Bettinger and Michael Kremer. *Long-Term Consequences of Secondary School.* Harvard University Press, 2004.

Becker, Gary. "The NCAA: A Cartel in Sheepskin Clothing." *Businessweek* (Sept. 25, 1989), p. 24.

Boudreaux, Don. "Open Letter to the President of a Teachers' Union," May 9, 2010. http://cafehayek.com/2010/05/open-letter-to-the-president-of-a-teachers-union.html.

Brennan, Geoffrey and Robert D. Tollison. "Rent Seeking in Academia," in Buchanan, James M., Robert D. Tollison, and Gordon Tullock, eds., *Toward a Theory of the Rent Seeking-Society.* College Station: Texas A & M University Press, 1980, Ch. 21.

Buchanan, James M. and Nicos E. Devletoglou. *Academia in Anarchy: An Economic Diagnosis.* New York: Basic Books, 1979.

Costrell, Robert M. "The Fiscal Impact of the Milwaukee Parental Choice Program in Milwaukee and Wisconsin, 1993–2008," School Choice Demonstration Project Milwaukee Evaluation Report #2, February 2008, University of Arkansas. http://www.uark.edu/ua/der/SCDP/Research.html.

Doyle, Denis P., Brian Diepold, and David A. DeSchryver. "Where Do Public School Teachers Send *Their* Kids to School?" Washington DC: Thomas B. Fordham Institute, 2004.

Fizel, John and Rodney Fort, eds. *Economics of College Sports.* Westport, CT: Praeger Publishers, 2004.

Frank, Robert H. *Choosing the Right Pond.* New York: Oxford University Press, 1985.

Friedman, Milton, "The Role of Government in Education" in Robert A. Solo, ed. *Economics and the Public Interest,* New Brunswick, NJ: Rutgers University Press, 1955.

Gallego, Francisco A. "School Choice, Incentives, and Academic Outcomes: Evidence from Chile," Econometric Society 2004 Latin American Meetings 39. Econometric Society. http://repec.org/esLATM04/up.17368.1080314323.pdf.

Glewwe, Paul, Michael Kremer and Sylvie Moulin. "Textbooks and Test Scores: Evidence from a Prospective Evaluation in Kenya." Mimeo, Harvard University, September 2000 (cited in Angrist et al., 2002).

Greene, Jay P. and Greg Forster. "Public High School Graduation and College Readiness Rates in the United States," *Texas Education Review* (Winter 2003–4).

Greene, Jay P. and Marcus A. Winters, "When Schools Compete: The Effects of Vouchers on Florida Public School Achievement," Manhattan Institute Education Working Paper, No. 2. August 2003.

Hsieh, Chang-Tai and Miguel Urquiola. "When Schools Compete, How Do They Compete? An Assessment of Chile's Nationwide School Voucher Program." NBER Working Paper No. W10008 (January 2002). http://ssrn.com/abstract=453802.

Merrifield, John, *School Choices: True and False.* Oakland: The Independent Institute, 2002.

Munger, Michael. Libertarian Candidate for Governor Platform, 2008. http://munger4 ncgov.com/?q=node/2.

PROBE Team. *Public Report on Basic Education in India.* Oxford: Oxford University Press, 1999.

Rauch, James E. and Peter B. Evans, "Bureaucratic Structure and Bureaucratic Performances in Less Developed Countries." *Journal of Public Economics* 75(1) (January 2000), pp. 49–71).

Steindel, Frank G. "University Admission Requirements as Rent Seeking," *Public Choice* 65 (1990), pp. 273–79.

Sykes, Charles J. *PROFSCAM: Professors and the Demise of Higher Education.* Washington DC: Regnery Gateway, 1988.

Wahlberg, Herbert J. 2007. *School Choice: The Findings.* Washington DC: Cato Institute.

13

Political Pursuit of Private Gain
Environmental Goods

SACRIFICING IMMEDIATE SELF-INTEREST for long-term environmental interest has been the message of activists, academics and politicians since the first "Earth Day" celebration in 1970. Enormous amounts of attention and resources are devoted annually to "saving" the environment, reducing pollution, preserving wildlife, creating more environmental amenities, keeping fit, vacationing in the wilderness and purchasing fashionable hiking shoes, backpacks, bicycles, and ski equipment. Morally enraged attacks on industrial polluters and obscene profiteers are fashionable in dinner table conversations. Humans, we are told, do not live on bread alone; poetry, the mind, and environmental amenities must also be cultivated in civilized societies. In short, what economists label as externalities, social costs, or neighborhood effects have become a staple of daily conversation.

This concern over the amenities of life is made possible, paradoxically, because of the tremendous economic growth engendered by capitalism. As material goods have become more plentiful, their marginal value has, as the law says, diminished; at the same time, the "quality of life" attributes have increased in value, posing further allocative choices. The problem becomes one of determining what combination of material and quality of life goods we wish to consume. For example, poor people place higher values on scarce material things, while richer people seek scarce, more costly amenities. But, any sacrifices from preserving environmental amenities are expected to be shared by all, rich and poor alike.

Public opinion polls show continuing support from all income classes for the government to "do something" about environmental degradation and to protect environmental amenities. But the methods government officials have chosen and continue to choose, as the analysis of Chapters 3 and 4 would predict, are often failures. Some policies are simply symbolic and make few if any meaningful changes. Others create the illusion of creating improvement while actually making things worse. Other policies succeed at protecting or improving environmental amenities but at costs that are greater than the value of the amenities.

A Primer: From Pigou to Coase

One of the most commonly cited economists who addresses environmental concerns is A.C. Pigou. He discussed the problem of "saving the environment" extensively in the 1920s and said, for example, "Smoke in large cities inflicts a heavy uncharged loss on the community, in injury to buildings, vegetation, expenses for washing clothes and cleaning rooms, expenses for the provision of artificial light, and in many other ways" (Pigou, 1920, 184, quoted in Yandle, 1998, 125–26).

Paul Samuelson's 1950s essays on public goods formalized and made clearer the nature of public goods and why markets may fail to provide them in adequate amounts. Samuelson and others using a similar analysis tell us that voluntary action in large groups and markets will fail to produce the socially optimal level of those private goods having external costs or benefits in production and/or consumption. As explained in Chapter 5, the standard argument is that markets overproduce a good when external costs exist since not all costs are incurred by the producers and consumers of the good. In effect, damaged third parties subsidize consumers of the good. Conversely, the market underproduces a good whenever external benefits exist because all benefits are not captured by market demand for the product. In competitive markets, especially those consisting of large numbers of people, there will be little or no incentive for individuals to voluntarily do anything about negative externalities; everyone's incentive is to free ride.

This discussion will become more precise by considering some elementary graphics, for they enable a pinpointing of what Pigou, Samuelson, and others identify as the nature of the problem and possible solutions. Consider Figure 13.1. Let the curve ABC represent the marginal spillover costs of an industry and the curve DBE represent the marginal costs of abatement by the industry. In an uncontrolled market the industry will emit a total of OE_M units of pollution

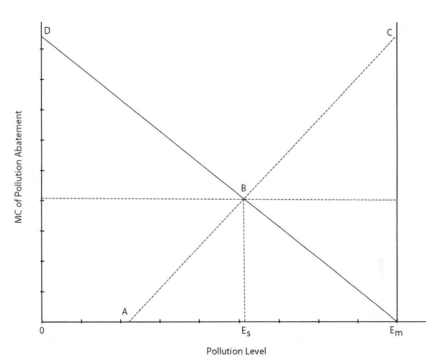

Figure 13.1 Controlling Pollution

even though the socially optimal level is OE_S where the two sets of marginal costs are equal.

The Pigouvian solution to the market failure described in Figure 13.1 is to apply one of two extensive and forceful governmental actions to remedy the situation. The first, preferred by most U.S. environmental groups and politicians, is to mandate OE_S. This approach, known as "command and control," is characteristic of most of the U.S. environmental legislation enacted during the 1970s and 1980s such as the Clean Air Act and the Clean Water Act. The second response is to tax the polluter by the amount of OT or BE_S. Taxing schemes are widely used in Europe to manage sewage collection and treatment and are being implemented throughout Latin America.

Pigouvian analysis claims a tax will encourage industrialists to produce the correct combination of products and pollution. Each firm will reduce its level of pollution until the marginal cost of abatement equals the tax rate. Any further reduction of pollution would be more costly than paying the tax, so EO_S is the optimal level. Presumably, the marginal cost of abatement will be equalized for all firms minimizing the costs of pollution control.

Economists tend to favor the taxing approach over a mandated outcome approach because enforcement costs are lower and innovation is encouraged. But many environmental activists consider pollution to be immoral in the same way that Baptists or Mormons might consider prostitution to be immoral. For these environmentalists, taxing an immoral activity is at best a social statement of indifference to environmentally destructive behavior. At worst, they believe such taxes condone environmental destruction. Taxing an activity fails to stigmatize it the way prohibiting or controlling it does, at least in the minds of the environmental elite. Both taxing and controlling are bound to be highly inefficient.

Consider the simple case of a paper mill discharging waste into a stream. Mandating OE_S is confoundingly complex. Politicians or regulators need to estimate demand for paper at various prices; assume the demand curve will not change; and estimate downstream damage, the costs of treating water downstream rather than at the paper mill, and the demand for different levels of clean water among the many different downstream users. What if there are many rivers in a region? To arrive at OE_S, a government entity must calculate the appropriate rule or tax for each producer by considering all users of the products produced, all downstream water users, and the effects of multiple externalities across the region. The government must also establish a system for monitoring and enforcing compliance (Yandle, 1998, 127–29).

Another problem facing regulators is that industries may respond in ways that are totally unexpected. Pollution charges or rules based on the volume of wastewater discharged may cause dischargers to concentrate their discharges in smaller amounts of water. Charges based on concentration of substances may encourage dischargers to increase the volume of wastewater discharged in order to dilute the concentrations and avoid the rules or charges (Huber, et al., 1998, 43).

A third problem concerns the policy itself. What if the policy is wrong-headed, based on incorrect information, or is in the hands of ideological zealots? Finding a more efficient way to do bad things is not an improvement. Fred Smith, founder of the Competitive Enterprise Institute and occasional user of rhetorical extravagance, often says, "Having a sharper guillotine is not necessarily a good thing."

It is an elementary but crucial fact that externalities, both good and bad, are *unintended* consequences of *useful* actions. Polluters do not go into business in order to pollute; they go into business to make money by satisfying consumer demands. Private firms as well as individual citizens take account of their own direct business costs in making decisions; they do not often take account of social effects. As a consequence, the prices attached to products reflect only the former and not the latter costs. That is what economists mean when they write of divergences between private and social costs. The market does not require such accounting when some portion of the natural environment is open for public use; air for example. Dumping pollution into the air rather than paying to control it reduces costs. Since commonly owned property is owned by no one, the results are clear—it will not be cared for as well as private property. Everyone has a powerful incentive to dump; few have sufficient incentives and power to prevent others from dumping. A resource owned by everyone is treated as if no one owned it. That is why we notice litter on public streets and sidewalks. Smokers find it convenient to drop their cigarette butts on the ground while none of us wishes to incur the costs of thwarting them. Wherever streets and sidewalks are kept clean, it is because cities have employed a street cleaning department and/or rely on private businesses whose potential customers seem to value ready, clean access to their shops.

In his 1960 paper, "The Problem of Social Cost," Ronald Coase shattered Pigouvian analyses and offered an entirely new way of approaching social costs and the policies needed to deal with them. David Friedman (2000, p. 36) describes how things went when Coase first presented his new approach to understanding externalities to economists at the University of Chicago:

> That view of externalities, originally due to Pigou, was almost universally accepted by economists until one evening in 1960, when a British economist named Ronald Coase came to the University of Chicago to deliver a paper. He spent the evening at the house of Aaron Director, the founding editor of the *Journal of Law and Economics*. Counting Coase, fourteen economists were present, three of them future Nobel Prize winners.

When the evening started, thirteen of them supported the conventional view of externalities described above. When the evening ended, none of them did. Coase had persuaded them that Pigou's analysis was wrong, not in one way but three. The existence of externalities does not necessarily lead to an inefficient result. Pigouvian taxes do not in general lead to the efficient result. Third, and most important, the problem is not really externalities at all. It is transaction costs.

Externalities, Coase explained, are reciprocal, which means they are not necessarily inefficient. Viewing external costs as simply the costs produced by polluters and consumed by victims misses the reciprocal nature of many externalities. If I move downwind from your dairy farm, I smell your cows and can be infested by flies during certain months. Surely you and your cows are at fault. But if I did not move to that location, I would not be damaged. We are jointly at fault. Coase's point is that legal rules that assign blame to you or to me can be inefficient. From the point of strict economic efficiency, the person able to prevent the problem at lower cost should do so. Coase (1960, p. 2) explained: "We are dealing with a problem of a reciprocal nature. To avoid the harm to B would inflict harm to A. The real question to be decided is: should A be allowed to harm B or should B be allowed to harm A?"

Coase rejected Pigou's taxes as unnecessary. As long as the dairy farmer and the neighbor can develop mutually agreeable and enforceable contracts, the market will determine efficiency. It does not even matter who gets the property rights initially. If property rights are well defined and we can bargain we will arrive at efficient solutions. If I have a right to not smell your cows, you can bargain with me to purchase that right or my property. You can also invest in better treatment facilities to eliminate smells and flies. If you have the right to produce smells and flies, I can purchase that right from you or pay for your treatment facilities. Either way, we reach an efficient outcome that reflects our values.

Coase did not, however, claim that markets would handle everything. He identified two causes of inefficiency—insufficiently developed property rights and high transaction costs. You and I may be able to agree on an efficient solution, but could one hundred of us agree, or thousands of us? We are back to the public goods problem, but now realize that solving the problem means focusing on transaction costs, not externalities. Solutions to transaction cost problems may be very different than solutions to externality problems.

Taking Coase seriously requires that analysts recognize they have been asking the wrong questions about environmental issues. And asking the wrong questions will lead them to recommend taxes or regulation. The wrong questions are dictated in the first place by an incorrect diagnosis of the sources of environmental problems, in the second place, by concentrating on the notion of externalities instead of reciprocal costs, and, in the third place, by political considerations honored by politicians and bureaucrats. Welfare economists must take the blame for the first two problems but cannot be held responsible for the necessities of electoral politics.

Coase based his analysis on the common law, which originated in the unwritten or customary laws of England and was later applied to England's colonies. As we described in Chapter 8, common law is court-made as opposed to legislature-made law. It is based in custom, usage, and precedence and is the legal system's analogue to prices in that it provides condensed information, not about scarcity and value but about cases, incentives, and outcomes.

The common law applied strong rights and responsibilities to property. The right to use and enjoy one's property is connected to a responsibility to not harm others' ability to do the same with their property. This concept was so embedded in English common law by the seventeenth century that the maxim from a 1611 English court, "Use your own property so as not to harm another's," was being applied to air pollution cases. By 1885 English courts were saying:

> Prima facie no man has the right to use his own land in such a way as to be a nuisance to his neighbour, and whether the nuisance is effected by sending filth on to his neighbour's land, or by putting poisonous matter on his own land and allowing it to escape to his neighbour's land, or whether the nuisance is effected by poisoning the air which his neighbour breathes, or the water which he drinks, appears to me wholly immaterial.
>
> If a man chooses to put filth on his own land he must take care not to let it escape on to his neighbour's land. (*Ballard v. Tomlinson*, 1885, 126)

Under the common law, if the victim of pollution convinces the court his property is harmed by another's actions, the court issues an injunction and determines damages. The victim's property rights trump the polluter's actions and if the polluter wishes to continue his actions he must buy the property right from the victim.

The American and Canadian systems of law were firmly based on the common law and the common law protected people's rights. Downstream users were protected from upstream polluters, including cities dumping their sewage into the stream. Upstream landowners were protected from flooding by a downstream dam builder. Farmers could sue industrial plants and win. Judges made polluters clean up or shut down.

One illustrative case is that of *Whalen v. Union Bag & Paper Co.* (1913). Union Bag and Paper built a new plant at an expense of more than $1 million and employed 500 people. The plant, however, polluted a creek making it impossible for use by a downstream farmer, Whalen, to continue to use the water for irrigating crops and watering livestock. Whalen sued the mill and the court ordered Union Bag and Paper to pay Whalen damages of $312 per year and to stop harmful pollution within a year. On appeal, Union Bag and Paper's damages were reduced to $100 and the injunction against polluting was lifted. According to the appellate court, the economic value of the mill to the area was greater than the value of the water to Whalen. The New York Court of Appeals reinstated the injunction, stating that economic value is not a good reason for violating someone's rights. The court went on to say, "Neither courts of equity nor law can be guided by such a rule, for if followed to its logical conclusion it would deprive the poor litigant of his little property by giving it to those already rich."

The New York Court of Appeals implicitly understood Coase's point about externalities because they asked, in effect, should A be allowed to harm B or should B be allowed to harm A and the answer to the question was not who had the most economic power but who owned the property rights. Once it was clear that Whalen owned the right to clean water, the paper company could negotiate with him and other landowners along the stream to purchase the right to pollute. Once they obtained such a right they could then pollute but then it is not an externality. Think of it as invited pollution rather than the uninvited pollution that sparked the original lawsuit.

One other important feature of the common law and the environment is that because common law solutions are local and specific they allow for adaptation and experimentation. By contrast, national legislation imposes a one-size-fits-all solution to problems everywhere regardless of cost of outcome.

Choosing Inefficient Policies

But, you might ask, what about burning rivers in Ohio, Love Canal, water pollution, and global environmental problems, if property rights and the common law are so effective? The answer is that, except in the Love Canal case,[1] there were no clear property rights that could be used by the common law.

By 1970 property rights and the common law were being used by every major city in the United States to define public property rights to air quality. Some states were forming multi-state compacts to define rights. Air and water quality were improving across the country. But, environmental concerns ran ahead of improvement and created opportunities for political entrepreneurship for interest groups, politicians, and bureaucrats. They tended to prefer highly complex—but often inefficient—regulations, taxes, and subsidy schemes. Unfortunately, each of these policies places a heavy burden on our capacities to gather and process information and multiplies the administrative costs of supervising polluters. At the same time, command and control or taxation solutions ignore the incentives and capacities of private parties to bargain with one another.

Politicians may prefer direct controls, because controls enhance their own power and because many voters mistakenly believe that regulation through law is the simplest and most effective way to discourage anti-social behavior. Since politicians must honor electoral myths, passing a law seems to demonstrate their deep concern and forcefulness in attacking outstanding problems.

---

1. Most of what everyone knows about Love Canal is incorrect. Love Canal was an abandoned canal used in the 1940s and 1950s by Hooker ElectroChemical Corporation as a place to dump chemical wastes. Hooker covered it with an impermeable clay cap. The local school board wanted the property and, under pressure, Hooker sold the landfill for $1 and warned that the property should be only used for a park or parking lot and that the clay cap should never be breached. Portions of the property were sold to developers who breached the clay to put in utilities, including water and sewer lines, and the chemicals followed the utilities to people's homes and to the surface (Bailey, 2004—Reason OnLine March 24, 2004, http://www.reason.com/rb/rb032404.shtml).

Whenever large numbers of people are involved in polluting, politicians are notably reluctant to enact tough anti-pollution legislation. They are reluctant, for example, to make drivers the culprits in auto pollution and traffic accidents. Industry serves as a convenient scapegoat. Bureaucrats, too, prefer environmental controls to market solutions; controls provide them with something useful to do along with a ready claim to larger budgets to meet further unmet social needs. They may be seen as dedicated servants of the public, hard-working officials protecting the environment; that they restrict the choices and behavior of others is of lesser concern. And, while their activities may be costly in the long run and, worse, ineffectual, few people notice the long run. Since higher costs of abatement appear to fall on the wealthy, corporate "malefactors" rather than the small taxpayer and consumer, politicians and bureaucrats gain support among voters.

In addition to the political attractiveness of illusory control policies, conventional approaches ignore the technical problem of identifying the optimal level of pollution. Without this information, calculating the appropriate size tax or level of control expected to bring social costs and benefits into line is impossible. Moral suasion on the part of government presents even more problems for it calls for nothing less than an ethical revolution. Besides being impractical, such a government policy is devoid of a mechanism to achieve the optimal level of emissions. Still, governments resort to moral suasion where enforcement is impossible (littering) or where immediate action is required in brief emergencies (temperature inversions in Los Angeles). Outright bans may be more reliable than moral suasion so long as they are limited in scope. But outright bans cannot work if the ban affects nearly everyone, as is the case with emissions from internal combustion engines. In any event, such prohibitions are unlikely to achieve the optimal amount of the externality—unless, of course, the optimum is zero pollution. In general, risk-averse governments have chosen the ban when the cost of discovering the optimum level was in itself prohibitive and they had to choose an arbitrary level between zero and unchecked, highly dangerous pollution.

Setting standards seems to be the most popular policy, at least in the United States. Whether the standards pertain to resource inputs, emissions, or ambient standards they all have a serious drawback; they are likely to be extremely and, in part, unnecessarily costly. Since it is inordinately difficult for governments to catch, prosecute, and convict violators, administrative costs are high. And, compliance costs are also apt to be high because standards must be tailored to the special circumstances of each polluter. Governments faced with this administrative nightmare, therefore, enact uniform standards but enforce them selectively.

Governments may also use a variety of subsidy instruments including income tax credits, accelerated depreciation privileges, low-interest loans, and exemptions from various taxes to purchasers of emission abatement equipment. These are only partial bribes and are, therefore, highly ineffective in encouraging the installation of emission equipment. A substantial private sacrifice on the part of the emitters is still required. Such programs also introduce an opportunity for rent seeking producers to have their control equipment mandated as the type that must be used, even though it may not be the least costly or most efficient.

The U.S. Clean Air Act of 1970 and its 1977 Amendments provide a useful guide to the politics of environmental protection. Coal-fired generating plants produced about one-half of all electric power generated in the United States and, according to Environmental Protection Agency estimates, produced 65 percent of the sulfur oxides emitted. Sulfur oxides (sulfur dioxide—SO_2—in particular) were the pollutants believed to be the major cause of acid rain, so reducing their production was a major goal of the clean air legislation. In fact the act required that SO_2 emissions be reduced to no more than 1.2 pounds of SO_2 per million BTU of energy produced.

What the act did not specify until the 1977 amendments was how the reductions were to be attained. Utility companies could install flue gas desulfurization mechanisms (scrubbers) in the smokestacks, wash crushed coal to remove most of the sulfur-bearing particles (coal washing), or burn coal with lower sulfur content. The least effective and most costly of the alternatives was scrubbing, whereas the least costly was burning low sulfur coal.

But burning low-sulfur coal presented a political problem because most of the nation's low sulfur coal is located in the mountain states while the high sulfur coal is found primarily in the East and Midwest. If utilities shifted to low-sulfur western coal in order to meet the clean air standards, jobs would be lost in the eastern coalfields where the United Mine Workers Union's membership is concentrated. Thus, the Clean Air Act Amendments of 1977 became a legislative battle over regional protectionism.

Environmental groups joined the battle on the side of Eastern "dirty coal" interests. The National Clean Air Coalition, the Environmental Policy Center, the Sierra Club, and the Natural Resources Defense Council supported mandating scrubbing *regardless of the coal's sulfur content*. Some environmentalists apparently favored forced scrubbing as a means of reducing the amount of strip mining in the West. Another rationale was the belief that scrubbing might reduce emissions below the 1.2-pound target.

Forced scrubbing, however, only applies to new plants; plants existing prior to the legislation were allowed to continue to emit four or five pounds of SO_2 per MBTU. Since adding scrubbers increases the cost of a new power plant by about 15 percent, old plants continue to be kept in production far longer than they would be otherwise. Incidentally, this "old plant effect" outweighs the extra benefits on air quality of forcing all new plants to scrub.

As modified by the 1977 Amendments, the Clean Air Act was a model of the political symbolism I discussed in Chapter 4. Environmental groups won new standards; politicians, notably Senator Howard Metzenbaum of Ohio, appeared to protect the environment; and the United Mine Workers in the eastern coalfields reduced the competition for their jobs. See Ackerman and Hassler's *Clean Coal/Dirty Air: or How the Clean Air Act Became a Multibillion-Dollar Bail-Out for High-Sulfur Coal Producers* (1981) for the definitive description and analysis of the politics of the 1977 Amendments.

Clean Air Act amendments since 1977 have allowed for some innovations that I will discuss later. The Clean Air Acts are hundreds of pages long, and Environmental Protection Agency (EPA) regulators have added thousands of pages of regulations that are based on compliance with particular processes, not on actually improving the air.

A simple, effective Clean Air Act by contrast, would be only a few pages long. It would stipulate standards states must meet, identify how reaching those standards will be measured, and establish penalties for failure. But a simple Clean Air Act would not provide the emotionally satisfying symbolism that drives so much of politics. It also would not contain exemptions for established producers nor would it protect jobs in Eastern and Midwestern coalfields.

Today's Clean Air Act substitutes complying with process for standards, measurement, and penalties. The core element of this process-focused regulation is the State Implementation Plan (SIP). A state produces a SIP to show the EPA how it will comply with federal standards. The typical SIP is thousands of pages long, meaning that there are thousands of state and federal regulators and contractors involved in "creating, maintaining, amending, and reviewing SIPs" (Schwartz, 2004) .

The SIP process focuses on whether the state's SIP has been approved by the EPA, not on whether the state actually improves air quality. States without approved SIPs are heavily fined. States with approved SIPs but who fail to meet air quality standards established by the SIP get an extension from the EPA for meeting the standards and are required to write a new SIP. Mountains of paper (or megabytes of emailed documents) move back and forth between state capitols and Washington DC. Thousands of federal and state bureaucrats and their private contractors keep busily employed. State politicians are able to complain loudly about onerous federal rules. Meanwhile billions of dollars are spent to solve non-problems while real sources of emissions are ignored (Schwartz, 2004).

Many point to the dramatic reductions in SO_2 during the past nearly four decades as evidence that the Clean Air Act has been a great success. But air pollution had been declining before the first Clean Air Act was passed in 1970. What is more, a careful study of similar counties affected by Clean Air Act rules and those that were not affected found "the null hypothesis of zero effect (of the Clean Air Act) cannot be rejected" (Greenstone, 2004). The same author, however, did find that particulate matter (but not SO_2) "declined substantially more in regulated than in unregulated counties during the 1970s and 1980s" (Chay and Greenstone, 2005). So, the regulations based on the Clean Air Act and its several amendments reduced some forms of pollution but not others.

One question to ask is whether the regulations affected improvements already underway. By using seventy years of data, Indur Goklany (1999) found that state and local efforts to clean the air were well underway before the 1970 law was passed. In fact, the rate of improvement slowed as the law started to be implemented. Goklany concluded that economic growth, technological change, and local governments were mainly responsible for the improvements in air quality. David Schoenbrod (2004), New York Law School professor and cofounder of the Natural Resources Defense Council, wrote the following for the back cover of Goklany's book:

Indur Goklany has the audacity to question the premise upon which the federal EPA has built its ever-growing power—that states and cities would fail to control pollution if not under Washington's thumb. By unearthing fascinating records from the first 70 years of this century and bringing them to life, he shows convincingly that America was cleaning up its environment just as fast before EPA came along as afterwards. By taking a cool look at the facts, Goklany reveals the environmental emperor to be wearing hardly a stitch of clothing.

Yes, air quality has improved and continues to improve but whether that improvement is caused by national clean air rules is not clear. Goklany's data suggest the United States has continued a trend that began at least by the beginning of the last century. It is clear that national clean air rules are the source of complex, ponderous administrative systems emphasizing process, not results.

Donning Coase-Colored Glasses[2]

During the past few years policy-makers and some interest groups discovered there are ways to move beyond a Pigouvian analysis and direct regulation by approaching the world with a Coasean analysis. By looking at environmental challenges through Coase-colored glasses, analysts will see problems and, therefore, solutions, differently. And although Coasean analysis may appear to be limited to small groups or narrow problems, it applies quite broadly.

Trading Dirty Air

The 1990 Clean Air Act included some Coasean innovations by creating a cap-and-trade program. Under the Title IV program, emitters were allowed to meet emissions caps any way they liked including buying "excess" emissions reductions from other sources able to cut back more than the amount required by the legislation. In effect, the legislation created tradable pollution permits. It also contained banking provisions that allowed companies that decreased emissions below their cap to save those allowances for future uses.

2. This title is taken from Terry L. Anderson 2004. "Donning Coase-Coloured Glasses: A Property Rights View of Natural Resource Economics." *The Australian Journal of Agricultural and Resource Economics,* 48:3, pp. 445–62.

Despite a host of problems a public choice analysis would predict—who establishes the cap, how secure the permit is, rent seeking by emitters and interest groups—the program has produced some impressive results. For one thing, cap-and-trade shows just how impossible it is for a centralized, Pigouvian system to measure costs. Pre cap-and-trade average costs exceeded $1500 per ton. The EPA estimated cap-and-trade would reduce emission control costs by about $700 per ton. Industry analysts estimated cap-and-trade would reduce costs to about $1300 per ton. The reality was far different as costs from 1995 to 2000 were just $150 per ton and costs under the second phase are about $250 per ton (Schwartz, 2004).

Cost savings were so badly estimated by EPA and industry because there is no *a priori* way to measure the creativity of power plant operators once they had an incentive to find new ways to reduce emissions instead of an incentive to meet technology requirements or regulator-defined procedures. That creativity included

innovations in power plant operation, rail transport and logistics models that included the cost of pollution per kilowatt-hour from each boiler, financial instruments for selling coal with SO_2 pollution allowances included, and scrubber technology that drastically reduced the cost of reducing SO_2 emissions from coal-fired power generation (Schwartz, 2004, email).

American Enterprise Institute analyst Joel Schwartz (2004) concludes from the cap-and-trade story that "regulators or any central planners can never know enough about the details of any activity, industry, or process to identify the least-cost (or even anywhere near the least-cost) approaches for achieving environmental protection." Because regulators and legislators can never know enough, establishing the "right" regulations or Pigouvian tax rates is impossible. Cap-and-trade, however, reduces regulators' roles to establishing and monitoring the caps. Market processes then establish prices and innovation follows.

Water Markets

One of the best examples of applying Coase to environmental issues concerns policies for water quality and quantity (see Gardner and Simmons, 2012 for cases).

Markets in water became a possibility in the arid American West as Congress became unwilling to support more massive water subsidies. The Western Governors' Association, for example, called for an increase in water marketing—allowing water to be bought and sold. Water marketing could really begin to allocate and conserve water currently supplied in federal projects if current water allocations were converted into property rights and issued to existing irrigators. Currently, water allocations not used are taken away from the irrigator so he or she has little incentive to conserve or to seek out those who place a higher value on an alternative use of the water. Allowing farmers to sell water at a profit, by contrast, enforces conservation as farmers waste water at the expense of personal income. Municipalities, in-stream recreational users, other farmers, and transport users could all buy water for their purposes.

In many Western states the law only recognizes property rights to water diverted from a stream. If water is left in the stream someone else can claim it. The Montana legislature changed the law so that private groups or public agencies can lease water from someone who previously diverted the water. The group or agency is allowed to leave the water in the stream for recreational or ecological purposes. By changing the definition of the property right from one requiring diversion to one allowing the water to be left in the stream, Montana moved beyond Pigouvian discussions of externalities and into Coasean discussions of exchanges.

Oregon also allows water to be left in streams without the owner forfeiting the water right. As a result, the Oregon Water Trust was created to keep water in streams that used to suffer from inadequate stream flow or no flow at all during parts of the year. They accomplish their efforts through market exchanges by purchasing water rights outright, trading hay to farmers who leave water in the stream instead of diverting it to water their own hay fields, and funding irrigation efficiency projects. Again, this Coasean approach accomplishes its goals through exchanges instead of regulations or taxes.

The nation that most explicitly uses Coasean water policy is Chile. Chile established the Water Code of Chile in 1981, which created tradable water use property rights, including the right to transfer water from one sector to another, such as from agriculture to mining. The result is that Chile has become a model for how to use property rights to allocate scarce resources. Some problems, such as high transaction costs and disagreements over the initial allocation of rights, continue to exist. As in most markets, there are charges of monopoly power and hoarding but these seem to be caused by inadequate government institutions. One study of the Chilean experience claims that markets and property rights allocate water well because "it transfers water from low value to higher value activities" and that "it puts the burden of information collection on water users and avoids problems of asymmetric information common in centrally planned situations" (Harris, 2003).

Other Environmental Markets

Water markets and markets for emissions are two of the more dramatic applications of property rights and market principles; there are many others, some of which also test the credulity of conventional thinkers. One example is markets in wildlife. Markets for wildlife are widely employed in other nations including seemingly "socialist" Britain where private clubs hold fishing rights to certain streams and rivers. The owners of these valuable resources maintain them in far better condition than are commonly held properties.

Much of Africa's wildlife is threatened with extinction, except on private game ranches, a few national parks, and the "communal" lands where villages are given property rights to the wildlife. Until recently Zimbabwe's Marxist regime actively promoted private game ranching as a means of preserving wildlife and bringing in desired foreign money. In one variation of game ranching, Southern African nations granted property rights to wildlife, including elephants, on the communal lands. The villages are able to sell a portion of their wildlife to hunters. The result? In the face of a doubling of human populations, elephant populations have increased 225 percent since 1989—the year Western nations imposed an ivory trade ban on all of Africa. Southern African countries opposed the international ivory trade ban because they claimed their programs for moving wildlife into markets was far more effective than programs to remove them from markets. In the countries that ban native populations from "owning" and selling hunting rights to elephants—in Kenya for example—elephant populations declined by seventy-five percent. Income from hunting has quadrupled and Southern Africa's elephants benefit 90,000 households. Their problem is that now there may be too many elephants for the available forage, so they may need to sell more hunting safaris, even in the national parks (Child, 2005).

The 200,000-acre Deseret Ranch in northern Utah illustrates how markets can work for wildlife. For several years the wealthy owner used the ranch for tax write-offs and did not particularly care if the ranch produced a profit. But once he had used up his tax benefits he told the ranch manager the employees' salaries would only come out of ranch profits. No profits, no jobs. Just as in the case of power plant managers whose incentives changed dramatically once they could trade emission permits, the cowboys got creative. The ranch manager told me, "You would be surprised how many ideas a cowboy with just two teeth in his head can come up with given the right incentives."

Today the ranch manages cows, sheep, deer, elk, and bison for a profit. Because they can control access by hunters and because they control the habitat, they are able to manage the elk and deer much as they manage the cows, sheep, and bison and charge significant fees for hunting. Although the ranch contains just six-tenths of one percent of the elk habitat in the state, it produces 15 percent of Utah's elk. The elk and deer herds have better age-class stratification than those on public lands. The average mule deer buck on the ranch, for example, is a four-point (western count) with a 22-inch spread. On the public lands, by contrast, the average is a two-point with a 12-inch spread.

The reason that the elk and deer on Deseret Ranch appear "hardier" than the elk and deer on public lands is simple—private property arrangements. Elk, whales, buffalo, snail darters, and birds will all increase in proportion to the property rights held in them by profit-oriented businessmen. There is no shortage of dogs, cats, horses, sheep, cows, chicken, and pigs.

It has also been proposed, notably by Milton Friedman (1962), that our public parks be sold to private investors. Richard Stroup (1990) went one step further and suggested that the national parks be given to "park endowment boards" managed by the leadership of such environmental organizations as the Sierra Club and Audubon Society as privately held property. Stroup contends the parks will be better managed, not because the board's members care more for the natural resources than does the Park Service, but because the board would soon adopt such efficient practices as increasing the park fees. Fees would reduce the damages of overuse by the price mechanism, not by fiat.

Furthermore, the boards would also begin to "exploit" other currently unused resources found within the parks including oil and coal deposits, timber, etc. Revenues from these sales would doubtless be used to maintain and improve the recreational resources and services of the parks as well as acquire new properties. As Americans' preferences move away from plastic goods to natural amenities, Stroup believes the market for park and environmental services will become a growth industry. One need only note that private entrepreneurs are already in the recreational business: ski-lodges, motels, hotels, private lodges, golf and tennis clubs, and RV parks are but a few of the facilities everyone takes for granted.

Why, then, must parks be in the public domain? And, why are so many public parks in disrepair, dangerous, and accorded low status? Perhaps, property rights are misplaced. The Nature Conservancy has for more than four decades purchased and protected ecologically valuable properties for preservation and public use. I have hiked the lovely trails of a Conservancy property located along the Oregon coast, not far from Salishan Lodge. Salishan is one of the top five lodges in the nation and is, itself, a sensitive owner and manager of beautiful forests, ocean beaches, not to speak of restaurants, tennis courts, golf course, hiking trails, and art galleries. The Nature Conservancy, Salishan Lodge, Deseret Ranch, and Zimbabwe's elephants are just a few examples that suggest private property holders can be at least as, if not more, dedicated and efficient at protecting the environment than public agencies.

A Note of Caution

Although markets can address water, sunshine, air, and pollution problems, we cannot simply assume that all is well. The Coase theorem has abstract problems that are not easily shed, and even if they were, we would still face considerable political problems of implementation. At the abstract level, critics have pointed to some highly restrictive conditions including the fact that transaction and administrative costs must be on the low side. Others have argued that the assignment of the initial rights has profound wealth effects with everyone wanting the original title. The original allocation is also critical because in general the amount that someone will pay to acquire something (say, pollution rights) is often less than the amount that must be paid to give it up. Who has the right to demand compensation is exceedingly important.

For pollution, a crucial political decision is the total amount of pollution permitted within an area. This choice may and should be influenced but not dominated by scientific considerations. In democratic processes, citizens are being asked to collectively determine the absolute pollution levels. As we learned in earlier chapters, arriving at a common decision is neither easy nor likely to be optimal. And, there have been bitter political battles over attempts to change the levels. These battles have, in many instances, spilled over into the rules governing the air shed until the regulations made it nearly impossible for the pollution market to function.

Even with these difficulties, when compared to the alternatives of taxation, subsidies, and regulation, markets for pollution have much to commend them. One problem with taxation is obvious: who will become the tax setters and how will the many tax rates be set? Another problem with the tax scheme is its failure to encourage the kind of entrepreneurship and creativity stimulated by property rights. Any regulation system is bound to become immensely complex and subject, of course, to political battles at every session of the legislature or city council.

The worst consequence of political controls is that they do not get at the heart of the emissions problem; they deal with symptoms. I have argued that the basic problem is incompletely assigned property rights. Markets for emissions provide a way of requiring emitters to pay the costs they impose on others. By emitters I mean the ultimate consumers of goods that give rise to emissions. The prices they pay must include the social costs not now taken into account in price setting. Markets for emissions accomplish that end with a minimum of red tape, coercion, and money outlays.

In most of the foregoing examples of looking at environmental policy through Coase-colored glasses there was no assumption that market transactions perfectly capture all of the effects they create. In fact, I assume that the essential role of private entrepreneurs is to operate in that space composed of unaccounted-for effects. It is in that space that entrepreneurs find opportunities to create value, to create gains from trade. Their efforts are easier when property rights and legal rules are clear or can be made at least clearer.

Climate Policy as Politican Environmentalism

Possibly the biggest challenges to private environmental entrepreneurs are environmental problems that cross international boundaries—the transaction costs of dealing in different legal structures and property rights systems are simply huge. The rent-seeking benefits from *political* entrepreneurship in cross boundary problems are also huge. An example is the potential for climate change caused by humans producing greenhouse gases. Although there are many human outputs that might affect climate change, the ones most generally focused on are greenhouse gases, particularly carbon dioxide. As carbon dioxide is released to the atmosphere, primarily through consuming fossil fuels, it accumulates to levels that many climate models predict will cause significant warming—hence the term "global warming." What is more, in terms of effects on atmospheric concentrations, it does not matter whether a ton of carbon dioxide is produced in New York, or Rome, or Beijing because of atmospheric mixing the effects are globalized, not localized.

Government officials wanting to "decarbonize" their economies in order to stabilize atmospheric carbon dioxide concentrations are in an n-person prisoner's dilemma. The world might be better off if all countries agreed to reduce their carbon emissions, but any one country taking major steps to do that without other countries following suit is simply reducing its own wealth and not affecting overall carbon dioxide concentrations in any climatically meaningful way. A country making that choice is taking the "sucker" payoff while other countries free ride. And that "sucker" payoff can be very expensive since there are no easy or inexpensive ways to decarbonize.

International agreements complete with reporting and enforcement mechanisms are potential ways to get out of the climate dilemma and the agreement under which most of the developed world has operated is known as the Kyoto Protocol, which was adopted in 1997 and implemented in 2005. By 2010, 191 countries had ratified and signed the agreement, under which 37 developed nations and the European Union member nations committed themselves to reduce greenhouse gases with the intent of returning to 1990 emissions levels by 2012. Besides putting the responsibility for reducing emissions on developed countries, the Kyoto Protocol committed the developed world to provide billions of dollars of aid to developing countries for emissions control. The developing world is exempt from reducing emissions, including China, India, and Brazil who are among the top-ten emitters of greenhouse gases—China is the top producer. The one developed country that rejected the Kyoto Protocol is the United States where the U.S. Senate voted 95–0 in 1997 to inform President

Clinton that they would not ratify it. The Kyoto agreement to reduce emissions expires in 2012 and Japan, Russia, and Canada announced in 2010 that they would not sign on for a second commitment unless China and poorer nations would agree to make cuts in their own emissions.

A public choice analysis of climate change politics predicts that the necessities of electoral politics will drive the climate change policy debate on the national level. Bureaucrats will use the process to increase budgets and influence, interest groups will seek political rents and use the process to pursue ideological commitments having nothing to do with climate, voters will remain generally uninformed but sympathetic to "doing something," and entrepreneurial politicians will maximize their chances of re-election by catering to both bureaucrats and special interests. It would be surprising if the process operated in any other way.

The "Conference of Parties" of the United Nations Framework Convention on Climate Change meets annually and the venues are nice, very nice. The list so far includes Berlin, Geneva, Kyoto, Buenos Aires (twice), The Hague, Bonn, Marrakech, New Delhi, Milan, Montreal, Nairobi, Bali, Poznan, Copenhagen, and Cancun. These are continuing rounds of meetings where politicians, bureaucrats, and green activists talk about reaching international accords about what steps all countries will take but these meetings continue to produce little more than an agreement to continue the process another year. Of course there are, as in the 2010 Cancun meetings, non-deals reached for industrialized countries to send billions of dollars per year to developing countries (no source for the funds was identified) and delegates to the meeting pretend the funds will materialize. Country representatives make non-binding pledges on carbon emissions and everyone pretends to believe the pledges will actually be kept. Any new treaty signed will be pointlessly weak or impossible to get through the U.S. Senate.

There are winners in this game. Some are the bureaucrats and NGO staff who act as political entrepreneurs as they hold pre-meeting meetings, hire more staff, and circulate new papers on the dangers of climate change, which justify their budgets and activities. They benefit from having the negotiation process continue, and continue, and continue. Thus, delegates to the meetings claim success at each round of meetings and talk about the long journey toward eventually reaching "a legally binding global climate framework," as the European Union's top climate official put it in the 2010 Cancun meeting.

Other winners are politicians who need some symbol to show their green constituents. As long as the meetings and promises of reform continue, the politicians can hold them up as successes. The head of the UN Framework Convention on Climate Change quite candidly explained the process when he was asked whether it mattered that Australia had passed its promised emissions trading legislation before the 2009 Copenhagen meetings. He said, "Quite honestly, no. What people care about in the international negotiations is the commitment that a government makes to take on a certain target" (Pielke Jr., 2010, 111). That is, *promising* to do something is at least as effective as actually *doing* it.

Other potential winners are company executives and hedge fund managers who hope to gain protections and other market advantages, even cartel power, from any of the agreements. If the right agreements are reached the companies will have investments protected and their markets made more secure. No wonder General Electric, Dow Chemical, General Motors and Duke Energy are part of the U.S. Climate Action Partnership, the coalition promoting carbon cap-and-trade in the United States. The Partnership even authored most of the 2010 American Power Act sponsored by Senators John Kerry and Joe Lieberman.

One way to understand the continuing process is through the Bootleggers and Baptists metaphor in which environmentalists are the Baptists and companies, trade association, and countries that seek favors under the Protocol's rules are the bootleggers. Politicians are the political entrepreneurs who bring the two groups together. Bruce Yandle, the originator of the bootleggers and Baptists metaphor, examined the Kyoto Protocol in 1998 and again in 2010 and noted,

> Somewhat unexpected coalitions of environmentalists and energy producers still sing together from green hymn books that call for final implementation of the Kyoto-blessed cap-and-trade greenhouse gas controls. However, there is a difference to be observed in how the singers make their music: The interest groups have learned to harmonize better. For example, a U.S. Climate Action Partnership, formed by some leading industrial firms and environmental groups, lobbies strenuously in support of federal cap-and-trade legislation. The industrial players are firms that will gain market share in resulting restructured energy markets. They are green in more ways than one—as in money. Contributions rise for

the environmental groups when they sing in harmony. Environmental organizations are also green in more ways than one (Yandle, 2010,).

Yandle pointed out that under the Kyoto Protocol developed countries make promises and even take actions to decarbonize while China, India, Brazil, and others increase their carbon output. He compared that situation to people patching holes in one end of a leaky boat while other people are boring larger holes in the other end. He concluded, "As was the case in 1998, this last observation suggests there is more to the story than emissions control. The themes of favor-seeking and wealth transfers still seem to explain outcomes."

A favorite rent-seeking proposal is to mimic successful regional cap-and-trade policies by creating a world-wide, carbon cap-and-trade system. The European Union has already created its own cap-and-trade system and the 2010 American Power Act would have created one for the United States if it had passed. Carbon cap-and-trade enthusiasts talk about carbon trading under such a system as if it makes decarbonizing nearly free. Germany's environment minister claimed, for example, that because of carbon trading Germany could close nuclear plants and replace them with eight to twelve new coal-fired plants. That is, they could close plants that produce no carbon emissions and replace them with ones that generate a lot of carbon emissions. The minister explained that by purchasing offsets, "You can build a hundred coal-fired power plants and don't have to have higher carbon emissions" (Pielke Jr., 2010, 111). In his role as political entrepreneur, the minister combined both coal and environmental interests to maximize his political payoff.

Offsets can come from companies who reduce their own carbon output and, therefore, have credits to sell. Others come from changes in agricultural practices and from rain forest preservation (the forests are carbon sinks). Most offsets are based on claims about what would otherwise have happened. These claims are really just stories about an unknowable future. The "savings" in these stories are turned into marketable carbon credits that European Union producers can purchase in order to exceed legally mandated caps on their emissions.

Political entrepreneurs in the NGO realm have also discovered opportunities to profit from this trend towards carbon offsetting. The World Wildlife Fund, for example, hopes to be able to sell some of the $60 billion of offsets that can be gained by offering guarantees to protect large portions of the Brazilian rain forest.

The World Wildlife Fund, private foundations, the World Bank, investment fund managers, and the Brazilian government are all involved in lobbying to have the potential offsets in Brazil recognized by the governing body of the UN Framework Convention on Climate Change as tradable credits. The scheme is impressive in its scope as it designates 9.5 million acres of rainforest to be protected from deforestation. These proposed credits will not reduce carbon production since that portion of the rain forest is in no danger of being deforested. Countries like Germany can, however, build many more coal-fired electricity generating plants by purchasing offsets from the rain forest. Thus, if the proposal is approved, WWF and its allies gain a huge financial transfer from carbon emitters while not providing any climate benefit. In fact, carbon emissions will increase.

Unintended consequences and even outright fraud exist within the European Union's cap-and-trade system. Companies in India and China, for example, produce HFC-23, a potent greenhouse gas that is used in the semi-conductor industry and as a refrigerant. Once the European Union allowed companies to pay the Chinese and Indian companies to destroy the gas in exchange for carbon credits, a lively market developed. The unintended consequence is that the carbon credits were worth more than the gas itself, so the producers increased production in order to have more credits to sell (Pielke Jr., 2010, 110). The Chinese government also manipulated the Europeans into providing wind-farm subsidies for wind projects which would have been built without the subsidies and for projects that are not even connected to the electrical grid. About one-third of China's wind turbines are not connected to the grid and were apparently built just for the credits.

The HFC-23 and Chinese wind-farm subsidies are two examples among many of how international cap-and-trade programs can and will be manipulated. Do not expect that the problems with cap-and-trade will cause such programs to be replaced with much better policies. The reason is rather simple: there is an increasing potential of billions of dollars to be made whether or not there is any positive effect on emissions. The proposed WWF project, for example, has $60 billion at stake. There are many more projects where powerful bootlegger interests are aligning themselves with environmental Baptists to make themselves better off.

Several other problems exist. Even if the developed countries meet their Kyoto pledges there will be no significant effect on global warming—climate models predict there would be just a few hundredths of a degree difference by

2050. Also, pledges from the developed to developing world are weak and symbolic. They are weak in that they are not binding; they are just unenforceable promises. They are symbols designed to appease the apparent desires of rationally uninformed voters. They also have politically unworkable conditions attached to them such as the $100 billion in aid to developing countries pledged in Cancun. Since that aid is unlikely to be delivered to developing countries, their leaders will feel free to promote policies that continue to increase carbon output.

The even bigger political problem is the fundamental restructuring of the developed world's economies that would be necessary to decarbonize at promised rates. That is, of course, the desire of many climate change activists who are using climate change as a reason to attempt to transfer wealth from rich to poor nations. German economist and Intergovernmental Panel on Climate Change (IPCC) official Ottmar Eddenhofer, explained prior to the Cancun conference in an interview with the Global Warming Policy Foundation (Potter, 2010):

> First of all, developed countries have basically expropriated the atmosphere of the world community. But one must say clearly that we redistribute de facto the world's wealth by climate policy. Obviously, the owners of coal and oil will not be enthusiastic about this. One has to free oneself from the illusion that international climate policy is environmental policy. This has almost nothing to do with environmental policy anymore, with problems such as deforestation or the ozone hole . . . Basically it's a big mistake to discuss climate policy separately from the major themes of globalization. The climate summit in Cancun at the end of the month is not a climate conference, but one of the largest economic conferences since the Second World War.

In a paper prepared for the Cancun conference Professor Kevin Anderson, Director of the Tyndall Centre for Climate Change Research, said the only way to reduce global emissions enough, while allowing the poor nations to continue to grow, is to halt economic growth in the rich world over the next twenty years. He called for World War II-type rationing of electricity in order to force people to conserve (Gray, 2010).

Calls for economic pain run up against what Roger Pielke Jr. in his 2010 book *The Climate Fix* called "the iron law of climate policy." The iron law is that economic objectives will have more weight in politics than will environmental objectives. Pielke pointed to a 2009 U.S. poll to illustrate about support for potential increased household costs from a climate bill. The poll found that a majority would accept an annual increase of $80 but that support dropped by half at $175 per year. At an increase of US$770 per year, opponents outnumbered supporters nearly 10 to one. Pielke concludes that any successful policy for decarbonizing economies must provide clear short-term benefits commensurate with the short term costs. If policies do not coincide with people's economic goals the policies will fail.

Given that current and proposed climate policies run up against the iron law of climate policy and are rent seeking opportunities that provide symbolic (non-)agreements, is there a meaningful climate policy? No one has yet developed a way to establish property rights to air or climate and cap-and-trade policies attempt to create something from nothing—magic carbon credits in exchange for promises to not develop. What is left aside from adapting if negative climate changes occur? Many economists suggest a Pigouvian carbon tax. There is even an informal group known as the Pigou Club that supports the U.S. Congress raising taxes on gasoline by 10 cents per year over a decade so that the tax eventually reaches $1 per gallon. The plan is far less complex than the rent-seeking-filled cap-and-trade bills proposed in Congress. The proponents claim it would reduce carbon production, make CAFE standards meaningless as people voluntarily seek higher MPG vehicles, put the costs where they should be—on consumers, and could substitute for some income taxes. Of course all the caveats identified earlier in this chapter about not knowing what is the appropriate tax; difficulties of monitoring emissions; unexpected responses by consumers; and the possibility that the tax is wrongheaded, based on incorrect information, or in the hands of ideological zealots still apply. But much of the rent-seeking and meaningless symbolism that are integral parts of large-scale cap-and-trade systems would be avoided.

The most innovative tax idea comes from Ross McKitrick (2008), a professor of economics at Canada's University of Guelph who specializes in environmental economics and policy analysis. He is skeptical about the claims regarding human-caused climate change and has published many scientific articles on the subject. His proposal, however, ought to appeal to believers and non-believers alike. He proposes a carbon tax that increases or decreases depending on the amount of warming that actually happens in the tropical troposphere, which is the lowest layer of the atmosphere. He suggests the tropical troposphere because climate models predict that is where there will be the first and strongest signals of human-caused global warming. Although he suggests a relatively low tax of about $5 per ton of carbon dioxide as a baseline, the tax will increase dramatically along with temperature and would reach $200 per ton by 2100 if some of the climate models are correct. If they are not correct, the tax could fall to zero.

There are at least four strongly positive features of McKitrick's proposal. First, the tax rate starts low enough to not bump up against the iron law of climate policy. Second, no one has to gamble in advance about whether the climate models are correct. Increasing warming produces increased taxes per ton of carbon dioxide produced. Decreasing or no warming reduces the taxes. Third, the tax will cause investors and producers to be forward looking rather than looking to government for political rents. Today's tax rate will not affect today's behavior as much as expectations about future tax obligations. They must plan today for rates ten and twenty years out and they will incorporate expected future taxes into their planning. Fourth, tying tax rates to temperature will create a new market for private-sector climate modeling as firms seek reliable information to build into their planning processes. Competition among climate modelers in this new market would remove climate modeling from a political arena with its short time horizons into a private arena with a large range of time horizons. And actual warming or cooling would be the measure of a good model, not politicians, bureaucrats, or NGO officials.

Conclusions

Current environmental policies are based on antipathy for business, support for increasing government intervention and regulation, and a belief that the ecology and economy are conflicting systems. I have suggested just the opposite: environmental protection is best achieved by extending property rights to environmental resources and relying on market transactions. Economy and ecology harmonize when property rights are clear.

From the earlier chapters it should be clear why I believe that only a private, decentralized system can enlist the dispersed knowledge necessary for wise resource management, and why a property rights system is the best way to create the incentives for people to act on that information. The information and incentive problems so easily handled by markets are at the heart of government mismanagement.

Obviously, there are many difficulties with extending markets and property rights to environmental goods now controlled politically or that cross political boundaries, but those difficulties are not unique to the environmental arena. The creative student might attempt to apply lessons from successful privatization programs worldwide to extending property rights to the environment.

Bibliographical Notes

The overproduction of words about the environment is analogous to the externalities environmental activists are so concerned about. Perhaps, word pollution should be subjected to the very harsh policies that mainstream environmentalists are so eager to have applied to others for much of the literature is the policy equivalent of garbage. There are, however, a handful of works that are valuable, including some famous essays. The first essay is Ronald Coase's extraordinary "The Problem of Social Cost," first published in 1960 by the *Journal of Law and Economics* 3 (October 1960), 1–44. Without using mathematics or even much economic jargon, Coase correctly diagnosed the nature of externalities and, therefore, what needed to be done about them. That essay plus his 1937 piece on the nature of the firm garnered him the Nobel Prize. In another essay, "The Lighthouse in Economics" (1974), Coase examined the claim that lighthouses were public goods and, therefore, could not be provided privately. He found, contrary to conventional wisdom, that lighthouse services could be and were provided by private enterprise. English lighthouses were built, operated, financed, owned, and sold by private individuals whose agents collected tolls at English ports. Coase's lighthouse study suggests markets may fail less easily than thought by many theorists.

A less famous but most influential article is Steven N. S. Cheung's piece with the intriguing title, "The Fable of the Bees: An Economic Investigation," in *Journal of Law and Economics* 16 (1973) in which the Coasean tradition is further refined and applied. Here the externalities—beneficial—of bees and beekeepers are explored in an imaginative exercise of the mind.

A few books deserve citation. Terry Anderson and Donald Leal published *Free Market Environmentalism* (New York: Palgrave) in 1991, and it is now in a second edition. It is the systematic exploration of how to apply markets and property rights to the environment. The authors explore topics as diverse as homesteading the oceans and the history of the American West.

Another extremely interesting and devastating attack on mainstream environmentalism is the book by Bjorn Lomborg, *The Skeptical Environmentalist: Measuring the Real State of the World* (Cambridge: Cambridge University Press, 2001). Lomborg notes that his title "is a play on the world's best known book on the environment, *The State of the World.*" A new version of that book is published each year by Worldwatch Institute and has sold more than a million copies. Read *The State of the World* (New York: W.W. Norton, 2007) and then read Lomborg. Probably no book has stirred the mainstream environmental community to more vitriolic attacks than has Lomborg's. The attacks and his responses are available on his website at http://www.lomborg.com/.

To read a wide variety of authors as they examine Community-Based Natural Resource Management (CBNRM) in Africa, find a copy of Brian Child's edited volume, *Parks in Transition: Biodiversity, Rural Development and the Bottom Line* (London: Earthscan, 2004). Child, who has a PhD in economics from the London School of Economics, has spent his life in Southern African wildlife management. An email received from him in May 2007 said,

> I am in Namibia looking at CBNRM . . . CAMPFIRE (Zimbabwe's version of CBNRM) is still doing well, especially where it has devolved to the level of real face-to-face democracy. In fact, I am about to get two Zim students to look at why CAMPFIRE was so robust, but the similar work I did in Zambia collapsed almost immediately . . . Must go—working on dial-up in a remote area.

Another book well worth reading is *Who Owns the Environment?* (Lanham, Maryland: Rowman and Littlefield, 1998) edited by Peter J. Hill and Roger E. Meiners. All the chapters are worth reading, but two stand out. The first is Bruce Yandle's "Coase, Pigou, and Environmental Rights." It explains Coase better than Coase does. The second is Elizabeth Brubaker's "The Common Law and the Environment: The Canadian Experience." It is the best single source I know for understanding common law applications to the environment.

The best book to date on climate policy is *The Climate Fix: What Scientists and Politicians won't tell you about Global Warming* by Roger Pielke Jr. Pielke argues that climate policies must be compatible with economic growth or they will fail. He injects a large and needed dose of pragmatism into the climate policy debates. He is also somewhat Hayekian in his approach as he promotes what he calls "oblique approaches" and decentralized, incremental policies. Something that sets him apart in the climate debate is what one reviewer noted was a respect for "the dignity of humans that obliges us to respect individual choices and help those in poverty improve their lives."

Bibliography

Ackerman, Bruce A. and William T. Hassler. *Clean Coal—Dirty Air.* New Haven: Yale University Press, 1981.

Anderson, Terry and Donald Leal. *Free Market Environmentalism.* New York: Palgrave, 1991.

Ballard v. Tomlinson 1885 LR 29 Ch.D 115.

Chay, Kenneth Y. and Michael Greenstone. "Does Air Quality Matter? Evidence from the Housing Market." *Journal of Political Economy* 113 (April 2005, pp. 376–424.

Cheung, Steven N. S. "The Fable of the Bees." *Journal of Law and Economics* 16 (1973) pp. 11–33.

Child, Brian. *Parks in Transition: Biodiversity, Rural Development and the Bottom Line.* London: Earthscan, 2004.

Coase, Ronald H. "The Lighthouse in Economics." *Journal of Law and Economics,* 17 (2): (1960), pp. 357–76.

Coase, Ronald H. "The Nature of the Firm," *Economica,* 4 (16): (November, 1937), pp. 386–405.

Coase, Ronald H. "The Problem of Social Cost," *Journal of Law and Economics,* 3 (October, 1960), pp. 1–44.

Friedman, David. *Law's Order: What Economics Has To Do with Law and Why It Matters.* Princeton: Princeton University Press, 2000.

Friedman, Milton. *Capitalism and Freedom.* Chicago: University of Chicago Press, 1962, p. 31.

Gardner, B. Delworth and Randy T. Simmons, eds. *Aquanomics: Water Markets and the Environment,* New Jersey: Transaction Publishers, 2012.

Goklany, Indur. *Clearing the Air: The Real Story of the War on Air Pollution.* Washington, DC: Cato Institute, 1999.

Gray, Louise. "Cancun Climate Change Summit: Scientists Call for Rationing in Developed World." *The Telegraph,* Nov 29, 2010. http://www.webcitation.org/5u145RnTn.

Greenstone, Michael. "Did the Clean Air Act Amendments Cause the Remarkable Decline in Sulfur Dioxide Concentrations?" *Journal of Environmental Economics and Management* (2004) 47.

Harris, Guillermo Donoso. "Water markets: Case Studies of Chile's 1981 Water Code." *Ciencia e Investigación Agraria* 33 (2): (2006), pp. 151–71.

Hill, Peter J. and Roger E. Meiners. *Who Owns the Environment?* Lanham, MD: Rowman and Littlefield, 1998.

Huber, Ruitenbreek and Seroa da Motta. 1998, cited in Kraemer, R.A., Pielen, B. and A. Leipprand, 2003: *Economic Instruments for Water Management: Extra-Regional Experiences and Their Applicability in Latin America and the Caribbean*, in: Inter-American Development Bank—Regional Policy Dialogue (Hrsg.): Environment Network—Economic Instruments for Water Management: Experiences from Europe and Implications for Latin America and the Caribbean, Regional Policy Dialogue Study Series, Washington D.C., Inter-American Development Bank—Regional Policy Dialogue: 3–55.

Lomborg, Bjorn. *The Skeptical Environmentalist: Measuring the Real State of the World.* Cambridge: Cambridge University Press, 2001.

McKitrick, Ross. "A Simple State-Contingent Pricing Rule for Complex Intertemporal Externalities." *Energy & Environment*, Volume 19, Number 5, pp. 707–11, September 2008. http://ssrn.com/abstract=1154157.

Pielke, Roger, Jr. *The Climate Fix: What Scientists and Politicians Won't Tell you About Global Warming.* New York: Basic Books, 2010.

Portney, Paul R. "Air Pollution Policy," in Portney, Paul R., ed., *Public Policies for Environmental Protection.* Washington, DC: Resources for the Future, 1990, pp. 27–96.

Portney, Paul R. "Policy Watch: Economics and the Clean Air Act," *Journal of Economic Perspectives,* 4 (Fall, 1990), pp. 173–81.

Potter, Bernard, IPCC Official: "Climate Policy Is Redistributing The World's Wealth." November 14, 2010. http://thegwpf.org/ipcc-news/1877-ipcc-official-climate-policy-is-redistributing-the-worlds-wealth.html.

Schwartz, Joel 2004. "Finding Better Ways to Achieve Cleaner Air." American Enterprise Institute for Public Policy Research, *Environmental Policy Outlook* (September–October 2004).

Stroup, Richard L. "Rescuing Yellowstone from Politics: Expanding Parks while Reducing Conflict," in Baden, John A. and Donald Leal, eds. *The Yellowstone Primer: Land and Resource Management in the Greater Yellowstone Ecosystem.* San Francisco: Pacific Research Institute for Public Policy, 1990, pp. 169–84.

Whalen v. Union Bag & Paper Co. 208 N. Y. 1.

Worldwatch. *The State of the World.* New York: W. W. Norton, 2007.

Yandle, Bruce. "Bootleggers, Baptists, and Global Warming." *PERC Reports:* Volume 28, No. 2, Summer 2010. http://www.perc.org/files/PRsummer10.pdf.

Yandle, Bruce. "Who Owns the Environment?" in *Who Owns the Environment,* Peter J. Hill and Roger E. Meiners, eds. Lanham, Maryland: Rowman and Littlefield, 1998.

14

Political Pursuit of Private Gain
Coercive Redistribution

THAT MEMBERS OF occupational groups, including well-paid professionals and highly successful businessmen, seek still greater wealth and income should be no great surprise; they are simply *Homo economi,* or wealth-maximizing citizens operating in a capitalist and democratic society. That they have a comparative advantage in rent seeking has been shown in some detail. What we have yet to consider are the wealth-maximizing activities of those who have not and are not doing well in the private economy. Some of these individuals made bad choices; some were born with disabilities; some became ill and cannot fend for themselves; some suffer "bad luck"; some are born in "hopeless" social circumstances; others are improvident; and still others prefer leisure or lower-paying work. In any event, there are some citizens who cannot readily care for themselves. What is to be their fate in a capitalist economy governed by democratic processes?

Adam Smith's hidden hand provides neither an apparent nor an appropriate way of demonstrating genuine concern for others. Still, most people appear to have some semblance of concern for others, especially those who are close and may share a commonality such as family, race, religion, nationality, occupation, or class. Such bonds of potential identification may provide motivation to offer care and wherewithal. Altruism is a well-established fact of human existence; its prevalence is easily observed but difficult to measure because it occurs in so many private ways. The most prevalent means are so common they are taken for granted; we refer especially to mothers and fathers whose sacrifices are seemingly without bounds. Obviously parents consider a child worth more than the now estimated $500,000 it takes to raise and see one through college.

At another level we may learn that substantial amounts are given ($308 billion in 2008 according to the Center on Philanthropy at Indiana University) to charitable causes and organizations and about 75 percent of that comes from individuals. While such giving is substantial it is not likely to identify or provide decent care and income to all those in distress. Much of the charitable funds go not to the destitute, but to civic organizations and activities such as museums, universities, Boy Scouts and Girl Scouts, the Sierra Club, and so on. That the cost of care for millions of unfortunate people is high goes without saying, but equally important is the public good element in altruism and its concomitant free-rider potential and incentives. Coerced contributions from people who would otherwise not give, offers one a means of solving the free-rider dilemma. Indeed, and contrary to much opinion, those who initiate redistributive action are not always the intended recipients, but rather potential donors. Whereas beneficiaries of redistribution are usually unable to muster sufficient political resources, the well-off donors possess the needed political resources—information, tax incentives, status, income, etc. By enacting state-directed welfare programs for the less well-off, wealthy donors accomplish two things of immediate importance to themselves: increases in the income of the poor and a reduced personal share in providing the higher benefits. State coercion for the good of the less well off hardly seems an imposition since those promoting the reforms do not know the taxpayers, or their burdens. And, of course, the taxpayer will hardly know how much she is, in fact, paying for support of the poor. Even if she knew, she may approve of the policy and sacrifice as part of a biblical command, a civic responsibility, or offering the public appearance of doing good.

Expenditures on social welfare programs have grown dramatically for the past several decades. A decent concern for alleviating poverty, even when combined with self-interest, does not exhaust possible explanations of growing welfare budgets. Marxists, as well as some public choice analysts, contend (and not without reason) that state expenditures on the less well off are rational responses on the part of capitalists to buy off disgruntled and potential revolutionists. Such payments are considered part of the "social capital" of capital economies. While social unrest may be reduced by such policies we doubt that "the capitalists," in fact, consciously act as a group to bribe the poor. They too face a free-rider problem. Instead, we see other powerful groups having shared interests in expanding the welfare expenditures of government including bureaucrats who administer programs, politicians who provide funds, and intellectuals who justify redistribution.

Many of our current social welfare programs were enacted during the New Deal when the normal low unemployment rolls were suddenly increased by millions of otherwise responsible, hard-working people. These working and middle class groups demanded that government do something about their plight—a plight not of their own doing. Politicians responded and were rewarded by votes and reelection. Regardless of their ultimate failure in reducing unemployment (still nearly one in five was unemployed in 1938), President Roosevelt and the Democratic Party were hailed for their efforts and commitments by those who believed themselves befriended by New Deal policies. A new and loyal generation of Democratic voters was created. While self-interest was a powerful motivator of voter support for welfare policies, it was also true that self-interest was generalized into an ethic for equality based on "entitlements." Subsequent intellectuals on the Left provided appealing arguments for democratic equality to counter the traditional inequality and personal responsibility characteristics of the market. Having helped create the growth industry of redistribution, redistributionist intellectuals also increased demand for the use of their scarce polemical skills.

As New Deal and later Great Society redistributive programs proliferated, new agencies came into being and created jobs for those who wanted to do good as well as those who wished subsequently to do well for themselves. Since the taxpaying public will ordinarily not tolerate outright grants or cash transfers, detailed, cumbersome controls were deemed mandatory. And the bureaucrats, even those whose sole motivation was to do good, profited from having to administer the detailed controls and red tape demanded by taxpayers. Doing good costs money; doing more good costs more money.

Not all who join government as bureaucrats share the convictions and motivations of their "more" benevolent counterparts. Some even develop a curious antipathy for the people they serve while others want nothing more than a secure job and an easy day. Sooner or later, the highly motivated egalitarian ideologue succumbs to bureaucratic routine or is replaced by a self-interested career aspirant. This routinization of benevolence deprives both the do-gooder and the beneficiary of pride, a fact that all reformers ought but seldom respect. Still, it seems appropriate to assume that most bureaucrats choose to work in agencies of their preference and that a person who joins the Department of Defense prefers to work on defense while a person caring about the problems of the poor chooses to work in a social welfare agency. If this is the case, it confirms the proposition that personal motivations reinforce selfish bureaucratic propensities for enlarging budgets; that is, doing more good things requires a larger budget. I am also inclined to the belief that most people wish to interpret their self-concerns as other-directed concerns. The mutual reinforcement of these beliefs serves on the one hand to improve employee performance but also overall bureaucratic inefficiency, i.e., the highly motivated energy of individuals is allocated into socially undesirable projects.

An ideology of equality and entitlement borne of desperate conditions has now taken such hold that even able supporters of effective capitalistic institutions are placed on the defensive. U.S. presidents find themselves in the uncomfortable position of having to justify their actions to reduce budgets while providing counter-claims that they had actually increased welfare expenditures and the number of citizens protected by such programs. In any case, claims for democratic equality tend to prevail over efficiency and economic inequality. The very wealthy must usually conceal their status especially if founded on inherited wealth. The birthdays of the capitalists are not celebrated. Clearly, a person wishing to defend market institutions that generate social good not out of good intentions, but from selfish motives, has a devilish problem on his hands. So long as this remains the case, the ideology of capitalism will remain on the defensive.

The Quest for Equality: Some Inconvenient Facts

The facts about government redistribution from the better to the less well off will, ironically, disturb both those who value and detest inequality. As for the facts, by 2007, 53 percent of all U.S. citizens received direct benefits mostly from the federal government (Trumbull, 2007). Benefits deemed public goods and therefore available to all such as defense, highways, and education were not included in the estimates. Most beneficiaries were and remain middle-class, entitled to benefits regardless of their private income. Social Security, Medicare, railroad retirement benefits, unemployment compensation, educational assistance and veterans' benefits are the best-known transfers.

In addition to the middle-class recipients, low-income recipients are aided by need-based programs more commonly understood as welfare. According to the U.S. Census Bureau's Survey of Income and Program Participation (Palumbo, 2010), 24 percent of U.S. households received aid from one or more means-tested programs during an average month in 2008 compared to 16 percent in 1984. The survey showed that about 45 percent of Americans lived in a household in which at least one member received benefits from one or more government-sponsored social welfare program. Conservatives are disturbed by these expenditures because they document an extraordinary dependence on government of nearly 50 percent of the nation. Similarly the same figures may disturb both liberal and radical because they suggest the continual failure of capitalism and a liberal society to adequately provide for its citizens. The latter critics may also contend that social welfare expenditures while substantial in the aggregate are highly deceptive, because actual benefits received (especially by welfare recipients) are considered woefully inadequate to sustain a decent life. Although there is truth in both these views, there are more devastating criticisms to be voiced.

Although social expenditures have increased notably during the past fifty years, little equalization has been accomplished. This inconvenient fact is further buttressed when one takes into account the tax side of the ledger. Billions of dollars are taxed reducing the welfare of those taxed but not enhancing that of recipients. In short, while vast amounts of money are transferred from one pocket to another (44 percent of all U.S. government spending at all levels), many transfers have the peculiar habit of moving within the same rather than across income groups. In other words, members of the same income classes support one another as well as pay the cost of transference.

More depressing still is the "leaky-bucket" phenomenon (Okun, 1975); a dollar authorized for the poor usually means they get something less with administration, administrators, and suppliers taking the difference. Based on 2005 Census Bureau statistics, it would take an average expenditure of $2,299 per individual in families and $5,295 per individual not living in families to bring the incomes of the 37 million living below the government's official poverty line out of poverty. In 2004, federal outlays for Temporary Aid for Needy Families totaled $18 billion, compared with $24 billion for Food Stamp benefits, $30 billion for Supplemental Security Income benefits for nonelderly recipients, $33 billion for the Earned Income Tax Credit, and $114 billion for the federal share of Medicaid spending on benefits for nonelderly people. Adding these together and dividing by the 37 million individuals living below the official U.S. poverty line results in an average expenditure of $7,775 per person—far more than is necessary to bring these individuals above the poverty line. Clearly the welfare bucket has huge leaks.

The Tax Policy Foundation (a joint venture of the Urban Institute and Brookings Institution) estimated that only about half of Americans paid any income taxes when they filed their returns in April 2010. They had enough credits, deductions, or exemptions to cancel any tax liability or they simply did not make enough money. And although people in every income category received transfer payments, people earning less than about $50,000 profited from their fiscal interactions with the federal government. That is, when taxes are subtracted from transfer payments, they were net beneficiaries. And, interestingly, those who lose are the higher income earners. Those families earning more than $100,000 paid, on average, nearly $60,000 in taxes, while receiving less than $7,000 in transfer payments. This raises a most important point: why do the wealthy permit this loss to occur and why the transfer to the less well off? One answer, already given, is that the wealthy may have a sense of noblesse oblige and/or altruistic impulses. Another, also noted above, is that the wealthy are taking out "social insurance" to preserve their position. And still another explanation is based on the notion that the better off are simply minimizing the costs of inevitable redistribution. Unfortunately, motives are not easily attributed. Explaining the existing ratios of private and public redistribution and why certain programs are adopted rather than others is important but unresolved.

Although certain obvious group gains from redistribution have been realized, little progress toward general equality has been achieved. The terrible truth is that most of our anti-poverty programs are misplaced and perverse; a poverty class has been perpetuated if not created by a public policy based on being generous. Being politically generous in the short run, however, solves neither the problem of why people are poor nor why they remain poor. The only realistic policy is one that encourages private economic growth thereby increasing employment opportunities and real income. But being for growth usually requires public policies that are interpreted by many as initially favorable to the well off. Reduced inflation rates, higher savings, greater investment, improved competitive markets: all provide increased welfare but only indirectly and in the long term. Such policies do not seem to offer immediate assistance to teen-age kids in poverty, the poor single parent, or the person for whom crime seems a rational pursuit among severely limited legitimate opportunities.

Redistribution in the Real World of Democracy

The answers to the foregoing questions are really quite simple and, once the basic premises of the analysis are accepted, everything follows in a straightforward manner. People make use of government as they do all social institutions: for the purpose of advancing their own welfare, and this is accomplished, primarily by demanding special benefits and dispersing their costs among others. Even in seeking more general or essentially public goods they may profit through being a supplier to government of those goods. And, of course, they seek to minimize their share of the tax burdens. Since no citizen by himself can achieve these goals, coalition partners are sought, partners just sufficient in number to win (a minimal winning coalition) and sometimes individually "weaker" than the person seeking allies. A minimal-winning-size coalition ensures that the costs of the rent seeking will be less than the sought-after gains of income redistribution while the "weakness" condition maximizes one's share of the winnings. The problem of course is that everyone becomes a member of many coalitions and is forced therefore to pay out substantial rent seeking and protection costs as well as increased benefits for all other coalitions. In short, we all run the risk of having our own benefits outweighed by the increasing costs of supporting the gains of countless others. But this is a highly uncertain calculation; we simply do not have an accurate public accounting system to handle all the transactions.

It is important to emphasize that, in our polity, redistribution is accomplished by direct and indirect transfers and that most indirect transfers are unintentional. Subsidies for corn ethanol, for example, also subsidize seed and equipment sellers and corn farming labor. They also direct corn toward ethanol plants and away from food processors, such as those that produce corn flour for tortillas. Ethanol subsidies, therefore, apparently reduce the amount of corn available for food. Even direct expenditures on pure public goods generate unwanted redistribution. Equal consumption necessarily means that some citizens must "consume" more than they wish, while others are coerced into consumption levels short of their ideals. Thus, no public expenditure or tax instrument is ever revenue neutral. Private market choices are necessarily affected.

Because all fiscal and monetary policies are redistributive (see Chapter 15), they are controversial, and because none are ever simple in their workings, it is apparent that redistribution will take place in such a manner that identifying all beneficiaries and taxpayers is most difficult. Accordingly, few simplistic predictions about redistribution from higher to lower income groups ("vertical redistribution") will hold true. Redistribution may be horizontal, that is, within a single class grouping, and may proceed upward as well as downward in the overall class "structure." As to horizontal redistribution, cross-subsidies such as urban postal users subsidizing rural users provide a beautiful example. Then, too, an individual may sometimes do very well while at other times not so well. That is one reason, but hardly the only one, why the Congress enacts "transition rules" to ease unexpected burdens resulting from important changes in tax laws. Whenever vast new government programs come into being the consequences are apt to be widespread, consequential, and somewhat unpredictable. And worse, neither the beneficiary nor the harmed may have any good idea of their fate or how it was decided. The macro or aggregate results summed up by income category are usually not terribly helpful in explaining unique outcomes for individual citizens. Each person's own situation is usually bewilderingly complex and unique.

Despite these general cautions, it would appear that certain generalizations can be made about who gets what. In the first place, most social scientists, and especially political scientists, claim that transfers generally move from the less to the more organized citizens. Interest group analysis in political science has long maintained that it can be no other way, and modern public choice confirms that earlier proposition. The argument in support of the idea is the familiar claim that special interest organizations have all the political advantages including incentives, organization, resources, votes, and weaker opponents. At the same time the politician has a powerful incentive to not only comply but also positively advance the concerns of the demanders.

But there is one notable fact that cannot be overlooked nor minimized when discussing redistribution to the less well off; they are not normally thought to be politically powerful. If this is the case, how are we to account for vast public expenditures for the advancement of low-income people? Public choice scholars have confronted this theoretical dilemma in a variety of ways but mostly by arguing some version of contractual theory in which risk-averse voters choose either to insure themselves over the long period of income fluctuation or that the wealthier citizenry attempts to protect their status by using public funds to bribe the discontented. There is an intellectual appeal to the contractual approach but it is clear, first, that citizens are never offered such clear-cut voting choices and, second, that politicians make partial policies in the immediate context of electoral and legislative struggles. They do not vote directly on overall welfare policy; rather they confront special welfare programs dealing with specific difficulties facing specific groups.

In dealing with these issues it is fairly clear that the truly poor do receive substantial benefits but receive far fewer than those immediately above them. Welfare policies deal with specific contingencies such as unemployment; mothers with dependent children and an absent husband; old age; and mental illness. Those citizens who suffer from incurable conditions such as mental retardation or physical disabilities must obviously depend upon the goodwill of others. But even here there are interested persons including the family and public bureaucrats, as well as private philanthropic agencies wanting others to help. While obvious altruism is involved, self-interest is not thereby precluded. A welfare industry exists consisting of not only the aided and potential beneficiaries, but an entire bureaucratic apparatus—both public and private—to deliver services, income, and benefits-in-kind. Nor should we overlook rent seeking producers who supply resources employed by the industry. Whenever surplus food programs, school lunch, etc., are debated in the Congress, our highly subsidized farmers and their lobbyists are among the conspicuous logrollers. Promoting the welfare of the farm sector is not incompatible with advancement of the urban poor. But advancing the welfare of both may be and most likely is achieved by the least efficient means.

Even if altruism provided a fully satisfactory explanation for public welfare, we are left with thorny problems of explaining how much welfare, for whom, and by what means. While private donors supply immense amounts of charity, much of it comes from relatively small numbers of wealthy people and their organizations. Of course, the mere existence of public welfare is an important cause of the low overall rates of charitable giving; why give voluntarily when you will in any case be forced to pay taxes? And, indeed, the tax laws are designed to encourage greater contributions. The fact remains, most people are unwilling to implement their public charitable impulses.

Distributive Justice in a Transfer Society

The volume of involuntary transfers in contemporary democracies is, as we have seen, overwhelming. That volume can and should be reduced and redirected in significant ways. State redistribution is not morally superior to that of markets or private charity. In fact, political distribution is at once both more impersonal and personally arbitrary than is the case with private institutions. Large-scale redistribution necessarily involves large-scale bureaucracies with all their inefficiencies and impersonal treatment of the individual. At the same time, discretionary choices on the part of legislator and bureaucrat make the citizen peculiarly dependent on what can only be viewed as arbitrary decisions. Those who choose to live by the state make a precarious choice. In short, while markets produce distributive outcomes that do not satisfy all, the polity can rarely satisfy anyone for long. Rent seekers, whether traditional producer groups or low income claimants, must devote far too much of their time and resources to unproductive activity merely to protect what they have. Fervent pursuers of equality are apt to be bitterly disappointed because they are frequently outmaneuvered by wealthier rent seekers. When the poor are taxed to support the middle and upper classes it is not only galling but, perhaps, poetic justice for those who seek redress via the state.

But the worst consequence is the sacrifice of individual liberty entailed by governmentally guaranteed income flows. To protect one citizen it becomes necessary not only to control another, but also to add insult to injury by reducing her income arbitrarily. Coerced, collective altruism also fails to dignify the donor or recipient since coercion promotes mutual resentment. Finally, collective aid is not altruistic but coerced and the good feeling from voluntarily giving is lost when giving is coerced; taxation and entitlement do little to build social capital and probably are destructive of it.

And who is to speak for those providing unequal inputs when greater outcome equality prevails? Is it not an injustice to reward equally those offering superior skill, hard work, and greater contributions to society and those possessing less skill, less motivation, and making lesser contributions to others? Why should the free rider be paid the same as the dedicated, hard-working contributor? I doubt that, without recognition, contributors will continue to make the same efforts with the same beneficial effects. Some may even come to believe they are suckers. The high salaries paid to Tiger Woods, Nicole Kidman, Denzel Washington, Lady Gaga, and innumerable transitory rock stars are not only earned but constitute a measure of the esteem in which they are held by appreciative fans. I do not hold them in the same esteem; still I should not wish to deny them high incomes when countless others are more than willing to purchase expensive tickets to see and hear them in live performances. The willingness of American youth to pay top dollars to African-American entertainers has quite possibly done more to equalize race relationships than all governmental policies together (see Nozick, 1974). In fact, our imperfect markets have done more to advance the material well being of the less fortunate than all that government could ever hope to achieve. By allowing inequality whenever it serves to improve the lot of the least advantaged, even John Rawls (1971) finds justification for inequality.

Aside from the more purely economic consequences of seeking greater equality, I doubt whether the pursuit of that end is in fact what most Americans want. What is wanted is greater equality of opportunity, a preference documented in countless public opinion polls. Aside from a reduced role for government in pursuit of that ideal I believe that a freer private economy will generate more opportunities than will any politically feasible or likely combination of governmental policies seeking income equality.

Americans' desire to protect their privacy and rights to be different is impressive. Protagonists of equality never, it seems, make clear precisely what, other than wealth and income, should be equalized. Must everyone dress alike? Live in the same houses with the same furniture? Eat the same meals? These are not rhetorical questions to be dismissed as the mouthings of irritable, impatient self-important professors. If de Tocqueville's observation concerning the increasing marginal importance of differences as equality is achieved is true, the egalitarian faces a serious dilemma. If everyone had the same income they would still trade possessions because their diverse preferences or tastes in consumption would require trades. Invidious comparisons cannot be avoided even in the equal society.

Most of all, I appeal for a new approach to distributive questions. For too long the egalitarians have dominated the debate, set the issues, selected the premises, and thereby put others on the defensive. Those who entertain any skepticism about political redistribution have been branded as uncaring, insensitive, and elitist. A reshaping of the agenda of debate is desperately needed. "What causes poverty?" is the wrong question. The right question is "What causes wealth?" Not everything in life is a zero-sum game in which the powerful necessarily dominate choices. The fact that some possess more wealth than others does not imply a capacity to coerce others. Wealth is accumulated by activities that increase opportunities available to others. One need only consult the online yellow pages or Google to see the enormous number of businesses that were created by the inventions as disparate as the automobile, snowmobile, computer chip, and home exercise machines. Nearly all of these businesses are *small,* making small annual profits, but in the aggregate, they employ millions of well-paid workers and serve the expanding needs of countless consumers.

These firms came into existence not by governmental dictate but by entrepreneurial aspirations and skills of otherwise ordinary people. A complex, large economy such as ours offers an extraordinary array of opportunities but mostly it offers the liberty to invent opportunities; to perceive and create "wants" where none exist. And for those entrepreneurs in need of investment funds there are monies to be had. Banks and investment firms actively seek outlets, as do families in the pursuit of profit. The material well-being and self-regard of hundreds of millions of people have been advanced far more by the mundane daily workings of imperfect markets than those of governments bent on redistribution and equality.

Bibliographical Notes

Much of politics in the twentieth century pertained to the efforts of some to have market distributions of wealth and income redistributed by political actors and processes. The term welfare state is frequently employed to describe what has taken place in democracies. For liberals, this development has been a welcome one. I believe it to be an unfortunate trend that I hope is peaking and possibly diminishing. In any case, the literature on what has occurred and whether it has been good or bad is voluminous. I do not pretend to have read more than a small fraction of what has been written.

Two of my favorites are not particularly well known but deserve to be: Yair Aharoni's *The No-Risk Society* (New York: Chatham House Publishers, 1981) and Dan Usher's *The Economic Prerequisite to Democracy* (New York: University of Columbia Press, 1981). The first book catalogues and discusses a vast array of government programs that shift the risk from individuals and businesses to society, that is, to others. Dan Usher's book rather incisively argues that the market is a far better institution for distributive questions than are our political processes. He also contends that democracy is unstable because of the incentives and opportunities presented to all citizens to plunder one another. Majority rule is one of the facilitating rules or institutions.

Two books that deal with improving the lives of the poor are by Peruvian economist Hernando de Soto, *The Mystery of Capital: Why Capitalism Succeeds in the West but Fails Everywhere Else* (New York: Basic Books, 2000) and *The Other Path: The Economic Answer to Terrorism* (New York: Basic Books, 1989). In these books, de Soto argues that the real problem facing poor countries is that they do not have the necessary network of laws that will allow poor people to turn their assets into liquid capital. In Egypt, for example, de Soto shows that the poor have 55 times as much wealth as all the direct foreign investments ever made in the country, but because they do not have title to their land and are excluded from markets, they remain poor. He and several associates founded the Institute for Liberty and Democracy in Lima, Peru, with the following mission:

> Four billion people in developing and post-Soviet nations—two thirds of the world's population—have been locked out of the global economy: forced to operate outside the rule of law, they have no legal identity, no credit, no capital, and thus no way to prosper. The Institute for Liberty and Democracy (ILD), based in Lima, Peru, has created a key that can open the system to everyone—a time-tested strategy for legal reform that offers the majority of the world's people a stake in the market economy.

The two Big Books that must be confronted are, of course, John Rawls's *A Theory of Justice* (Cambridge: Harvard University Press, 1971) and Robert Nozick's *Anarchy, State, and Utopia* (New York: Basic Books, 1974). These two volumes by men who were distinguished colleagues in Harvard's Philosophy Department set forth the foundations for judging fairness and for explaining the minimal state. The basic questions of each are different, but they manage, nevertheless to define them in such a way that the books are competitors in how to think about justice and the modern state. Both books have stimulated much scholarly response and will endure.

References

Aharoni, Yair. *No Risk Society.* New York: Chatham House Publishers, 1981.

Center for Philanthropy at Indiana University. "Giving USA 2010." Giving USA Foundation. http://www.givingusa2010.org/.

de Soto, Hernando. *The Mystery of Capital: Why Capitalism Succeeds in the West but Fails Everywhere Else.* New York: Basic Books, 2000.

de Soto, Hernando. *The Other Path: The Economic Answer to Terrorism.* New York: Basic Books, 1989.

Institute for Liberty and Democracy. "Who We Are." ild.org.pe. http://www.ild .org.pe/who-we-are.

Nozick, Robert. *Anarchy, State, and Utopia.* New York: Basic Books, 1974, pp. 161–63.

Okun, Arthur M. *Equality, and Efficiency: The Big Tradeoff.* Washington, DC: The Brookings Institution, 1975.

Palumbo, Thomas. *Economic Characteristics of Households in the United States: Third Quarter 2008.* Current Population Reports, p. 70–119. U.S. Census Bureau, Washington, DC, 2010.

Rawls, John. *A Theory of Justice.* Cambridge: Harvard University Press, 1971.

Trumbull, Mark. "As US Tax Rates Drop, Government's Reach Grows," *Christian Science Monitor,* April 16, 2007, Section 4, p. 1. http://www.csmonitor.com/2007 /0416/p01s4-usec.html.

Usher, Dan. *The Economic Prerequisite to Democracy.* New York: Columbia University Press, 1986.

15

Micro-Politics of Macro-Instability

ECONOMIC INSTABILITY PERSISTS despite the best efforts of our political leaders, other public figures, and economists. Although pure and permanent stability may not be desirable, many people seem to place a very high value on reducing, if not eliminating, business cycles. Whenever something is valued highly and widely but remains unrealized, there arises a strong need to explain the discrepancy.

As outlined in Part I, economic instability is thought by many to be an inherent tendency of the market economy. Many older Keynesians and most Marxists who share this pessimistic if not apocalyptic vision have defined the problem for decades; that they mislead makes little difference. Like Schumpeter, I, too, believe that market economies are unstable but that the resultant instability is the byproduct of some otherwise highly desirable and unavoidable properties of the economy. Schumpeter (1942) summed it up, aptly, as a "perennial gale of creative destruction." Business cycles are not to be denied; they were, are, and always will be with us. Unfortunately, a once-resilient market economy is now so buffeted by political forces that the most important cause of modern economic fluctuations is not the economy but the polity. Readers of the *Wall Street Journal* know all too well that their fortunes are often decided less by Wall Street than by Washington DC, less by the profit and loss column than by the vote calculus.

Governmental failure or politically generated instability is a consequence of two basic factors characterizing politics: economic ignorance and the self-interests of political decision makers including voters, interest groups, politicians, and bureaucrats.

Neither economic ignorance nor conflicts of interests keep politicians from attempting counter business cycles. They announce and promote policies with confidence, often with staff economists in the background cheering them on. There are two broad areas of countercyclical policy: fiscal and monetary. Fiscal policy consists of manipulating taxation and government spending policies in order to affect aggregate demand. Fiscal policy is rooted in the familiar equation of Y=C+G+I+NX (where GDP or output = Y, Consumption = C, Government Spending = G, Investment = I, and Net Exports =NX). Fiscal policy gives politicians two powerful tools to use attempting to control business cycles while maximizing votes and enacting preferred policies. If Y=C+G+I+NX, and Y drops as it does in a recession, politicians can respond by increasing one of the elements on the other side of the equation. Reducing taxes during a downturn will, in this model, increase C and I, therefore increasing Y. Reducing taxes is popular among politicians who prefer smaller government and/or are up for reelection. Reducing taxes "sells" at election time. But among politicians who want government in general to grow and/or have special projects they want funded, spending tax dollars is highly attractive—especially if the tax dollars being spent are those of future taxpayers who are not yet voters. The incentive, then, is to spend and more important, to deficit spend. As G increases so does Y and the economy recovers quickly and avoids a bust.

Of course there is another side to the business cycle—the boom. Booms are a problem because they promote over-investments and mal-investments and spur inflation. In the end they go "bust." Historical examples include Holland's famous 1630 "tulip mania," the dot-com bubble in the late 1990s, and the lending and mortgage crisis of 2008 in the United States. What politicians should do during a boom, according to Keynesians, is decrease C, I, and G by increasing taxes and reducing spending; even running a budget surplus. Neither of these policies is attractive to politicians who wish to remain in office.

Monetary policy is the regulation of interest rates and the money supply by some monetary authority. In the United States that authority is the Federal Reserve Board, which acts as a central bank. During an economic downturn, the Federal Reserve follows an expansionary policy of increasing the money supply and lowering interest rates.

During an economic boom, the Federal Reserve uses a contractionary policy of decreasing the money supply and increasing interest rates. Politicians worry a great deal about the autonomy of central bankers and often wish the bankers would do more to help reelection efforts. Economists who work for the Federal Reserve enjoy a great deal of power and prestige.

This brief and simplified description of fiscal and monetary policy could have been in the chapter about the Idealized State (Chapter 2) because the description is idealized. As taught in most introductory principles of economics texts politicians and their advisors cannot know what to do to counter a business cycle nor how to do it. They are like the captain of a great ship that refuses to follow a straight course, so he constantly nudges the rudder one way or another in order to correct course. However "steering" the economy is not like steering a ship and politicians and their advisors not only cannot know what to do to counter a business cycle or how to do it. Lacking knowledge or ability might cause regular citizens to act cautiously. For politicians and bureaucrats, it means the sphere of action is far wider than it would be if they were constrained by knowledge and understanding.

Uninformed Governments

Let us begin with a generous recognition of the task confronted by government: the world is a highly uncertain place while the theories and information provided by economists on macro-policy, especially, are woefully deficient. No one knows the workings of the economy in the sense that physicists know their universe; one reason is the lack of economic "constants." Even when macro-economists agree on the relevant variables they cannot agree on long-term forecasts or even short-run predictions. Data are rarely current, often incomplete and seldom very reliable. Sizeable ranges of uncertainty must be attached to all estimates and one must expect that unexpected shocks—mostly political— can occur at any time to upset even the most finely tuned and sophisticated monetary and fiscal advice. Knowing the current state of the economy is never likely to be very easy or reassuring for anyone. Since we can neither undo the past nor know the future, large and frequent errors are expected.

Even if we were able to capture an accurate picture at any one time, we would soon discover that it was outdated. Data are costly and time-consuming to collect and the necessary collective action required to act on that information is often slow and uncertain. The time lags between adopting, say, an expenditure program and implementing it are apt to number in months and even years. It takes time for government spending to get through the bureaucracies and ripple through the economy, usually too much time.

Scholars and politicians have assumed that we know the effects of policy changes, that is, if a tax rate is altered, or a certain sum of public money is to be spent on a particular type of activity that we can then trace out the economic impact of those changes. The fact of the matter is that we have little reason to be confident. For example, some in the Reagan Administration thought the Reagan tax cuts would pay for themselves with increased tax revenues from increased demand and supply. Paul Krugman, who later was awarded a Nobel Prize in Economic Science, criticized the tax cuts calling them an "inflation time bomb" (Krugman and Summers, 1982). Neither the wildly optimistic nor pessimistic were correct. The Federal Reserve, with the explicit support of Reagan himself, tamed inflation through a tight money supply policy. There were large budget deficits but only because the cumulative increase in defense spending during the Reagan years was larger than the increase in budget deficit. That is, without the military build-up the total deficit would have fallen (Niskanen and Moore, 1996). It seems that both the optimistic supply-siders and the pessimistic Keynesians were seriously in error.

President George W. Bush attempted to stop a slide in the economy in 2008 when he asked Congress to authorize a $168 billion tax cut. People received their shares of the tax cut as rebate checks with individuals receiving up to $600 and those with dependent children receiving up to $300 per child. Bush and his advisors hoped the recipients would spend their rebates, thereby boosting C. Only about one-third was spent on new consumption; the rest was used to pay down debt or put into savings. Consumers sometimes refuse to act as politicians and their advisors want them to.

Then, too, we really do not know either the effects or sequence of major budgetary deficits; some argue that they are all bad, including inflation and the crowding out of private investment, while others contend that at times they may be good and still others claim that they are essentially neutral. Such confusion seems to non-economists as inexplicable. No wonder most presidents show little enthusiasm for their meetings with the Council of Economic Advisers.

To make things still worse, some theorists maintain that without major shocks governments are unable to "outsmart" people with changes in economic policy. Whatever countercyclical fiscal and monetary policies might be adopted are defeated because informed, rational citizens respond with counteractions to protect themselves in the market. Since policy is negated it is wasteful. Unless a new policy is a complete surprise it will fail to achieve the desired effects. Investors, for example, attempt to anticipate a rate change by the Federal Reserve. If they anticipate correctly, they can build the change into their investment strategy so that when the change happens it has almost no effect. If one accepts this rational-expectations analysis, macro-policy is largely futile.

With less threatening premises, the economic advisor is still in difficulty because knowledge of the right variables does not easily translate into advice on how much spending and taxing is enough. How drastic must policies be to achieve desired effects? And what if consumer expectations change as a result of policy changes? In short, macro-policy advice is something economists should offer with humility rather than confidence. Ironically, leftist thinkers whose distaste for economics is well known are the very persons demanding the most from economists. Their planning, manipulating, and controlling of economies and, therefore societies, require economic knowledge that is unobtainable; neither economists nor governments are omniscient or omnicompetent.

Self-Interest in Instability

Although students of international politics have long known that governments take advantage of and manipulate foreign events for their own purposes, economists and even political scientists have only lately begun to appreciate the role of political self-interests in economic instability. Ordinary citizens are well aware of the fact that campaigning politicians base their efforts on the presumed state of the economy, but few realize how politicians in office attempt to use governmental policy to influence elections. To some extent, politicians have created a political-business cycle. Spending and taxing policies designed to improve their own electoral chances contribute to exaggerated economic fluctuations. And market fluctuations, in turn, provide rhetorical ammunition for politicians wanting to inject the government still more into economic life. Actually, stability in politics benefits neither the politician nor the bureaucrat; neither would have the wealth, income, power nor status that accrue when there is more to do and nothing is done. Paradoxically, politicians become more important, have more money to spend, and derive more ego rewards if the economy is believed to work poorly. Bureaucrats may be expected to demand larger budgets when contending with economic insecurity. We note, too, that Keynesian economists find more work and status when fighting unemployment or even inflation than in studying a steady-state economy, while public choice analysts have a self-interest in complaining about large and active governments.

For politicians, fighting unemployment, if not inflation, is rewarding. Fighting unemployment brings out politicians' compassion and enables more money to be spent on activities they think might help, or at least will help someone in their district or state. Lowering taxes and spending more money creates not only economic but political good for the politician. Appearing to fight inflation and deficits is also politically astute. Actually fighting them may be political suicide. Since politicians recognize that most people view inflation as a bad most of the time they rail against it. But inflation also increases the revenues of government usually at a rate faster than the rate of inflation. If prices rise by, say, 10 percent, revenues will increase by, say, 15 percent. The discrepancy comes about because of progressive rate structures. The more one earns the greater the rate of marginal taxation. Politicians appreciate this feature of the tax structure because it provides automatic revenue increases without having to publicly pass tax increases. So, politicians, including the conservatives, have somewhat ambivalent feelings about reducing taxes.

Inflation also presents politicians with the opportunity to campaign for governmental controls over the economy, a self-serving policy supported by some liberal and many new left economists. Wage and price controls have exerted a fatal fascination for centuries. If prices rise, the uninformed believe that controls will in fact stop further increases. From such myths controls are born and a bureaucracy to administer them.

Politically Manipulated Business Cycles

Sabotaging the economy is not deliberate. It is an inadvertent product of politically purposive actions inspired by political incentives. Instead of alleviating cyclical difficulties the sum-total of economic policies often promotes disorder beneficial to a few citizens but mostly to the welfare of the political classes. These self-interests manifest themselves in a political business cycle.

Incumbent governments have shown a distinct propensity to adopt inflationary policies during the year or two prior to elections—not because they wish to increase inflation but in order to decrease unemployment—a good in most voter minds. Spending to diminish unemployment, especially if accompanied by budgetary deficits, has the unfortunate effect of increasing pressure on the price level. Although pre-election unemployment is artificially lowered, inflationary tendencies assert themselves after the election and in so doing anger increasing numbers of citizens. Anti-inflationary policies then seem in order, and a cycle of contrary or restrictive policies is established over the electoral cycle. Politicians who attempt to pursue a steady course of averaging out both unemployment and inflation rates might achieve economic success, but such a course most certainly would not constitute political success. Politicians are not solely to blame, however, for voters actually prefer the succession of policies generating the instability they presumably do not want. Voters, it seems, act as though the immediate present is more important than vague memories of the past and a still more vague and uncertain future. Thus, voters are economically myopic.

The political business cycle can be illustrated in simple fashion as in Figure 15.1, where the rates of inflation and unemployment are arrayed on the vertical dimension and the electoral periods on the horizontal line. The optimal political business cycle or mix of two lines indicates the course of unemployment and inflation rates. The rate of inflation rises over the electoral period and should reach its maximum just after an election, while the rate of unemployment should fall continuously between elections. Rational politicians will attempt to dampen inflation shortly after an election, and they do so with policies that necessarily increase the unemployment rate. This highly stylized model does not, however, accurately portray the actual, messy course of events but it does serve to show typical intentions and policy choices. Although politicians are indeed powerful they cannot usually fine-tune the fiscal and monetary policies necessary to give effect to the model shown in Figure 15.1. The facts of the matter are that power is diffused, information is limited, and the citizenry soon learns that they can partially counter this obvious Machiavellian electoral strategy by anticipating and planning for it.

It should be noted, nevertheless, that several empirical studies have shown the existence of a political business cycle. For example, Frey and Schneider (1981) found systematic evidence for the period of 1959 to 1974 in the United

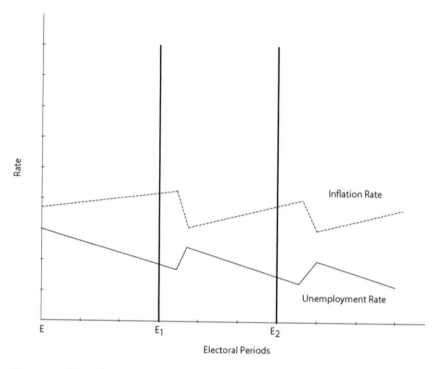

Figure 15.1 The Political Business Cycle

Kingdom. They discovered that a fall in the inflation rate of 1 percent increased the government's lead by 0.6 percent while a fall in unemployment by 1 percent increased the lead by a remarkable 6 percent. Fighting unemployment is definitely a superior political strategy, or at least it was during the period studied. All governments over this period in the UK were found to expand expenditures and reduce taxation when their leads in popularity were lower. When their popularity was much higher they were able to pursue more ideological policies without fear of retribution by voters (Frey and Schneider, 1981). Grier (2008) found similar evidence of "sizeable opportunistic" political business cycle effects in the United States since 1960. The greatest opportunities come from promoting income growth in the last two quarters before an election. Income growth rather than GDP growth appears to motivate voters, which allows skillful politicians to pursue an ideological agenda early in their terms with little penalty from voters as long as incomes grow immediately prior to the election. The data from U.S. presidential elections are illuminating. Average incomes grew 1.5% more in presidential election years than in other years from 1947 to 1977. The increase during presidential election years has been 1.4% since 1948 (Achen and Bartels, 2004).

Evidence of the political business cycle is also strongly suggested by the monetary policies pursued by the presumably independent Federal Reserve Board from 1959 through 1981. Except for the chairmanship of Alan Greenspan (Chairman, 1987–2006), the Federal Reserve was "abnormally expansionary" in the months prior to a presidential election if the incumbent president is from the party that initially appointed the Chairman of the Federal Reserve (Abrams and Iossifov, 2006). Apparently there are. In fact, in that case, we might expect that there are interactions between presidential policies and policies adopted by the Federal Reserve.

A Note on Supply-Side Economics

Although much was written during the last three decades on "supply-side" economics and its notable role in the policies of Reagan, G. H. W. Bush, and G. W. Bush, relatively little attention has been accorded its political relevance. A discussion of the political business cycle affords a convenient opportunity if not invitation to do so. While the economic virtues of this "old wine poured into new bottles" strategy are certainly debatable, there can be little debate about the political attractiveness of a program of policies based on the Laffer Curve. A policy promising to increase government revenues by reducing tax rates is bound to win widespread favor for both tax reductions and yet increased revenues for the government. That is exactly how President G.W. Bush argued for tax reductions in a 2006 speech. He said, "You cut taxes and the tax revenues increase." He was echoed by Senate Budget Committee Chair Judd Gregg who said, "These tax cuts pay for themselves" (Center on Budget and Policy Priorities). As is so often the case in economics, measuring the precise effects has proven devilishly difficult; as a result everyone can maintain their own faith without much fear of falsification by empirical tests. In any case, supply-side economics may be viewed, for all practical purposes, as the extreme right's ideological equivalent to the traditional Keynesian faith in macroeconomics. Both provide the necessary rationale for combining what are perceived to be "good" economics with "good" politics.

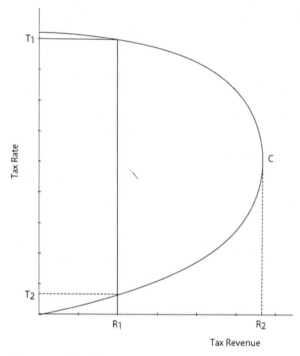

Figure 15.2 Tax Revenue

Just how this all comes about may be shown in the form of the famous Laffer Curve, which attempts to relate the rate of taxation with the size of governmental revenues. Figure 15.2 is a reproduction of that relationship (see also Figure 11.1 and the accompanying discussion).

This diagram is of interest not only because of the substantive content but also because of its political implications. In the diagram, we see that, except for that point at which maximum revenues are obtained, all other quantities of revenue can be obtained by either of two rates of taxation, a higher and lower rate. Thus, R_1 can be achieved with either rates T_1 or T_2. If this general analysis is correct, we should expect that a vote-maximizing government would prefer the lower rate (T_1) since that would minimize collection costs and taxpayer anger. It should be noted, too, as one reads the curve from left to right, that as the tax rate increases revenues increase to a maximum found at C, but thereafter tax rate increases lead to a fall in total revenues. The latter occurs because taxpayers find less incentive to work and greater incentives to avoid paying taxes. Presumably, at the lower rates they will continue to work hard as well as pay their taxes. Another way of saying this, in more technical terms, is that the activity that is being taxed will decline at a faster percentage rate than the tax rate itself increases. While it is in politicians' interest to use the lower rate, given revenue "needs," it is also quite possible that the higher rates may prevail. Taxes are enacted for other reasons than revenue and politicians and their advisors are often poorly informed and necessarily, shortsighted. And, lest we forget, taxes are sometimes supported as appropriate punitive measures as is the case with some environmental and all sin taxes. Of course, once a tax is enacted it is difficult to repeal.

There are now quite convincing data that, given the current tax structure in the United States, tax cuts do not "pay for themselves" by generating more tax revenue than is lost from the cut. Martin Feldstein, former chairman of Reagan's council of economic advisors, while pointing out many positive supply-side effects, estimates that a government recovers about one-third of the revenue it loses from a tax cut. Proponents celebrate that taxpayers get to keep more of the money they earned and point to the one-third of tax revenue regained while opponents point to the two-thirds lost. What the Laffer Curve adds to the tax debate is not that tax cuts pay for themselves, but that they are not as costly as a static analysis predicts.

Micro-Basis of Macro-Policies

Students of microeconomics or price theory have long bemoaned the tendency of Keynesian macroeconomists to ignore well-established principles of individual choice and behavior when devising spending and taxing policies. The great aggregates of macro analysis—$Y=C+G+I+NX$—are so defined that their composition appears neutral. All a government needs do is construct a gigantic econometric model showing how government-induced changes in one or more of the aggregate variables will produce beneficial alterations in the others. The individuals and firms making up the real economy are ignored because their choices are thought to be infinitely amenable to policy changes. The trouble is that macro-level changes must be consonant with the micro-foundations of individual choice. Since human nature cannot be ignored, incentives, prices, information, and expectations must be included for they shape individual responses to changing environments. Fortunately, we need not create some new economics that will take account of individual choice; two hundred years of microeconomics has provided a solid basis on which to assess and base macro-policies. Conditioned by years of Keynesian supremacy, many economists and others ignore these verities. Elementary principles of the market are really quite universal and, as I have taken pains to point out, are applicable far beyond the marketplace. Here I am concerned with the relevance of the market for macro-policy.

Taking the market seriously leads to quite different macro-policies than those to which we have been accustomed. But what is the micro-wisdom? In the first place, macro-policy should be based on the axiom that individuals are maximizers and mostly of their own income and wealth or welfare. How they respond depends on relative prices and taxes and not the overall price level or aggregate averages and aggregate policies. In short, effective policies must take into account the detailed composition of the great aggregates. Nowhere is this truer than in the composition of the labor force.

Unemployment policies not based on the changing nature of the population and nature of unemployment are doomed. Unfortunately, much earlier Keynesian analysis had been fixated on the Great Depression when the bulk of the unemployed were adult men. Today's unemployed tend to be youth and/or individuals in families containing employed workers. These individuals are not skilled, trained workers; rather they lack skills and/or job experience or have the wrong skills. They remain unemployed because they are not employable in their present state. Then, too, many who find themselves unemployed have become so because of personal choice and are really between jobs. Fortunately for them their unemployment is brief and cushioned by personal savings, family resources, and a variety of welfare programs and unemployment insurance. The new microeconomics suggests that these facts negate a great deal of Keynesian policy; unfortunately one of the costs of these policies is to prolong unemployment and thereby further distort the allocation of resources. Since leisure is now made much less costly to both employee and employer, incentives are perversely affected; employment is discouraged. In the Netherlands and the United Kingdom it hardly pays to look for work when for two or more years one can receive monthly incomes nearly equal to the earned wages. How to deal with people between jobs and those without skills or having outmoded skills must surely be different than dealing with the massive involuntary unemployment of the 1930s.

At the same time economists are revitalizing the old explanations of unemployment, they are also rethinking some other old lessons and their application to new circumstances, namely, decisions to save and invest. In short, much American policy enacted since the Depression has discouraged savings and investment. These policies are based on both a theoretical condemnation of savings and an obvious political strategy favoring borrowers. Consumption, savings, and investment are, according to Keynesian analysis, separate, uncoordinated decisions containing the seeds of their own destruction. In a depression savings constitute an individually rational course of action leading to collective disaster. According to Keynes there can be too much saving, insufficient investment, and too little consumption. Since saving is now deficient, investment is also deficient. Far too many public policies have contributed to this bleak outlook.

Because the tax code has permitted borrowers to deduct interest costs from their taxable income, borrowers have been encouraged through tax subsidies to perpetuate their habit. I am among the millions whose borrowing via home mortgages and credit cards has been considerably eased by these tax subsidies. Those who choose to save find, on the other hand, that they will be penalized because their earnings will be taxed not once but twice, first when income is earned and again when that invested income earns interest—even when the interest income was lower than the inflation rate. Naturally, the demand for borrowed money is increased, as personal private indebtedness clearly demonstrates.

That capital formation has become a major problem for Americans is no surprise. With the federal government competing for funds, private businesses find themselves "crowded out" of the capital market. A reduction in government borrowing would do much to ease the situation. But at the individual level potential savers and investors find that incentives to save and invest have been skewed to such an extent that they simply save and invest less than is desirable. Another beneficial provision would be to allow income earned from interest accounts to be exempt from taxation. Corporate tax rates should be reduced and government forced to rely more on consumption taxes. Such actions are consistent with the micro-foundations of price theory as well as social psychology. Reward those behaviors that are socially beneficial and tax the inefficient choices.

Although these reforms will help, so long as government engages in massive borrowing, saving and investment will be penalized. This must be because government has but three ways of financing deficits—taxes, borrowing, or printing money—and all tend to discourage work and productivity. If government raises taxes it reduces the incentive to work; if government borrows it competes with private borrowing and raises the interest rates; and finally if government indulges in printing more money it creates inflation with all its attendant problems for more risky investment decision. Although laudable, these policy proposals confront persistent biases in our political institutions, biases stemming from powerful perverse incentives. Since governmental decisions are rarely based on the economic criteria of marginal costs and benefits we have no definitive way of knowing whether the GDP is increased or decreased by more public and less private spending. In comparing alternative spending programs analysts are left at a loss because they cannot scientifically decide whether building public housing is more important than, say, adding a new bomber to the Air Force.

Keynesian fiscal policy, at least as presented by textbook writers and popularizers, maintains that spending and taxing policies can be manipulated in the interests of fighting both depressions and inflation. Such is not the case; however objective the economist may be, fiscal policy lends itself to fighting depression rather than inflation. Reducing taxes and increasing public expenditure is bound to be politically expedient to a degree unattainable by increasing burdens and reducing spending.

Likewise, monetary policy finds itself inflation- rather than recession-oriented. Still, politicians are not happy about having to restrain the supply of money. And whatever combination of fiscal and monetary policies may constitute economic sense, the politician must pay close attention to the distributive details of aggregate measures of consumption and supply. Fiscal policies are translated into specific legislation having a vital impact on the composition of output and demand. *Whose* investments are affected cannot be a matter of overall fiscal efficiency. *Whose* consumption is affected, how, when, to what extent, are all basic questions for politicians to be answered by their vote calculus. Much the same considerations apply to monetary policies. Aside from these general considerations we must realize that members of government not only have political self-interests in destabilization—compounded by economic ignorance—but that the very organization of the United States federal government frustrates effective stabilization.

Countless critics, including members of Congress, have long maintained that the budget is *uncontrollable*. If the budget is uncontrollable, who made it so? And, if the budget is uncontrollable how can Keynesian policies form the rationale of government stabilization? The realization of this dilemma, disheartening as it may be to fine-tuners, has led Congress to follow not Keynes but political rules of thumb derived from electoral necessities. Students of Congressional budgeting have shown rather forcefully that Congress does not and cannot under existing rules compare one spending program with another; one taxing measure against another. The task is simply too great. Accordingly, they begin with the President's political budget proposal and previous budgets and simply legislate sufficient monies to placate various interests. Except for defense expenditures few members of Congress ever question spending proposals by colleagues. A new member quickly learns that the best advice is that of former Speaker Sam Rayburn: "to get along, you must go along." Likewise, embattled presidents seeking reelection will use every available dollar to buy the votes of powerful interests.

These several considerations lead to the conclusion that while government may occasionally assist in stabilizing segments of the economy it does not and cannot stabilize the economy. Government is chiefly responsible for inflation and it has contributed mightily to our growing unemployment and continuous misallocation of scarce resources. One agency encourages and provides for the improvement of tobacco growing while another warns smokers of the health hazards of smoking. One agency works to increase the productivity of farmers while simultaneously limiting acreage and buying up surpluses to store at enormous cost. Then, at campaign time, some politicians exclaim that 20 million Americans are hungry and homeless. Another agency entrusted with public lands wastes timber and other resources when the price of those same resources is increasing. Such is the real political world of fiscal and monetary policies. Aggregate demand and supply remain intellectual and political problems.

Supposed deficit reduction is an art form for skillful politicians. They engage in a form of fiscal illusion in which they appear to reduce spending but are, in fact, actively protecting their Congressional districts, states, or special-interest friends. They even admit to making cuts that are all "smoke and mirrors." A budget reduction plan promoted in 2010 by Representative Paul Ryan (R, Wisc.) provides guidance as to how it is done. Ryan, the ranking member of the House Budget Committee, prepared what he called "a Road Map for America's Future" that addressed issues from healthcare to Social Security to tax reform. He then asked the Congressional Budget Office to "score" the plan—to evaluate the plan's economic effects. According to the CBO, following Ryan's Road Map would balance the budget and eliminate the federal deficit by 2080. That result is only obtained, however, by Ryan instructing the CBO to assume that tax revenues would equal at least 19 percent of GDP during that period (the average since 1945 has been 18.2 percent) and assuming major changes in Social Security, Medicare, Medicaid, and other social programs. President Obama was even more optimistic than Representative Ryan. In his first address to a joint session of Congress (2009), he promised to cut the $1.2 trillion federal budget deficit in half in four years while not raising taxes on 98 percent of American families. I expect that he and other politicians will continue to fine-tune their smoke and mirrors.

One budget strategy followed at least since Ronald Reagan was president is known as "starve the beast." The assumption is that an effective way to shrink the size of government is to cut its revenue stream. Presumably politicians will have an aversion to deficits that are somehow "too high" so they will reduce spending as a response to tax cuts. Unfortunately for its proponents, there are no data supporting starving the beast as a budget-cutting strategy. In fact, tax cuts apparently increase spending! A study of the four major tax decreases (1948, 1964, 1981, and 2001) found that each was followed by increased spending (Romer and Romer, 2007). One reason could be the one suggested in the discussion above that spending and taxing decisions are made independently of each other, so we political observers should not expect tax cuts to cause spending cuts. In fact, it provides no link in voters' minds between spending and taxes, so demanding greater spending and lower taxes is rational. Another possibility is that tax cutters and spenders end up working together implicitly, if not explicitly through "shared fiscal irresponsibility" (Romer and Romer, 2007). Shared fiscal irresponsibility would be an understanding among politicians wishing for greater government spending to see tax cutting without accompanying spending cuts as a message that deficits do not matter. If the conservatives can be fiscally irresponsible, then so can the liberals! And promises of future spending increases might be necessary to get sufficient votes for today's tax cut to pass.

Micro-Politics and Macroeconomics

The "Crash of 2008" created a great deal of hand wringing among politicians, the public, and academics. While professors argued about whether it was a sign of market failure or government failure, politicians led first by President Bush and then by President Obama plunged forward with massive spending and regulatory programs. The once generally discredited argument that government spending creates prosperity was back. If C is down, increase G! But as noted above, even if increasing G is the right thing to do, what is the right amount? Does it matter if government dollars flow through social programs or construction projects? What are the effects on private investment and private job creation? Would the Congress and bureaucrats design policies that would have any of the desired effects? No one knew the answers to these questions although many claimed they did.

Economic systems are complex and information is incomplete and even unknowable, so unknowable that excellent analysts still argue about the causes of the Great Depression, when it ended, and why. If the past is such a mystery how can anyone pretend to know the future?

This chapter began by claiming that macro-instability is exacerbated by economic ignorance and political self-interest. Economic instability may be good as it indicates that people are reallocating resources to better uses, and such reallocations take time and even some pain. Attempting to stop the reallocation does not stop the pain; it usually just postpones it by putting off the inevitable. And the pain is worse and more drawn out if politics interferes with the self-correcting mechanisms in markets. Stabilizing the economy is a fanciful dream, yet voters continue to demand supposed stabilization policies and politicians continue to enact them. One analysis of the Crash of 2008 by the authors of one of the leading introductions to economics principles textbooks (Gwartney et al., 2008) reacted to the political responses with the following:

> Suppose we observed a country with regulations that had financial markets in disarray, widespread subsidies to the politically powerful, huge

budget deficits, and hastily constructed political action based on dooms-day threats. If this were happening in another country, we would recognize that it was the result of a breakdown in political decision-making. If the country had some semblance of a market economy, we would call it "crony capitalism." Is this descriptive of the United States today?

The United States may not have achieved crony capitalism but political responses to the Crash of 2008 clearly show how micro-incentives drive macro-policy

Bibliographical Notes

Despite the importance of macroeconomics and all the political discussions about macroeconomic policy, there is no single, readily accessible volume dealing with the political elements involved in policy-making. This being the case, I suggest a few books that are classics on the general topic containing various discussions—some technical—that examine the micro-political foundations of macroeconomic policies. The first is the wide-ranging and well-written *The Economic Consequences of Democracy* (New York: Holmes and Meier Publishers, 1977) by the brilliant English journalist Samuel Brittan. The chapters on English politics are dated, but the book contains many fascinating discussions on economics and democracy including the politics of spending and taxing.

One of the very few books on macroeconomics by a political scientist is the well-known *Political Control of the Economy* (Princeton: Princeton University Press, 1978), by Yale's Edward R. Tufte. The book is both scholarly and technical so if the reader is an undergraduate the going may be a bit tough; but most of it is readable and most of it in accordance with the ideas in the present book.

Easily the most important book for the readers of this chapter is the Buchanan and Wagner volume *Democracy in Deficit* (New York: Academic Press, 1977. Republished by Liberty Fund Press as Volume 8 in *The Collected Works of James M. Buchanan,* 2000), a far-ranging analysis of the political legacy of John M. Keynes. No other work demolishes Keynes and his followers as well as this one. The first third of the book deals with the history of how Keynes's ideas came to dominate academic and other circles while the next third deals with the public choice aspects of Keynes's work, that is, how the ideas got translated into political strategies and policies. Finally, the authors consider and advocate constitutional reform to negate the baleful Keynesian doctrines and polices. The book was an eye-opener for me; it will be for others as well.

Finally, I cite a recent collection edited by Thomas D. Willett called *Political Business Cycles: The Political Economy of Money, Inflation and Unemployment* (Durham: Duke University Press, 1988). This well-reviewed book contains some twenty-one chapters dealing not only with political business cycles but also with many other interesting topics highly germane to this discussion. Some of the chapters are not easy reading but most can be grasped by non-economic specialists. Two of the best ones are Chapters 1 and 3 by the editor and King Banaian for they explain the various public choice models that have been advanced to understand macroeconomic policies as products of a political process.

For much of the last twenty-five years the political-business cycle was presumed to be a dead idea, as analysts had been able to find little evidence of it. Political scientists tended to discount it because the theory assumes that voters will vote based on short-term, rather than long-term interests. Students of public choice have never shared the vision of voters being sensible. Recent years have seen renewed interest in the political business cycle as new studies found strong evidence of political manipulations of the economy for political gain. The article by Grier, the article by Achen and Bartels, and the article by Abrams and Iossifov that I cited in the discussion above are just three examples. Even though there is a renewed interest in political business cycles, there are no good, new books to suggest.

One non-traditional work I strongly suggest is "Fear the Book and Bust," a video distributed over the Internet by Russell Roberts and John Papola. The authors call the video "a Hayek vs. Keynes Rap Anthem," and it is indeed a confrontation between the ideas of Keynes and Hayek done as a rap video. The video was posted on YouTube in January 2010, and by April 15, 2011 the English language version had more than two million hits. It has been reposted to YouTube in ten different languages. The English language version is at http://www.youtube.com/user/EconStories. A sequel titled "Fight of the Century: Keynes vs. Hayek Round Two was released in early 2011. By June it had nearly 1 million hits. Watch both videos. Share them with your friends.

References

Abrams, Burton A. and Plamen Iossifov. "Does the Fed Contribute to a Political Business Cycle?" *Public Choice* 129 (2006) pp. 249–62.

Achen, Christopher and Larry Bartels. "Musical Chairs: Pocketbook Voting and the Limits of Democratic Accountability." Working Paper, Princeton University (2004). Available at http://www.princeton.edu/~bartels/chairs.pdf.

Anderson, Martin. *An Economic Bill of Rights.* Stanford: Hoover Institution, 1984.

Brittan, Samuel. *The Economic Consequences of Democracy.* New York: Holmes and Meier Publishers, 1977.

Buchanan, James M. and Richard E. Wagner. *Democracy in Deficit.* New York: Academic Press, 1977. Republished by Liberty Fund Press as Volume 8 in *The Collected Works of James M. Buchanan,* 2000.

Center on Budget and Policy Priorities. "Tax Cuts: Myths and Realities." Center on Budget and Policy Priorities. http://www.cbpp.org/cms/?fa=view&id=692 #m1.

Feldstein, Martin. "Rethinking Social Insurance." *American Economic Review* 95 (2005): 1–24.

Frey, Bruno and Friedrich Schneider. "A Political-Economic Model of the UK: New Estimates and Predictions," *Economic Journal* 91 (1981), pp. 737–40.

Grier, Kevin. "US Presidential Elections and Real GDP Growth, 1961–2004," *Public Choice* 135 (2008) pp. 337–52.

Gwartney, James, David Macherson, Russell Sobel, and Richard Stroup. "Special Topic: Crash of 2008." http://commonsenseeconomics.com/Activities/Crisis/CSE.CrashOf2008.pdf.

Krugman, Paul and Larry Summers, "Inflation During the 1983 Recovery," U.S. Government Memorandum, September 9, 1982.

Niskanen, William and Stephen Moore. Cato Institute Policy Analysis No. 261: Supply-Side Tax Cuts and the Truth about the Reagan Economic Record, October 22, 1996.

Papola, John and Russell Roberts. *Fear the Boom and Bust,* 2010. Music Video. http://www.youtube.com/user/EconStories.

Payne, James L. *The Culture of Spending: Why Congress Lives Beyond Our Means.* San Francisco: Institute for Contemporary Studies, 1991.

"Rayburn Is Dead; Served 17 Years As House Speaker." *New York Times* (November 17, 1961). http://www.nytimes.com/learning/general/onthisday/bday/0106 .html.

Romer, Christina D. and David H. Romer. Do Tax Cuts Starve the Beast: The Effect of Tax Changes on Government Spending (October 2007). NBER Working Paper No. W13548. http://ssrn.com/abstract=1024965.

Ryan, Paul. *Roadmap for America's Future,* 111th Cong., H.R. 4529.

Schumpeter, Joseph A. *Capitalism, Socialism, and Democracy.* New York: Harper & Brothers, 1942, Ch. 7.

Tufte, Edward R. *Political Control of the Economy.* Princeton: Princeton University Press, 1978.

U.S. Statistical Abstract. 1992.

PART V

Political Implications of Public Choice

ONLY ONE CHAPTER comprises this final section. There are so many things it could have included—regulatory reform and constitutional reform for example. Instead of making particular recommendations, I identify some general themes as a way of encouraging our readers to think of the specifics. In particular, I am interested in inspiring thought about the third world. Five billion of the earth's six billion people live there and are trapped in hierarchical societies where status determines outcomes. I hope that contracts and markets will replace status, exchange with strangers will replace exchanging within narrow neighborhood and kin groups, and finally, for the scarce resource, freedom, to be nurtured and allowed to flourish.

16

Creating a Climate for Liberty

> To act on the belief that we possess the knowledge and the
> power which enable us to shape the processes of society
> entirely to our liking, knowledge which in fact we do not
> possess, is likely to make us do much harm.
>
> —Friedrich A. Hayek

ONCE NAIVETÉ AND good intentions are replaced by an understanding of the reality of politics, it becomes time to consider changes. In
this chapter I suggest some general themes for change. They call for a greater
reliance on property rights, market processes, and private institutions and are
wholly in keeping with the American political heritage of limited, decentralized
government, and I believe will make a more rational and peaceful polity. They
are limiting government, letting markets handle problems, trying freedom,
and establishing the rule of law.

Limiting Government

In Chapter 29 of the Book of Genesis, Jacob went off in search of a wife.
While visiting his uncle Laban, Jacob met Laban's daughter Rachel, fell in
love, and asked for her hand. Laban required seven years of labor as a bride
price and Jacob agreed to the deal. After seven years the wedding night finally
arrived. Jacob woke up the next morning to discover that he had consummated
marriage not with Rachel, but with Leah, her older sister.

Political scientist Aaron Wildavsky (1982) used this story to explain what
happened in the United States as we pursued our good intentions through

government. He claimed that America "fell in love with the Rachel of social reform and found itself instead married to the Leah of big government." Americans believed those who argued that governments could and would fix market failures. Americans believed that the political class would turn good intentions into good policies.

Good intentions and good policy, however, seldom go hand-in-hand in politics. And why should we expect them to? In a 1997 interview (Hazlett, 1997) about his tenure as editor of the *Journal of Law and Economics,* Ronald Coase said, "What we discover is that most regulation does produce, or has produced in recent times, a worse result." When pushed to identify what he would consider a good regulation and an example of a not-so-good regulation, he responded:

> This is a very interesting question because one can't give an answer to it. When I was editor of *The Journal of Law and Economics,* we published a whole series of studies of regulation and its effects. Almost all the studies—perhaps all the studies—suggested that the results of regulation had been bad, that the prices were higher, that the product was worse adapted to the needs of consumers, than it otherwise would have been. I was not willing to accept the view that all regulation was bound to produce these results. Therefore, what was my explanation for the results we had? I argued that the most probable explanation was that the government now operates on such a massive scale that it had reached the stage of what economists call negative marginal returns. Anything additional it does, it messes up. But that doesn't mean that if we reduce the size of government considerably, we wouldn't find then that there were some activities it did well. Until we reduce the size of government, we won't know what they are.

When Coase's interviewer asked for an example of a good regulation, Coase replied that he could not remember any regulation that is good. He said, "Regulation of transport, regulation of agriculture—agriculture is a, zoning is z. You know, you go from a to z, they are all bad. There were so many studies, and the result was quite universal: The effects were bad."

One reason the results were bad "from a to z" is that the invisible hand of politics seldom produces the good results of the invisible hand of markets. Adam Smith's greatest accomplishment was demonstrating that the invisible hand of the market converts self-interests into collective good. We sometimes forget that he also explained how the visible hand of government converts self-interests into collective harm, even when the self-interests are meant to help others. In the *Theory of Moral Sentiments,* Smith explained,

> . . . a certain spirit of system is apt to mix itself with that public spirit which is founded upon the love of humanity, upon a real fellow-feeling with the inconveniences and distresses to which some of our fellow-citizens may be exposed. This spirit of system commonly takes the direction of that more gentle public spirit, always animates it, and often inflames it, even to the madness of fanaticism (VI.II.40).

That is, public-spirited people who love humanity may do some awful things out of their desire to direct their fellows. Smith worried about these "men of system" who tried to use political society to do good. He explained,

> The man of system . . . is apt to be very wise in his own conceit, and is often so enamored with the supposed beauty of his own plan of government, that he cannot suffer the smallest deviation from any part of it. He goes on to establish it completely and in all its parts, without any regard either to the great interests or to the strong prejudices which may oppose it; he seems to imagine that he can arrange the different members of a great society with as much ease as the hand arranges the different pieces upon a chessboard; he does not consider that the pieces upon the chessboard have no other principle of motion besides that which the hand impresses upon them; but that, in the great chessboard of human society, every single piece has a principle of motion of its own, altogether different from that which the legislature might choose to impress upon it. If these two principles coincide and act in the same direction, the game of human society will go on easily and harmoniously, and is very likely to be happy and successful. If they are opposite or different, the game will go on miserably, and the society must be at all times in the highest degree of disorder (VI.II.42).

My students often believe, at least at the beginning of the semester, that the solution to social and political problems is to elect good people. "Isn't the problem," they ask, "that there are too many bad people in political office?"

They assume that the men of system have bad intentions. I tell them that it is far worse than they imagined. The problem is not bad people but people who are trying to do good! It is tempting to attack political activists, bureaucrats, or politicians as being evil, venal, or stupid. The reason it is tempting is that the solution to the problems would be so simple. We would just need to elect better politicians or hire better-trained bureaucrats. But the truth is more difficult and far more frightening. Liberty gets run over by the tyranny of good intentions.

Good intentions are a large part of the human experience and ought to be promoted in *private* relationships. But bringing good intentions into the public sphere often chips away at liberty. Those who intend well are not content doing well in just their own lives; they want to bring their good intentions to your house and mine. They want to help us make the world a better place, whether we want to or not. People we do not even know want to tax us if we want to smoke a cigarette in the back yard, they want to protect us from ourselves by forcing us to wear a seatbelt and buy cars with airbags.

In the Spring 2003 edition of *Regulation,* Penn Jillette (of the magician act Penn & Teller) explains the problem of good intentions:

> When I was a 17-year-old longhaired freak, I thought there was a "war machine" and a "pig power structure." Believing in evil power is more reassuring than chaos. Even if it's someone evil, at least someone is in control. Now, that I'm a 47-year-old longhaired freak, I don't think there's any conspiracy. I don't think Bush wants to do Iraq just for oil. Sadly, I believe the bigger horror: He thinks he's doing the right thing. Cynicism is youth's reassurance. I think people are good, and that's worse. Believing people are doing what they think is best is infinitely sadder.

Penn Jillette and I would be happier if people stopped trying to do good through politics and paid more attention to their own lives than to ours. It appears that people took John Kennedy far too seriously when he said, "Ask not what your country can do for you—ask what you can do for your country." As Milton Friedman pointed out, "neither half of that statement expresses a relation between the citizen and his government that is worthy of the ideals of free men in a free society." "What your country can do for you" is a paternalistic vision of the state that contradicts our vision of what it means to be free and responsible. "What you can do for your country" implies that the country is something bigger than the mass of individual citizens.

One of my favorite examples of good intentions gone astray is the effect of state university paternalism on university students. In Chapter 12 I explained that universities are complex bureaucratic organizations that produce goods and services that are financed by means other than the market. The university combines students as consumers who do not buy with faculties or producers who do not sell and taxpayers or owners who do not control. The results are predictably irrational.

Many if not most professors argue that students cannot and should not be treated as consumers. That is one reason that the University of Phoenix, a private non-traditional university, frightens so many professors. At "real" universities, we are providing an education, not a product they claim. They may be correct, but what is the message they are sending to their students? They are not showing confidence in them as free beings. They are not encouraging a range of choices or increasing students' control over their own destinies. Professors are saying that they know best so sit back and accept their monopoly-driven answers to your questions and please do not ask to see course evaluations. They know what is good for you. They are people of system who know where you should be on the chessboard.

Let Markets Handle It

One of the more impressive accomplishments of the Western world was developing, recognizing, and defending contracts. This was impressive because contractual relationships replaced those relationships conditioned by status. Contract allows for dynamism and change while status maintains stagnant and traditional societies. Sir Henry Sumner Maine (1902) explained in his classic work, *Ancient Law,* "[T]he movement of the progressive societies has hitherto been a movement from Status to Contract."

To the moderns in the developed world, contract is so much a part of our lives that we forget how advanced and radical it is. Contract means that people make up the rules that govern their relationships with each other without having to rely on tradition and status to dictate the terms. Relying on tradition was necessary to survive in the pre-industrial world but surviving and thriving today rely on contracts. Contracts imply trading with strangers and making reciprocal commitments through time. They are the basis of markets.

My reliance on and enthusiasm for contract law and markets may seem simplistic in the sense that I keep saying, "let the market handle it, even when markets supposedly fail." I arrive at that simple, realistic, but not simplistic answer because in the vast majority of cases government intervention makes things worse, and the more complex the government intervention the worse things become. Remember that in Chapter 4 "worse" was defined as a reduction of Pareto efficiency, as a loss of wealth.

When I argue for markets I am rejecting one-size-fits-all solutions to perceived problems. I am rejecting centralized, expert rule because experts never have the information, knowledge, ability, or incentives to know what ought to be done. Rejecting experts means accepting the amazingly complex systems of human interaction.

Letting the market handle it reaffirms the title of this book and my argument that much of what modern societies rely on politics to accomplish are simply "beyond politics." Not that government will completely fail in its objectives, but it will accomplish far less and at far more cost than if markets were allowed to work. Educating children, reducing traffic congestion, protecting water sources and supplies, reducing pollution to appropriate levels, rebuilding after natural disasters will all be dealt with more efficiently and fairly by markets than by collective choice. Political processes, after all, are driven by rent-seeking, vote-maximizing, and bureaucratic behavior.

In a December 2006 *National Journal* article in memory of Milton Friedman, Clive Cook had the following to say about markets and popular knowledge about them:

> Much of what is wrong with popular attitudes to capitalism comes down to one thing: a lack of wonder at what uncoordinated markets can achieve. Going to a grocery store for the hundredth or thousandth time is a pretty humdrum experience. As a rule it isn't going to elicit much of an intellectual response—though if it does, the response might be one of two kinds. The commentator Robert Kuttner once wrote of

his dismay at the great number of breakfast cereals on offer in his local grocery. What a waste, was his point; who could possibly need all these different cereals? Can't we arrange things more intelligently? This is a leftist kind of response: "Put somebody sensible in charge and plan things better." The liberal response (in the proper sense of "liberal") is different: "How amazing that all these choices are available, so that every taste is catered to, and it's all so cheap."

Many believe, like Kuttner, that they can identify better outcomes than those arrived at by markets. But that is the truly simplistic conclusion. Cook's conclusion is far more complex. He recommends letting millions of creative people with their individual knowledge, preferences, and understandings voluntarily cooperate in creating solutions to problems and products that none of us individually could foresee. That is the wonder of markets—the seemingly "uncoordinated" actions of strangers are coordinated through markets.

Saying, therefore, "let the market handle it," is to say that solutions to most problems are beyond politics—beyond coordinated, centralized, expert-driven processes. It requires being humble enough to say, "I do not know what ought to be done." Only complicated, voluntary, decentralized interactions will produce competing answers and competition among those answers will determine what works best in the current circumstances.

But, what about market failures such as the path dependence of QWERTY keyboards being chosen over the faster, superior DVORAK keyboards or public goods problems like providing lighthouses or bees pollinating orchards, all among the most commonly cited examples of each kind of perceived market failure? The problem is that all three examples fail to survive examination. Ronald Coase (1974) examined the history of lighthouses in Britain and found that lighthouses, especially those in the most difficult places to build, were built and maintained privately for many years. The lighthouse owners were allowed to collect tolls when ships reached port. Another economist, Steven Cheung (1973), conducted a similar study of beekeeping and apple growing in Washington State. He found that there was a market for the unintended externality of bees pollinating apple trees in their search for pollen. In that market, orchard owners paid beekeepers for the bees' services. Cheung titled his article "The Fable of the Bees" and the article exploding the myth of the QWERTY keyboard was titled "The Fable of the Keys." Economists Stan Liebowitz and Stephen Margolis (1990) found that experiments comparing the keyboards with each other find that neither design of keyboard has a clear advantage over the other. Claims that DVORAK demonstrates market failure continue, however, just as do similar claims about bees and lighthouses. These examples indicate we should be wary of other sightings of market failures.

As should be clear by now, perceived externalities cannot be prima facie justifications for government action. Government responses seldom make things better, regardless of the mythology built up about the need for those responses. What is more, if we apply Coase's insight that externalities are reciprocal, most proposed government interventions do not even address the underlying issues. Finally, most externalities are not caused by failed markets; they are caused by underdeveloped or poorly specified property rights.

Try Freedom

Letting markets handle it leads to my next proposal, that countries around the globe really try freedom. In the popular mind, democracy and economic freedom are so linked as to be the same concept. They are not. Democracy refers to how political decisions are made. It is the freedom to participate in the polis. Economic freedom is about the freedom to pursue your own interests, to voluntarily exchange with others, to profit and lose from your choices. Thus, highly democratic countries can offer their citizens very little economic freedom, as was the case in India for many years, and non-democratic countries can offer their citizens a great deal of economic freedom as has been the case in Hong Kong and Singapore. The important point about economic freedom and politics, whether more or less democratic, is political interference in markets must be limited.

For several years Canada's Fraser Institute has published an annual report titled, "Economic Freedom of the World." The report is now published annually by a network of institutes in more than 70 countries with the objective to measure "economic freedom in an accurate, comprehensive, and objective manner." The lead authors of the annual report are economists James Gwartney and Robert Lawson. In the first annual report (1966) they defined economic freedom:

Individuals have economic freedom when property they acquire without the use of force, fraud, or theft is protected from physical invasions by others and they are free to use, exchange, or give their property as long as their actions do not violate the identical rights of others. An index of economic freedom should measure the extent to which rightly acquired property is protected and individuals are engaged in voluntary transactions.

Gwartney and Lawson, along with their research teams, use thirty-eight variables to measure economic freedom. Their index measures (1) size of government: expenditures, taxes, and enterprises, (2) legal structure and security of property rights, (3) access to sound money, (4) freedom to trade internationally, and (5) regulation of credit, labor, and business. In the 2007 report they included 141 nations in their index. They highlighted the indicators of well-being between countries that are economically free and those that are not (Gwartney and Lawson, 2009, p. 4):

- Nations that are economically free out-perform non-free nations in indicators of well-being.
- Nations in the top quartile of economic freedom have an average per-capita GDP of US $32,443, compared to US $3,802 for those nations in the bottom quartile.
- The top quartile has an average per-capita economic growth rate of 2.24 percent, compared to 0.9 percent for the bottom quartile.
- In nations of the top quartile, the average income of the poorest 10 percent of the population is US$9,105, compared to $896 for those in the bottom quartile.
- Life expectancy is 79.12 years in the top quartile but 59.4 years in the bottom quartile.
- Nations in the top quartile of economic freedom have an average score of 1.6 for political rights on a scale of 1 to 7, where 1 marks the highest level, while those in the bottom quartile have an average score of 4.4.
- Nations in the top quartile of economic freedom have an average score of 1.6 for civil liberties on a scale of 1 to 7, where 1 marks the highest level, while those in the bottom quartile have an average score of 4.1.

• Nations in the top quartile of economic freedom have an average score of 84.8 out of 100) for environmental performance, while those in the bottom quartile have an average score of 64.5 (exhibit 1.19).

Gwartney and Lawson note that many of the relationships highlighted above "reflect the impact of economic freedom as it works through increasing economic growth." They also stress that "some of the variables that influence economic growth may also influence political factors like honesty in government and protection of civil liberties" so there may not always be a direct causal relationship between economic freedom and the variables highlighted above. Their data illustrate, however, the striking differences between countries with more and less economic freedom.

Establish the Rule of Law

As formerly communist countries attempted to liberalize many told them there were three things they needed to do: "Privatize, privatize, privatize." Milton Friedman was one who made that recommendation but later decided he had been wrong. What was more basic, he said, was to establish the rule of law. Without the rule of law, privatization in many countries failed miserably. Friedman (2002) pointed to Russia as an example. He said, "Russia privatized but in a way that created private monopolies—private centralized economic controls that replaced government's centralized controls."

The rule of law is necessary for markets and, therefore, privatization, to work for three reasons. First, it regulates government power by making it less arbitrary and less available for abuse by rulers. Second, it makes all persons equal before the law; it makes the law respect us as equals. Third, it means there will be formal processes to establish justice by consistently applying general rules. Under the rule of law, individuals can organize their lives, make plans for the future, and resolve disputes without relying on violence or status.

Without the rule of law, attempts to improve the lot of the developing world will just move pieces around the chessboard, accomplishing little. An amazing amount of entrepreneurship already exists in the developing world, but as noted in Chapter 6, much of the capital controlled by the world's five billion poor people is dead because property rights are not recognized and they do not have the legal structure necessary to allow entrepreneurs to bring capital, ideas, and labor together efficiently. They cannot get credit and use collateral. They cannot create firms to take advantage of the division of labor. Hernando de Soto, author of *The Other Path: The Invisible Revolution in the Third World* and *The Mystery of Capital: Why Capitalism Triumphs in the West and Fails Everywhere Else* (2004) notes that there are four billion people living on less than $3 a day,

> . . . who are poor, who are entrepreneurs, and who are completely excluded from the global economy, because of lack of law. . . . If you're poor and all you've got basically is a piece of land and a place where you work, whether you're street vending or milking a cow, there is nothing more precious to you than your property. But to preserve it without the law you've got to satisfy tribal chiefs, crooked cops, corrupt politicians, bad judges, your difficult neighbors, and even the terrorists.

Hernando de Soto's Institute for Liberty and Democracy and similar institutes around the world are working with government leaders to quantify just how much third-world capital is held by the poor outside the law. They have found that the world's poor own over $9 trillion of dead capital, that typically 70 to 90 percent of a country's citizens are excluded from the formal legal system, and that dead capital in that country's extralegal economy is more than all the foreign investment or aid. Eighty percent of Mexicans, for example, are in the extralegal economy. They own 6 million businesses, 134 million hectares of land, and 11 million buildings. The businesses, buildings, and land are worth an estimated $315 billion, which, according to de Soto, "is seven times the value of Mexican oil reserves and 29 times the value of all foreign direct investment since Spain left" (de Soto, 2004).

The public choice problem is how to get third world leaders to allow or create the legal and enforcement changes necessary to create the rule of law. Among the American Founders there was a shared understanding about the value of life and liberty and that the pursuit of happiness required the rule of law to protect persons and property. Citizens of developing countries do not have that shared understanding and many of them are too busy just surviving to pursue political and legal change. But the developed countries could change their approach to foreign aid. Instead of providing roads, bridges, airports, ports, irrigation projects, dams, and other direct investments, they could encourage and help develop legal systems that will allow markets to operate. Successful market economies are, after all, legal constructions.

I am not saying the U.S. and others should be exporting democracy. Instead, I suggest something much more humble than that. I suggest encouraging countries in their efforts to convert dead capital into fungible property rights and create legal institutions to protect those rights. They should help countries create the systems necessary for individuals to establish an officially recognized identity and address so they can be recognized by the formal sector. Once the current holders of dead capital have that official recognition, they can replace the kin relationships and status that are characteristic of the informal sector with contracts with people outside their own families or neighborhoods. Then the first world needs to trade with them. Once liberal institutions are in place so that markets function, political freedoms will follow.

Conclusion

As I noted in the preface, I wrote a brief article about Bill Mitchell after his death for the journal *Public Choice*. I quoted Mitchell from an unpublished statement of his. It serves as an appropriate conclusion:

[Forty] years of reading and thought have revised not only my old understandings of markets and polities but have strongly influenced my values and the criteria I use in judging institutions. I should add that the Vietnam War and the conspicuous failure of many domestic programs have also left their mark on my thinking about the real world. I now value individual liberty more than ever and equality less. I now value the capacity of humans to create and decide as I never did before. Thus, I value institutions that promote individual choice and abhor those that place undue and unagreed upon constraints on the right to freely interact and contract. I worry about the increasing collectivizing of our lives, but I also take heart from the denial of totalitarian models by the very beings who must live with their real world counterparts. Arendt and others who could not conceive of rebellion and resistance and, indeed, revolution in such lands, never knew the resilience of humans. And, if there be an Iron Law of Oligarchy, then surely there is also an Iron Law of Freedom and, maybe, Democracy, too. History, it seems, is one of protracted struggle for liberalism: Freedom from serfdom; from monopoly; from crippling controls of government; from privilege; and for freedom of trade and association. The struggle is never-ending.

Bibliographical Notes

Economic Freedom of the World, co-authored by James Gwartney and Robert Lawson and published annually by the Fraser Institute, is the most comprehensive index of economic freedom available. The full dataset as well as a PDF version of the annual report is available at www.freetheworld.com. Since its initial publication in 1996, the report has been the basis of more than 200 scholarly articles. The great contribution of Gwartney and Lawson is that they developed, and continue to develop, an index based on objective characteristics of each country's economy. They do not teach things I did not suspect, but they provide data sets that allow an objective assessment of the state of economic freedom.

One of the best modern writers on politics, economics, and culture is Virginia Postrel. In *The Future and Its Enemies: The Growing Conflict over Creativity, Enterprise, and Progress* (Touchstone, 1999) she has written a manifesto for a dynamic, as opposed to a static, world. Although people today are wealthier, healthier, and have more opportunities than ever before, there is a constant chorus from the academic and political worlds lamenting our condition. Postrel attacks that chorus. She, like Hayek, knows that we really do not know our future. What we can know is the curiosity and excitement of living at a time and in places where there can be, in Hayek's words, "the party of life, the party that favors free growth and spontaneous evolution."

An excellent discussion of the "wonder" of markets and the price system, to use a term Hayek used, is in Russell Roberts novel, *The Price of Everything: A Parable of Possibility and Prosperity.* His discussion of how prices allocate graphite among its competing uses pays homage to Leonard Read's essay, "I Pencil. " Among the many insightful points is this one, "Know that there is no free lunch. Play with prices and you will bring disorder. You will lose the benefits of the flow of knowledge and resources that prices choreograph without a choreographer." Order without design, cooperation without coercion, and harmony among competing desires are concepts taught masterfully in the novel.

References

Cheung, Steven N. S. "The Fable of the Bees: An Economic Investigation." *Journal of Law and Economics* 16 (April 1973): 11–33.

Coase, Ronald H. "The Lighthouse in Economics." *Journal of Law and Economics* 17 (October 1974): 357–76.

Coase, Ronald H. "Looking for Results." *Reason* (January 1, 1997).

Crook, Clive. "On Milton Friedman's Unfinished Work." *National Journal,* 38:49 (December 9, 2006), 15–16.

de Soto, Hernando. "Bringing Capitalism to the Masses," *Cato's Letter,* 2 (Summer 2004).

Friedman, Milton. *Capitalism and Freedom.* 40th Anniversary ed. Chicago: University of Chicago Press, 2002.

Friedman, Milton. "Economic Freedom Behind the Scenes," Preface to *Economic Freedom of the World: 2002 Annual Report,* Vancouver, B.C.: Fraser Institute. http://www.freetheworld.com/2002/0EFW02frntmttr.pdf on 2007-11-22.

Genesis 29. 15–31. King James Version of Bible.

Gwartney, James and Robert Lawson. *Economic Freedom of the World: 2007 Annual Report.* Vancouver, B.C.: Fraser Institute. http://www.freetheworld.com/2007/EFW2007BOOK2.pdf.

Hayek, Friedrich A. von. "The Pretence of Knowledge." Lecture, Nobel Prize Award Ceremony from The Nobel Foundation, Stockholm, December 11, 1974.

Hazlett, Thomas W. "Looking for Results: Nobel Laureate Ronald Coase on Rights, Resources, and Regulation." *Reason Magazine* (January 1997). http://www.reason.com/news/show/30115.html.

Jillette, Penn. "One of the Things We're Saying—is Give Peace a Chance," *Regulation Magazine,* 26, no. 1 (Spring 2003): 68. http://www.cato.org/pubs/regulation/regv26n1/v26n1-final.pdf.

Liebowitz, Stan J. and Stephen E. Margolis. "The Fable of the Keys," *Journal of Law and Economics,* Vol. 33, 1 (April 1990), 1–27.

Maine, Sir Henry Sumner. *Ancient Law, Its Connection with the Early History of Society And Its Relation to Modern Ideas,* with an introduction and notes by Sir

Frederick Pollock. 4th American from the 10th London ed. New York: Henry Holt and Co., 1906. http://oll.libertyfund.org/title/2001/138159/2629423.

Postrel, Virginia. *The Future and Its Enemies: The Growing Conflict Over Creativity, Enterprise, and Progress.* New York City: Free Press, 1999.

Read, Leonard. *I, Pencil.* 1st ed. New York: Foundation For Economic Education, 2010.

Roberts, Russell. *The Price of Everything: A Parable of Possibility and Prosperity.* Princeton: Princeton University Press, 2009.

Smith, Adam. *An Inquiry into the Nature and Causes of the Wealth of Nations.* Indianapolis: Liberty Fund, Inc., 1981. Reprint. Originally published: Oxford: Clarendon Press, 1979. (Glasgow edition of the works and correspondence of Adam Smith, vol. 1).

Smith, Adam. *The Theory of Moral Sentiments.* 1790. Library of Economics and Liberty. http://www.econlib.org/library/Smith/smMS.html.

Wildavsky, Aaron. "Progress and Reform" in *Progress and Its Discontents,* Gabriel A. Almond, Marvin Chodorow, and Roy Harvey Pearce, eds. Berkeley: University of California Press, 1982.

Index

About the Author

RANDY T. SIMMONS is Senior Fellow at the Independent Institute, Professor of Economics and Director of the Institute of Political Economy at Utah State University's Jon M. Huntsman School of Business, and former Mayor of Providence, Utah. He received his Ph.D. in political science from the University of Oregon, and he is a member of the Board of Directors of the Utah League of Cities and Towns and a Member of the Utah Governor's Privatization Commission.

Professor Simmons's books include *Beyond Politics: Markets, Welfare, and the Failure of Bureaucracy* (with William Mitchell) and *The Political Economy of Culture and Norms: Informal Solutions to the Commons Problem*. A contributing author to various volumes such as *Re-Thinking Green: Alternatives to Environmental Bureaucracy*, he is the author of scholarly articles that have appeared in numerous journals, and his popular articles have been published in newspapers and magazines across the United States.

Independent Studies in Political Economy